TO IMPROVE THE ACADEMY

TO IMPROVE THE ACADEMY

Resources for Faculty, Instructional, and Organizational Development

Volume 30

Judith E. Miller, Editor

James E. Groccia, Associate Editor

POD

Professional and Organizational Development
Network in Higher Education

JOSSEY-BASS
A Wiley Imprint
www.josseybass.com

TO IMPROVE THE ACADEMY

To Improve the Academy is published annually by the Professional and Organizational Network in Higher Education (POD) through Jossey-Bass Publishers and is abstracted in ERIC documents and in Higher Education Abstracts.

Ordering Information

The annual volume of *To Improve the Academy* is distributed to members at the POD conference in the autumn of each year. To order or obtain ordering information, please contact:

John Wiley & Sons, Inc.
Customer Care Center
10475 Crosspoint Blvd.
Indianapolis, IN 46256
Phone: 877-762-2974
Fax: 800-597-3299
E-mail: custserv@wiley.com
Web: www.josseybass.com

Permission to Copy

The contents of *To Improve the Academy* are copyrighted to protect the authors. Nevertheless, consistent with the networking and resource-sharing functions of POD, readers are encouraged to reproduce articles and cases from *To Improve the Academy* for educational use, as long as the source is identified.

Instructions to Contributors for the Next Volume

Anyone interested in the issues related to instructional, faculty, and organizational development in higher education may submit manuscripts. Manuscripts are submitted to the current editor early in

December of each year and selected through a double-blind peer review process.

Correspondence, including requests for information about guidelines and submission of manuscripts for Volume 31, should be directed to:

James E. Groccia, Ed.D.

Director, Biggio Center for the Enhancement of Teaching and Learning

Auburn University

Auburn, AL 36849

Phone: 334-844-8530

Fax: 334-844-0130

E-mail: TIA@auburn.edu

Mission Statement

As revised and accepted by the POD Core Committee, April 2, 2004

Statement of Purpose

The Professional and Organizational Development Network in Higher Education is an association of higher education professionals dedicated to enhancing teaching and learning by supporting educational developers and leaders in higher education.

Mission Statement

The Professional and Organizational Development Network in Higher Education encourages the advocacy of the ongoing enhancement of teaching and learning through faculty and organizational development. To this end, it supports the work of educational developers and champions their importance to the academic enterprise.

Vision Statement

During the twenty-first century, the Professional and Organizational Development Network in Higher Education will expand guidelines for educational development, build strong alliances with sister organizations, and encourage developer exchanges and research projects to improve teaching and learning.

Values

The Professional and Organizational Development Network in Higher Education is committed to:

- Personal, faculty, instructional, and organizational development
- Humane and collaborative organizations and administrations
- Diverse perspectives and a diverse membership
- Supportive educational development networks on the local, regional, national, and international levels
- Advocacy for improved teaching and learning in the academy through programs for faculty, administrators, and graduate students
- The identification and collection of a strong and accessible body of research on development theories and practices
- The establishment of guidelines for ethical practice
- The increasingly useful and thorough assessment and evaluation of practice and research

Programs, Publications, and Activities

The Professional and Organizational Development Network in Higher Education offers members and interested individuals the following benefits:

- An annual membership conference designed to promote professional and personal growth, nurture innovation and change, stimulate important research projects, and enable participants to exchange ideas and broaden their professional network
- An annual membership directory and networking guide
- Publications in print and in electronic form
- Access to the POD Web site and listserv

Membership, Conference, and Programs Information

For information, please contact:

> Hoag Holmgren, Executive Director
> The POD Network
> P.O. Box 3318
> Nederland, CO 80466
> Phone: 303-258-9521
> Fax: 303-258-7377
> E-mail: podoffice@podnetwork.org
> Web: podnetwork.org

CONTENTS

SECTION THREE
Broadening the Campus Context

SECTION FOUR
Developing Our Craft

ABOUT THE AUTHORS

The Editors

Judith E. Miller is executive director of assessment at the University of North Florida. A former biology faculty member, she currently teaches an online course in college teaching for faculty and graduate students. In 1998, she received the Outstanding Undergraduate Science Teacher award from the Society for College Science Teachers; in 2002 she was named the Massachusetts CASE Professor of the Year by the Carnegie Foundation for the Advancement of Teaching; and in 2004 she won Worcester Polytechnic Institute's Trustees' Award for Outstanding Teaching. Miller is the coeditor (with Jim Groccia and Marilyn Miller) of *Student-Assisted Teaching: A Guide to Faculty-Student Teamwork* (2001) and (with Jim Groccia) of *On Becoming a Productive University: Strategies for Reducing Costs and Increasing Quality* (Anker, 2005) and *Enhancing Productivity: Administrative, Instructional, and Technological Strategie*s (1998). She has published and presented extensively on active and cooperative learning, learning outcomes assessment, team teaching, and educational productivity. She may be contacted at j.miller@unf.edu.

James E. Groccia is director of the Biggio Center for the Enhancement of Teaching and Learning and associate professor in the Department of Educational Foundations, Leadership, and Technology at Auburn University. In addition to faculty development work, he teaches graduate courses on teaching and higher education and coordinates the university's graduate certificate in college and university teaching. He is a former POD Network president and core committee member. Groccia received his doctorate in educational psychology and guidance from the University of Tennessee. He has presented at dozens of national and international conferences, conducted hundreds of workshops worldwide, has served as an advisor and consultant to institutions nationally and abroad, and has authored numerous articles and book chapters on teaching and learning issues. He is the author of *The College Success Book: A Whole-Student Approach to Academic Excellence* (1992). He is the coeditor (with Judith Miller and Marilyn Miller) of *Student-Assisted Teaching: A Guide to Faculty-Student Teamwork* (2001) and (with Judith Miller) of *On Becoming a Productive University: Strategies for Reducing Costs and Increasing Quality* (2005) and *Enhancing Productivity: Administrative, Instructional, and Technological Strategies* (1998). He may be contacted at groccje@auburn.edu.

The Contributors

Terre H. Allen is professor of communication studies and director of California State University Long Beach's Faculty Center for Professional Development. She has published articles and book chapters on group communication, communication in instruction, interpersonal communication, and instructional technology, and facilitated meetings and retreats for groups in business, nonprofit, and higher education. Terre is a consultant and instructional designer and has coauthored USAFunds Life Skills, a book series on financial literacy and student success. She may be contacted at tallen@csulb.edu.

Julianna V. Banks is a scholar of higher education leadership and policy studies. She has conducted research on social and educational issues with private, nonprofit, and government organizations. Her research focuses on access and equity in education, and faculty and student socialization. A research fellow with the Center for Urban and Multicultural Education at Indiana University–Purdue University Indianapolis, she was recently recognized for her contributions to equity for women in higher education. She may be contacted at jvbanks@indiana.edu.

Jeffrey L. Bernstein is professor of political science at Eastern Michigan University. He is coeditor (with Michael Smith and Rebecca Nowacek) and contributing author of *Citizenship Across the Curriculum* (2010). His work has appeared in the *Journal of Political Science Education*, *Journal of the Scholarship of Teaching and Learning*, *Political Research Quarterly*, *Politics and Gender*, and numerous edited volumes. He has served as secretary of the International Society for the Scholarship of Teaching and Learning. He may be contacted at jeffrey.bernstein@emich.edu.

A. Jane Birch is assistant director for faculty development at Brigham Young University. Among other programs, she directs an eighteen-month new-faculty program and a semester-long workshop on scholarly productivity. She helps faculty make connections between their religious faith and professional work, and develop a broad vision of their work and assist students in making meaning, finding purpose, and connecting to what is important. She may be contacted at jane_birch@byu.edu.

Krishna K. Bista is a doctoral student at the Center for Excellence in Education, Arkansas State University. His interests are global and comparative education, learning styles, and English as a Second Language (ESL). His writings appear in the *Journal of English for Specific Purposes, The Educational Forum,* and *Journal of ESL.* He holds master's degrees in postsecondary education, English, and teaching English as a Second Language. He may be contacted at Krishna.Bista@smail.astate.edu.

Allison P. Boye is director of the Teaching Effectiveness And Career enHancement (TEACH) program at Texas Tech University. Her work includes graduate student and faculty development as well as leading pedagogical seminars and faculty reading groups. Her recent publications focus on peer observation, instructor response to feedback, and adaptation of active learning; her other research interests include millennial students, teaching writing, and gender. She may be contacted at allison.p.boye@ttu.edu.

Beth L. Brunk-Chavez is an associate professor of rhetoric and writing studies at the University of Texas at El Paso, where she is the director of first-year composition and an associate dean in the College of Liberal Arts. Her research interests are writing with technology, digital collaboration, grading and assessment, and course and program redesign. Her work has appeared in a number of journals and edited collections. She may be contacted at blbrunk@utep.edu.

Dannielle Joy Davis is an associate professor of educational leadership, policy, and law at Alabama State University and has studied and conducted research in Ghana, South Africa, Egypt, Germany, the

Netherlands, and Belgium. Her interdisciplinary K–20 research examines the experiences of marginalized groups in educational settings and the role of organizational policy and practice in the promotion or inhibition of egalitarian academic and occupational outcomes. She may be contacted at djdavis@alasu.edu.

Shelda Debowski is Winthrop Professor of Higher Education Development and the director of organizational and staff development services at the University of Western Australia. Her past roles include president of the International Consortium for Educational Development and the Higher Education Development Society of Australasia. Widely published in faculty development, she has extensive experience in leading teaching and learning centers and in supporting academic leadership, research, and organizational development. She may be contacted at Shelda.Debowski@uwa.edu.au.

Bonnie S. Farley-Lucas is director of faculty development and professor of communication at Southern Connecticut State University, where she also directs the Curriculum Innovation Program. Her research includes faculty-student communication, gender in the workplace, work-family processes, organizational development, and interpersonal conflict. She earned a Ph.D. in organizational communication from Ohio University and an M.S. in organizational behavior from the University of Hartford. She is co-owner and executive producer for Synthetic Cinema International. She may be contacted at farleylucab1@southernct.edu.

Beth A. Fisher is the associate director of the Teaching Center and a lecturer in women, gender, and sexuality studies at Washington University in St. Louis. Her work at The Teaching Center focuses on helping graduate students improve their teaching and prepare for academic positions and on developing teaching methods that can help students improve their writing skills. She teaches courses in American literature and gender studies. She may be contacted at bfisher@wustl.edu.

Ernetta L. Fox received her M.A. in costume history and design and M.F.A. in costume shop management from the University of South Dakota, and her M.L.S. from Southern Connecticut State University.

She serves as the director of disability services at The University of South Dakota. She may be contacted at Ernetta.Fox@usd.edu.

Regina F. Frey is the director of The Teaching Center and a professor of the practice in chemistry at Washington University in St. Louis. She teaches general chemistry and a first-year course on women in science. Her research focuses on group-oriented, student-centered STEM pedagogy. She collaborates on scholarship projects with departments (chemistry, education, and psychology) and other Washington University centers (Science Outreach and Cornerstone: The Center for Advanced Learning). She may be contacted at gfrey@wustl.edu.

Tara Gray is associate professor of criminal justice and the founding director of the Teaching Academy at New Mexico State University (NMSU). She has been honored at NMSU and nationally with seven awards for teaching or service. She has published three books, including *Publish and Flourish: Become a Prolific Scholar* (2005). Gray has presented faculty development workshops in more than thirty states and in Mexico, Guatemala, Thailand, Saudi Arabia, and the United Arab Emirates. She may be contacted at tgray@nmsu.edu.

Laura Henderson is the evaluation specialist in the Office of Academic Planning and Assessment at the University of Massachusetts Amherst. She designs, executes, and manages evaluation processes for a variety of campus initiatives, employing qualitative social research methods in support of evidence-based decision making. She holds master's degrees in applied anthropology from Oregon State University and cultural anthropology from University of California, Santa Barbara. She may be contacted at lhenderson@acad.umass.edu.

Anne Herrington is distinguished professor of English and site director of the Western Massachusetts Writing Project at the University of Massachusetts Amherst. With Kevin Hodgson and Charles Moran, she coauthored *Teaching the New Writing: Technology, Change, and Assessment in the 21st-Century Classroom* (2009); with Charles Moran, she coedited *Writing, Teaching, and Learning in the Disciplines* (1992) and *Genres Across the Curriculum* (2005). With Marcia Curtis, she wrote *Persons in Process: Four Stories of Writing and Personal Development in College* (2000). She may be contacted at anneh@english.umass.edu.

Susan R. Hines is the director of faculty development at Saint Mary's University of Minnesota, Twin Cities, where she also teaches in the Ed.D. leadership program. Her research interest for the past five years has focused on faculty development program evaluation. She holds an Ed.D. in leadership and has been a college teacher for twenty-six years. She may be contacted at shines@smumn.edu.

Mark A. Hohnstreiter serves as the advancement officer for the Teaching Academy at New Mexico State University. He assists the academy in seeking philanthropic funds and helping to create better awareness for the academy. He has been a professional fundraiser (certified fundraising executive) since 1982, including major roles at the University of Chicago, Northwestern Memorial Hospital, Saint Louis University, Presbyterian Healthcare Foundation, and the University of New Mexico. He may be contacted at mhohnstr@nmsu.edu.

David A. Horne is professor of marketing and director of M.B.A. programs at California State University Long Beach. His research has been published in the *Journal of Consumer Affairs, International Journal of Service Industry Management, European Journal of Innovation Management, Research in Consumer Behavior, Psychology and Marketing,* and *Current Issues in Research and Advertising.* He coedited *Earth, Wind, Fire, and Water: Perspectives on Natural Disasters,* a book about consumers' recovery from disasters. He may be contacted at dhorne@csulb.edu.

Teresa A. Johnson is instructional consultant for assessment and the scholarship of teaching and learning in the University Center for the Advancement of Teaching at The Ohio State University. She is a lecturer in education policy and leadership and teaches a course on college teaching. Her current research interests are course and curriculum design, articulation of learning outcomes, and evaluation of teaching strategies. She may be contacted at johnson.674@osu.edu.

Alan Kalish is director of the University Center for the Advancement of Teaching and adjunct assistant professor of education policy and leadership at The Ohio State University. He has studied, both qualitatively and quantitatively, transitions from graduate school to faculty life and teaching and learning in higher education. His current interests are peer review of teaching, preparing future faculty, scholarship of teaching and learning, and assessment of academic support units. He may be contacted at kalish.3@osu.edu.

Bruce C. Kelley is founding director of the Center for Teaching and Learning at the University of South Dakota, where he also holds faculty rank as an associate professor of music. He received his Ph.D. in music theory from The Ohio State University. He specializes in course design and music of the American Civil War. He may be contacted at Bruce .Kelley@usd.edu.

Sally L. Kuhlenschmidt has been director of the Faculty Center for Excellence in Teaching at Western Kentucky University since 1994. She received her Ph.D. in clinical psychology from Purdue University. Her current research interests include assessment of faculty development and using technology to enhance development. She may be contacted at sally .kuhlenschmidt@wku.edu.

Thomas F. Nelson Laird is an assistant professor of higher education at Indiana University, Bloomington, where he manages the Center for Postsecondary Research's Faculty Survey of Student Engagement. His work focuses on improving collegiate teaching and learning, particularly the design, delivery, and effects of student experiences with diversity. He may be contacted at tflaird@indiana.edu.

Kathryn E. Linder is the assistant director at the Center for Teaching Excellence at Suffolk University and a former doctoral intern at The Ohio State University's University Center for the Advancement of Teaching. She received her Ph.D. in women's, gender, and sexuality studies from The Ohio State University. Her research interests include cultural studies of education, youth studies, and alternative pedagogies. She may be contacted at klinder@suffolk.edu.

Amanda E. Major is pursuing an Ed.D. in educational leadership, policy, and law at Alabama State University. She earned certification in professional learning and performance from the American Society of Training and Development Certification Institute, certification as an associate in project management from the Project Management Institute, a master's degree in industrial and organizational psychology from Louisiana Tech University, and a bachelor's degree in interdisciplinary studies from the University of Texas at Dallas. She may be contacted at amandamajor@ myasu.alasu.edu.

Ingrid M. Martin is professor and chair of marketing at California State University at Long Beach. Her research has examined issues in the areas of consumer goals and branding, as well as consumer risk and public policy issues around risk communication and risk mitigation behaviors. She has coauthored numerous journal articles, conference proceedings, and four book chapters. She serves as the chair of the college's M.B.A. program curriculum committee. She may be contacted at imartin@csulb.edu.

Laurie A. Maynell is an instructional consultant at the University Center for the Advancement of Teaching at The Ohio State University and an instructor with the ESL Spoken English Program. Her area of focus is supporting international teachers. Her research interests include issues that international faculty in the United States face, intonation in spoken language, and language processing. She can be contacted at maynell.1@ osu.edu.

Leslie G. McBride is associate vice provost for teaching, learning, and assessment in the Center for Academic Excellence at Portland State University, where she is also an associate professor of community health. Her recent faculty development work and related publications have focused on institutional change and shifting faculty roles, the relationship of campuswide student learning outcomes to institutional change, and building capacity for sustainability through curricular and faculty development. She may be contacted at bqlm@pdx.edu.

Bonnie B. Mullinix balances the roles of curriculum coordinator with Greenville Technical College, senior consultant with the TLT Group, and copresident of Jacaranda Educational Development. An adult educator with over thirty years of national and international experience, she has served as faculty, faculty developer, and assistant dean in five higher education settings and established two teaching and learning centers. Her professional work focuses on educational innovation, technologies, evaluation, and participatory, learner-centered approaches. She may be contacted at bbmullinix@gmail.com.

Yolanda Flores Niemann is vice provost at Utah State University. Her research interests include the effects and social-ecological contexts of stereotypes, the psychological effects of tokenism, and overcoming obstacles to higher education for low-socioeconomic-status group members. Notable book publications include *Presumed Incompetent* (in press), *Black/Brown Relations and Stereotypes* (2003), and *Chicana Leadership* (2002). She is working on a book on the experiential differences between white faculty and faculty of color. She may be contacted at Yolanda .fniemann@usu.edu.

Linda B. Nilson is founding director of the Office of Teaching Effectiveness and Innovation at Clemson University, a previous editor of *To Improve the Academy* (Vols. 25–28), and author of *Teaching at Its Best: A Research-Based Resource for College Instructors*, now in its third edition (2010) and *The Graphic Syllabus and the Outcomes Map: Communicating Your Course* (2007). She conducts workshops and gives keynote addresses at conferences, colleges, and universities both nationally and internationally. She may be contacted at nilson@clemson.edu.

Rebecca S. Nowacek is assistant professor of English at Marquette University. She is a coeditor (with Michael Smith and Jeffrey Bernstein) and contributing author of *Citizenship Across the Curriculum* (2010). She is also the author of *Agents of Integration: Understanding Transfer as a Rhetorical Act* (2011). Her work has appeared in *College Composition and Communication*, *College English*, and *Research in the Teaching of English*. She may be contacted at rebecca.nowacek@marquette.edu.

Edward B. Nuhfer is faculty developer with tenure at California State University Channel Islands. He thanks Cynthia Desrochers, Steve

Fleisher, Mitch Handelsman, Tom Jones, Barbara Millis, Mike Pavelich, Carl Pletsch, James Rhem, and the wonderful staff at his previous institution. These are people of great heart, supporting success and survival daily. His current scholarship includes fractals, science literacy, and a student success guide coauthored with his fellow CSU faculty developers. He may be contacted at ed.nuhfer@csuci.edu.

Carolyn B. Oxenford was founder of the Marymount University Center for Teaching Excellence in 2006. Prior to directing the center, she was chair of the psychology department and a practicing clinician. Oxenford received her Ph.D. in clinical psychology from Emory University. Her current research interests include performance anxiety and teaching effectiveness. She may be contacted at carolyn.oxenford@marymount.edu.

Megan M. Palmer is an assistant dean for faculty affairs and professional development at the Indiana University (IU) School of Medicine. She holds faculty appointments in general internal medicine at the IU School of Medicine and in educational leadership and policy studies at the IU School of Education in Indianapolis. Palmer has published on student engagement in higher education, college choice, faculty development, and faculty vitality. She may be contacted at mmpalmer@indiana.edu.

Sunay V. Palsole is the director of instructional support at the University of Texas at El Paso. A geophysicist by academic training, he has been involved in academic technology for over fourteen years. His research interests are in developing and mapping sociotechnical systems and uses of technology in the service of academic areas. He has presented and published in these areas in a variety of national and international forums. He may be contacted at sunay@utep.edu.

Kathryn M. Plank is associate director of the University Center for the Advancement of Teaching and adjunct assistant professor of education policy and leadership at The Ohio State University. She received her Ph.D. in English from The Pennsylvania State University. She teaches a graduate course on college teaching and coordinates faculty learning community programs. Her research interests include program assessment, teaching consultation, diversity, educational technology, critical thinking, and team teaching. She may be contacted at plank.28@osu.edu.

Kara Provost is professor of academic enrichment and coordinator of the first-year honors program at Curry College. She teaches composition and interdisciplinary first-year honors seminars, conducts creative writing workshops for adults and children in the community, and leads two creative writing groups with peers. Her poetry has been published in literary magazines. Her first chapbook of poetry, *Nests*, was published in 2006. A second collection is due out in spring 2011. She may be contacted at kprovost0907@post03.curry.edu.

Tony Ribera is a doctoral candidate in higher education and student affairs at Indiana University, Bloomington, where he works with surveys of student engagement in his role as project associate for the NSSE Institute. His research focuses on the adoption of a scholarship of teaching and learning among multiple constituencies in higher education, particularly faculty and student affairs professionals. He may be contacted at aribera@indiana.edu.

Elizabeth Roderick is associate director for the Center for Advancing Faculty Excellence at the University of Alaska Anchorage (UAA), where she oversees initiatives for diversity, sustainability, and twenty-first-century trends in higher education. She is director of the UAA/Alaska Pacific University Difficult Dialogues initiative, edited *Alaska Native Cultures and Issues: Responses to Frequently Asked Questions* (2010), and is an internationally recognized singer and songwriter. She received her B.A. in American studies from Yale University and her M.A. in social psychology from Alaska Pacific University. She may be contacted at aner@uaa.alaska.edu.

Stephanie V. Rohdieck is the assistant director and coordinator for graduate teaching assistant programs in the University Center for the Advancement of Teaching at The Ohio State University, where she earned her master's degree in social work administration. She is a lecturer in education policy and leadership and teaches a course on teaching support for graduate teaching assistants. Her current research interests are graduate teaching preparation, teaching portfolio development, diversity, teaching awards, and teaching consultation. She may be contacted at rohdieck.1@ osu.edu.

Margaret M. Sargent is associate professor of communication at Southern Connecticut State University. Specializing in organizational and interpersonal communication, she teaches courses in both theoretical and applied contexts. Her research includes faculty-student interaction, doctor-patient communication, and language and social interaction. She earned a Ph.D. in interpersonal communication from Southern Illinois University and an M.A. in organizational communication from Northern Illinois University. In 2009, she was awarded SCSU's J. P. Phillip Teaching Award for outstanding teaching. She may be contacted at sargentm1@southernct.edu.

Joshua S. Smith is professor of educational psychology and director of the Center for Urban and Multicultural Education at Indiana University–Purdue University Indianapolis. His research examines transitions from middle to high school and from high school to college. He works with schools and community-based organizations to evaluate educational programs. He has been principal investigator on over thirty externally funded research grants and has published in the area of student development and educational transitions. He may be contacted at jss2@iupui.edu.

Justin M. Smith recently completed his Ph.D. in human sciences with a focus on leadership in higher education from the University of Nebraska–Lincoln. He currently serves as the coordinator of the Fides Program at the University of South Dakota in the Center for Teaching and Learning. The program is funded by a congressionally directed grant from the Fund for the Improvement of Postsecondary Education with the purpose of identifying and addressing the academic needs of wounded warriors through faculty and staff workshops. He may be contacted at Justin.M.Smith@usd.edu.

Michael B. Smith teaches history and environmental studies and is coordinator of the School of Humanities and Sciences Community Service Program at Ithaca College. He is a coeditor (with Jeffrey Bernstein and

Rebecca Nowacek) and contributing author of *Citizenship Across the Curriculum* (2010). His work has appeared in *Learning and Teaching: The International Journal of Higher Education in the Social Sciences*, *Environmental History*, *Feminist Studies*, and *The Historian*. He may be contacted at mismith@ithaca.edu.

Michael E. Solt is dean of the College of Business Administration at California State University, Long Beach, where he develops innovative programs and supports the scholarly and creative activities of college faculty. He also serves as director of the Ukleja Center for Ethical Leadership at CSULB. Solt has authored and coauthored numerous national and international publications and has consulted for a variety of businesses and organizations. He may be contacted at msolt@csulb.edu.

Mary Deane Sorcinelli is associate provost for faculty development and professor of educational policy, research, and administration at the University of Massachusetts Amherst. She has served as president of the Professional and Organizational Development (POD) Network in Higher Education. Her research interests include academic career development, mentoring, teaching, and faculty development, both national and international, all of which are integrated in her coauthored (with Ann E. Austin, Pamela L. Eddy, and Andrea L. Beach) book, *Creating the Future of Faculty Development* (2005). She may be contacted at msorcinelli@acad.umass.edu.

Martha L. A. Stassen is director of assessment at the University of Massachusetts Amherst, where she supports faculty efforts to design curricular and assessment strategies that enhance student learning. Her research includes the impact of diversity in higher education, engaging faculty in learning assessment, and the student outcomes associated with living-learning community participation. She serves as president of the New England Association for Educational Assessment. She may be contacted at mstassen@acad.umass.edu.

Janelle DeCarrico Voegele is assistant director of teaching and learning in the Center for Academic Excellence at Portland State University. She has a master of arts degree in communication studies and is a doctoral student in the educational leadership program in the Graduate School of Education at Portland State. She is working on her dissertation focused on faculty experiences with blended (hybrid) learning. She may be contacted at voegelej@pdx.edu.

Sherree A. Wilson is assistant dean of the faculties at Indiana University–Purdue University Indianapolis, where she focuses on the recruitment and retention of less-represented faculty, collaborates with campus leadership to advance diversity, facilitates dual-career assistance for faculty and staff, and provides career development consultation to graduate students. She is also assistant clinical professor in Indiana University's Higher Education Student Affairs program. Her research focuses on the advancement of faculty of color in higher education. She may be contacted at sawilson99@gmail.com.

Lisa A. Wittenhagen served in the U.S. Marine Corps for six years. While serving, she earned her B.S. in human resource management from Park University. She went on to complete her M.B.A. and is currently pursuing a doctoral degree in organizational management, both from the University of Phoenix. She serves as an instructional designer for the Fides Program, a congressionally directed project funded by the Fund for the Improvement of Postsecondary Education for the purpose of helping faculty better serve student veterans with disabilities. She may be contacted at Lisa.Wittenhagen@usd.edu.

PREFACE

Editors of *To Improve the Academy (TIA)* are often asked how they arrive at the thematic divisions that appear as part titles in the Contents. Surely there must be some advance decisions made, and if so, couldn't these themes be shared with prospective authors? As both a beginning associate editor and a stickler for structure, I too was incredulous when Linda Nilson, the previous editor of *TIA,* told me that the process is organic—that the editors develop the themes based on the content of the accepted manuscripts. Finally, in my fourth year on the editorial team, I have come to embrace the organic theory of the Contents.

This volume contains twenty-two contributions from authors across an array of institutions on a variety of topics. Reflecting the times in which we live and work and the evolution of our profession, we received fewer manuscripts than in the past on topics of individual faculty development and more on topics of institutional and professional concern. We have organized the chapters in this volume to reflect the various levels at which our work as developers has impact—on our colleagues, our campuses, and our craft. In addition, we included a special part that highlights how faculty development is evolving to serve its increasingly diverse constituencies.

The contributions to this volume reflect both the challenges that higher education faces and the maturation of our practice as faculty, staff, and organizational developers. They also reflect the fact that even when addressing challenges, we as a profession always seem to do so with optimism and energy.

Section One: Promoting Our Colleagues' Professional Success

Chapter One, by Kathryn Linder, Stephanie Rohdieck, Alan Kalish, Teresa Johnson, Kathryn Plank, and Laurie Maynell, describes an opportunity for graduate students interested in the field of educational development as a career to serve as educational development interns. The authors report that teaching center staff, participating graduate student interns, and the field of educational development all benefited from the internship model.

In Chapter Two, Sunay Palsole and Beth Brunk-Chavez address the challenges of preparing faculty to develop hybrid courses that serve new generations of learners. They describe a digital academy to help faculty interweave online elements with face-to-face teaching.

In Chapter Three, Dannielle Davis, Kara Provost, and Amanda Major share their experiences as leaders of faculty writing groups. They emphasize that not only can writing groups empower faculty to successfully meet research obligations, but they also have a wide-ranging impact on work-life balance and faculty retention.

In Chapter Four, Leslie McBride and Janelle Voegele write about a faculty learning community focused on tenure and promotion. They used academic portfolio development as a common reference point for addressing tenure and promotion issues, and in the process faculty shared insights and perspectives about the value of diverse forms of scholarship.

Jeffrey Bernstein, Rebecca Nowacek, and Michael Smith close out Part One in Chapter Five by arguing that citizenship themes can be incorporated into a wide variety of classes, including some in disciplines not considered traditional homes for civic education. They describe how faculty development centers can play a critical role in helping faculty integrate citizenship into the curriculum and evaluate the learning that occurs in their citizenship-oriented classes.

Section Two: Supporting Institutional Priorities

Bonnie Farley-Lucas and Margaret Sargent interviewed thirty-three undergraduates regarding faculty behaviors, statements, and practices that contributed to and discouraged out-of-class communication between faculty and students. They report in Chapter Six that they found that in-class communication sets the stage for whether students approach faculty outside class.

Allison Boye worked with three instructors who had limited control over the curriculum and pedagogy in their courses. In the process, she writes in Chapter Seven, she discovered that not only can faculty developers help instructors realize change on an individual level, but they can promote change at the departmental and big-picture levels as well.

In Chapter Eight, Beth Fisher and Regina Frey write about a laboratory research group model, common in the sciences, that they adapted to foster the scholarship of teaching and learning (SoTL) among a group of faculty in the sciences. This group has bridged communication and knowledge gaps among science and social science faculty and science education specialists, fostered the development of collaborative SoTL projects, and laid the groundwork for broader institutional support of SoTL.

In Chapter Nine, Thomas Nelson Laird and Tony Ribera examine institutional encouragement of and faculty engagement in SoTL across forty-nine U.S. colleges and universities. Their results suggest that institutional encouragement of and faculty engagement in the public dissemination of teaching investigations lag behind encouragement and engagement in other aspects of SoTL.

Martha Stassen, Anne Herrington, and Laura Henderson map in Chapter Ten the definitions of critical thinking used on their campus and in national assessment instruments and find considerable variation. The mapping process not only helps campuses make better-informed decisions regarding their responses to accountability pressures; it also provides a stimulus for rich, evidence-based discussions about teaching and learning priorities related to critical thinking.

In Chapter Eleven, Terre Allen, David Horne, Ingrid Martin, and Michael Solt describe the process of a revision of a master's of business administration curriculum. The process was notable because faculty development and faculty governance worked together to provide continuous assistance, opportunities for frequent discussion, periodic review, and faculty programming to achieve curriculum and course redesign.

Section Three: Broadening the Campus Context

Krishna Bista investigated the perceptions of international undergraduate and graduate students about possible causes for academic dishonesty. In Chapter Twelve, she reports that previous learning style, English language proficiency, unfamiliarity with American academic cultures, the relationship between student and teacher, and the availability of technical and educational resources were causes of academic dishonesty.

Bruce Kelley, Ernetta Fox, Justin Smith, and Lisa Wittenhagen discuss in Chapter Thirteen the implications of the fact that almost 2 million veterans returning from military service in Iraq and Afghanistan will soon enroll in postsecondary education and that up to 40 percent of these veterans are estimated to have disabilities. They suggest various strategies for faculty developers to help faculty better serve these incoming veterans.

Carolyn Oxenford and Sally Kuhlenschmidt review in Chapter Fourteen evidence on faculty stress and impairment and help faculty developers recognize signs that mental health issues may be affecting faculty performance. They make suggestions to help faculty developers work effectively with colleagues who are coping with psychological impairments.

In Chapter Fifteen, Megan Palmer, Julianna Banks, Joshua Smith, and Sherree Wilson describe Next Generation @ IUPUI, an intensive one-year leadership program at their institution designed to develop the leadership potential of faculty of color. In addition to addressing higher education administration theories and trends, participants receive individualized coaching and mentoring to develop a broad network of peers.

Yolanda Niemann explores in Chapter Sixteen the impact of token status on faculty of color. She describes the personal, psychological, and career-damaging impacts of tokenism and provides guidelines for professional development professionals that may diffuse these negative impacts by assisting department heads to mentor faculty of color.

In Chapter Seventeen, Elizabeth Roderick describes the Difficult Dialogues partnership between two universities that sought to improve the learning climates on both campuses by making each more inclusive of minority voices and ways of knowing and safer places for the free exchange of ideas. The results were transformative, establishing an atmosphere where all viewpoints were respected, and freeing both faculty and students to explore new ideas.

Section Four: Developing Our Craft

Mary Deane Sorcinelli, Tara Gray, and Jane Birch describe in Chapter Eighteen integrated approaches to professional development that support faculty in many areas, including orientation, mentoring, scholarly writing, time management, career advancement, leadership, and service. They suggest ways that centers can create programming that goes beyond instructional development and supports a more expansive range of faculty work.

In Chapter Nineteen, Mark Hohnstreiter and Tara Gray describe a comprehensive model by which their teaching center raises funds from faculty and others. They find that the payoff from a fundraising effort is huge, not only in terms of money, but in terms of the personal investment of participants, both valuable in difficult economic times.

Susan Hines investigated faculty development program evaluation practices at thirty-three established, centralized, university-funded teaching and learning centers. In contrast to her prior study that revealed that limitations of time, resources, and assessment knowledge resulted in superficial evaluation practices, she reports in Chapter Twenty that established centralized centers have significantly stronger practices for evaluating their services.

In Chapter Twenty-One, Linda Nilson, Ed Nuhfer, and Bonnie Mullinix synthesize and identify patterns among more than thirty cases furnished by faculty developers who experienced career disruptions such as center closures. They offer evidence-based counsel to developers on how to recognize potential hazards and mitigate damage.

Shelda Debowski concludes the volume in Chapter Twenty-Two with a reflective review of the need to review and reform the role of faculty development. She argues that the faculty developer's portfolio needs to expand to include support for academic research, career management, and leadership roles, as well as organizational development strategies to complement existing individual and instructional approaches.

To Improve the Academy offers professionals engaged in faculty development the opportunity to share expertise, research, and best practices to enrich efforts to support the enhancement of higher education teaching and learning. *TIA* represents the true spirit of the POD Network in the unselfish sharing of our wisdom and expertise to enrich our profession and those with whom we work: colleagues and students, teachers and learners. This volume joins those that have preceded it in recording our evolving knowledge of what works and bringing our collective wisdom to bear on promoting improvement in faculty, instructional, and organizational development.

ACKNOWLEDGMENTS

A volume of this type would not be possible without the dedication and enthusiasm of myriad members of the community whose work it reflects and documents. We received fifty-four manuscripts, all of them with significant merit, and fortunately we were able to trust our reviewers to help us make some very hard choices. We distributed 220 reviews across seventy-seven reviewers. Many experienced reviewers from *To Improve the Academy, Vol. 29* signed on again for this volume, as did many people who had also submitted manuscripts, and many new colleagues volunteered to join us. The reviews we received were, for the most part, timely, thorough, thoughtful, and constructive. Taken together, the four reviews of each manuscript reflected the diversity of perspectives that is one of the many strengths of our organization. Many authors whose manuscripts were ultimately rejected expressed their thanks for helpful comments that would inform continuation of their work.

Those reviewers who worked so diligently to bring you the best possible *To Improve the Academy, Vol. 30* are Roberta Ambrosino, Dorothe Bach, Donna Bailey, Gabriele Bauer, Danilo Baylen, Delores Bertoti, Victoria Bhavsar, Donna Bird, Phyllis Blumberg, Jim Borgford-Parnell, Susanna Calkins, Chris Clark, Jeanette Clausen, Eli Collins-Brown, Bonnie Daniel, Michele DiPietro, Sally Ebest, Donna Ellis, Bonnie Farley-Lucas, Beth Fisher, Christopher Garrett, Judy Grace, David Green, Jace Hargis, Nira Hativa, Jason Hendryx, Jennifer Herman, Sue Hines, Linda Hodges, Katherine Hoffman, Mikaela Huntzinger, Sallie Ives, Wayne Jacobson, Doug James, Kathleen Kane, Bruce Kelley, Bruce Larson, Marion Larson, Jean Layne, Virginia Lee, Jean Mandernach, Jean Martin-Williams, Jeanette McDonald, Sal Meyers, Theresa Moore, Bonnie Mullinix, Ed Neal, Linda Noble, Ed Nuhfer, Leslie Ortquist-Ahrens, Patrick B. O'Sullivan, Michael Palmer, Donna Petherbridge, Patty Phelps, Susan Polich, Michael Potter, Gerald Ratliff, Stewart Ross, Brian Rybarczyk, Gertina van Schalkwyk, Beez Schell, Connie Schroeder, Peter Shaw, Jennifer Shinaberger, Cecilia Shore, Shelley Smith, Lynn Sorenson, Susan Sullivan, Suzanne Tapp, Brigitte

Valesey, Karen Ward, Stacie Williams, Eva Wong, Mary Wright, Jon Young, and Donna Ziegenfuss.

Thanks are due to Hoag Holmgren, executive director of the POD Network, for supporting our efforts, and to David Brightman and Aneesa Davenport of Jossey-Bass for their prompt responses and gentle reminders. My sincere appreciation goes to the University of North Florida for providing logistical support for this endeavor. Special thanks are due to Summer Sullivan for her efficiency, diligence, and sharp editorial eye.

My collaboration with associate editor Jim Groccia has been both productive and enjoyable—all that I had hoped and expected, and far more. This volume is truly a team effort, and its quality and comprehensiveness are attributable in no small measure to his work. With the completion of this volume, I pass *To Improve the Academy* into his capable hands.

Judith E. Miller
University of North Florida
Jacksonville, Florida
March 9, 2011

ETHICAL GUIDELINES FOR EDUCATIONAL DEVELOPERS

Preamble

As professionals, educational developers (faculty, teaching assistant, organizational, instructional, and staff developers) have a unique opportunity and a special responsibility to contribute to the improvement of the quality of teaching and learning in higher education. As members of the academic community, they are subject to all the codes of conduct and ethical guidelines that already exist for those who work or study on campuses and those who belong to disciplinary associations. Educational developers have special ethical responsibilities because of the unique and privileged access they have to people and often to sensitive information. This document provides general guidelines to inform the practice of professionals working in educational development roles in higher education.

Educational developers in higher education come from various disciplinary areas and follow different career tracks. Some work as educational developers on a part-time basis or for simply a short time, but for others educational development is a full-time career. The nature of their responsibilities and prerogatives as developers varies with their position in the organization, their experience, interests, and talents, and with the special characteristics of their institutions. This document attempts to provide general ethical guidelines that should apply to most developers across a variety of settings.

Ethical guidelines indicate a consensus among practitioners about the ideals that should inform their practice as professionals, as well as those behaviors that would constitute misconduct. Between the ideal of exemplary practice and misconduct lies a gray area where dilemmas arise: choices may seem equally right or wrong; different roles and/or responsibilities may place competing, if not incompatible, demands on developers; or certain behaviors may seem questionable but no consensus can determine that those behaviors are examples of misconduct.

It is our hope that these guidelines complement typical programmatic statements of philosophy and mission and that educational developers can use the guidelines effectively to promote ethical practice. This document describes the ideals of practice, identifies specific behaviors that typify professional misconduct, and provides a model to think through situations which present conflicting choices or questionable behavior.

Guidelines for Practice

Ideals of Practice

Ideals that should inform the practice of educational developers include the following areas of professional behavior: providing responsible service to clients, demonstrating competence and integrity, assuring that the rights of others are respected, maintaining the confidentiality of any information regarding contact with clients, and fulfilling responsibilities to the profession of educational development as a whole. It is expected that educational developers will understand and integrate these ideals into their daily practice. Even though the following categories are viewed as ideals of practice, many of the individual statements are quite concrete and practical, while others encourage educational developers to attain a high standard of excellence.

Educational developers evince a high level of responsibility to their clients and are expected to:

1. Provide services to everyone within their mandate, provided that they are able to serve all clients responsibly;

2. Treat clients fairly, respecting their uniqueness, their fundamental rights, dignity and worth, and their right to set objectives and make decisions;

3. Maintain appropriate boundaries in the relationship, avoid exploiting the relationship in any way, and be clear with themselves and their clients about their specific role;

4. Protect all privileged information, obtaining informed consent from clients before using or referring publicly to client cases in such a way that the client could be identified;

5. Continue service only as long as the client is benefiting, discontinue service by mutual consent, and suggest other resources to meet needs they cannot or should not address.

Competence and Integrity

Aspects of competence and integrity discussed in these guidelines include the behavior of educational developers, the skills and the boundaries they should respect and enforce, and the need for them to assure the rights of their clients. Educational developers should also interact competently and with integrity in relationships with their co-workers, supervisees, and the community.

BEHAVIOR

In order to assure evidence of competence and integrity, educational developers should:

a. Clarify professional roles and obligations;

b. Accept appropriate responsibility for their behavior;

c. Make no false or intentionally misleading statements;

d. Avoid the distortion and misuse of their work;

e. Clarify their roles and responsibilities with each party from the outset when providing services at the behest of a third party;

f. Accept appropriate responsibility for the behavior of those they supervise;

g. Model ethical behavior with co-workers and those they supervise and in the larger academic community.

SKILLS AND BOUNDARIES

To practice effectively educational developers need an awareness of their belief systems, personal skills, and personal knowledge base and cognizance of their own and their clients' boundaries. Ethical practice requires that educational developers:

a. Be reflective and self-critical in their practice;

b. Seek out knowledge, skills, and resources continually to under-gird and expand their practice;

c. Consult with other professionals when they lack the experience or training for a particular case or endeavor or if they seek to prevent or avoid unethical conduct;

d. Know and work within the boundaries of their competence and time limitations;

e. Know and act in consonance with their purpose, mandate, and philosophy, integrating the latter insofar as possible;

f. Strive to be aware of their own belief systems, values, biases, needs, and the effect of these on their work;

g. Incorporate diverse points of view;

h. Allow no personal or private interests to conflict or appear to conflict with professional duties or clients' needs;

i. Take care of their personal welfare so they can facilitate clients' development; and

j. Ensure that they have the institutional freedom to do their job ethically.

CLIENTS' RIGHTS

Because educational developers work in a variety of settings with a variety of clients and interact within different teaching and learning contexts, they must be sensitive to and respectful of intellectual, individual, and power differences. Educational developers should thus:

a. Be receptive to different styles and approaches to teaching and learning, and to others' professional roles and functions;

b. Respect the rights of others to hold values, attitudes, and opinions different from their own;

c. Respect the right of clients to refuse services or to request the services of another professional;

d. Work against harassment and discrimination of any kind, including race, ethnicity, gender, class, religion, sexual orientation, disability, age, nationality, etc.; and

e. Be aware of various power relationships with clients (e.g., power based on position or on information) and not abuse their power.

Confidentiality

Educational developers maintain confidentiality regarding client identity, information, and records within appropriate limits and according to legal regulations. Educational developers should:

a. Keep confidential the identity of clients, as well as their professional observations, interactions, or conclusions related to specific clients or cases;

b. Know the legal requirements regarding appropriate and inappropriate professional confidentiality (e.g., for cases of murder, suicide, or gross misconduct);

c. Store and dispose of records in a safe way; and comply with institutional, state, and federal regulations about storing and ownership of records; and

d. Conduct discreet conversations among professional colleagues in supervisory relationships and never discuss clients in public places.

Responsibilities to the Profession

Educational developers work with colleagues in the local, national, and international arena. In order to assure the integrity of the profession, they:

a. Attribute materials and ideas to their creators or authors;

b. Contribute ideas, experience, and knowledge to colleagues;

c. Respond promptly to requests from colleagues;

d. Respect colleagues and acknowledge collegial differences;

e. Work positively for the development of individuals and the profession;

f. Cooperate with other units and professionals involved in development efforts; and

g. Are advocates for their institutional and professional missions.

Professional Misconduct

The professional misconduct of educational developers would reflect gross negligence and disdain for the Guidelines for Practice stated above. Unethical, unprofessional, and incompetent behaviors carried out by educational developers should be brought to the attention of the association. Individual educational developers should take responsibility if or when they become aware of gross unethical conduct by any colleague in the profession.

Ethical Conflicts in Educational Development

CONFLICTS ARISING FROM MULTIPLE RESPONSIBILITIES, CONSTITUENTS, RELATIONSHIPS, AND LOYALTIES

Educational developers may encounter conflicts that arise from multiple responsibilities, constituents, relationships, and loyalties. Because educational developers are responsible to their institutions, faculty, graduate students, undergraduate students, and to themselves, it is inevitable that conflict will arise. For example, multiple responsibilities and relationships to various constituencies, together with competing loyalties, may lead to conflicting ethical responsibilities. The following examples point out situations in which conflicts may arise and identify the specific conflict.

Example 1: An instructor is teaching extremely poorly and students in the class are suffering seriously as a result. *Conflict:* In this situation the educational developer is faced with a conflict between the responsibility of confidentiality to the client-teacher and responsibility to the students and the institution.

Example 2: A faculty member wants to know how a teaching assistant with whom the educational developer is working is progressing in his/her consultation or in the classroom. *Conflict:* In this situation the educational developer is faced with a conflict between responding to the faculty member's legitimate concern and with maintaining confidentiality vis-à-vis the teaching assistant.

Example 3: The educational developer knows first hand that a professor-client is making racist or sexist remarks or is sexually harassing a student. *Conflict:* In this situation the educational developer is faced with a conflict between confidentiality vis-à-vis the professor-client and not only institutional/personal ethical responsibilities but responsibility to the students as well.

Example 4: A fine teacher who has worked with the educational developer for two years is coming up for tenure and asks that a letter be written to the tenure committee. *Conflict:* In this situation the educational developer is faced with a conflict between rules regarding client confidentiality and the educational developer's commitment to advocate for good teaching on campus and in tenure decisions.

In such instances of conflict educational developers need to practice sensitive and sensible confidentiality. It is best that they:

1. Consult in confidence with other professionals when they are faced with conflicting or confusing ethical choices.

2. Inform the other person or persons when they have to break confidentiality, unless doing so would jeopardize their personal safety or the safety of someone else.

3. Break confidentiality according to legal precedent in cases of potential suicide, murder, or gross misconduct. In such cases, to do nothing is to do something.

4. Decide cases of questionable practice individually, after first informing themselves to the best of their ability of all the ramifications of their actions.

5. Work to determine when they will act or not act, while being mindful of the rules and regulations of the institution and the relevant legal requirements.

CONFLICTS ARISING FROM MULTIPLE ROLES

Educational developers often assume or are assigned roles that might be characterized as teaching police, doctor, coach, teacher, or advocate, among others. They are expected to be institutional models or even the conscience for good teaching on their campuses. Yet, in their work with professors and graduate students, they endeavor to provide a "safe place" for their clients to work on their teaching. Another potential area for conflict arises from the fact that educational developers may serve both as faculty developers and as faculty members. As developers, they support clients in their efforts to improve their teaching; in their role as faculty they often serve on review committees that evaluate other faculty. Either role may give them access to information that cannot appropriately be shared or communicated beyond the committee or the consultation relationship (even if it would be useful for the other role).

An important area of potential conflict exists in the case of the summative evaluation of teaching. Departmental faculty and campus administrators (chairs, deans, etc.) are responsible for the assessment of teaching for personnel decisions. Educational developers should not generally be placed in this situation because of the confidentiality requirements noted in the section on Guidelines for Practice. In general, educational developers do not make summative judgments about an individual's teaching. In particular, they should never perform the role of developer and summative evaluator concurrently for the same individual unless they have that person's explicit consent and with proper declaration to any panel or committee involved. However, educational developers may:

1. Provide assessment tools

2. Collect student evaluations

3. Help individuals prepare dossiers

4. Educate those who make summative decisions

5. Critique evaluation systems

Conclusion

This document is an attempt to define ethical behaviors for the current practice of educational development in higher education. In creating this document the association has referred to and borrowed from the Ethical Guidelines of the American Psychological Association, the American Association for Marriage and Family Therapy, Guidance Counselors, the Society for Teaching and Learning in Higher Education in Canada, and the Staff and Educational Development Association in the United Kingdom. The association will continue to refine these guidelines in light of the changes and issues that confront the profession. The guidelines will be updated on a periodic basis by the Core Committee of the Professional and Organizational Development Network in Higher Education.

TO IMPROVE THE ACADEMY

SECTION ONE

PROMOTING OUR COLLEAGUES' PROFESSIONAL SUCCESS

GRADUATE STUDENT INTERNSHIPS AS A PATHWAY TO THE PROFESSION OF EDUCATIONAL DEVELOPMENT

Kathryn E. Linder, Suffolk University

Stephanie V. Rohdieck, Alan Kalish, Teresa A. Johnson, Kathryn M. Plank, Laurie A. Maynell, The Ohio State University

Educational developers can help create a cadre of well-prepared new professionals by mentoring them during graduate study. Through an educational development intern position, we created a mentorship opportunity for graduate students interested in the field of educational development as a career opportunity. Teaching center staff, participating graduate student interns, and the field of educational development benefited from the model.

Although graduate students are often mentored within the field of educational development through opportunities such as graduate assistantships in teaching and learning centers, more extensive and structured formal training experiences for graduate students are rare. In this article, we argue that through an educational development intern position, teaching centers can create a mentorship opportunity for graduate students who are interested in the field of educational development as a career opportunity. While all graduate student positions in teaching centers may create allies or new professionals for the field serendipitously (Gosling, McDonald, & Stockley, 2007; Meizlish & Wright, 2009), the internship position we describe is meant to intentionally train new professionals who want to pursue a career within educational development.

The Literature on Mentoring New Developers

In the past decade, educational development scholars have begun to study their own training and pathways into the field (Chism, 2007; Gosling et al., 2007; McDonald & Stockley, 2008, 2010; Meizlish & Wright, 2009; Stefani, 1999). With the exception of Meizlish and Wright (2009), these studies do not include thoughts on training and mentoring graduate students into careers as educational developers.

While scholars point to the importance of having multiple pathways into the field (Gosling et al., 2007; Stefani, 1999), new educational developers have expressed their desire for mentorship before and as they are entering the field (Jensen, 2002). Despite training programs from organizations such as the Professional and Organizational Development (POD) Network, which offers annual one-week and one-day workshops for new professionals, scholars have found that developers are entering the field with little experience. Indeed, Chism (2007) found that developers often receive "on-the-job" training without any prior preparation (p. 1).

The literature on acculturation to the academic profession suggests that formal, sequential, serial, and affirming forms of socialization tend to lead to more successful outcomes for those seeking to join the profession (Tierney & Rhoads, 1994). Recent research has pointed to the value of similarly structured activities for professionals entering the field of educational development to gain both content knowledge and hands-on experience (Chism, 2007; McDonald, 2010). Scholars in the field have also begun to argue for the importance of "growing our own" (Meizlish & Wright, 2009, p. 386), encouraging teaching centers to take on the responsibility of training and mentoring new professionals into the field.

Mentorship initiatives such as the POD internship grant program have illustrated the success of intentional pipeline support in which opportunities are created for graduate students and faculty members to be trained as educational developers. Ouellet and Stanley (2004) found not only that the POD internship grant program benefited teaching centers that participated, but also that the program "does appear to serve as a catalyst for engaging interns further in faculty and instructional development careers" (pp. 215–216). For centers at institutions with graduate student populations, the opportunity exists to mentor new professionals from the beginning of their academic careers.

With no specific higher education program devoted to training future educational developers (Gosling et al., 2007; Knapper, 2010; McDonald & Stockley, 2008), graduate students interested in the profession must often pursue whatever activities are available to them through their campus teaching center or other campus organizations that support teaching and learning. These opportunities may include volunteer facilitator positions for workshops or events or paid positions as administrative staff or graduate assistants within a teaching center. Because "the educational developer has become a recognized professional role which has moved from the fringes to the mainstream of higher education" (Gosling et al., 2007, p. 4), we believe that centers should consider offering graduate students structured mentorship opportunities to learn more about educational development as a career choice within the larger academy.

A Doctoral Internship Program at The Ohio State University

The University Center for the Advancement of Teaching (UCAT) at The Ohio State University developed a two-year doctoral internship position in 2007. The center is a moderately sized development unit, employing five permanent full-time consulting staff, a program coordinator, an office manager, a visiting consultant, and several graduate and undergraduate students. Through conversations and interactions with senior graduate students who had previously worked with our office, the staff identified potential candidates for the internship who were interested in exploring educational development in higher education as a career and invited them to apply for the position. Candidates were then interviewed by staff and selected based on their career path plans, their level of teaching experience, their indication of a genuine interest in the field, and their time to degree. One intern was selected for the first cycle (2007–2009), one for the second cycle (2009–2011), and one for the third cycle (2011–2113). All of our interns to date have been senior graduate students who have graduated on schedule; our most recent intern graduated before completing the internship after accepting a job in educational development.

The UCAT doctoral intern position consists of a twenty-hour-per-week paid graduate administrative associateship and independent study. The intern is expected to assume both research and administrative tasks, while also assisting professional staff in the teaching support mission of the office. Although the intern has many similar job tasks to our other graduate associates (GAs), such as consultation, workshop facilitation, and research responsibilities, the intern assumes a greater leadership role in a wider range of center activities.

Each intern first meets with and interviews each UCAT staff member to learn about various aspects of UCAT's work. The intern also learns about each staff member's educational development responsibilities and philosophy and entry into the field. Throughout the two-year term, the intern continues to meet monthly with UCAT's director to discuss the progress of the mentorship and to ask questions that have arisen about educational development during this training. At each meeting, the intern produces a monthly reflection paper on her or his experiences and receives feedback on her or his training. After the first year, the intern is given the opportunity to pursue a writing project of choice: the first-year intern transitioned her monthly reflection papers into writing an article, and the second-year intern transitioned her papers into drafts of a philosophy of practice for use on the job market. In each of six areas of doctoral internship training and mentorship—events, consulting, learning communities, teaching, teaching center administration, and general professionalization activities—our interns receive direct feedback from staff on performance, client feedback in the form of event assessment surveys and an annual client survey on consultation services, and anonymous client feedback solicited for an annual performance review.

Events

The academic year at UCAT begins with our annual university-wide teaching orientation for more than five hundred new graduate teaching associates. Both interns have helped UCAT staff redesign orientation curriculum, facilitate sessions at the orientation, train graduate student facilitators, and work with various orientation committees.

Throughout the year, our center also offers both campuswide and departmental workshops that are designed and presented by individual consulting staff. Since this is an integral component of teaching center services, both interns have been involved in all stages of workshop planning. As an introduction to the workshop experience, each intern went through a training process that included observing a workshop facilitated by a staff member, cocreating content and agendas, cofacilitating the workshops, and ultimately independently facilitating a workshop with feedback from staff observers and campus participants.

The hiring of our second intern in summer 2009 coincided with our university's beginning the process of converting from a quarter-based to a semester-based system. To facilitate this large-scale transformation, our teaching center created a fifteen-hour institute on course design and another on curriculum design. The intern thus had an opportunity to participate in the design and implementation of a long-term event series from its earliest planning stages through its assessment and revision.

The UCAT staff believed it was important to provide the interns with a full and realistic experience of the skills consultants need to successfully design and facilitate campuswide events and an understanding of the complex nature of such events in terms of public relations, content, goals, logistics, and staffing. Our choice to involve the interns with large-scale events from start to finish allowed staff to contextualize each event in terms of both the center's role within the university and the purpose of the event within the larger mission of our teaching center.

Consulting

Individual teaching consultation is a significant component of educational development and one of the core services that our center provides. In order for our interns to receive a foundational understanding of the intricacies of the consultation experience as well as the complexity of the consultant-client relationship, they go through a shadowing and debriefing process that is required of all new staff and graduate student consultants.

The training procedure is similar to that described for events. The three-step process follows the developmental path of new practitioners as they build knowledge and confidence before working with faculty and graduate student clients independently. First, the intern shadows several staff members on a number of consultations, sitting in on the meetings and taking notes on the interactions without interacting with the client. The staff members and intern then debrief the consultation, discussing questions the intern has for the staff members about choices made in the interaction, the rationale for the choices made, and ways that the intern may have done things differently had he or she been the consultant.

The second step in the training process is co-consultation: the intern is brought into a consultation that a staff member usually leads. The intern eventually becomes an equal participant in the interaction by asking clarifying questions, answering client questions, and offering recommendations. This intermediate step allows the intern to gain confidence interacting with clients as part of a team.

The final step in the training is for the intern to conduct consultations independently but with staff members present. The intern has complete autonomy as to the direction of the consultation, and the staff member in the room takes notes on what the intern has done well and ideas for improvement. The additional benefit of this step is that the intern can bring the staff member into the conversation or ask questions if necessary. Intern progression through these three steps depends on intern skills as well as the consultation needs of the center. After the intern completes all three steps to staff satisfaction, the intern can then consult with clients independently.

In addition to shadowing, the intern attends monthly codevelopment meetings where we discuss client cases, training progression, and relevant literature, as well as engage in case scenarios and role-play activities designed to strengthen the intern's consultation skills. The interns have found that these codevelopment meetings have the benefit of building community with other GAs in the office who are frequently working on different projects from the intern. Building community around consultation experience allows all participants in the codevelopment sessions to contribute their thoughts and ideas for tough cases (for example, clients who come to the center without a specific reason or graduate students with very low teaching evaluation scores).

The training procedure for interns is very similar to that of new consultants and GAs, although there are several important differences. First, rather than working with one staff member, interns are asked to shadow and co-consult with multiple staff members so they are exposed to a wide variety of models. Also, whereas the procedure we have outlined for consultants and GAs typically occurs over a full year, interns follow an accelerated schedule. Finally, the debriefing portion is usually more in-depth for interns than for other graduate students. Interns may also be given tougher consults than their GA peers and are asked to co-consult with staff members on faculty consultations about individual teaching needs, as well as collaborate with staff to provide departmental consultation.

Learning Communities

In addition to facilitating large events, workshops, and individual consultations, our center's staff members coordinate instructor learning communities. These learning communities meet monthly throughout the academic year, and participants present their accomplishments at an annual breakfast that celebrates their work.

Our first-cycle intern became involved with our graduate teaching fellows learning community because the staff member who ran that program took an extended leave. The intern scheduled and attended all meetings, helped create agendas, independently facilitated several of the meetings, and consulted with learning community members as needed. Because the intern was involved in the community from the very beginning, participants reacted positively toward the shared facilitation in their end-of-year feedback.

Our second-cycle intern expressed an interest in working with our center's midcareer learning community in order to become familiar with services for experienced faculty. Because of the small size of the group (nine members, one of them a faculty facilitator), the staff agreed that it would be best for the intern to attend meetings as a participant rather than a facilitator so that the dynamic of the group's structure did not change. The community welcomed her participation in the discussions and expressed interest in her career development.

Since learning communities are very much participant driven, these experiences gave our interns the opportunity to observe and practice a diverse set of facilitation skills. The challenge in facilitating learning communities is often to provide guidance and boundaries while still allowing the group to set its own agenda and encourage discussion to evolve organically. In particular, the staff wanted each intern to observe the listening skills, flexibility, and ability to bring in resources that are necessary components of facilitating a faculty learning community.

Teaching

During the 2010 winter quarter, one of the consultants was revising a graduate course on college teaching, and the staff decided this would be an appropriate learning experience for the intern. In collaboration with the staff member teaching the course, the intern codesigned the syllabus, reading list, lesson plan, assessment activities, and course wiki system. In addition to team teaching with the staff member, the intern independently designed and taught two of the ten class sessions. Team teaching provided a unique professionalization experience for both the staff instructor and intern.

Because the teaching experience was such an intensive collaboration, there were effective opportunities for experimenting with team-teaching styles, developing rapport as cofacilitators, and learning from each other's pedagogical philosophies. The debriefing that followed each class session provided ample opportunity to discuss the rationales for and impact of instructional choices. Because neither the staff member nor the intern had cotaught before, both left the experience with an additional skill set that simultaneously offered personal fulfillment and professional value.

Teaching Center Administration

During the first cycle (2007–2009) of our internship program, the intern was engaged in conversations about the administration of the unit and attended numerous staff meetings. However, because the first intern was quite clear in exit interviews that some of our decision-making processes remained opaque, the second intern was treated from the beginning as a full member of the core staff team. She attended almost all staff meetings, was given an annual review, and participated in our administrative decision-making discussions whenever and wherever appropriate. During the second cycle of the internship, for example, UCAT hired a visiting consultant, a new program coordinator, a new graduate associate, and several new graduate student facilitators for our university-wide teaching orientation. Our second intern was included in the review of applications and materials, the interview processes, and the hiring discussions for each of these positions.

Interns have also been given program coordination responsibilities, including our graduate interdisciplinary specialization in college and university teaching. In addition to collecting syllabi for courses in this program, interns responded to questions from interested graduate students and updated the program website with information as needed.

Finally, interns are given the opportunity to observe university committee meetings with the director of our center and other members of the staff. We have found that these committee shadowing opportunities allow the intern to learn more about the university's structure, the relationship between the teaching center and other administrative offices, and the kinds of administrative decisions to which teaching centers contribute.

Professionalization Activities

Each of our interns attended two POD conferences. In their first year, they traveled to the conference as an attendee to observe the presentations, network with other graduate students, and participate in the pre-conference workshop for new consultants in the field. In their second year, together with staff, interns prepare proposals on components of educational development.

Attending the annual POD conference also helps interns to experience the scholarship that is valued within the educational development community. Because our interns represent the interdisciplinarity of our field (thus far, one from education and the other from women's studies), attending a national conference allows them to see a variety of potential research projects. While other graduate students within our center may also participate in scholarly activities, their level of engagement in research is usually limited to supporting the staff's larger projects. Our interns, however, are encouraged to conduct research projects independently and in collaboration with staff and to submit their efforts for publication. In their initial training and as part of their more individualized research projects, both interns read widely within the field of educational development in order to contextualize their internship experience.

Our interns are also trained to develop technology skills that are becoming increasingly relevant to our field, such as Web design and the use of databases. In the second cycle of our mentorship program, our intern was trained on the design and implementation of wikis for interdisciplinary institutes in course and curriculum design, as well as wikis' use for structuring student learning experiences.

The Benefits for Interns

Throughout the two cycles of our mentorship program, based on feedback received through intern monthly reflection papers and exit interviews, we have found that the internship position meets at least four specific needs for graduate students interested in exploring educational development as a career.

Hands-On Experience

At the end of their two-year experience in our office, each intern was especially grateful for the opportunity to observe and have hands-on experience with workshops, consulting, large-event coordination, teaching, a variety of administrative tasks, and the facilitation of learning communities. Interns felt that the opportunities to talk through assessment practices of teaching centers, measure the effectiveness of services, and ask questions about their experiences before, during, and after they facilitated various activities were powerful components of their training.

Mentoring and Debriefing

Both interns appreciated being mentored by multiple staff members with different backgrounds, professional styles, and problem-solving approaches. The open conversations between interns and faculty members concerning instructional decisions, student engagement, and course planning were especially valuable to the first intern, who commented,

"These conversations led to an appreciation of the multiple disciplines on campus, a grasp of students' experiences at a large research university, and an understanding of work-life challenges for faculty."

A Contextualized Introduction to the Field

Through the expectation that interns read widely within the field and begin to add to the research of educational development, they found that their work experience was contextualized in a variety of ways. Our first intern commented that she "appreciated the opportunities to frame teaching and learning in terms of student understanding. Considering the student experience from a university, program, and classroom perspective underscored the value of educational development as a growing field."

Our second intern, on returning from a job interview in the field, expressed her thanks that the internship exposed her to the underlying philosophies of practice in our center and of the field, including rationales for client confidentiality, the limitations of our center's mission, and the ethical obligations of consultants. Her awareness of these larger educational development concerns helped her more clearly articulate her personal philosophy of practice.

Formalized Skill Building Through Intentional Training Activities

Interns appreciated building their skills as educational developers through structured training rather than through self-teaching. From the beginning, staff envisioned a distinct sequence of planned activities that lead to a specified role in the organization and illustrate the complexities and challenges of work in educational development. Each intern learned that becoming a consultant involves building skills over time, recognizing one's strengths and weaknesses, and honing one's abilities to work with teaching center clients in a variety of environments.

The Center Perspective

After two cycles of this internship program, the UCAT staff have identified both benefits and challenges to mentoring graduate students into the field using this method.

Benefits

Perhaps the most obvious benefit to an internship program is having an extra staff member who, within a few months (depending on his or her background), can contribute to the center. After an introductory period, our interns handle basic, straightforward teaching center tasks (for example, small group instructional diagnoses and making short promotional presentations) as well as assist staff in tackling projects that frequently haunt staff to-do lists but fail to be accomplished due to work overload.

As consultants, we often hear our clients say that they are amazed at how much they learn from teaching, and the internship program has reinforced this statement. Having an intern on staff provided opportunities for reflection on our practice by stimulating conversations that may have occurred only because there was an intern in the center. Aspects of the mission of a teaching and learning center, such as confidentiality and the importance of voluntary client participation, are often embedded in daily practice but not explicitly discussed unless new staff are present. Discussing our center's mission and purpose on a regular basis as each new cycle of the internship program is initiated has led to many larger-scale conversations about our center's strategic plan.

Having the intern shadow consultations has benefited both intern and consulting staff. Because consultation is so often done behind closed doors and under strict policies of confidentiality, it is all too often a skill that is developed in isolation. Just as we encourage instructors to open the classroom door and engage in a community of teachers, as consultants it is equally important to share and learn from one another. Although we frequently discuss the consultation process or specific consultations with colleagues, we have found that the presence of an intern creates an added structured opportunity for reflection and growth.

When discussing consultation with an intern, staff members are frequently required to articulate a rationale for decisions made about what to do and say (or not say). In some cases, intern questions have forced us to explore actions that have become so automatic that we are barely aware of them. In addition, debriefing after shadowed consults helps us think about other intervention options. Since the intern has shadowed several different consultants, she or he is often the link between different styles and approaches and can bring them into the conversation. Having a third person in the room gives a unique opportunity to hear another person's perspective on our words or actions and to see ourselves as our clients may see us. All of this helps us to become more self-aware and intentional in our practice.

Challenges

One administrative challenge was differentiating the internship position from other graduate associate positions. We learned that we had to clarify to staff and students that although both positions share job tasks, the intern is provided a wider range of experiences, is expected to take more of a leadership role in some of those tasks, and is simultaneously engaged in a study of the field. Those clarifications come at the start of employment for both interns and GAs, during staff meetings, and in individual meetings with GAs.

The other challenge we have encountered is the necessity of finding time to integrate, collaborate with, train, and supervise each intern. With any mentorship or training, time needs to be devoted to making sure the intern gains necessary skills and knowledge to be able to work independently. Monthly meetings with staff members; regular planning meetings about events, consultations, and other tasks; and impromptu discussions about the educational development field and job market all take time. Without these meetings and discussions, however, we have found that both the intern and the center staff can too easily lose focus or momentum and miss important learning opportunities. By organizing meeting times and delineating which staff will attend to specific discussions, we believe this challenge can be easily overcome.

Conclusion

We have found that the benefits of an internship program outweigh the challenges. However, because our internship program is still in its infancy, with only two interns having completed the program, our staff is just beginning to discuss formal mechanisms to measure the long-term success of this training and mentorship structure. Going forward, we plan to develop a set of measures of success for the internship structure that includes the following items:

• *Regular staff review of interns.* While interns are employed by our center, we ask that staff regularly review them through annual reports and throughout their participation in various events and training modules. These staff check-ins allow us to make sure each intern is receiving a wide range of experiences by working with several staff members.

• *Exit interviews.* Interviews with our former interns regarding their mentorship experience will assess a number of facets of the experience:

  • *Completeness.* Do our interns believe that their training prepared them for what they are encountering in the field? Do any components of their training need more depth or breadth?

  • *Challenge.* Are the interns challenged and intellectually stimulated by their work in our office? Are there areas where they would have liked to have received further training?

- *Support.* Do we support our interns appropriately as potential new professionals as they train to enter a career track that may be different from what they originally planned? Is the field contextualized appropriately for interns as they prepare to find a job in educational development?

- *Information regarding future employment.* We will continue to track where our interns are employed after they leave our institution. Do they enter the field of educational development? What kind of position and at what level of skill are they hired?

- *Longitudinal interviews.* We plan to stay in touch with our interns in the long term so that we can see their progress and celebrate their accomplishments as colleagues. If our interns enter the community of educational developers, these interviews will probably be conducted regularly at POD gatherings.

Although we do not yet have long-term assessment data for our program, the initial feedback that we have gathered from both the interns and the staff with whom they have worked suggests value in the process. We believe that our doctoral internship program benefits the field of educational development as former interns enter the workforce. Intern exposure to guided reflection, the scholarship of teaching and learning, and the philosophies of educational development in advance of joining the field may allow smoother transitions into their positions as new professionals.

Based on our experience, we highly recommend that other teaching centers develop the opportunity to employ and mentor graduate student interns into the field of educational development. Our hope is that internship programs for graduate students will serve the field by creating a larger number of well-prepared new professionals. In the future, a comparison of outcomes from several internship systems may help us further determine the critical features of mentorship programs for new professionals.

REFERENCES

Chism, N.V.N. (2007, October). *A professional priority: Preparing educational developers.* Paper presented at the 32nd annual meeting of the Professional and Organizational Development Network in Higher Education, Pittsburgh, PA.

Gosling, D., McDonald, J., & Stockley, D. (2007). We did it our way! Narratives of pathways to the profession of educational development. *Educational Development, 8*(4), 1–6.

Jensen, J. D. (2002). If I knew then what I know now: A first-year faculty consultant's top ten list. In K. H. Gillespie (Ed.), *A guide to faculty development: Practical advice, examples, and resources* (pp. 92–98). San Francisco, CA: Jossey-Bass.

Knapper, C. (2010). Plus ça change . . . Educational development past and future. In J. McDonald & D. Stockley (Eds.), *New directions for teaching and learning: No. 122. Pathways to the profession of educational development* (pp. 1–5). San Francisco, CA: Jossey-Bass.

McDonald, J. (2010). Charting pathways into the field of educational development. In J. McDonald & D. Stockley (Eds.), *New directions for teaching and learning: No. 122. Pathways to the profession of educational development* (pp. 37–45). San Francisco, CA: Jossey-Bass.

McDonald, J., & Stockley, D. (2008). Pathways to the profession of educational development: An international perspective. *International Journal for Academic Development, 13*(3), 213–218.

McDonald, J., & Stockley, D. (2010). *New directions for teaching and learning: No. 122. Pathways to the profession of educational development.* San Francisco, CA: Jossey-Bass.

Meizlish, D. S., & Wright, M. C. (2009). Preparing advocates for faculty development: Expanding the meaning of "growing our own." In L. B. Nilson & J. E. Miller (Eds.), *To improve the academy: Vol. 27. Resources for faculty, instructional, and organizational development* (pp. 385–400). San Francisco, CA: Jossey-Bass.

Ouellett, M. L., & Stanley, C. (2004). Fostering diversity in a faculty development organization. In C. Wehlburg & S. Chadwick-Blossey (Eds.), *To improve the academy: Vol. 22. Resources for faculty, instructional, and organizational development* (pp. 206–225). San Francisco, CA: Jossey-Bass.

Stefani, L. (1999). On becoming an academic developer: A personal journey. *International Journal for Academic Development, 4*(2), 102–110.

Tierney, W. G., & Rhoads, R. A. (1994). *Faculty socialization as a cultural process: A mirror of institutional commitment* (ASHE-ERIC Higher Education Report No. 93:6). Washington, DC: George Washington University, School of Education and Human Development.

2

THE DIGITAL ACADEMY

PREPARING FACULTY FOR DIGITAL COURSE
DEVELOPMENT

Sunay V. Palsole, Beth L. Brunk-Chavez,
University of Texas at El Paso

New generations of learners necessitate new ways of teaching, and hybrid courses can help institutions leverage technologies to improve teaching and learning. The adoption of a new instructional paradigm, however, requires attention to the faculty's ability to create and deliver effective courses. The University of Texas at El Paso has developed the Digital Academy to help faculty interweave online elements with face-to-face teaching. The model is pliable and portable in its application to other universities.

University educators are challenged to engage and educate a generation of learners who were born into the digital age, grew up with digital technologies readily available, think and learn very differently from previous generations of students, and are highly engaged with technology in multiple ways (Howe & Strauss, 2000; Palfrey & Gasser, 2008; Tapscott, 1999). Given the technological attitudes and experiences of the digital generation, it is no surprise that these students enter universities with significant expectations regarding the use of technology to support their learning. However, students' expectations of learning anywhere, anytime, and with a variety of technological tools may exceed their instructors' abilities to use technology innovatively and effectively (Roberts, 2005). At the same time, universities are experiencing growing enrollments and therefore an increasing demand for classroom space, putting tremendous pressure on them to meet scheduling demands.

These dual demands of shifting student learning styles and limited space are certainly challenging, but they also generate an opportunity for faculty developers to work with instructors toward creatively and efficiently transforming the delivery of university courses while continuing to maintain high academic standards. Much can be achieved by rethinking traditional classroom spaces and replacing face time by leveraging various technologies to deliver content and encourage interaction online (National Center for Academic Transformation, 2005). One solution is to move selected courses into a hybrid environment. Hybrid, or blended, delivery combines the best features of online learning and face-to-face teaching (Sands, 2002). Although variations are possible, students enrolled in hybrid courses generally meet one day a week in a classroom and shift a significant portion of the work into an online environment such as a course management system or wiki. Therefore, hybrid delivery of courses enables universities to reduce the need for classroom space by 50 percent or more and provide students with the opportunity to learn in a more flexible anytime, anywhere environment.

The Challenges of Shifting to Hybrid Delivery

While campuses embrace the multiple benefits that hybrid courses provide, the reality is that many college faculty are not prepared to teach in this blended environment. They are content specialists but not yet "computer-empowered users," whom Selber (2004) described as being able to "integrate computers . . . productively, and [to] cope reasonably well in dynamic environments" (p. 46). Instructors need to be computer-empowered users who can "confront skill demands, collaborate online, and explore instructional opportunities" (Selber, 2004, p. 46). Therefore, faculty developers can play an integral role in gauging the technological literacies of faculty who are sometimes intimidated by learning new technologies or have difficulty translating what they do well in the physical classroom to an online environment. In addition, instructors who are empowered users in the traditional classroom often learn that these strengths alone are not sufficient for making the transition to a hybrid course. To teach a successful hybrid class, instructors need to do more than know how to use technology. They must also reenvision their instruction and be willing to replace the traditional sage-on-stage approach with more student-centered pedagogy.

Cho and Berge (2002) identified major barriers that most faculty face when creating and delivering hybrid or online courses, no matter what their comfort level with technology, including administrative structure, evaluation of effectiveness, quality of social interaction, student support services, access, faculty compensation, time, and legal issues. When moving a traditional class to a hybrid environment, such obstacles can become a great source of frustration for instructors. The Digital Academy, a series of faculty engagement and training workshops that immerses instructors in the course model they are developing, can help alleviate these frustrations. By assuming the roles of both instructor and student within the Academy, faculty can become comfortable in the design and delivery of their own hybrid courses.

The Digital Academy

Since the early 2000s, many outstanding articles and books have been published to assist faculty in making the transition from face-to-face to hybrid courses, and many studies have helped us understand what pedagogies and online tools work most effectively. Although these are useful on their own, collectively they form a disparate bundle of information that needs to be brought together as a cohesive, structured whole. So when faculty at the University of Texas at El Paso expressed interest in teaching hybrid courses, instructional support services (ISS) saw value in creating a community of faculty learners who work together to design, develop, and eventually deliver hybrid courses. The Academy was formed, and in order to ensure effective teaching, the provost's office required that all faculty new to hybrid courses participate.

One of the initial steps was for ISS faculty developers to create a general framework and guiding principles for hybrid courses at our university. Academy participants learn that no matter the discipline, hybrid courses should not be run as two separate and distinct teaching environments. Rather, the face-to-face and online activities, engagements, and learning strands should interweave and inform one another. The work students do in class should directly relate to and inform the work students do online, and vice versa; the two modes of instruction must be truly blended.

In addition, we determined that instructors need support in embracing and implementing student-centered instruction, effective and timely intervention and feedback, peer-to-peer interaction, and multiple input sources within a highly interactive learning context. The success of a hybrid course depends on an instructional design that supports specific learning outcomes, allows flexible delivery, and encourages both student and instructor participation (Dudeney, 2001; Laird, 2003; Sharp, 2005). Establishing these general principles from the start enabled ISS faculty developers to determine goals for the Academy.

Academy Goals

Based on our hybrid framework and general principles, the central goals of the Academy are to help participants organize and then prepare to deliver hybrid courses in their program. To do this, the Academy focuses on four subgoals of assisting faculty:

- Modifying and applying teaching techniques for hybrid environments
- Applying practical knowledge of basic courseware management environments
- Developing strategies to engage students in a hybrid setting
- Developing effective student assessments for hybrid learning

Academy Participants

Each Digital Academy enrolls between eight and twelve participants. The first Academies were focused on specific programs such as first-year composition and the entering student program because there was a critical mass of interested instructors within these programs. While we initially felt that having participants with similar backgrounds would be productive, the Academies were altered when we realized that having a broad mix of backgrounds led to more robust and open feedback. Current Academies are run using an open call for proposals, so faculty from education may be in an Academy along with engineering, liberal arts, and science faculty. Participants have reported that they enjoyed meeting and networking with colleagues from different colleges and backgrounds, and they felt that they received valuable feedback on their instructional design and interactivities when paired with someone who was not familiar with their field of expertise.

Academy Content

Instructional tasks and readings vary depending on the strengths, weaknesses, disciplinary focus, and experience of the participants, but each Academy generally covers the following topics:

- *Building content:* Writing content for and with digital media; using the tools within the learning management system; using external tools; chunking content
- *Considering copyright:* Understanding copyright concerns and rules when distributing content in digital formats

- *Building an effective course syllabus:* Identifying key learning outcomes; uncovering hidden goals; providing a structure for class performance and rules
- *Selecting technology:* Experiencing different technologies and adapting technologies to achieve desired outcomes; evaluating technologies; considering student-driven adoption strategies
- *Mapping the course:* Approaching the course from a student perspective; creating visual maps of the course and identifying gaps in goals, assessments, and content; creating navigation schema for students
- *Encouraging student engagement:* Developing strategies for engaging students in online and face-to-face environments; connecting in-class activities to online activities and vice versa; considering alternative assessments, reward structures, and competition within the classroom; establishing instructor presence in online settings; using Web 2.0 tools (Twitter, Facebook) to create a social network within the course
- *Developing assessments:* Writing effective assessments to measure learning outcomes; developing formative and summative assessments; adopting a culture of assessment; adopting various assessment tools in a learning management system; using external applications (Articulate, StudyMate)
- *Managing the course:* Developing effective strategies to handle student concerns; considering workload issues and time constraints; setting course management goals; cycling student feedback into a continuous improvement loop; creating time lines for course updates; creating efficiencies using the grade book tool

Academy Structure

With such a robust list of goals, the first versions of the Academy consisted of two face-to-face workshops a month for one semester. However, we realized that this format created a significant disconnect for participants and that they required several follow-up sessions on both pedagogical strategies and technologies for course creation. Faculty developers felt that participants would be more engaged in the content of the workshops if they were offered in a compressed format and if more of the work were completed online. In addition, we determined that offering compressed Digital Academies for a week while classes were not in session would

Figure 2.1 The Digital Academy Model

allow participants to focus on course redesign instead of being distracted by their current teaching and grading responsibilities.

Although the Academy was compressed, the intensity of the interaction allowed faculty developers to expand the topics addressed and better integrate the theoretical with the practical. Reshaping the format to more closely reflect a hybrid course (50 percent face-to-face and 50 percent online) helped participants understand the student experience of being enrolled in one. The Academy now weaves the two seemingly disparate but complementary elements of hybrid courses to save time and model the experience. Figure 2.1 illustrates how the workshops interweave the face-to-face and online components.

In this compressed hybrid model, participants meet for five hours a day Monday through Friday. During the morning, instructors first participate in an "experience session" when they experience different interactions (content modules, crossword interactions, Webquests, and so on) that students may also experience in a hybrid course. These activities are designed to get participants thinking about student engagement and course design. The experience session is followed by a "think session," which addresses the pedagogical and theoretical aspects of course redesign. During this time, instructors are engaged in the previously assigned readings through active discussions in a face-to-face classroom setting. They are also given the assignment of redesigning existing elements of their face-to-face course by considering a variety of potential technological tools and then gathering feedback from their peers in the Academy.

The afternoon "learning the technology sessions" are spent discussing and applying technologies needed to achieve outcomes identified in the morning sessions. To integrate face-to-face meetings with online work, participants are given time to engage in online portions of the Academy course at the end of the session. They then have homework to complete before the next class meeting. Often this is a reading assignment followed by online discussions, as well as creation of one element in their new hybrid course module. By continuing through this cycle, participants

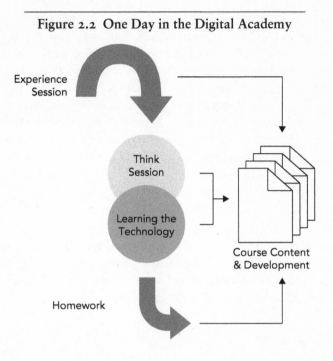

Figure 2.2 One Day in the Digital Academy

build at least one complete course module that includes content, engagement exercises, and discussion questions. To test the efficacy of the modules as they are being developed, at least two other Academy participants are enrolled as students within them and are asked to provide feedback. This feedback is then cycled into the development loop, thus leading to the improved quality of the module before it is delivered inside a hybrid course. Figure 2.2 illustrates each day's structure.

Although each Academy is designed to attain similar goals, the schedule and focus may change based on participant preparedness and experience with formal course design principles and technology use. The level of technology instruction and application is made more complex if most of the incoming participants are fairly comfortable with technology and are empowered users. This ensures a learning environment no matter what level of expertise participants have before the Academy begins.

Academy Completion

The end result of the Academy is that each participant creates a course module to be evaluated using the framework outlined by Chickering and Ehrmann (1996). The Academy emphasizes the principles of contact between students and faculty, reciprocity and cooperation among students, use of active learning techniques, high expectations, and respect for diverse talents and ways of learning. Beginning in the semester following the Academy, participants are expected to teach at least two technology-enhanced courses (less than 50 percent online), followed by fully hybrid courses (50 percent or more online) in successive semesters. Academy participants receive various incentives for completion including stipends ($1,000 to $1,500), travel money ($500), or new computers (ranging in price from $750 to $1,500). The incentive is awarded after the hybrid course is delivered.

Outcomes

Over the past five years, nearly one hundred faculty have participated in the Digital Academies offered every summer and during some winter intersessions. We have collected a variety of data and feedback from Academy participants and students enrolled in their classes.

Faculty Feedback

Eighty-seven faculty responded to the feedback survey. Approximately 83 percent felt that the experience expanded their knowledge about hybrid courses, and 93 percent felt that the Academy prepared them to develop and effectively teach their own hybrid courses. Seventy percent of participants expressed confidence in their ability to teach with technology to the extent that they forwent the technology-enhanced course and taught a hybrid course immediately. We gathered the following answers from the questions on the survey instrument:

- "Before participating in the Academy, my knowledge of teaching online, hybrid, and technology-enhanced courses could best be classified as":

    None: 21 percent

    Introductory: 0 percent

    Moderate: 43 percent

    Extensive: 23 percent

- "After participating in the Academy, my practical knowledge about teaching online, hybrid, and technology-enhanced courses satisfactorily increased."

Strongly agree: 49 percent

Agree: 23 percent

Disagree: 5 percent

Strongly disagree: 0 percent

- "The Academy effectively taught me the following about teaching online, hybrid, and technology-enhanced courses, and these things helped me in developing and teaching my course(s) (check all that apply)."

  How to rewrite course objectives that can be effectively achieved in an online, hybrid, and technology-enhanced course environment: 67 percent

  How to implement some digital tools (for example, software, hardware, Web 2.0 tools) to promote active learning: 85 percent

  How to develop authentic assessments of student learning for online delivery: 51 percent

  How to engage students online and build an online learning community: 74 percent

  How to plan the structure and content in an online, hybrid, and technology-enhanced course: 78 percent

  How to structure my course so that I can use the tools to improve my efficiency and balance instructor presence in the course with use of instructor's time: 69 percent

In addition to survey data, success of the Academy is illustrated through the following statements from Academy participants. A lecturer in history said: "The Academy really helped me see that my subject—which I thought really needed me in the classroom to be successful—could be changed to reduced class time and actually enhance the student learning. I can be a bit more creative with their assignments, which has made this interesting for the students and me." An education professor felt that the process of formally creating a hybrid course caused her to redesign her face-to-face courses to incorporate more online elements.

Finally, faculty satisfaction is borne out by the increased number of hybrid courses offered on campus. We believe that if Academy participants were not satisfied with the courses, they would not continue to teach them or encourage others to do so. The total number of officially scheduled hybrid courses has increased from 13 sections in academic year 2004–2005 to more than 250 in 2009–2010. We have also noticed an increase in the offerings of technology-enhanced courses: more than eighteen hundred sections in academic year 2009–2010. Informal data collected from faculty who offer these courses suggest that this may be the result of Academy participants' encouraging their colleagues to teach with technology.

Student Feedback

While instructor satisfaction and increased offerings are important measures, the success of the Academy is ultimately measured in terms of student satisfaction and learning. Therefore, we include student surveys in our feedback loop to help inform future iterations of the Academy. Surveys have measured student comfort levels with software applications, as well as general anxieties about use of technology in the classroom. Surveys also measured student reactions to the hybrid course format. Initial outcomes indicated that over 85 percent of students surveyed would take hybrid courses again, and over 90 percent of those same students would recommend that other students take hybrid courses. Qualitative data gathered with the student surveys suggest that students experience an increase in both knowledge and comfort with technology, in particular the learning management system and other classroom technologies. Informal student data collected from students in hybrid courses and analysis of the grade spread in hybrid courses compared to face-to-face classes suggest that hybrid courses are as engaging as face-to-face classes, with no significant differences in learning outcomes and grade spread. Follow-up data that analyzed student writing in all of the writing courses suggest that student retention and quality of reflective work are better in hybrid than in face-to-face courses.

Overall Outcomes

Some academic units such as the first-year composition program, developmental English, and education have found hybrids to be so successful that they now offer all sections of specific courses as hybrids to improve the students' technological literary and save on classroom space. For example, all sections of the first-year composition course—more than ninety of them—can be taught in existing computer lab spaces instead of in the more tightly scheduled classroom spaces. There has been an increasing demand to move some doctoral courses in education and geosciences to hybrid because faculty have found that this instructional format builds a community of learners who stay connected to course content and continue to be trackable outside the classroom discussions.

Starting a Digital Academy

Offering an Academy is an effective way of helping groups of faculty learn how to design and teach hybrid courses. We believe the experiences and data presented here speak to the value of instituting a structured faculty development Academy that immerses participants in the hybrid teaching environment. Before instituting a Digital Academy, faculty developers should consider time commitment, faculty and administrative buy-in, transferability across technologies, portability across disciplines and courses, campus-specific factors, and sustainability over time.

Time Investment

The Academy does have significant time investments associated with its design and delivery. The initial two academies had a substantial time investment of over four hundred net hours as developers were considering all elements at once: content, delivery, faculty relations, and technologies.

As content has stabilized and the mode of delivery has been tested and proven, time commitment has diminished. However, over one academic year, faculty developers spend approximately 220 hours in researching and adding new ideas to content, delivering content, providing follow-up support, and assessing courses and students. Faculty spend about 50 to 60 hours a week attending the Academy (face-to-face and online), working on homework, and working on course development. Although this may seem like a huge time commitment for faculty developers, the net payoff is high compared to providing one-on-one consultations and a series of workshops with sporadic attendance where tracking of outcomes becomes difficult and faculty get distracted by other issues.

Ensure Faculty and Administrative Buy-In

Before engaging in course development efforts, faculty developers need to secure administrative buy-in and become aware of possible incentives such as course reductions, research support, or summer stipends. Faculty buy-in is also important for ensuring robust involvement and program growth. Providing student survey data along with research on the efficacy of hybrid and online courses helps to make the case for adoption. Over time, successful online instructors can be tapped to lead workshops within their departments or colleges to encourage the development of more courses. Without these key elements of support, sustaining training efforts can become an issue.

Transferability Across Technologies

Traditional courses have common instructional tools; the same is true for hybrid courses. However, an Academy must consist of more than a series of application-specific how-to workshops. Sustainability is one reason; as we know, technologies constantly change, so what is usable for one semester may not be a viable or supported option in the next. The most significant reason to support hybrid teaching across technologies, however, is that using technology should not take precedence over achieving learning goals. Participants should first be asked to consider course learning objectives and goals and then to consider the technologies that will help achieve those goals. Faculty should also be encouraged to find what works, but not to become wedded to one technology. In addition, it is important to encourage the use of technologies that are supported by the institution through licensing and technical support.

Portability Across Disciplines and Courses

To create a "culture of use" (Brunk-Chavez & Miller, 2009), Academy leaders need to build a "portable model simple and dynamic enough to be a framework for developing an Academy, but one that [does] not make up a completed, static structure" (p. 14). Some topics should remain common across all Academies, including syllabus reenvisioning, content planning and design, structured assessment, and need-based adoption of technologies. However, within this structure, flexibility needs to be provided for adaptations depending on the leaders' objectives and participants' needs. Another way to facilitate portability is to chunk all Academy content so that it is packaged in small, self-contained portions that can be reused and reshaped for future Academies.

Campus-Specific Factors

An integrated model, where pedagogical strategies and technological training coexist, is the necessary solution for enabling faculty to design hybrid content and interactions for students. Because of our focus on course redesign and pedagogy, the Academy is independent of specific learning management systems (the Academy has been delivered using WebCT 4.2, Blackboard 8.1, Moodle, and Sakai) or any other technologies, and is thus portable to other universities. For example, for an Academy delivered in Chile, our pre-Academy surveys indicated a strong preference for open source tools. Therefore, the Academy facilitators located and prepared recommendations for open source technologies that participants could use to engage their students in learning activities. The structure of the Academy allowed faculty developers to be flexible in meeting the needs of the local population.

Sustainability

For the Academy to sustain momentum across campus, it is imperative to have strong faculty buy-in and participation in terms of attendance and in the design and delivery of future Academies. While faculty developers often develop a strong sense of ownership of their "product," the key to sustainability is letting the product be reshaped by its users. Over time, the Academy has become largely faculty led, with ISS staff playing a support role in research and delivery. We find that content delivery by faculty colleagues is sometimes not perfect, but it can engage faculty participants at a deeper level.

Assessment and Continuous Improvement

Assessment and continuous improvement apply to both the Academy and the individual hybrid courses delivered. It is important that all faculty who are teaching hybrid courses conduct a learning outcomes analysis with an improvement focus. We encourage the forming of partnerships in Academies so participants look at one another's data and provide improvement-focused feedback. ISS staff, of course, help the faculty make changes to their course as requested and needed. We also encourage refresher workshops for all faculty who were involved in the Academy as participants and facilitators.

Conclusion

Training faculty in learning management technology and online and hybrid pedagogies can be a daunting task, and yet this is just what may be required to create a strong foundation of hybrid courses and well-versed, experienced hybrid instructors at any university. Increasingly diversified student populations, as well as growing enrollments, create an immediate demand for such training, though often the required paradigm shift in faculty pedagogy is ignored in the name of efficiency. The Digital Academy, an integrated model where technology training and practical teaching strategies coexist, is a solution for enabling faculty to create and deliver effective hybrid courses.

REFERENCES

Brunk-Chavez, B., & Miller, S. (2009). The hybrid academy: Building and sustaining a technological culture of use. In D. N. DeVoss, H. A. McKee, & R. Selfe (Eds.), *Technological ecologies and sustainability*. Logan: Utah State University Press. Retrieved from http://ccdigitalpress.org/ebooks-and-projects/tes

Chickering, A., & Ehrmann, S. (1996, October). Implementing the seven principles: Technology as lever. *AAHE Bulletin, 49*(2), 3–6. Retrieved from www.tltgroup.org/programs/seven.html

Cho, S. K., & Berge, Z. L. (2002). Overcoming barriers to distance training and education. *USDLA Journal, 16*(1). Retrieved from www.usdla.org/html/journal/JAN02_Issue/article01.html

Dudeney, G. (2001). The Internet and the language classroom. *EIT Journal, 55*(1). Retrieved from www.dudeney.com/consultants-e/webquests/resources.html

Howe, N., & Strauss, W. (2000). *Millennials rising: The next great generation*. New York, NY: Vintage.

Laird, P. G. (2003, May). *Flexible design, development, and delivery: Using the e-course manual to simplify faculty transitions to online education*. Paper presented at the Council for Christian Colleges and Universities Technology Conference, Jackson, TN.

National Center for Academic Transformation. (2005). *Program in course redesign*. Retrieved from www.thencat.org/PCR.htm

Palfrey, J., & Gasser, U. (2008). *Born digital: Understanding the first generation of digital natives*. New York, NY: Basic Books.

Roberts, G. R. (2005). Technology and learning expectations of the Net generation. In D. Oblinger & J. Oblinger (Eds.), *Educating the Net generation*. Boulder, CO: Educause. Retrieved from www.educause.edu/Resources/EducatingtheNetGeneration/TechnologyandLearningExpectati/6056

Sands, P. (2002). Inside outside, upside downside: Strategies for connecting online and face-to-face instruction in hybrid courses. *Teaching with Technology Today, 8*(6). Retrieved from www.uwsa.edu/ttt/articles/sands2.htm

Selber, S. (2004). *Multiliteracies for a digital age*. Urbana: Southern Illinois University Press.

Sharp, V. (2005). *Integrating technology into classroom teaching*. New York, NY: McGraw-Hill.

Tapscott, D. (1999) *Growing up digital: The rise of the Net generation*. New York, NY: McGraw-Hill.

3

WRITING GROUPS FOR WORK-LIFE BALANCE

FACULTY WRITING GROUP LEADERS
SHARE THEIR STORIES

Dannielle Joy Davis, Alabama State University

Kara Provost, Curry College

Amanda E. Major, Alabama State University

Faculty writing groups can promote both the work-life balance and productivity of members of the professoriate. The benefits of such development initiatives expand beyond productivity to include retention, promotion, and improved teaching. Through the development of writing groups, faculty developers can empower faculty to meet research obligations, establish equilibrium in their work practices, and maintain work-life balance.

With scholarship being one of the three pillars of faculty tenure and promotion, faculty and administrators have an impetus to publish scholarship and support such efforts, respectively. Yet writing and publication compete for attention with more immediate academic work obligations: teaching and service. Some faculty, especially those early in their careers, lack the experience and motivation needed to become prolific writers. Writing groups can remove such barriers to publication.

Writing groups vary from collaborative writing groups to circles of writers who individually author their own pieces. These groups may have interdisciplinary, discipline-specific, or interprofessional focus. The size can range from two to multiple members, and a university may have one group

---

Many thanks to Dominique N. Gibson for technical assistance with later drafts of this chapter.

or many. Groups form for different reasons under a range of conditions, with their main focus or purpose changing with the needs of the group. Nevertheless, one purpose remains clear: to engage in scholarly writing.

The reflections of four faculty members about their writing group experiences were captured by Pasternak, Longwell-Grice, Shea, and Hanson (2009). These faculty decided to participate in writing groups because they sought social structure to help them make meaning of their writing. They identified revising support, inquiry-based learning, and a forum for learning through writing as benefits of their participation. Their departments supported writing groups by providing approval, financial and logistical support, facilitation, and mentoring.

On a large scale, about two-thirds of the faculty at a large state institution participated in interdisciplinary research writing circles, each composed of three to four faculty (Gillespie et al., 2005). These research circles were specifically designed to facilitate junior faculty members' adjustment to tenure-track positions. A senior faculty member organized the circles and coordinated group membership. Each member received thirty minutes of the group's time. Sessions began with the writer explaining the type of feedback she or he wanted, followed by the group reading three pages of the work and giving noncritical oral feedback. Member self-reflections and evaluations by research circle participants revealed that reader interest and feedback promoted productivity and motivated improvements in writing perspective and style. Furthermore, participation facilitated acculturation of junior faculty to the research process and helped them see the link between scholarly practices and teaching. Overall, the research circles facilitated faculty writing and an interdisciplinary community that resulted in increased creativity and professional development.

Administrators at an Australian university allocated part of the research budget to establish writing groups as a professional development strategy to meet policy objectives (Lee & Boud, 2003). The writing groups were organized by faculty members' level of experience; for example, one group consisted of new researchers and another of those who had published. Faculty from multiple disciplines took turns fulfilling each role in their respective groups. From detailed records of the groups' activities, reflections, and evaluations, it became clear that in addition to the normal business of developing research skills and writing to meet objectives, the groups all addressed emotional dimensions of development and change, identity formation, and knowledge of the research process.

Another study featured a multidisciplinary collaboration among an associate dean as coordinator and seven tenure-track faculty members who met each month to group-edit draft manuscripts (O'Malley et al., 2006). Over a two-year period, the format evolved to accommodate group needs. Instead of group editing, the group paired colleagues for co-mentoring feedback on writing with different dyads for each group meeting. By the end of the two-year period, the group had reviewed eighteen manuscripts. Group members identified beneficial outcomes that included publications, improved scholarship, empathy for other writers, collaboration opportunities, professional accountability, and development of meaningful personal research agendas. Participants further reported that the group strengthened their ability to balance scholarship demands with other demands of academic life.

Faculty members seek ways to balance their personal lives with the work requirement of publishing, which is sometimes perceived as an extraneous activity to complete during off-hours (Hochschild, 1997). Writing communities have the potential to foster more efficient and focused writing efforts than individual writing, thereby providing faculty more time to focus on other work or life obligations. For instance, faculty participating in group writing activities at a writing retreat reported more motivating, enjoyable, and productive experiences than they normally encountered at work (Davis, Chaney, Edwards, Rodgers, & Gines, 2011), abating the usual stress around professional writing that has the potential to spill over into life negatively or contribute to work-life conflict (Olson-Buchanan & Boswell, 2006). A positive writing experience stems from the establishment of a collaborative community of writers, the space and time for writing (Johnson & Mullen, 2007), and a safe physical and psychological work environment. Satisfaction gained from participating in writing groups serves as a reward for engaging in writing activities, thereby improving the chances that participants collaborate or write again while easing the stress of work and life in general.

The need to balance work and life prompts faculty to find creative ways to accomplish required writing. Specifically addressing the barriers to writing that female medical doctors experienced, Candib (2006) states that the "problems of women's writing have a gendered past as well as a gendered present" (p. 2). For women, a host of related factors impede writing, including a lack of self-confidence, family responsibilities, and high levels of professional service. Candib (2006) explains that women are challenged to turn their "susceptibility to relatedness, usually construed as a weakness, into a strength" (p. 14). She goes on to say that writing-in-relation (by writing to a partner, group, class, or another) allows women a way to both nurture a relationship and complete writing. Writing communities offer faculty an outlet to uphold their relationships in and out of work and write at the same time, thereby balancing their work-life obligations.

Although writing groups differ in composition, size, scale, purpose, and outcomes, they have commonalities as well. Members participate in scholarly learning through writing, a skill set that has the potential to transfer from the faculty-writing community member to the students whom the faculty instruct. Writing communities offer collegiality, tenure and promotion support, development of independent research skills, and enjoyment.

The journey toward work-life balance in today's academic culture often feels like swimming upstream. Many faculty face challenges in balancing teaching, research, and service responsibilities with their personal lives. We describe the writing group leadership experiences of the first two authors, an African American female academic from a historically black institution (HBCU) and a Caucasian female from a predominantly white institution (PWI). Both authors are Generation Xers, born between 1965 and 1980. Their interest in work-life balance and the use of writing groups to promote that balance are informed by their generational outlook.

An HBCU Faculty Member's Story

Interest in forming my first writing group as a postdoctoral fellow stemmed from my need to recreate the structure and accountability I experienced while writing my dissertation. I started by inviting collaborators on a grant proposal to join me as group members. We met weekly for the primary purpose of completing the proposal. Following submission of the proposal, we continued to meet regularly for both collaborative and individual academic writing. Facilitating and participating in the group promoted both strong collegial relationships and productivity in the form of submissions of manuscripts and proposals. The participants in this first writing group were six black female faculty, representing the fields of education and engineering, at a predominantly white institution. All except one were junior tenure-track faculty. We met weekly for two hours at a time. While our initial collaboration involved review of written materials, ultimately the group evolved into a write-on-site group. Although we made no written purpose statements or agreements, we all vowed to attend each weekly writing session and encourage others toward their goals.

My subsequent organization of and participation in writing groups as a tenure-track faculty member helped my continued productivity.

Specifically, the formal and informal accountability prompted by the writing groups helped me maintain productivity while experiencing major life issues. During one pretenure year, I became pregnant, and my father and father-in-law both passed away. Any one of these constitutes a major life event. Yet despite these personal challenges, my writing goals continued to be met and my publication record remained competitive, consistent with my prior output of at least two publications per year.

In addition to my increased writing output, an unanticipated benefit of the writing groups was the professional networking and peer mentoring I experienced. Meeting regularly with faculty within and across disciplines offered new ways of viewing my own work and opened opportunities for collaboration regarding writing, publishing, and teaching. Because participants were at various stages of their careers, intergenerational mentoring occurred.

As faculty, we all reflect our individual life experiences and training. The University of Illinois at Urbana-Champaign, my alma mater, had a strong social justice orientation. For many years I have been active in Sisters of the Academy, an international organization of black female academics and administrators. These professional experiences, as well as my own personal experiences of immersion in African cultures, shape the way I view academic life. While Western culture largely mirrors an individualistic meritocracy, I am very community minded. My orientation toward the collective is an important element of my long-term interest in and work with writing groups.

I know from years of interactions with other academics that some lack confidence in their writing abilities, resulting in reluctance to publish. However, nonacademic experiences have developed my intellectual tough skin and confidence that I have transferred into my life as a writer. For instance, as a graduate student, I studied dance at the University of Ghana at Legon in West Africa for six months and spent weeks studying dance with natives in Senegalese villages. My Senegalese teachers changed my life, in that they literally forced me to acknowledge my talents and to confidently share them within the community "circle." They would not allow the band of drummers (all standing in a circle) to stop drumming until I demonstrated mastery of what I had learned to the entire village— solo. It was intimidating, but it worked. I still remember the wonderful feeling of validation upon successfully mastering what I learned, coupled with applause, cheers, and hugs from proud teachers and members of the local community. This experience continues to permeate my life as an academic writer through its influence on the development of my persistence and ability to weather the ups and downs of the publishing process.

This tenacity complements my worldview, which is informed by my generational outlook. Some scholars suggest that a generational shift is occurring in academe, with senior faculty holding on to former ways of work and new faculty looking for more balanced work lives while adhering to excellence in their fields (Davis, Green-Derry, & Wells, 2009). I remember going to a conference for academics where I learned of another academic who reconsidered her work habits upon seeing a picture of herself that her child drew at school. The drawing was of a woman working on a computer, and only the back of her head was shown. She reflected that if this is how her child saw her, she needed to make changes to promote balance between her work and home lives. This story stays with me, a new academic mom, particularly when I am working on a deadline in my son's presence. What picture will he draw of me in the future? Fortunately, writing groups have resulted in my writing during typical work hours (between 9:00 A.M. and 5:00 P.M.) and engaging in less binge writing, a practice that leads to less output in the long run (Boice, 2000).

Informally coaching other writing group members has prompted me to practice what I preach and sparked my interest in learning more about writing strategies. Now I waste far less time on procrastinating, worrying, and writer's blocks, which leaves more time for nurturing family relationships and doing community service. This interest in promoting balance reflects Trower's (2010) findings of Gen X faculty members' commitment to working toward full professional and personal lives. She writes, "Gen Xers . . . have been vocal about wanting increased flexibility, greater integration of their work and home lives, more transparency of tenure and promotion processes, a more welcoming, diverse, and supportive workplace/department, and more frequent and helpful feedback about progress" (para. 6). Lancaster and Stillman (2002) also note generational workplace differences. They associate with Gen Xers (born between 1965 and 1980) a high value placed on collaboration, autonomy, the desire for clear feedback, the expectation that the workplace should be flexible to accommodate the balancing of occupational and personal goals, and a willingness to change jobs. Collaboration and clear feedback are major components of writing groups. In essence, writing groups support the generational outlook of Gen X members by offering a supportive community of authors. The following poem, which I wrote as a journal entry, reflects this generational stance:

On Being a Generation Xer and Black in Academe
   The symbol: X,
   That of anonymity,

Or critique of the status quo,
We work against eXploitation.
As our X illustrates civic partnership,
Pursuing eXcellence of the mind and spirit.
X . . .
The neXus of eXactly two lines,
The yoga of a generation's intellectual thoughts, academic words and
political deeds.
Critical, engaging, eXtraordinary scholars and family women,
EXceeding limits guided by eXemplars.
Yes we can,
Yes we will,
Forever be. . .
Gen X.

A PWI Faculty Member's Story

I wear many hats inside and outside my professional role as a faculty
member. I am a teacher; a scholar of pedagogy; a poet who regularly pub-
lishes and gives readings; a visiting poet-in-the-schools; a creative writing
teacher in the community; a leader and member of two active writing
groups (one inside and one outside the college); a parent; and a runner.
Although I do not attempt to be my students' friend or mother, I think
allowing them to glimpse areas of my life beyond the classroom such as
through reading and discussing a poem I recently published, having them
see my children's artwork when they come to an advising appointment
in my office, or exchanging suggestions for good jogging routes nearby
can help them negotiate their growth into adulthood. What we do in the
classroom is vital, but experiences outside class are critical to my own
and our community's authenticity, growth, and well-being. Initiating a
faculty creative writing group at Curry College is both an outgrowth of
this philosophy and a way I maintain work-life balance and coherence.

When I left a full-time faculty position and began a multifaceted position at a new institution, I knew I would have to develop additional
strategies to carve out time for writing, reading, publishing, and performing poetry. I saw starting a writing group at my new institution as a way
to nurture my connection to creative writing and maintain my balance as
I took on a new job with both administrative and teaching responsibilities and negotiated my family roles as a spouse and parent. Being new
to campus, I felt a creative writing group would provide a good venue to
build a community with like-minded individuals.

Soon after coming to Curry, I met several faculty who were also creative writers. I asked them and my department chair about others who wrote and invited a group of faculty to join a creative writing group to support each other's efforts and provide feedback on work in progress. Although no such writing group existed on campus at the time, the institution promoted peer mentoring in general through a faculty peer support program, which encouraged faculty to form mentoring relationships and rewarded participation by allowing us to include peer mentoring as an aspect of service in our promotion files. Now in its fourth year, our creative writing group has grown from five to eight members and has increased meeting frequency from monthly to biweekly. Before we invited new members, we agreed on and circulated expectations for participation in the group. I established a rotation so individuals would know when to submit work, ensuring that everyone had equal opportunities for feedback. A few days before we meet, participants generally distribute via e-mail several poems or a prose piece so members can read submissions ahead of time. During meetings, the writer often reads the poem or an excerpt from a prose piece, followed by comments and discussion of the work. Sometimes the writer also receives written feedback from group members.

A wonderful attribute of the group is its diverse membership. Our eight members represent gay, straight, black, white, married, single, parents, full- and part-time academics, faculty new to Curry and those with many years at the institution. The two men include one librarian and an editor of the college's arts and literary magazine. Our disciplines include education, English, women's and gender studies, developmental composition, history, African American studies, and honors studies. Some of us write poetry, some of us fiction, some memoir or hybrid forms that blend personal, creative, and scholarly writing in various genres.

The group has been professionally and personally beneficial in more ways than I had initially imagined. One of the primary benefits has clearly been supporting work-life balance: the group provided all of us with impetus to carve out writing time and affirmed the value of the creative, social, and emotional aspects of our being. The group has been a positive force in other ways as well, including acting as a testing ground for work that has gone on to be published or presented at conferences; helping us solve teaching dilemmas within a supportive community of fellow educators; building collegiality; and strengthening our knowledge of other programs and departments at the college—all while being highly pleasurable, even fun!

The members of the creative writers' group have elaborated on the group's value in their own words. Melanie Long, an associate professor in politics and history and coordinator of African American studies, eloquently testified to how the group contributes to work-life balance by providing members with creative, professional, social, and emotional support. She says the writers' group offers

> a place where colleagues can "feed their souls" through creative writing. I cannot express how much this group means to me as some-one who generally feels overwhelmed by the amount of nonteaching work required. . . . This group provides a place where you can breathe and share your creative work with your peers and discuss it in sup-portive and substantive ways that are often impossible in the class-room. The group continues to provide support, boost self-confidence and offer a sense of collegiality that is vital to helping faculty reach their full potential as scholars.

Similarly, Karen Mato, a senior lecturer in English, describes the writers' group as being "a great gift to me personally," noting that it provides "a way to keep my writing current while teaching," as well as opportunities "to learn from my colleagues' teaching in action" as we engage in thoughtful conversation about one another's work.

Daniel Mills, acting director of the library, describes the group's con-tribution to community building, stating that it fosters our "continuing, developing self-awareness as a community with an active literary life." Mills also testifies to how the group supports faculty development by furthering intellectual and creative growth, sometimes leading to concrete outcomes such as publications, presentations, or readings. He comments that the writing group

> has been absolutely invaluable to me, in terms of my develop-ing work as a poet. It's no exaggeration to say that without this group . . . I would not have found a forum enabling me to make the kind of progress I have made or achieve the confidence to do so. This includes developing the ability to witness and comment on other people's work. The work of the writers' group has also been brought forward to other members of the campus through several presentations.

Gabe Regal, a full-time faculty member who teaches in both English and women's and gender studies, sums up the pleasure and renewal all of us experienced as a benefit of participating in the creative writing group when she comments that it has been "one of my most rewarding and enjoyable experiences at Curry. . . . It inspires me and teaches me on many levels."

Discussion

The featured writing groups were prompted by an interest with connecting with other faculty. They transformed potentially isolating experiences of writing into collegial, enjoyable experiences. These experiences contributed to the engagement of participants within their academic fields as a whole through increased publications and presentations.

Writing groups played a role in promoting productivity and work-life balance for the faculty featured in this work. In addition, they offered group members an opportunity to strengthen or establish professional relationships. Our experiences suggest that ongoing faculty writing groups can have significant benefits in the form of increased publications, presentations, and grant applications; providing a safe space for pedagogical problem solving; building collegiality; and contributing to overall work-life balance for faculty.

Both writing group leaders are members of Generation X. Differences between the silent generation (born 1925–1944), baby boomers (born 1945–1962), Generation X (born 1963–1980), and millennials (born 1981–2001) hold potential to have a positive or negative influence on collegiality among faculty and staff in university settings. Differences in perception are most evident between the silent generation, who married at younger ages and respected authority or hierarchies, versus Gen Xers, who question authority and have either remained single or married later in life (Bickel & Brown, 2005) and value work-life balance. The development of writing groups and interest in promoting healthy balance in their careers and personal lives reflect the featured authors' generational group.

The diversity of the Curry College group in terms of gender, sexual orientation, race, and rank brought to the discussion different perspectives on work. Preliminary feedback from a diverse array of individuals is particularly important when seeking publication and making effective presentations at conferences.

Recommendations for Faculty Developers

Regardless of institutional type, faculty developers may want to implement similar writing groups to promote academic productivity, work-life balance, and occupational satisfaction among faculty, thereby retaining faculty members and promoting their professional development. We offer our specific recommendations for faculty developers:

- *Build motivation.* Regularly offering workshops on writing productivity and publication strategies suggests the importance of scholarship at an institution. Faculty developers can also share with faculty research on the benefits of accountability and writing groups.

- *Lay the groundwork.* Faculty developers and administrative leaders must assess faculty concerns regarding writing and publication and use this information to inform programming. Institutions can facilitate the formation of such groups by providing networking opportunities, valuing peer mentoring in promotion and tenure decisions, and offering resources such as space and funding for writing group meetings and for events where faculty can present work developed through the group.

- *Build an infrastructure.* Leaders' support of work-life balance strengthens the likelihood of faculty participation. Academics with heavy teaching loads and who are overwhelmed with long meetings receive the unconscious message that research and writing are not institutional priorities. Differentiated teaching loads, teaching releases for the purpose of scholarship development, and a one-hour limitation on meetings create work cultures that provide space for innovation and subsequent scholarship.

- *Support the process, but only as much as it needs.* For faculty writing groups to be successful, they should be voluntary and driven by goals that all members agree on, formally or informally. Some groups may find it helpful to set out written expectations or objectives; such statements may evolve with the needs of the group. Faculty developers may act as facilitators or provide guidance to faculty interested in serving this role. Ideally the facilitator, whether a faculty developer or faculty member, should have experience in the publishing process.

Faculty writing groups create a safe space for members to take creative and intellectual risks and to be their authentic, full selves. Such initiatives yield the institutional benefits of scholarly productivity, informed pedagogy, and faculty who feel in control of the multiple demands on their time.

REFERENCES

Bickel, J., & Brown, A. J. (2005). Generation X: Implications for faculty recruitment and development in academic health centers. *Academic Medicine, 80*(3), 205–210.

Boice, R. (2000). *Advice for new faculty members: Nihil nimus.* Needham, MA: Allyn & Bacon.

Candib, L. M. (2006). Writing troubles for women clinicians: Turning weakness into strength through writing-in-relation. *Families, Systems, and Health, 24*(3), 302–317.

Davis, D. J., Chaney, C., Edwards, L., Rodgers, G., & Gines, K. (2011). *Academe as extreme sport: Black women excel and network through faculty development programs.* Manuscript submitted for publication.

Davis, D. J., Green-Derry, L., & Wells, J. (2009). Leadership in K–12 learning communities: Activism and access via inter-generational understanding. In C. A. Mullen (Ed.), *Leadership and building professional learning communities* (pp. 205–213). New York, NY: Palgrave Macmillan.

Gillespie, D., Nives, D., Kochis, B., Krabill, R., Lerum, K., Peterson, A., & Thomas, E. (2005). Research circles: Supporting the scholarship of junior faculty. *Innovative Higher Education, 30*(3), 149–162.

Hochschild, A. R. (1997). When work becomes home and home becomes work. *California Management Review, 39*(4), 79–97.

Johnson, W. B., & Mullen, C. A. (2007). *Write to the top: How to become a prolific academic.* New York, NY: Palgrave Macmillan.

Lancaster, L. C., & Stillman, D. (2002). *When generations collide.* New York, NY: Harper Business.

Lee, A., & Boud, D. (2003). Writing groups, change and academic identity: Research development as local practice. *Studies in Higher Education, 28*(2), 187–200.

Olson-Buchanan, J. B., & Boswell, W. R. (2006). Blurring boundaries: Correlates of integration and segmentation between work and non-work. *Journal of Vocational Behavior, 68*(3), 432–445. doi:10.1016/j.jvb.2005.10.006

O'Malley, G. S., Bates, A., Latham, N., Lucey, T., Meyer, B., Spycher, E., & Wedwick, L. (2006). Promoting scholarship through writing groups. *Academic Exchange Quarterly, 10*(4), 171–175.

Pasternak, D. L., Longwell-Grice, H., Shea, K. A., & Hanson, L. K. (2009). Alien environments or supportive writing communities? Pursuing writing groups in academe. *Arts and Humanities in Higher Education, 8*(3), 355–367. doi:10.1177/1474022209339958

Trower, C. A. (2010). A new generation of faculty: Similar core values in a different world. *Peer Review, 12*(3). Retrieved from www.aacu.org/peerreview/pr-su10/pr_su10_NewGen.cfm

4

REFLECTING TOGETHER ABOUT TENURE AND PROMOTION

A FACULTY LEARNING COMMUNITY APPROACH

Leslie G. McBride, Janelle DeCarrico Voegele,
Portland State University

What happens when faculty representing various disciplines and career stages reflect together on the tenure and promotion process? How does the learning community they form facilitate development of their academic portfolios, and what insights into various forms of scholarship does it provide? This chapter addresses these questions. It describes the learning community over a five-month period, explains how academic portfolio development was used as a common reference point for addressing tenure and promotion issues, and summarizes insights and perspectives shared among faculty members as they tried to understand the value of diverse forms of scholarship.

Boyer's (1990) landmark book, *Scholarship Reconsidered,* called into question the restricted approach toward scholarship taken on most college and university campuses and argued convincingly for the value of multiple forms of scholarship, including the scholarship of teaching. Although academics have found the four complementary types of scholarship in Boyer's extended model (discovery, integration, application, and teaching) both affirming and liberating, junior faculty members have hesitated to stray too far from either disciplinary norms or department expectations regarding the type of scholarly work they should produce for a successful promotion and tenure review.

At Portland State University (PSU), hesitancy on the part of new faculty is particularly apparent in regard to scholarship that focuses on service-learning and civic engagement—what Ward (2003), in an extension of Boyer's work, refers to as the scholarship of engagement. In new faculty orientation sessions and during individual promotion and tenure consultations, new and untenured faculty inevitably express curiosity about the scholarship of engagement and its value compared to traditional scholarship. They are particularly interested in learning how their disciplinary colleagues regard the scholarship of engagement and about the kind of support it typically receives during promotion and tenure review (O'Meara & Rice, 2005; Ward, 2003).

At the Center for Academic Excellence at PSU, we responded to such concerns by designing a faculty learning community with an embedded academic portfolio development component. We used participants' initial consideration of how to organize their portfolios and what to include in their written narratives as a common reference point for exploring the range of scholarly activity present within the group. This approach stimulated deeper inquiry into diverse forms of scholarship and, as a result of learning community discussions, participants gained helpful insights into the faculty review process.

PSU is an urban university that enrolled nearly twenty-eight thousand full- and part-time students in 2009. It has nearly fifteen hundred full- and part-time faculty and offers 213 degree programs. The university's motto, "Let Knowledge Serve the City," carries a great deal of meaning for both faculty, who refer to it regularly in the context of their work, and administrators, who build on it when establishing priorities, fundraising, and during promotional campaigns. Recently identified in the *Chronicle of Higher Education* as one of five "smaller institutions that have either honed great reputations in their markets or are on the rise" (Carlson, 2010, p. 1), PSU has been recognized for its service-learning and senior capstone programs; its learning communities, internships, and cooperative learning; and, related to these, its outstanding community involvement. In 1996, PSU institutionalized support for the scholarship of community engagement by including appropriate explanations and examples in a revision of university promotion and tenure guidelines. More recently, a year-long process involving key administrators produced a 2007–2009 vision statement describing PSU's leadership in engagement.

The academic portfolio learning community project emerged out of this campus context. As director and assistant director for the university's faculty development programs, we wanted to support faculty members' attempts to understand and respond to institutional expectations for engagement and service to the city, while at the same time attending to disciplinary norms and expectations for scholarship within academic units. Building on previous work that explored shifting institutional norms pertaining to definitions of scholarship on our campus (Rueter & Bauer, 2005), we wanted to better understand how faculty interpreted these expectations.

Although the process-driven learning community framework we decided on was time intensive and at times unwieldy, we chose it because of the relatively untapped potential of faculty learning communities for rendering the tenure review process more transparent (Cox, 2004). We also wanted to explore how development of academic portfolios (Seldin & Miller, 2009) and investigation of scholarship of teaching, learning, and engagement literature within a learning community framework would contribute to members' understanding of the promotion and tenure process. We assumed that an implicit understanding of this process would emerge when learning community discussions were coupled with the work that faculty did on their individual academic portfolios between meetings. We also assumed that this understanding could be made more explicit through group reflection activities that focused attention on participants' developing understanding of promotion and tenure.

The AIM Model

For sixteen years, faculty and staff working in the Center for Academic Excellence have used a learning community approach to encourage innovative teaching and scholarly activity. This approach, currently referred to as the Academic Innovations Mini-Grant (AIM) program, has focused primarily on the scholarship of teaching and learning and the scholarship of engagement. However, the same approach has also been used to encourage faculty to participate in projects they might not be able to pursue without staff and resource support. Incorporating community-based learning into established courses, transitioning from traditional classroom to blended or fully online course formats, and developing innovations in program assessment are three examples of faculty innovation and curricular change supported by AIM groups.

Currently AIM provides the organizational support for three to five faculty learning communities each year. These groups typically involve ten to fifteen members who meet together once a month for five to six months, although the overall time frame and frequency of meetings reflect each group's basic goals. Facilitation duties are often shared between a faculty developer and a member of the group. Participating faculty receive stipends ranging from five hundred to fifteen hundred dollars for regular participation and development of a work product that is described in general terms in the call for proposals. Past work products have included curricular and course redesign in such areas as community engagement, sustainability, and blended learning; scholarship of teaching (or engagement) manuscript drafts; and written reflections in *Our Voices,* an annual publication on teaching and learning at PSU produced by the center. Although we encourage faculty participation in AIM learning communities by offering stipends, we also listen carefully to the felt needs that faculty express and attempt to integrate our understanding of these into AIM program themes. When appropriate, we align AIM themes with institutional priorities and strategic initiatives. Often these overlap. For example, campus priorities related to engaged scholarship, coupled with faculty curiosity regarding levels of support this scholarship received across departments, proved to be important incentives for participation in the AIM academic portfolio group.

Within the normal range of topics or goals that AIM groups pursue, those of the academic portfolio groups were somewhat different. These groups offered participants the opportunity to focus for a brief time on themselves—their career goals, their faculty responsibilities, and their research and scholarship—and share insights and resulting work in a learning community framework. We describe how the two groups were organized, their schedule, and details of specific activities in the next section.

AIM Academic Portfolio Groups

The call for AIM academic portfolio proposals was distributed during fall 2008 and again in fall 2009. Ten faculty members applied and were accepted each year. The sixteen tenure-track, two tenured, and two fixed-term faculty represented professional schools (business, education, engineering, social work, and urban and public affairs); liberal arts; fine and performing arts; honors; and general education. A member of the library faculty also participated. Of the twenty participants, three were men. Some participants were in their first year at PSU; others were anticipating promotion and tenure review during the following academic year. One participant, returning to the faculty after serving a five-year term as associate dean, was pursuing promotion to full professor. In response to the first call for proposals, a tenured full professor and an untenured assistant professor in the same professional school applied as a team, proposing to develop a teaching portfolio (the junior member) and a literature review on the use of student evaluations in promotion and tenure decisions (the senior member). Their goal was to better understand the relative merits and contributions of each approach to the tenure and promotion process and to share what they learned in presentations to their colleagues.

Both groups met monthly from January through May and followed the same general schedule. We assumed more active leadership roles than usual within a faculty learning community format because most members were junior faculty who had many questions about the promotion and tenure process and were experiencing varying degrees of stress related to it. Our first priority was to establish an environment in which participants felt comfortable asking questions about various aspects of the promotion and tenure process and sharing early drafts of their portfolio narratives. To encourage this, we provided ample time during the first meeting for participants to get acquainted. We also created a composite list of the group's reasons for participating, the benefits they expected to gain, and the collective goals members held for creating portfolio drafts. We distributed this list during the first session as a means of initiating discussion about the learning community process and what results participants might expect. Early on we also wanted to familiarize members with different portfolio types and introduce them to related literature. We asked them to read chapters from *Scholarship Reconsidered* (Boyer, 1990), selections from O'Meara and Rice's (2005) work tracing the history of efforts to redefine scholarship, and further elaborations on the scholarship of teaching (Hutchings & Shulman, 1999) and the scholarship of engagement (Ward, 2003). We encouraged learning community members to deepen their understanding of the types of scholarship described in these readings through general discussion and sharing accounts of disciplinary experiences.

The second session included a key activity, Will It Count?, designed to stimulate extended discussion about what made work scholarly and what constituted scholarship. Participants read descriptions of academic work in teaching, research, and service (both community and professional), discussed in small groups how colleagues in their respective units would value each example, and then discussed results with the entire group. Among the examples that participants considered were these:

- Published an article in a discipline-based refereed journal
- Published an article on student learning and technology in a refereed journal
- Published an article on assessment of community-based learning outcomes in the refereed journal *Community Partnerships*
- Published an article in a nonrefereed online journal

- Researched, drafted, and worked to pass legislation related to a scholarly agenda
- Wrote and received a grant examining the civic purposes and responsibilities of courses at a university
- Made regular contributions to a research-oriented blog
- Completed a comparative assessment of face-to-face and online learning
- Presented teaching, learning, and community-based research strategies at a national conference

Lively conversation ensued as participants shared their perspectives on work from each category and explained their opinions. As the discussion progressed, participants identified characteristics that strengthened the best examples and specified how weaker examples might be improved. Finally, the group considered how they could apply what they learned from Will It Count? to their own work. During this session, we also introduced basic portfolio types, making special reference to Seldin and Miller's (2009) book describing the academic portfolio. The wide variety of examples presented in the book stimulated participants' thinking about their own portfolios and provided background context needed to begin designing their own narrative statements.

Sessions 3 and 4 marked a shift in focus from general background information to the progress participants were making on their portfolio outlines and narrative themes. Participants shared basic organizational plans for their portfolios during the third session and described themes they were considering for inclusion in their narratives. In groups of three, they reported on their progress and responded to three basic questions: (1) What questions or approaches do you share in common with others in your group? (2) Based on your discussion, what is unique about your portfolio? and (3) What questions do you have about your portfolio work as a result of your discussion today? The summary discussion of this process indicated that members of the learning community were beginning to think seriously about the portfolio development process and that doing so was stimulating deeper insights into various aspects of their work.

Participants brought written drafts of their narratives to the fourth session. Once again, they divided into groups of three and spent their time reading and commenting on each other's drafts. Summary discussions at the close of session 4 indicated that participants found this process helpful. Listening to issues framed from different disciplinary perspectives and responding to questions posed by colleagues in other disciplines shed new light and fresh perspective on familiar academic themes. Participants' awareness of the range of meanings related to different forms of scholarship increased (Albers, 2007); over time, they reported sharing their new insights with colleagues in their home departments.

The fifth and final meeting of each academic portfolio learning community was an open forum to share with nonparticipating faculty what participants had learned. We included this forum as part of the overall framework to encourage each group's reflection over the entire process. Each year's learning community planned its forum to encourage discussion and consideration of the tenure and promotion process, the merits of academic portfolio development, and different forms of scholarship. As one of two final products for which participants were responsible, the forum also ensured their accountability to the AIM program as participants reflected together over what they had learned, set priorities as they developed forum goals, and considered the best design to achieve them. An average of thirty people attended each forum, including faculty, department chairs, deans and associate deans, and vice provosts. Those completing evaluation forms distributed at the conclusion of the 2009 forum indicated they found the information useful or very useful, and rated the overall presentation quality as outstanding. They wrote that as a result of attending the forum, they were more aware of variations in the promotion and tenure process across programs and of the range of definitions of scholarship used within them. A few commented that the forum renewed their interest in Boyer's (1990) vision for multiple forms of scholarship.

The only remaining responsibility for learning community participants at this point was completion of their academic portfolio outlines and the accompanying narrative statements for one section. Members of both groups struggled to fulfill this requirement. Some were overloaded by teaching and related student responsibilities that coincide with the end of an academic year. Others had simply procrastinated too long. At this point, the stipend of five hundred dollars played a key role, providing the additional motivation needed to persevere and complete the second work product.

Outcomes

Because of confidentiality concerns around tenure and promotion review, some outcomes from the AIM portfolio groups may never be known. Short-term outcomes, both expected and unexpected, related to portfolio development and increased understanding of the promotion and tenure process.

The expectation that each faculty member would develop an academic portfolio outline, including an expanded narrative for one section, provided some members added clarity and insight into their work. One member observed that in the press of daily responsibilities, she had lost sight of the larger pattern of her work. Working on her portfolio brought her back in touch with this pattern and helped her recognize the significance of work she had either forgotten or not recognized previously.

We also expected that the learning community process would render promotion and tenure review more transparent to members. Portfolio development, group discussion, readings, and group activities like Will It Count? did just that. Faculty described themselves as more confident of their ability to prepare a portfolio that would represent their work accurately, and they felt better prepared for the review process. Checking in with us early in the academic year following her AIM participation, one faculty member observed how much more confident she felt as she assembled her portfolio and entered the initial phase of her promotion and tenure review. When we asked her to elaborate, she used as an example her consideration of the peers she recommended as external reviewers. Because of participating in the AIM group, she was much more intentional about whom she recommended, considering their areas of expertise, the type of institution where they worked, and the nature of their responsibilities. She observed, "I never would have considered these factors, but after participating in the group, I realize they may make a difference in how my work is regarded."

We hoped that the conversations about promotion, tenure, and what constitutes scholarship that took place in the learning community would encourage group members to engage in extended conversations beyond the group. Previous research conducted on our campus revealed numerous indicators of progress toward understanding and acceptance of expanded forms of scholarship; however, agreement on the value of new forms of scholarly products continued to vary widely across campus (Rueter & Bauer, 2005). Several AIM members became leaders or mentors in their units, often facilitating conversations that furthered departmental understandings of the potential value of innovative academic products and processes. The participating library faculty member facilitated a department retreat on representation of diverse forms of scholarship. A faculty member in urban planning with experience engaging students in community-based projects met with her department chair to compare their interpretations of the scholarship of engagement and clarify implications related to tenure and promotion. In the process of updating her portfolio, a senior faculty member gained insight into her practice of designing and teaching innovative courses (one was Creativity in Business) and using innovative approaches to learning in the classroom. Realizing that her natural ability to innovate and her experience in curricular and course design made her a useful resource, she now shares her expertise in these areas with other faculty. Finally, the department chair and assistant professor who teamed up to focus on the relative use of teaching portfolios and student evaluations in the promotion and tenure process shared results of their inquiry with disciplinary colleagues, encouraging them to enlarge the review process to include scholarship of teaching indicators.

Insights and Lessons

We will no doubt experience more insights and learn more lessons as we continue to sponsor academic portfolio groups. Three lessons became clear to us so early in our work that we believe they are important to overall success.

Mutual Trust Is Essential to Establishing Effective Peer Support

The sense of trust that participants experience in the group facilitates honest, straightforward sharing of personal opinions and experiences related to various stages of academic review. Initially participants needed ample opportunity to explore common ground. Providing a written composite of members' goals and expectations for their learning community was one way of supporting this process. Participants discussed their scholarly agendas and their understanding of expectations held by their units, their deans, and the university. They were intensely interested in sharing stories of their personal experiences and checking their understanding of various policies and procedures with one another. Trust developed along the way, nurtured by adequate time to support these early conversations.

Support the Process and Outcomes of Deep Reflection

One of the strengths and outcomes of portfolio development is the deeper-than-usual reflection about teaching, scholarship, and service that it encourages. As participants reflected on work products in relation to their professional goals and their units' promotion and tenure guidelines, questions surfaced that reflected multiple levels and nuances of the process.

Different perspectives on "what counts" created lively discussions; comparison of personal records of accomplishment to written descriptions of responsibilities and disciplinary norms prompted soul searching; and, later, portfolio presentation and peer feedback sessions deepened members' understanding of how to frame the insights and creative solutions gained through their collective inquiry process. As facilitators, we searched out information to address questions arising from this multilevel reflection and review. We also developed focused questions to help guide peer feedback sessions as portfolios were developed; these played a helpful role in preventing discussions over individual portfolios from becoming too wide ranging.

Public Forum Is Key to Diffusion of Information

The public forum that constituted participants' fifth and final session was a key element in this program. Although participants were resistant to the idea initially, as they gained confidence from their own portfolio development, group discussion of various forms of scholarship, and a more extensive understanding of tenure and promotion practices, they gradually agreed that that there were good reasons to share what they had learned in a formal presentation. Planning for and holding the forum required further reflection and synthesis of knowledge gained as members decided what was important to cover and how to organize the forum for its greatest effect.

Conclusion

Cox (2004) and others have noted higher education's failure to authentically and effectively respond to requests from new faculty for a more comprehensible tenure system. Our initial efforts to combine a faculty learning community framework with academic portfolio development demonstrate a potentially effective way to address the alignment between institutional priorities and faculty reward structures.

During a particularly poignant moment when the group was deeply engaged in discussion, a participant described a senior faculty member's response to her question regarding how she might judge whether she had enough publications to her credit: "I was told, 'Ask the faculty member who recently has had a successful review how many publications he or she had and then just add one more.'" Participants grew quiet as they considered her comment; then, one by one, they began to chuckle as the absurdity of the end result gradually dawned. After the entire group had enjoyed a good laugh, it claimed as its slogan, "Just add one more!" and determined that it could come to a shared understanding of promotion and tenure requirements that would serve it much better. At that point, participants began giving serious consideration to what really counts in scholarship, teaching, and service.

Through the learning community format, review and discussion of literature describing scholarship in its different forms, and a clearer understanding of portfolio use and development, participating faculty have acquired the ability to recognize and help promote diverse forms of scholarship. Indeed, the learning community became much more than a group helping one another assemble an academic portfolio. Rather, the portfolio and learning community framework provided a departure point for a deeper, more significant faculty conversation about the promotion and tenure process, what counts toward advancement, and why.

REFERENCES

Albers, C. (2007). Developing a shared meaning of scholarship to enable the revision of a promotion policy. *International Journal for the Scholarship of Teaching and Learning, 1*(1). Retrieved from http://academics .georgiasouthern.edu/ijsotl/current.htm

Boyer, E. L. (1990). *Scholarship reconsidered: Priorities of the professoriate.* San Francisco, CA: Jossey-Bass.

Carlson, S. (2010, November 19). How to build a perception of greatness. *Chronicle of Higher Education,* pp. A1, A11–A13.

Cox, M. D. (2004). Introduction to faculty learning communities. *New directions for teaching and learning: No. 97. Building faculty learning communities* (pp. 5–23). San Francisco, CA: Jossey-Bass.

Hutchings, P., & Shulman, L. S. (1999, September/October). The scholarship of teaching: New elaborations, new developments. *Change, 31*(5), 10–15.

O'Meara, K., & Rice, R. E. (Eds.). (2005). *Faculty priorities reconsidered: Rewarding multiple forms of scholarship.* San Francisco, CA: Jossey-Bass.

Rueter, J., & Bauer, T. (2005). Identifying and managing university assets: A campus study of Portland State University. In K. O'Meara & R. E. Rice (Eds.), *Faculty priorities reconsidered: Rewarding multiple forms of scholarship* (pp. 187–208). San Francisco, CA: Jossey-Bass.

Seldin, P., & Miller, J. E. (2009). *The academic portfolio: A practical guide to documenting teaching, research, and service.* San Francisco, CA: Jossey-Bass.

Ward, K. (2003). *Faculty service roles and the scholarship of engagement.* San Francisco, CA: Jossey-Bass.

5

THE CITIZENSHIP IMPERATIVE AND THE ROLE OF FACULTY DEVELOPMENT

Jeffrey L. Bernstein, Eastern Michigan University

Rebecca S. Nowacek, Marquette University

Michael B. Smith, Ithaca College

By teaching the capacity for citizenship across the curriculum, colleges and universities can better serve their role as socially responsive institutions. We argue that citizenship themes can be more central to a wide variety of classes, including some in disciplines not considered traditional homes for civic education. Faculty development centers can play a critical role in helping faculty integrate citizenship into the curriculum and evaluate the learning that occurs in their citizenship-oriented classes. We offer guidelines for how learning communities can best serve these purposes.

Every fall the doors of our universities open to new students. During their time on campus, our responsibility is to educate them broadly (through general education requirements), help them build expertise in a few particular areas of knowledge (through major and minor requirements), offer them cocurricular opportunities to broaden their interests and build their leadership skills, and prepare them to pursue their careers and lives. In addition, universities must prepare students for their role as citizens in civil society by helping them develop the skills and dispositions of citizenship, broadly defined.

Advocating citizenship education is not a novel position in higher education (Battistoni, 2002; Bringle, Games, & Malloy, 1999; Carnegie Foundation, 2006; Colby, Ehrlich, Beaumont, & Stephens, 2003). Calls for "socially responsive knowledge" go back at least to Altman (1996), and arguably to Dewey (1916). Nevertheless, citizenship education remains uneven, often walled off in disciplinary silos. Despite gestures toward its value over the past twenty years, colleges and universities have not always transformed the call for citizenship education into curricular innovation. There is reason to be optimistic that such needed change is happening.

If the potential of citizenship education is to be realized, faculty development will have to assume a leading role. Faculty development professionals and the centers they lead are crucial to such efforts, particularly on campuses that cannot devote institutional resources to establishing a dedicated center. While there are many roads to citizenship education, we draw evidence and illustrative examples from our experiences in a cross-institutional learning community to argue for the power of the faculty learning community as one way to sponsor education for citizenship among faculty and, eventually, among students.

The Need for Citizenship Education

In recent years, respected scholars have spoken of the need to teach with an eye toward citizenship (Bok, 2008; Nussbaum, 2002; Schmidt, 2009). Nussbaum (2002) argues, for example, that the philosophical well-spring of higher education flows in the direction of citizenship education. Cultivation of our common humanity in the service of a functioning polity has "long been at the root of our aspirations, as we construct a higher education that is not simply pre-professional, but a general enrichment of and a cultivation of reasonable, deliberative democratic citizenship" (p. 291). Such academic discussions resonate powerfully with conversations in the public sphere, particularly regarding the need to inculcate the core values of civility. These various calls unite to sound a clarion that identifies citizenship education as an imperative for the academy.

In the public sphere, few officials have more eloquently emphasized the imperative of civility than Jim Leach, former member of Congress and current chair of the National Endowment for the Humanities (NEH). In one of his many speeches on the subject during the 2010 midterm election season, Leach argued:

> Citizenship is hard. It takes a commitment to listen, watch, read, and think in ways that allow the imagination to put one person in the shoes of another. Words matter. They reflect emotion as well as meaning. They clarify—or cloud—thought and energize action, sometimes bringing out the better angels of our nature, and sometimes, baser instincts. . . . Civility is an ancient virtue of civilized society. It is not simply or principally about manners. Rather it is about respectful

engagement with an understanding that we are all connected and rely upon each other.

The fact that Leach has made civility one of the cornerstones of his agenda as NEH chairman is significant. Even more significant is that Leach's definition of citizenship revolves around empathy, connectedness, and mutuality. As we shall see, thinking of citizenship in these terms not only gets to the core of what is necessary for sustaining human communities, but also makes it possible to teach citizenship in almost any discipline.

In recent years, lamentations like Leach's about the decline in civility have poured forth from the media, from the pulpit, at coffee shops, at town hall meetings, and in the halls of the academy. The academy has begun to address this, as evidenced by the work of the Association of American Colleges and Universities (most notably its Center for Liberal Education and Civic Engagement and its Civic Learning and Democratic Engagement initiatives; Dey, 2009; Knefelkamp, 2008), Imagining America, and dozens of initiatives within specific disciplines (Science Education for New Civic Engagements and Responsibilities in the sciences, for example, and the American Association of Higher Education's service-learning in the disciplines monograph series). This body of work makes it clear that the turn to citizenship education and civic engagement in the academy is more than mere words. But too often, civically engaged teaching and learning continues to be seen as the province of certain disciplines or the responsibility of a center on campus.

The key to overcoming this may lie, we believe, in empathy. Developing empathy, the foundation for civil society, can be the province of any discipline. When we can empathize with the perspectives of others, we become more attuned to collective needs and the sense of reciprocity that ennobles civic life (Bellah, Madsen, Sullivan, Swidler, & Tipton, 1985; Putnam, 1993; Rhoads, 1997). Without empathy, community frays—and the desire to sustain functioning communities is at the core of citizenship. Rifkin (2009) argues that empathy is the glue that has held civilization together; recognizing this dimension of human community is the first step toward solving the problems of the twenty-first century. Cultivating an expanded capacity for empathy is foundational to citizenship education and makes it possible to embrace citizenship education by emphasizing disciplinary content in new ways.

Our experience as co-inquirers working together in an interdisciplinary faculty learning community suggests that two things need to happen for citizenship education to become as well integrated into the curriculum as writing skills or numeracy. First, we need to cultivate models of citizenship education across the curriculum, expanding it beyond its perceived native habitats of history, political science, and sociology into the science, technology, engineering, and mathematics (STEM) disciplines, business schools, and other seemingly unlikely areas. Although we have noted some remarkable efforts to do this at the macrolevel, there is more that faculty developers can do at the campus level. Second, implementing citizenship education is only the first step. We need to be sure that as we infuse citizenship education across the curriculum, we develop a clear sense of what our learning outcomes will look like and have mechanisms in place for capturing, assessing, and studying student learning. Only after taking this second step will we be able to make a persuasive case for the effectiveness of our enterprise.

As scholars who have engaged in teaching citizenship across the curriculum and have engaged in rigorous investigations of our own classroom practice, we can offer our work as data. We draw on our own experiences to demonstrate how our participation in a faculty learning community enhanced our work and to suggest lessons for others who are considering engaging in such work.

From Individual to Community: Meeting the Challenges of Education for Citizenship Across Campus

Our prior classroom-based research (Smith, Nowacek, & Bernstein, 2010) indicates that students emerge from our individual classes with higher-than-usual levels of citizenship skills, such as the ability to sort through conflicting political information and the ability to disagree civilly. We also have evidence that our students emerge stronger on developing a sense of empathy, a tolerance for ambiguity and for questions that have no easy answer, and a willingness to see themselves as part of something larger than themselves. In short, we see our students beginning to make movement toward future citizenship behaviors.

As pleased as we are by these achievements, we each remain somewhat isolated on our campuses, frustrated with our limited ability to move our respective institutions toward more robust, cross-curricular citizenship education. We know from our conversations with collaborators on other campuses that our frustration is widespread. Our efforts to be more effective curricular change agents are constrained by two significant factors. First, we are limited by our institutional roles: we are each faculty members, working inside disciplinary homes without the benefit of administrative appointments. While we can accomplish much at the course or even the departmental level, we lack the reach and authority to sustain conversations about citizenship education across campus, much less implement initiatives to foster actual classroom experimentation. Second, while we each have allies in our quest to develop the teaching of citizenship across the curriculum, there are too few opportunities in the academy for allies in pedagogical and curricular innovation to find each other. The disciplinary silos in which we work limit interactions across campus; furthermore, joining with others to push our institutions to embrace the goal of teaching for citizenship necessarily becomes just one of many interesting and important initiatives competing for our time. Teaching and learning centers and faculty development professionals can become critical allies to faculty in these efforts.

As we individually pursued citizenship education goals, we were influenced by the supportive community we established as Carnegie Scholars with the Carnegie Foundation for the Advancement of Teaching in 2005–2006; ultimately this Carnegie experience can be described as a multidisciplinary, multi-institutional, residential faculty learning community (Cox, 2001; Cox & Richlin, 2004; Millis, 1990). In our learning community, we shared extended residencies that provided opportunities to read together, delve deeper into our projects, listen to and learn from our colleagues' presentations of their ongoing work, and engage in extended dialogue over shared meals and social outings. While this elaborate, well-funded model of a learning community is beyond the reach of most budgets, broader lessons can be drawn from it.

This learning community model is at the core of our recommendation for how faculty development centers can enhance citizenship education across campus. Originally we and the authors in our edited volume (Smith et al., 2010) approached citizenship education with different motivations. For some, educating tomorrow's democratic citizens was always front and center in our work and in our motivations for doing it (Bernstein, 2010; Geelan, 2010). Others were initially motivated by other problems, including students' inability to accurately self-assess their learning (Werder, 2010), their difficulty making empathetic connections to the literature of the Shoah (Holocaust) (Tinberg, 2010), and the challenges of developing a robust understanding of other cultures (Halualani, 2010). Over time, we found that our understandings of those problems were intimately linked with a richer conception of citizenship. Our learning community enabled us to find each other and illuminate these common themes.

As we coalesced into a learning community, we derived many benefits from the relationship. Foremost was a strong sense of solidarity and camaraderie.

As we swam against the prevailing tides of our disciplines, departments, schools, and the academy more generally, it was useful to have supportive colleagues with whom we shared a vocabulary and an ethos. There was always someone to e-mail for advice or call for support, or discuss what happened in class that day. The benefits of having a community of supportive peers are substantial for faculty working against the grain.

Beyond moral support is the question of institutional change. As we contemplate the institutional challenges that confront us, the three of us have pondered, more than once, how much we might be able to achieve were we working together on the same campus. We would be able to draw on the professional relationships we have built, our shared perspectives on citizenship education, the exciting intellectual differences in our approaches, and our cross-disciplinary borrowing of teaching approaches and assessment methods. If we had the opportunity to work together all the time, we are convinced we could be more effective than we are individually.

Indeed, as we look around our own campuses, we wonder how many of our colleagues share, unbeknown to us, a commitment to education for citizenship. How are we to find these colleagues, these potential partners? Faculty aiming to educate for citizenship can accomplish far more working together than they can working alone. Given the values that citizenship education seeks to foster, making this kind of pedagogical and curricular initiative a collective endeavor is all the more important. Because faculty development centers are potentially the place where communities of pedagogical practice receive the most support—and are often a physical space where disciplinary cross-fertilization in teaching and learning happens—these centers can sponsor significant breakthroughs in citizenship education.

Four Lessons Learned from a Faculty Learning Community on Citizenship

Based on our experiences, which form a case study of sorts, we offer guidance for faculty developers considering using faculty learning communities to build faculty capacity and institutional support for citizenship education. The literature on faculty learning communities (see, for example, Cox & Richlin, 2004) and on communities of practice (Wenger, 1998; Wenger, McDermott, & Snyder, 2002) offers a thorough review of how to create faculty learning communities. Here, we focus on the unique challenges and opportunities for these communities in the realm of citizenship education, offering specific suggestions for how learning communities might be structured and harnessed to provide maximum support to faculty working on citizenship education.

Embrace Diverse Definitions

Defining precisely what we mean by "citizenship education" or "civically engaged education" remains a challenge for anyone working in this area. Saltmarsh (2005) observes that "a lack of clarity about what is meant by the term 'civic engagement'" is ubiquitous whenever academics gather to discuss the subject. He suggests that "this lack of clarity fuels latent confusion about how to operationalize a civic engagement agenda on campus" (p. 52). We experienced this confusion when the participants in our learning community decided to extend and formalize our conversations by undertaking the project of writing a book: we tried to forge a shared definition, with little success. Definitional challenges briefly became an impediment to work in this area. They also, however, can become a source of strength.

Our definitions of what citizenship means, and what constitutes teaching for citizenship, evolved over many conversations over several years. We all began our work with a definition of citizenship in our heads and a sense of how we wanted to teach it in class. But as we saw how others taught citizenship, and how they articulated their goals for citizenship education in their classes, our individual understandings changed. Many of us learned to consider the role of different literacies, including scientific and quantitative literacy, in our understanding of citizenship, as a result of conversations with colleagues in the STEM disciplines (Burke, 2010; Fisher, 2010; Geelan, 2010). Many of our definitions pushed toward including an empathy component as we considered how one of our colleagues (Tinberg, 2010) used the literature on the Shoah to help his students explore how literature can develop their capacity for empathy. Although we cannot deny the allure of a compact, sound bite–friendly definition of citizenship, we have found that this messier, more capacious understanding has enriched our work in deeply rewarding ways.

We recommend encouraging faculty to share their own definitions of citizenship with the community. While definitions can, and should, be modified based on feedback from others, faculty should not be encouraged to all use the same definition in their classes. Likewise, we suggest encouraging faculty to investigate different aspects of citizenship development even in different sections of their classes. Ideally, discussions of the many valences of citizenship, and how they intersect across classes and within the same class, can become a source of generative discussions.

One way a faculty learning community might structure this discussion is around Shulman's (2008; see also Sullivan, 2004) work on habits of the mind, habits of the heart, and habits of practice. Each of our classes can help students learn essential knowledge for citizenship, whether these involve understanding how the political system works, how to evaluate scientific or quantitative arguments, or how to work with diverse groups of people to make collective decisions. Our classes can also help students develop dispositions of citizenship. We would all do well to cultivate in our students a tolerance for (and even a love of) problems that defy simple solutions, where the correct answer may be something about which reasonable people can disagree. Empathy, of course, remains a predominant disposition of citizenship, without which many other virtues are unattainable. Finally, we can strive to help our students practice the behaviors of citizenship through in-class simulations, group projects, or various forms of service-learning.

We would not suggest that faculty in a learning community ought to incorporate all of these aspects of citizenship into all in-class activities; that would easily overwhelm the courses we are teaching. But through a learning community, faculty can enrich their understanding of the many meanings of citizenship and think more about how to incorporate this diversity of perspectives into their classes. From an institutional standpoint, students can gain exposure to these varied perspectives through the sweep of their course work and emerge with a more complete picture of what citizenship can mean.

Use Citizenship Themes to Engage Students in Achieving a Course's Disciplinary Goals

Instructors are overworked and courses are already overstuffed with content, and these realities work against finding room to incorporate education for citizenship into classes across the curriculum. Our learning community has taught us that to be sustainable, education for citizenship cannot be an add-on in already content-rich classes. Rather it must become a vehicle through which already existing course-related goals are achieved. In this, we take our cue from the writing across the curriculum (WAC) movement. WAC acknowledges that certain departments have a critical, foundational role to play in the teaching of writing, just as political science and history have a foundational role to play in citizenship education. Teaching *with* writing, however, can be used outside composition classes as a tool to help teach the lessons of other disciplines (Bean, 1996). Writing lab reports in physics or position papers in political science are ways to use writing to teach through to the core of disciplinary knowledge. We believe an analogous process can be observed for citizenship.

Teaching biochemistry, as Fisher (2010) does, by focusing on diseases such as AIDS and Alzheimer's (and on the societal impact of these diseases) sacrifices little biochemistry content while helping to increase students' understanding of a major issue. Understanding the plight of those with these diseases also helps to cultivate the empathy that is critical to citizenship education. Fisher is one of many scientists who have discovered the power of this pedagogical twist (Rogers, Hamilton, Pfaff, & Erkan, 2010; Zobitz, 2009). Likewise, Mike Burke (2010) could teach the graphing of logarithmic functions using context-free values for x and y. He instead uses data sets based on real-world problems like nuclear waste disposal. By having his students use the rate of decay of radioactive material to calculate the length of time until it becomes safe, Burke allows students to learn mathematical principles as they gain a deeper understanding of a pressing social issue for global citizens of the twenty-first century. Along the way his students learn quantitative literacy, another important tool for citizenship education, within the context of learning mathematical functions in a precalculus class. Some math educators are even realizing their potential as force multipliers, as they help future primary and secondary teachers in training think about ways to integrate civic lessons into math (Jacobsen & Mistele, 2010).

These models make clear the broad applicability of citizenship education. When we start from the perspective that citizenship can be defined broadly, as requiring quantitative or scientific literacy, or empathy, or a tolerance for ambiguity, and that it can be taught in a wide variety of disciplines, the possibilities for using themes of citizenship to teach important course concepts expand dramatically. While different disciplines might excel at teaching different aspects of citizenship—we would not expect a poetry class to teach quantitative literacy, for example—all disciplines should be able to find aspects of citizenship to incorporate into their classes. At a course level, therefore, we argue that citizenship across the curriculum is eminently attainable. At a campus level, however, the challenges are greater, requiring the centralization and coordination that faculty development centers can provide.

Use the Learning Community to Enhance SoTL

We encourage scholarly investigations of student learning about citizenship through investigations grounded in the scholarship of teaching and learning (SoTL) (Bass, 1999; Hutchings & Shulman, 1999). Because teaching for citizenship and civic engagement pushes the envelope in terms of what is taught, and perhaps even sacrifices small amounts of course content in service to larger goals, these efforts need to document carefully what is being done and what students are gaining from the experience in order to convince skeptics of the worth of this enterprise. Fisher (2010) and Burke (2010) provide compelling examples of such documentation.

Furthermore, the learning community can become an important resource for instructors undertaking SoTL inquiries by facilitating "methodological trading zones" (Huber & Hutchings, 2005). Participating in the Carnegie Foundation's fellowship program brought us into close contact with colleagues wrestling with questions of how to examine and document the student learning that was taking place in their classrooms. In the methodological trading zone we established, faculty with expertise in survey research shared the benefits and techniques of quantitative methods, while those who used textual or discourse analysis in developing qualitative assessments of student learning opened up the possibilities of these methods for the scientists and social scientists. Each of us emerged with a greater set of methodological tools at our disposal. The traces of these exchanges can be found in each of our individual investigations. As one example, Nowacek, trained as a qualitative researcher of composition and rhetoric, has begun to use survey methods to study learning in her classes. This work is part of a collaboration with Bernstein, a quantitative political scientist who is now doing content analysis of student essays to study the impact of his pedagogical practices. This methodological trading continues to enhance our cross-disciplinary and cross-institutional conversations.

Embrace Student and Administrative Voices

A final bit of advice we offer to faculty developers considering a learning community is to involve a broad cross-section of people in the conversation. As Werder and Otis (2009) argue, students have a great deal to contribute to the scholarship of teaching and learning. Moreover, if a goal of these learning communities is to propagate this teaching approach across the curriculum, then the involvement of administrators, as well as professionals from divisions of student affairs, becomes an important piece of the puzzle. Faculty may have valid reasons for forming their own communities (such as to discuss specific pedagogical and epistemological matters in teaching citizenship and in evaluating the effectiveness of their approaches); other voices, however, ought to be part of the conversation in some way. Although we have not yet done as much with this theme as we would have liked (see, however, Gutman, Sergison, Martin,

& Bernstein, 2009) and were unable to do so during our joint residency, we believe this to be valuable advice for faculty wishing to form campus-based learning communities.

Implications

As the world continues to suffer from an economic crisis, accompanied by attendant (and resultant) increases in the cost of attending colleges and universities, the public is quite correctly asking more questions about what students gain from a college education. Accordingly, the attention colleges and universities have devoted to assessing student learning through their course work is well placed. In addition, we would argue that institutions of higher learning have an obligation to consider the kinds of people they are graduating. Have we graduated students capable of understanding the perspectives of those different from themselves? Have we graduated students willing to roll up their sleeves and exert effort, frequently difficult effort, to help heal and repair the world? In short, we must look at the students graduating from our institutions and ask whether they have the skills and dispositions of effective citizenship.

We also need to consider how to improve the capacity of colleges and universities to deliver on this citizenship education. Many professors are doing this work in their classes. We hope these efforts continue, and multiply, in the years and decades to come. But from an institutional standpoint, more needs to be done to ensure that the sum total of citizenship education on a campus exceeds the individual efforts faculty may be exerting in their classrooms. To that end, faculty development centers can serve as a locus of such efforts; faculty development centers have the ability to centralize, coordinate, and coalesce the efforts of individual faculty. Furthermore, we suggest the faculty learning community as a model by which this can occur. We hope the efforts of faculty development centers can move us closer to the goal of graduating civically engaged and capable citizens.

REFERENCES

Altman, I. (1996). Higher education and psychology in the millennium. *American Psychologist, 51*(4), 371–398. doi:10.1037/ 0003-066X.51.4.371

Bass, R. (1999). The scholarship of teaching: What's the problem? *Inventio: Creative Thinking About Learning and Teaching, 1*(1), 1–10.

Battistoni, R. (2002). *Civic engagement across the curriculum: A resource book for service-learning faculty in all disciplines*. Providence, RI: Campus Compact.

Bean, J. (1996). *Engaging ideas: The professor's guide to integrating writing, critical thinking, and active learning in the classroom*. San Francisco, CA: Jossey-Bass.

Bellah, R. N., Madsen, R., Sullivan, W. M., Swidler, A., & Tipton, S. M. (1985). *Habits of the heart: Individualism and commitment in American life*. Berkeley: University of California Press.

Bernstein, J. L. (2010). Citizenship-oriented approaches to the American government course. In M. B. Smith, R. S. Nowacek, & J. L. Bernstein (Eds.), *Citizenship across the curriculum* (pp. 13–35). Bloomington: Indiana University Press.

Bok, D. (2008). *A candid look at how much students learn and why they should be learning more*. Princeton, NJ: Princeton University Press.

Bringle, R., Games, R., & Malloy, E. (Eds.). (1999). *Colleges and universities as citizens*. Needham Heights, MA: Allyn & Bacon.

Burke, M. (2010). Enumeration, evidence, and emancipation. In M. B. Smith, R. S. Nowacek, & J. L. Bernstein (Eds.), *Citizenship across the curriculum* (pp. 132–146). Bloomington: Indiana University Press.

Carnegie Foundation for the Advancement of Teaching. (2006). *Higher education: Civic mission and civic effects*. Retrieved from www.civicyouth.org/PopUps/higher_ed_civic_mission_and_civic_effects.pdf

Colby, A., Ehrlich, T., Beaumont, E., & Stephens, J. (2003). *Educating citizens: Preparing American undergraduates for lives of moral and civic responsibility*. San Francisco, CA: Jossey-Bass.

Cox, M. D. (2001). Faculty learning communities: Change agents for transforming institutions into learning organizations. In D. Lieberman & C. M. Wehlburg (Eds.), *To improve the academy: Vol. 19. Resources for faculty, instructional, and organizational development* (pp. 69–93). San Francisco, CA: Jossey-Bass.

Cox, M. D., & Richlin, L. (2004). Developing scholarly teaching and the scholarship of teaching and learning through faculty learning communities. In M. D. Cox & L. Richlin (Eds.), *New directions for teaching and learning: Vol. 97. Building faculty learning communities* (pp. 127–136). San Francisco, CA: Jossey-Bass.

Dewey, J. (1916). *Democracy and education*. New York, NY: Free Press.

Dey, E. (2009). *Civic responsibility: What is the campus climate for learning?* Washington, DC: Association of American Colleges and Universities.

Fisher, M. A. (2010). Educating for scientific knowledge, awakening to a citizen's responsibility. In M. B. Smith, R. S. Nowacek, & J. L. Bernstein

(Eds.), *Citizenship across the curriculum* (pp. 110–131). Bloomington: Indiana University Press.

Geelan, D. (2010). Science, technology and understanding: Teaching the teachers of citizens of the future. In M. B. Smith, R. S. Nowacek, & J. L. Bernstein (Eds.), *Citizenship across the curriculum* (pp. 147–164). Bloomington: Indiana University Press.

Gutman, E. E., Sergison, E. M., Martin, C. J., & Bernstein, J. L. (2009). Engaging students as scholars of teaching and learning: The role of ownership. In C. Werder & M. M. Otis (Eds.), *Engaging student voices in the study of teaching and learning* (pp. 130–145). Sterling, VA: Stylus.

Halualani, R. T. (2010). De-stabilizing culture and citizenship: Crafting a critical intercultural engagement for university students in a diversity course. In M. B. Smith, R. S. Nowacek, & J. L. Bernstein (Eds.), *Citizenship across the curriculum* (pp. 36–53). Bloomington: Indiana University Press.

Huber, M. T., & Hutchings, P. (2005). *The advancement of learning: Building the teaching commons.* San Francisco, CA: Jossey-Bass.

Hutchings, P., & Shulman, L. S. (1999, September/October). The scholarship of teaching: New elaborations, new developments. *Change, 31*(5), 10–15.

Jacobsen, L., & Mistele, J. (2010). Please don't do "connect the dots": Mathematics lessons with social issues. *Science Education and Civic Engagement: An International Journal, 2*(2), 5–11.

Knefelkamp, L. L. (2008). Civic identity: Locating self in community. *Diversity and Democracy, 11*(2), 1–3.

Leach, J. (2010, August 5). Civility in a fractured society. *Denver Post.* Retrieved from www.denverpost.com/recommended/ci_15677293

Millis, B. J. (1990). Helping faculty build learning communities through cooperative groups. In L. Hilsen, R. Boice, N. Diamond, L. Gardiner, D. E. Morrison, & M. D. Sorcinelli (Eds.), *To improve the academy: Vol. 9. Resources for faculty, instructional, and organizational development* (pp. 43–58). Stillwater, OK: New Forums Press.

Nussbaum, M. (2002). Education for citizenship in an era of global connection. *Studies in Philosophy and Education, 21*(4/5), 289–303. doi:10.1023/A:1019837105053

Putnam, R. (1993). *Making democracy work: Civic traditions in modern Italy.* Princeton, NJ: Princeton University Press.

Rhoads, R. (1997). *Community service and higher learning: Explorations of the caring self.* Albany: State University of New York Press.

Rifkin, J. (2009). *The empathetic civilization: The race to global consciousness in a world in crisis.* New York, NY: Tarcher.

Rogers, M., Hamilton, J., Pfaff, T., & Erkan, A. (2010). Multidisciplinary collaborations in the traditional classroom: Wrestling with global climate change to improve science education. *Transformations: The Journal of Inclusive Scholarship and Pedagogy, 21*(1), 89–98.

Saltmarsh, J. (2005). The civic promise of service learning. *Liberal Education, 91*(2), 50–55.

Schmidt, P. (2009, September 30). Many at colleges feel students get too little civic education. *Chronicle of Higher Education.* Retrieved from http://chronicle.com/article/Many-at-Colleges-Feel-Students/48639/

Shulman, L. S. (2008). Pedagogies of interpretation, argumentation, and formation: From understanding to identity in Jewish education. *Journal of Jewish Education, 74*(1), 5–15. doi:10.1080/15244110802493289

Smith, M. B., Nowacek, R. S., & Bernstein, J. L. (Eds.). (2010). *Citizenship across the curriculum.* Bloomington: Indiana University Press.

Sullivan, W. M. (2004). *Work and integrity: The crisis and promise of professionalism in America* (2nd ed.). San Francisco, CA: Jossey-Bass.

Tinberg, H. (2010). We are all citizens of Auschwitz: Intimate engagement and the teaching of the Shoah. In M. B. Smith, R. S. Nowacek, & J. L. Bernstein (Eds.), *Citizenship across the curriculum* (pp. 73–90). Bloomington: Indiana University Press.

Wenger, E. (1998). *Communities of practice: Learning, meaning, and identity.* New York, NY: Cambridge University Press.

Wenger, E., McDermott, R., & Snyder, W. (2002). *Cultivating communities of practice: A guide to measuring knowledge.* Cambridge, MA: Harvard Business School Press.

Werder, C. (2010). Fostering self-authorship for citizenship: Telling metaphors in dialogue. In M. B. Smith, R. S. Nowacek, & J. L. Bernstein (Eds.), *Citizenship across the curriculum* (pp. 54–72). Bloomington: Indiana University Press.

Werder, C., & Otis, M. M. (Eds.). (2009). *Engaging student voices in the study of teaching and learning.* Sterling, VA: Stylus.

Zobitz, J. (2009, December). Quantifying the atmospheric impact of an urban biomass incinerator. *Science Education and Civic Engagement: An International Journal.* Retrieved from www.seceij.net/seceij/fall09/quantifying_atm.html

SUPPORTING INSTITUTIONAL PRIORITIES

6

ENHANCING OUT-OF-CLASS COMMUNICATION

STUDENTS' PERSPECTIVES

Bonnie S. Farley-Lucas, Margaret M. Sargent,
Southern Connecticut State University

Out-of-class communication between faculty and students is linked to student learning, engagement, and success. As the source for mentoring, advising, and supplemental instruction, out-of-class communication and its barriers require explicit attention. Using a faculty-student collaborative research approach, we interviewed a diverse group of thirty-three undergraduates regarding behaviors, statements, and practices that contributed to or discouraged out-of-class communication. We found that in-class communication sets the stage for whether students approach faculty outside class and that faculty misbehaviors and disconfirming communication in class almost inevitably lead to out-of-class avoidance.

Out-of-classroom communication is the wellspring for mentoring, academic advising, supplemental instruction, and, generally, favorable student-faculty relations. Out-of-class communication also includes faculty involvement in student organizations and all student-faculty discussions about non-class-related issues (Nadler & Nadler, 2001). Many universities require faculty office hours to facilitate this essential contact. Despite its central role in academic culture, out-of-class communication, particularly from a student perspective, receives less explicit research attention than it deserves. This chapter examines personal characteristics

Our thanks to the reviewers of the manuscript for this chapter for helpful feedback and to Southern Connecticut State University student interviewers Kierstin Pry, Allison Stankiewicz, and Lissette Agosto. This project was supported by a 2009 Connecticut State University Research Grant.

and behaviors of faculty that students experienced as contributing to, discouraging, or supporting out-of-class communication. Information gathered from students can help faculty attend to areas known to have a positive impact on teaching and can help faculty developers assemble workshops and professional resources to promote specific strategies that students experienced as helpful in their learning.

Student-Faculty Communication

Student-faculty communication is central to teaching and learning. Students rank student-faculty interaction as a high priority (Astin, 1993). They want to connect with professors and often cite the valued relational qualities of equality, mutuality, and respect (Garko, Kough, Pignata, Kimmel, & Eison, 1994). When students engage in out-of-class communication, student-teacher relationships are more interpersonal in nature (Dobransky & Frymier, 2004; Fusani, 1994). Indeed, one of the two environmental factors most predictive of positive change in college students' academic development, personal development, and satisfaction, and one of the five benchmarks of student engagement, is interaction between faculty and students (Astin, 1993; Kuh, Kinzie, Schuh, & Whitt, 2005; Light, 2001). Expressing care, building rapport, and creating positive learning climates all contribute to positive faculty-student interaction, and thus to student motivation and learning (Ambrose, Bridges, DiPietro, Lovett, & Norman, 2010; Chickering & Gamson, 1987; Meyers, 2009; Richmond, Gorham, & McCroskey, 1987). Because faculty-student interaction promotes student motivation and success, professors are advised to increase contact, maximize office hours, talk with students, and share experiences (McKeachie & Svinicki, 2010; Schoenfeld & Magnan, 2004).

Despite its many benefits, face-to-face faculty-to-student out-of-class communication is infrequent (Feldman & Newcomb, 1996). On average, first-year students interact with teachers outside class only once or twice a month, and seniors at research universities had no more interaction with faculty than first-year students did at liberal arts colleges (Schroeder, 2003). Electronic consultations by e-mail have largely replaced traditional office hours. Students favor e-mail contact with faculty for the ability to clarify course material, efficiency, availability, approachability, and personal and social reasons (Kelly, Keaten, & Finch, 2004; Waldeck, Kearney, & Plax, 2001). Faculty favor e-mail contact for efficiency, timeliness, ability to allow reticent students to communicate more freely, and potential for increased student engagement outside class (Duran,

Kelly, & Keaten, 2005). Given the primacy of e-mail contact, faculty face new challenges in building rapport with students.

Unfortunately, students do not always encounter positive faculty behavior. Teacher misbehaviors are defined as "those behaviors that interfere with instruction, and thus, learning" (Kearney, Plax, Hays, & Ivey, 1991, p. 310). Based on their analysis, Kearney et al. identified twenty-eight categories of misbehavior within three underlying dimensions: incompetence, indolence, and offensiveness. Incompetence, which refers to the lack of basic teaching skills, has nine categories of misbehavior: confusing lectures, apathy toward students, unfair testing, boring lectures, unintelligible accents, information overload, lack of knowledge on subject matter, inappropriate volume, and bad grammar or spelling. Offensiveness relates to how teachers verbally interact with students and encompasses sarcasm, put-downs, verbal abuse, unreasonable or arbitrary rules, sexual harassment, negative personality, favoritism, and prejudice. Indolence, a teacher's disregard for students, refers to being absent, tardy, unprepared and disorganized, deviating from the syllabus, returning student work late, and information overload.

Faculty misbehaviors have a negative impact on both students and faculty. Students report less learning, less engagement, and less enactment of recommended classroom behaviors when teachers misbehave (Dolin, 1995). Furthermore, students often interpret teacher misbehavior as intentional, and student motivation and judgments of teachers' effectiveness are both adversely affected by misbehavior (Kelsey, Kearney, Plax, Allen, & Ritter, 2004). Teacher misbehaviors are also linked to student resistance (Kearney, Plax, & Burroughs, 1991), teachers' lack of credibility (Banfield, Richmond, & McCroskey, 2006), and negative teaching evaluations (Schrodt, 2003). Assertiveness, responsiveness, student liking for the teacher, and affect toward the material are all negatively associated with teacher misbehavior (Banfield et al., 2006; McPherson, Kearney, & Plax, 2003, 2006; Myers, 2002; Wanzer & McCroskey, 1998).

Not surprisingly, students can encounter teacher misbehaviors out of class as well as in class. Such misbehaviors include inaccessibility to students, missing scheduled appointments, not showing up for office hours, and not making time for students when they need additional help (Kearney et al., 1991). Although there is scant research on faculty misbehaviors in out-of-class communication, the anticipated consequences can be quite negative. Common problems associated with e-mail contact include lack of response to requests for project clarification, impersonal responses to students' reports of illness or family emergencies, and condescending comments on students' work. Students can experience barriers to learning, public embarrassment, sexual harassment, frustration, and the violation of expectations for faculty professionalism, all contributing to impoverished learning (Farley-Lucas & Sargent, 2007).

Research Approach

This study aims to add depth to our understanding of out-of-class communication by privileging students' voices and highlighting their experiences. With an explicit focus on specific behaviors, interactions, and verbal statements that students experienced and defined as encouraging and discouraging of out-of class communication, we can make clearer connections to pedagogical practices that contribute to learning as well as to practices that contribute to disengagement, demotivation, and depersonalization. Specifying behaviors also allows an exploration of the nature, development, and consequences of particular classroom dynamics.

We addressed three key questions that emerged from the literature: (1) What personal characteristics and faculty behaviors have students experienced as encouraging out-of-class communication? (2) What personal characteristics and faculty behaviors have students experienced as discouraging out-of-class communication? and (3) What specific instructional strategies did students report as being effective in encouraging them to engage in out-of-class communication with their professors?

Method

To foster candid interviews and student research experience, three undergraduate interviewers were recruited, trained, and provided with uniform interview protocols. Each interviewed eleven undergraduates. When recruiting volunteers, they aimed for intentional diversity (Anderson & Jack, 1991), identifying and selecting participants for diversity of age, gender, ethnicity, major, and universities attended. Due to their limited experience with student-faculty communication, first-year students were not as heavily recruited as upperclass students. To protect identities, participants were asked to think about particular professors but avoid using names. To enhance anonymity, participants created their own pseudonyms, and tapes were submitted directly to a professional transcriptionist. Audiorecorded interviews averaged thirty-five minutes each, resulting in 402 pages of verbatim transcripts.

Participants

Thirty-three undergraduate students, representing a diverse population, participated. There were sixteen women and seventeen men. Self-described ethnicity identified Caucasian or white (eighteen), Hispanic (six), African American (two), Native American (one), Polish (one), "black and white" (one), "a regular walking U.N." (one), and three who declined to label themselves. Ages ranged from 19 to 32, with an average of 21.8 years. Sixteen majors were represented: thirteen in arts and humanities; ten in social sciences; seven in science, engineering, and mathematics disciplines; and three in education. Sixteen participants attended the same university only, fourteen were transfer students representing twelve institutions, and three attended other universities. Participants were two first-year students, eight sophomores, nine juniors, and fourteen seniors.

Analysis

Narrative analysis focuses on describing people's varying experiences and highlights participants' own languages and definitions (Geertz, 1983). Using inductive analysis (Anderson & Jack, 1991), interview transcripts were analyzed first to identify themes and trends for each participant, and then to identify themes and patterns across research questions. While participants varied in degree of detail provided, their experiences point to a wide variety of behaviors and instructional practices. Exemplars were selected according to three criteria: representativeness, the degree to which comments represent common perspectives or describe problematic interactions others experienced (similar views); intensity, the degree to which language reflects emotional, cognitive, or behavioral attachment to the category (strong views); and uniqueness, the degree to which comments capture unique viewpoints not previously expressed (different views) (Van Manen, 1990). Students' descriptive language adds authenticity to the study (Manning, 1997).

Behaviors Encouraging Out-of-Class Communication

Research question 1 addressed faculty's personal characteristics and behaviors that encourage students to engage in out-of-class communication. As seen in Table 6.1, participants provided 174 comments related to encouraging out-of-class communication, with ten key qualities discernable. Very clearly, in-class communication sets the stage for whether students approach faculty outside of class.

Table 6.1 Qualities That Encourage Out-of-Class Communication

Characteristic	Number of Students ($n = 33$)	Number of Statements ($n = 174$)
Positive personal qualities	21	36
Invited out-of-class communication	21	29
Caring	16	29
Offered or provided instrumental help	14	20
Positive interpersonal skills	10	13
Availability	8	16
Challenging	7	11
Express or discuss common interest	7	8
Good teacher in class	5	8
Recognizes students as individuals	4	4

Prior to outside connections, teachers must connect with students in class. Students variously described the most important characteristic that led them to engage in out-of-class communication as "showed empathy" or "caring about what students are dealing with." Those who showed interest in students' lives, and particularly those who showed interest in student success beyond classroom boundaries, received high praise. As one student commented, "She really wants you to understand and do well, not just for class." Along with caring behaviors, positive personal qualities encouraging interaction include "nice," "honest," "great sense of humor," "down to earth," "open," and "friendly." Similarly, faculty described as having good interpersonal skills, especially being a "good listener," encouraged out-of-class communication.

The most accessible teachers were described as inviting out-of-class communication, both implicitly and explicitly. Implicit invitations took the form of "being approachable" or "giving off that inviting feeling that we could meet anytime." Explicit invitations mostly stemmed from classroom introductions during the first class, with faculty actively creating a positive classroom climate. Often mirrored in the course syllabus, statements concerning the teacher's commitment to student success and expectations for conversations beyond classrooms were seen as indicative of teachers' welcoming student contact. Typically approachable teachers provided more time than official office hours, offering help at any time. Several reported teachers who invited feedback by e-mail or phone, and a few reported text messages.

Helpfulness was the next key theme. Once students approached professors out of class, they expected to receive the help they sought. Students reported receiving tangible assistance on projects, essays, and exams that led to improved understanding and, quite often, higher grades. Helpfulness extended to "being resourceful" and referring students to other on-campus resources.

Students are more likely to engage in out-of-class communication with faculty perceived as recognizing their individual needs. They appreciated faculty knowing their names and being aware of any special circumstances the students might be dealing with. Students shared positive anecdotes of faculty helping them cope with illness or absences, develop study strategies, and take advantage of opportunities to raise grades. At the same time, students are likely to engage in out-of-class communication with professors who challenge students, "raise the bar," and help students improve. As one stated, "They push you along, but don't hold your hand."

Positive out-of-class communication often transforms impersonal connections into more personal, caring relationships. With established lines of communication, students are more likely to present a positive face. They are more likely to care about professors' impressions of them, so they are less likely to miss class, and if they do, they are likely to provide justification. Professors who respond in caring ways to students' reports of illness or family or work demands further establish positive relational connections.

Quite often, students reported a relational shift that occurred when they could discuss more personal issues with instructors. Some reported seeing professors as potential mentors and advisors, and many established informal mentorships as a result of continued positive out-of-class communication. Some gained empathy and noted personal issues that professors were experiencing, such as losing a family member. Moreover, in positive student-faculty relationships, students reported working harder in class, gaining self-confidence, learning more about the discipline, and, in some cases, learning how to write or conduct research.

Student expectations of student-faculty relationships appear to undergo a transition from their first year through their senior year. During the first year, students reported feeling insecure, intimidated by faculty, and unsure how to connect. Therefore, faculty who facilitated interaction were evaluated highly. Some were described as "the reason I stayed" within academic programs or universities. Students in their third and fourth years were more likely to see faculty as individuals and more likely to engage in conversations about career-related or personal topics. More experienced students defined student-faculty relationships more instrumentally, particularly as they sought career-related information, networking, and letters of recommendation.

Behaviors Discouraging Out-of-Class Communication

Research question 2 explored behaviors and qualities discouraging out-of-class communication. As seen in Table 6.2, 105 statements related to discouraging out-of-class communication, yielding eight key qualities. Only one student out of the thirty-three participants reported that she had not experienced negative interactions with faculty. The other thirty-two participants described a wide variety of faculty misbehaviors, negative interactions, and unprofessional actions that led to less-than-optimal learning outcomes. The primary finding is that faculty misbehaviors and disconfirming communication in class almost inevitably lead to out-of-class avoidance.

When describing professors they would be most unlikely to interact with outside class, students first centered on negative personal characteristics:

Table 6.2 Qualities That Discourage Out-of-Class Communication

Characteristic	Number of Students ($n = 33$)	Number of Statements ($n = 105$)
Lack of availability/ unapproachable	15	23
Teacher misbehavior	11	12
Lack of interpersonal skills	10	18
Public embarrassment	8	13
Negative personal characteristics	8	11
Poor teaching	7	16
Lack of openness	5	6
Apathy toward students and teaching	4	6

"cold," "arrogant," "self-centered," egotistical," "standoffish," and "mean." Negative teachers were described as possessing a lack of warmth and empathy and as having poor interpersonal skills. Exemplars included "doesn't start conversations" and "can't talk to him due to his lack of eye contact."

Unapproachable professors projected that they "disliked students," communicated a lack of openness ("he looked like he didn't have time for us"), and, in some cases, explicitly stated their lack of availability. As one explained, "On the first day of class she told us all the ways to contact her that she would never respond." Unapproachable faculty are seen as "not helpful." In some cases, faculty made statements discouraging communication, such as, "I'm not here to be your friend," or, "If you have problems, take it to your TA and not me."

The other main finding regarding discouraging out-of-class communication was that poor teaching was associated with faculty misbehavior. Students reported emotional memories of faculty members who were condescending, "shot down my ideas in class," or "told me my ideas are wrong." Most damaging were personal insults and negative comments about students' intelligence or academic ability. Public embarrassment, dismissive comments, lack of respect for students, and threatening students with poor grades were commonly cited as strong repellents to out-of-class communication. Inappropriate humor or humor made at the expense of students was also likely to discourage out-of-class contact. Poor teaching, including lack of organization, unclear assignments, and nonspecific expectations for evaluation of assignments often contributed to an overall evaluation of "lack of professionalism." Often unprofessional behavior was associated with professors' lack of concern for learning. One student recalled a professor who "expected you to know everything" yet did not provide means to learn.

Apathy emerged as the last main characteristic with a negative impact on out-of-class communication. Students often expect professors to demonstrate both passion for their discipline and concern for students. Professors who "seemed unhappy" or "showed a lack of passion for their subject" were evaluated negatively. The overarching assumption was, "Professors should display passion, not work just to get a paycheck." Apathy toward students was reflected in the following: "He just writes on the board and doesn't care to interact with us. He doesn't care about us." Students logically conclude that apathy in class would be equated with apathy out of class, and apathetic faculty do not inspire further contact.

Students who experience negative in-class communication are less likely to pursue out-of-class contact and therefore less likely to experience learning, student success, and connectedness to a discipline. Students in this unfortunate position are presented with two negative outcomes: poor teaching and the lack of means to address the poor teaching. This dynamic is critical in students' first year because it may set expectations for more difficult or unprofessional professors, thus interfering with student success and retention.

With negative in-class communication, students reported less motivation to attend class or work on class assignments. This was particularly true if students experienced feelings of futility—that regardless of their effort, they would be graded harshly and receive a poor grade. Thus, students reported a higher likelihood of disengaging from the learning process. With respect to professors who repeatedly engage in student put-downs, the implicit message sent to students was that they should mimic professors' views in order to "survive a class," or, as one student said, "If you don't have the same opinion, you'll fail the class."

Strategies for Encouraging Out-of-Class Communication

Research question 3 explored specific instructional strategies students reported as effective in encouraging out-of-class communication with professors. They provided several concrete suggestions that faculty can use to inform their practice. Most obviously, faculty need to be present for office hours, keep scheduled appointments, and make time for students when they need help. Students expressed great appreciation for positive, one-on-one time, particularly when they received the help they expected. To facilitate "quick questions" when students are most likely to have them and allow brief exchanges, students expect professors to arrive early to class and stay after class.

Classroom management practices also contribute to out-of-class communication. Students responded well to syllabus statements inviting students to visit during office hours. Including a "by appointment" option is critical since it is quite likely that professors' office hours conflict with students' class or work schedules. Letting students know on the first day, with regular reminders throughout the semester, about availability for extra help was reassuring. Several students pointed out faculty who wrote their e-mail and office hours on the board every class. They were impressed by faculty who seemed to provide a "24/7 open door" by providing home phone numbers or cell phone numbers in case students ran into "emergencies." Although students "hardly ever" telephone a professor, they found this invitation to be a caring gesture. One student succinctly suggested, "Let us know that you enjoy talking with us, particularly about the course."

Students expect "respect," "positivity," and "professionalism" during class. When professors learned and used students' names, they felt "more valued," "more connected," and more likely to interact out of class. Students also suggested that faculty recognize and greet students when they encounter them around campus, and, if possible, exchange basic pleasantries.

Given that e-mail is the primary channel for academic and social connections, it is imperative that faculty respond promptly and politely. In addition to brief responses, a friendly opening and closing personalizes the communication. Students reported faculty sending periodic e-mails to the class offering assistance on projects as they progressed throughout the semester. Updates from faculty were seen as "very helpful" and as having a positive impact on students' performance. Blackboard and other learning management systems easily facilitate such contact.

In order to increase opportunities for one-on-one exchanges, students responded well to mandatory meetings. A few mentioned mandatory initial "meet-and-greets" held early in the semester to get acquainted and set goals. Midterm consultations held with each student to review progress helped motivate them to participate in class and earn higher grades. One-on-one meetings provided specific feedback on course projects. Students allowed to submit revisions prior to assigning a final grade on projects reported learning more about the writing process.

Discussion and Implications

In summary, explicit descriptions of students' experiences contribute to our awareness of classroom interactions and instructional practices that either encourage or discourage out-of-class communication and the related outcomes of each. Positive out-of-class communication begins inside the classroom with the level of competence a professor demonstrates, as well as students' perceptions of professors' caring and helpfulness. Outside the classroom, students benefit from faculty described as approachable and helpful and those who recognize students as individuals. Positive out-of-class communication transforms student-faculty relations from impersonal to interpersonal, opening doors for mentoring and advising. Conversely, professors' disconfirming communication and misbehaviors inside the classroom inevitably lead to out-of-class avoidance. Poor teaching is associated with faculty misbehavior and contributes to poor academic achievement and disengagement from the learning process. Students' specific suggestions for instructional practices are helpful for those wishing to engage students in academic discourse, facilitate deeper understanding, and serve as advisors and mentors.

This study complements literature highlighting the importance of out-of-class communication and the affective dimension of instruction, and it privileges students' perspectives. By identifying from a student perspective what constitutes positive out-of-class communication, faculty-student relationships, advisement, and mentoring can be strengthened. Associated outcomes are increased academic success, greater levels of integration and retention, more engaged learning, and increased satisfaction with academic experiences.

True to our intent, information gained from students was instrumental in developing workshops and resources that have been widely disseminated throughout our university. One workshop on out-of-class communication was conducted for faculty as part of our semester-wide offerings, and another workshop on best practices in student advisement was copresented with the academic advising office during our annual teaching academy. A short article was included in our faculty development electronic newsletter. A summarized list of students' top ten suggestions was included on the back of brochures distributed at a presemester faculty development forum and is included in new faculty orientation programs. Ultimately, faculty developers and faculty need to involve students and have a positive impact on them.

REFERENCES

Ambrose, S. A., Bridges, M. W., DiPietro, M., Lovett, M. C., & Norman, M. K. (2010). *How learning works: Seven research-based principles for smart teaching.* San Francisco, CA: Jossey-Bass.

Anderson, K., & Jack, D. C. (1991). Learning to listen: Interview techniques and analysis. In S. B. Gluck & D. Patai (Eds.), *Women's words: The feminist practice of oral history* (pp. 11–26). New York, NY: Routledge.

Astin, A. W. (1993). *What matters most in college? Four critical years revisited.* San Francisco, CA: Jossey-Bass.

Banfield, S. R., Richmond, V. P., & McCroskey, J. C. (2006). The effect of teacher misbehaviors on teacher credibility and affect for the teacher. *Communication Education, 55*(1), 63–72. doi:10.1080/03634520500343400

Chickering, A. W., & Gamson, Z. F. (1987, March). Seven principles for good practice in higher education. *AAHE Bulletin, 39*(7), 3–7.

Dobransky, N. D., & Frymier, A. B. (2004). Developing teacher-student relationships through out of class communication. *Communication Quarterly, 52*(3), 211–223. doi:10.1080/01463370409370193

Dolin, D. J. (1995). *Ain't misbehavin': A study of teacher misbehaviors, related to communication behaviors, and student resistance* (Unpublished doctoral dissertation). West Virginia University, Morgantown.

Duran, R. L., Kelly, L., & Keaten, J. A. (2005). College faculty use and perceptions of electronic mail to communicate with students. *Communication Quarterly, 53*(2), 159–176. doi:10.1080/01463370500090118

Farley-Lucas, B. S., & Sargent, M. M. (2007, July). *"Checking out mentally": Faculty misbehaviors and impact on students.* Paper presented at the international conference on Improving University Teaching, Jaen, Spain.

Feldman, K. A., & Newcomb, T. M. (1996). *The impact of college on students* (Vol. 2). San Francisco, CA: Jossey-Bass.

Fusani, D. S. (1994). "Extra-class" communication: Frequency, immediacy, self-disclosure, and satisfaction in the student-faculty interaction outside the classroom. *Journal of Applied Communication Research, 22*(3), 232–255. doi:10.1080/00909889409365400

Garko, M. G., Kough, C., Pignata, G., Kimmel, E. B., & Eison, J. (1994). Myths about student-faculty relationships: What do students really want? *Journal on Excellence in College Teaching, 5*(2), 51–65.

Geertz, C. (1983). *Local knowledge.* New York, NY: Basic Books.

Kearney, P., Plax, T. G., & Burroughs, N. F. (1991). An attributional analysis of college students' resistance decisions. *Communication Education, 40*(4), 325–342. doi:10.1080/03634529109378858

Kearney, P., Plax, T. G., Hays, L. R., & Ivey, M. J. (1991). College teacher misbehaviors: What students don't like about what teachers say or do. *Communication Quarterly, 39*(4), 309–324.

Kelly, L., Keaten, J. A., & Finch, C. (2004). Reticent and non-reticent college students' preferred communication channels for communicating with faculty. *Communication Research Reports, 21*(2), 197–209. doi:10.1080/08824090409359981

Kelsey, D. M., Kearney, P., Plax, T. G., Allen, T. H., & Ritter, K. J. (2004). College students' attribution of teacher misbehaviors. *Communication Education, 53*(1), 1–17. doi:10.1080/0363452032000135760

Kuh, G. D., Kinzie, J., Schuh, J. H., & Whitt, W. (2005). *Student success in college: Creating conditions that matter.* San Francisco, CA: Jossey-Bass.

Light, R. J. (2001). *Making the most of college: Students speak their minds.* Cambridge, MA: Harvard University Press.

Manning, K. (1997). Authenticity in constructivist inquiry: Methodological considerations without prescription. *Qualitative Inquiry, 3*(1), 93–115. doi:10.1177/107780049700300105

McKeachie, W. J., & Svinicki, M. (2010). *McKeachie's teaching tips: Strategies, research, and theory for college and university teachers* (13th ed.). Boston, MA: Houghton Mifflin.

McPherson, M. B., Kearney, P., & Plax, T. G. (2003). The dark side of instruction: Teacher anger as norm violations. *Journal of Applied Communication Research, 31*(1), 76–90. doi:10.1080/00909880305376

McPherson, M. B., Kearney, P., & Plax, T. G. (2006). College teacher misbehaviors. In T. P. Mottet, V. P. Richmond, & J. C. McCroskey (Eds.), *Handbook of instructional education: Rhetorical and relational perspectives* (pp. 213–234). Needham Heights, MA: Allyn & Bacon.

Meyers, S. A. (2009). Do your students care whether you care about them? *College Teaching, 57*(4), 205–210.

Myers, S. A. (2002). Perceived aggressive instructor communication and student state motivation, learning, and satisfaction. *Communication Reports, 15*(2), 113–121.

Nadler, M. K., & Nadler, L. B. (2001). The roles of sex, empathy, and credibility in out-of-class communication between faculty and students. *Women's Studies in Communication, 24*(2), 241–261. doi:10.1080/07491409.2001.10162436

Richmond, V. P., Gorham, J. S., & McCroskey, J. C. (1987). The relationship between selected immediacy behaviors and cognitive learning. In M. L. McLaughlin (Ed.), *Communication yearbook 10* (pp. 574–590). Thousand Oaks, CA: Sage.

Schoenfeld, A. C., & Magnan, R. (2004). *Mentor in a manual: Climbing the academic ladder to tenure* (3rd ed.). Madison, WI: Atwood.

Schrodt, P. (2003). Students' appraisals of instructors as a function of students' perceptions of instructors' aggressive communication. *Communication Education, 52*(2), 106–121. doi:10.1080/03634520302468

Schroeder, C. (2003, March/April). How are we doing at engaging students? Charles Schroeder talks to George Kuh. *About Campus, 8*(1), 9–16.

Van Manen, M. (1990). *Researching lived experience*. Albany: State University of New York Press.

Waldeck, J. H., Kearney, P., & Plax, T. G. (2001). Instructional and developmental communication and theory and research in the 1990s: Extending the agenda for the 21st century. In W. B. Gudykunst (Ed.), *Communication yearbook 24* (pp. 206–229). Thousand Oaks, CA: Sage.

Wanzer, M. B., & McCroskey, J. C. (1998). Teacher socio-communicative style as a correlate of student affect toward teacher and course material. *Communication Education, 47*(1), 43–52. doi:10.1080/03634529809379109

7

EFFECTING CHANGE
IN LIMITED-CONTROL
CLASSROOM ENVIRONMENTS

A CASE STUDY

Allison P. Boye, Texas Tech University

Many instructors face the dilemma of possessing little control over their own curriculum or even their own pedagogy. This chapter examines three instructors who were teaching the same course over several years, facing the same problematic issues beyond their control, and describes the role of faculty developers in helping effect practical change for those instructors and for the course. The findings of this study, using longitudinal data derived from student evaluations and qualitative responses from instructor interviews, suggest that faculty developers can help instructors realize change on an individual level as well as at the department and big-picture levels.

Louise, Alex, and Ashley all had problems teaching. Their students thought the course material was too difficult and often boring, and they frequently came to class with bad attitudes. Yet despite their desire to improve, these instructors felt disempowered to make any changes. For three years, faculty developer colleagues at my center and I worked with these three graduate student instructors (GSIs) who were teaching the same course: a large, required course in food sanitation. Each year we helped these instructors, who were also participants in our graduate student development program, try to navigate the pedagogical challenges of

I thank Suzanne Tapp for her invaluable insights and support during the completion of this project, as well as the instructors and faculty members who were involved, for allowing me to share their experiences.

the course, and we noticed that the same problems appeared each year. Unfortunately, most of the course's ongoing problems had less to do with the individual GSIs than with curricular and departmental issues that were out of their control.

Any faculty developers who have worked with GSIs or new or adjunct faculty have likely encountered instructors who are teaching something they have been told to teach, with little or no control over content, pedagogical, or logistical decisions. Those instructors might feel pressured to conform to a certain style of teaching that may or may not match their own preferences, or perhaps they are teaching content with which they are unfamiliar and must rely on another's material just to get by. This circumstance is certainly not unusual, but it surely changes the way a faculty developer is able to interact with and advise instructors who are seeking improvements in the classroom. This conundrum begs the question: If the instructor does not have the authority to make the changes that are really necessary for the most improvement, what can a faculty developer do?

The Perfect Storm: A Case Study

This case study focuses on GSIs, identified here as Louise, Alex, and Ashley, who taught the same course in food sanitation in the department of animal and food sciences over three different years (2006–2007, 2008–2009, 2009–2010). During each of those academic years, respectively, the GSIs were participants in a graduate student development program, the Teaching Effectiveness And Career enHancement Program (TEACH), at Texas Tech University, and they worked closely with faculty developers while teaching the course. As part of TEACH, each semester faculty developers observed the instructors in the classroom, provided feedback, and conducted a small group instructional diagnosis (SGID), a well-known form of midterm student evaluation in which individual as well as group consensus feedback is solicited (Clark & Redmond, 1982). As we worked with these GSIs, we noticed ourselves making many of the same suggestions, and students making many of the same complaints, year after year.

A Brief Overview of the Literature

Although little has been written about the lack of curricular or pedagogical control full-time faculty might face, GSIs and adjuncts are undoubtedly the most likely to lack control over their own teaching environment.

Literature confirms that adjunct instructors, often fearful of losing their positions, also suffer from limited academic freedom (Marshall, 2003; Schneider, 1999; Thompson, 2003). Much of the literature about GSIs confirms that they, like adjuncts, do not receive a great deal of training or support for their teaching (Association of American Universities, 1998; Gaff, 2002a, 2002b; Golde & Dore, 2001; Kuther, 2003; Meacham, 2002; Park, 2002; Weisbuch, 2004). Meacham (2002) in particular claims that lack of pedagogical preparation is a failure by universities not only for the graduate students, but also for the undergraduate students in their care. In a survey of perceptions of using GSIs, Park (2002) explores both the benefits and drawbacks. The notable drawbacks include confusion that may be created if the GSI teaches differently from the course leader, as well as tension fostered by the lack of ownership in the teaching process. Both concerns are related to the issue of control that the instructors in this case study experienced. In addition, Prieto and Meyers (1999) highlight the increase in self-efficacy or confidence that GSIs who receive support and training realized.

The literature also substantiates that resistance to faculty development and the difficulty of pedagogical change, such as that experienced by the instructors in this study, are not new. Common reasons for such resistance include concerns about not having the time to implement change, that help or change is unnecessary, or that the need for faculty development implies incompetence on the part of the instructor (Boice, 1984; Turner & Boice, 1986). Hodges (2006) notes that fear of risk taking can play a large part in impeding change and emphasizes the importance of small changes that do not remove instructors far from their comfort zones, while Hativa (2000) focuses on the significance of addressing personal beliefs about teaching with instructors. All of these issues are likely familiar to experienced faculty developers, and indeed they were taken into consideration when working with the instructors in this study.

One major concern in this case study was the faculty developer's ability to act as an agent of change, even in the face of such resistance. Several authors call for faculty developers to take a decidedly proactive approach toward becoming change agents on their campuses (Cook, 2001; Diamond, 2005; Fletcher & Patrick, 1998; Zahorski, 1993). Gardiner (2005) specifically asserts the importance of developing a sense of urgency for change. Cook (2001) further corroborates that faculty developers can be helpful partners in curricular change, given their position as objective observers and their ability to provide empirical evidence of the need for change. Finally, others (Boye & Meixner, 2010; Brookfield, 1995; Loughran, 2002; McAlpine & Weston, 2000) underscore the value of instructor reflection in the transformation and development process, something that we also demonstrated in this study.

What Students Had to Say

To determine if what appeared to be recurring problems with the food sanitation course truly were just that, content analysis was conducted of the individual comments from all six semesters of SGID data for the three graduate instructors. That analysis confirmed that each year, nine common themes continued to surface from student feedback, in almost exact proportions; each year, approximately 33 to 37 percent of the total student feedback related to nine common complaints (Table 7.1):

1. Amount of material
2. Difficulty of material or grading
3. Pace too fast

Table 7.1 Major Common Themes in Individual Student SGID Comments

Common Theme	Common Theme Comments, 2006–2007	Common Theme Comments, 2008–2009	Common Theme Comments, 2009–2010
Amount of material	17.5%	10.0%	15.6%
Difficulty of material or grading	15.7	23.8	25.4
Pace too fast	27.9	17.9	12.3
Desire for more interaction	24.9	32.2	31.4
Too much lecture or PowerPoint	5.7	3.8	12.8
Imbalance of majors and nonmajors	1.7	6.3	.82
Memorization versus application of material	2.2	1.7	0
Location of class	1.7	3.8	.27
Team teaching	2.6	NA	1.4
Percentage of total SGID comments related to common themes	33.5	32.7	37.2

4. Desire for more interaction

5. Too much lecture or PowerPoint

6. Imbalance of majors and nonmajors

7. Memorization versus application of material

8. Location of classes

9. Team teaching

Many of those common themes were related to issues outside the realm of control of the GSIs, for this course carried with it a host of unusual complicating factors. First, this course suffers from unbalanced demographics: although it is taught within the department of animal and food sciences, the instructors note that approximately 80 to 90 percent of the students come from the college of human sciences who are taking the course as required preparation for the national ServSafe exam before entering the restaurant and hospitality industries. Second, the animal and food sciences building is for all intents and purposes off-campus, a mile and a half away from the human sciences building. Walking between the two buildings takes about twenty minutes; taking the campus bus takes approximately seventeen minutes due to the five stops in between; either option takes far longer than the ten minutes allotted between classes. Therefore, the instructors typically start class late and finish early to accommodate students from human sciences. The class consists of 100 to 130 students each semester, and the classroom has fixed stadium seating with long tables and entrances at the front. The professor who coordinates the course and team-teaches with the graduate students is well established and respected, and in general, her lecture style dominates.

The yearly complaints from students about amount of material, difficulty of material, and application of material all clearly relate to the palpable divide between majors and nonmajors in the course. Many students, particularly human sciences students, did not understand the relevance of the vast amounts of material in the class, since it was their understanding that the course was meant solely as preparation for the ServSafe exam. One student wrote, "The endless barrage of microbiology terms is completely useless because it retains no context due to the vast majority of sanitation issues being solved with simple rules which can be retained in any on-the-job sanitation course." However, both the professor and graduate instructors verified that additional material was geared toward the more advanced animal and food science majors. Similarly, human sciences students repeatedly cried out for more direct application of the material to their own future careers, writing statements such as,

"I'd like to learn more about food procedures and things I will actually use in a kitchen/restaurant, NOT MEMORIZING things I will forget in 2 weeks." Some comments, which could not be separated into distinct pedagogical categories, but only as majors versus nonmajors, likewise gave strong voice to the tangible divide between animal and food science majors and human sciences majors each year, such as, "When taking this class [human sciences] majors and [animal and food science] majors should not have to take this class together. It should be separate."

The complaints about the rapid pace of the course are also somewhat related to the location of the classroom. The need to cover the vast amount of material in a relatively short time becomes even more complicated when each class period is shortened by ten to twenty minutes to allow travel across campus. Each semester, students would make comments such as, "I understand there is a lot of material to be covered, but the rushed feeling throughout lectures really just stresses me out and affects my ability to really learn the material." Students already struggling with difficult, unfamiliar material thus struggled even further with the brisk pace of instruction.

The concerns over excessive PowerPoint-driven lecture and a desire for more class interaction had much to do with not only the restrictive physical space of the classroom itself (perceived as unfavorable for learning activities that require movement or interaction), but also with fear experienced by some of the GSIs about straying too far from the traditional style of the course. One of the graduate instructors, for instance, revealed that she "felt it was best to mimic the instructor of record's style to maintain consistency," even though she wanted to try other activities and styles of teaching. While the students appreciated the structure and clarity provided by the use of PowerPoint, they did not like the monotony of feverishly scribbling notes and listening to lecture every class or, as one student wrote, "Slide after slide after slide after slide." Each year they also made comments asking for more variety and interaction in the class, such as, "I am a hands-on learner, so I would like to see more of that instead of constant lecture." Students in the course obviously shared many similar concerns, and interestingly, the GSIs did as well.

What GSIs Had to Say

To gain further insight into the course from the instructors' perspectives, feedback was also gathered during interviews with the three former GSIs by e-mail, before which they granted permission for use of their comments and information related to the course for this project.

Each instructor expressed similar frustrations with the tension created by the unbalanced demographics of the course. Each also echoed student concerns about the amount of material and the need to separate majors and nonmajors, making comments such as, "I would have reduced the amount of material or split the course into two separate sessions, with one being for science-based students, and the other being for the nonmajors. By doing this, I could adjust the type of material that was covered in the course and the way that the material was being presented to the students."

Further resonating with the tensions observed in Park's study (2002), one of the instructors stressed her unfulfilled desire to try out new teaching styles and vary the methods traditionally used in the course, especially in relation to the varying needs of the two groups of students. She remarked, "It was difficult not being able to change the style of teaching and method of presenting material to accommodate the students in the class. Facing a large group of uninterested and grumpy students each class period was difficult." The other GSIs confirmed the generally low morale or poor attitudes of disgruntled students in the class. Undoubtedly these graduate instructors were in tune with course issues that were creating unhappy students and had their own ideas about how to solve some of those problems; unfortunately, they felt they had no authority to do so.

What the Faculty Developer Can Do: Multiple Levels of Change

The food sanitation course is a perfect storm of sorts. Most courses, we hope, are not quite as complicated. Nevertheless, this case study focuses on the ultimate concern of what faculty developers can do to help instructors, like Louise, Alex, and Ashley, who have little control over their own curriculum and even pedagogy. The experiences of these instructors suggest that faculty developers can help such instructors realize multiple levels of change and growth.

Instructor-Level Change

The first level of change resides with the individual instructor. While the major changes needed might seem impossible, faculty developers must remember that there are elements within the instructor's control. While working with Louise, Alex, and Ashley, we helped them focus on what they could control and change at the moment and distinguish that from what they could not control. For instance, in our written feedback and discussion of our observations and the SGID, we purposely—even visually—separated the commentary that pertained specifically to the instructor from that which pertained to the uncontrollable course situation, and focused on the former. We maintained confidentiality and let the instructors determine if they wanted to share the feedback with their course advisor, hoping that if they did so, others in the department would have an opportunity to hear student feedback.

We furthermore assisted the instructors with tangible, immediate changes, such as how they designed and animated PowerPoint slides, since that was the major vehicle of instruction for all of them. We helped one instructor think through her classroom management style as she tried new strategies for handling the sometimes unruly, discontented students. And for another, we visited her classroom to provide feedback for her first attempt at a new small group activity.

While these interventions might seem inconsequential in light of the larger frustrations of the course, the instructors indicated that their impact was significant. One noted, for instance, that the faculty developers "gave [her] great ideas to use for getting a big group of students to participate" and that they were "very influential in the changes to [her] overall teaching approach." And just as Prieto and Meyers's study (1999) might have predicted, faculty developer support played an important role in improved self-efficacy, for another commented, "The TEACH staff gave me more confidence in my teaching style and methods. . . . The staff gave me many suggestions on how to handle the difficult students and how to be strong when faced with difficult situations." As such, we as faculty developers were able to meet some of the personal and pressing needs of individual instructors seeking instructional improvement.

Department- and Program-Level Change

As faculty developers, we are perhaps most comfortable working directly with individual instructors. Similarly, those instructors are likely used to dealing with their own departments regarding curriculum and program design, especially with respect to elements they may not feel they can change. What might be less common is the faculty developer working directly with the department to effect change when appropriate. Faculty developers have been urged to become more purposeful change agents (Cook, 2001; Diamond, 2005; Fletcher & Patrick, 1998; Zahorski, 1993), and this study demonstrated the positive effect of answering that call.

Given the large amount of consistent student feedback data available on the food sanitation course and the length of time our center had worked with course instructors, I decided the time was right to bring together the faculty with the most authority regarding the course: the course advisor from the department of animal and food sciences, who is in charge of designing the course, and the chair of the restaurant and hospitality industry management department, whose students make up the majority of the class. The goal was to present an overview of the data and facilitate a discussion about the status of the course.

I maintained a neutral position as the faculty developer while engaging with these faculty members. I did not call the meeting with the purpose of dictating what I thought should be done with the course; instead, I simply presented the data and said, "Here is what I have gathered about this course, and I thought you might find it interesting and want to talk about it together." That neutrality was crucial in preventing those department heads, who had not willingly solicited this interaction or feedback, from feeling ambushed or attacked; the goal was to help them maintain a feeling of control and an open mind, for I believe that only with openness can change be accomplished. I also maintained instructor confidentiality: I shared only the general overview of the SGID data and a few representative comments related to the common feedback themes.

Although I was unsure of how these department heads might respond to this unsolicited feedback, the meeting was ultimately a resounding success. The chairs spent only a few minutes skimming the data, confirming that they were both at least somewhat aware of the course's issues. They then immediately turned to me and asked for suggestions for change. In response, I returned to the data and what I had learned from the instructor interviews for support and made suggestions centered on the two major complaints: creating two sections of the course—one for majors and one for nonmajors—so that the material can be more tailored to student needs and placing the nonmajors class in the human sciences building. Within minutes, the department heads began collaborating to brainstorm ways to move the classroom and create a separate section, and they declared they could make it happen by the next fall semester. Finally, they proposed that we also collaborate on some future research about the changes. Altogether, in just thirty minutes, major pedagogical and curricular changes began to take form after years of frustration on the part of students and instructors alike. Those department chairs report that they continue to work together toward those suggested changes: new classrooms have been reserved for the fall in the human sciences building for the nonmajors section, and other faculty are excited about the developments.

An important lesson for faculty developers extending from this experience is that while these department heads clearly knew that change was needed, they required an objective outsider to motivate and facilitate that change by providing solid evidence and a rationale for change. As Cook (2001) points out, one benefit of faculty developer involvement in curricular revision is the objectivity and empirical data we can provide. As that objective observer, I also helped provide a greater sense of urgency, as Gardiner (2005) called for, and made sure to offer suggestions that were not only based on evidence but also were within the comfort zones of faculty in charge, making change easier to embrace (Hodges, 2006). Furthermore, although my objectivity and respectfulness played an important role in department head openness and the success of the meeting, they also expected me to offer suggestions since I called the meeting. Therefore, preparation is paramount for faculty developers who are aiming to take this proactive approach. This experience demonstrates that with the right combination of initiative, evidence, and consideration, higher-level change is in fact possible.

Change for the Future

The final level of change lies in the big picture for instructors who feel they do not have the authority to change their current classroom situation. Just as we did with Louise, Alex, and Ashley, and even when department- or program-level change is impossible, faculty developers can always help instructors think about the big picture of their teaching, beyond the current course that is out of their control and toward the future that will be in their control. A critical element in reaching toward that future change comes from the power of reflection (Boye & Meixner, 2010; Brookfield, 1995; Loughran, 2002; McAlpine & Weston, 2000). Reflection is a core value of the TEACH Program, and we encourage our participants to make it a career-long habit. Reflective practice has proven to be an especially powerful tool for instructors who feel disenfranchised from the courses they teach because it offers them an outlet for realizing that they can have a personal teaching philosophy and that their pedagogy can be different; thus, they can look forward to the time when they will be able to implement their own teaching philosophy on their terms.

Faculty developers at our center assisted Louise, Alex, and Ashley with several activities to help them engage in such big-picture reflection, first and foremost being the creation of teaching philosophy statements and teaching portfolios. The very process of thinking about their beliefs about teaching and how they would choose to act on those beliefs in the classroom, along with the support of faculty developers to help cultivate that reflection, provides instructors with an evocative outlet for self-realization. In other words, it helps give them a voice when perhaps they feel voiceless, and that is a compelling experience for anyone. Other valuable reflective activities for the instructors in the study included the hypothetical course redesign that Ashley completed—her answer to "how I would teach this course if I had complete control"—and Alex's focus on creating a list of strategies for teaching large enrollment courses.

Interviews with course instructors confirm the benefit of these efforts toward recognizing big-picture change and future control. One instructor commented that "her involvement with the TEACH Program and faculty developers profoundly assisted her in developing her own philosophy of teaching and determining what was most important to her." Another mentioned a more tangible benefit of these activities, crediting "the development of her teaching philosophy and portfolio with securing her current faculty position at another university." The GSIs in this study have since moved on from teaching the food sanitation course and can now happily put into practice their own personal philosophies of teaching.

Conclusion

Louise, Alex, and Ashley are certainly not the only instructors who might feel that they are in a no-win situation, teaching a class they feel they have no power to change. Although this case study focuses on experiences of GSIs, it represents the experience of instructors populating every campus, including new faculty, lecturers, and adjuncts. Involvement with these instructors and their supervisors reveals that regardless of appearances, faculty developers can effect change in a variety of practical ways. Faculty developers can bring a wealth of attributes to instructors in need, from the neutrality and confidentiality we offer in our consultation practices, to the empirical evidence we can provide. Through preparedness and thoughtful effort, we can help even those instructors in limited-control situations with small, immediate issues that still have significant impact on their personal satisfaction and professional growth. Moreover, we can become proactive agents for change on a larger scale, with the appropriate amount of convincing data and objectivity. And more than that, we can help frustrated instructors think about their teaching and discover their personal teaching philosophies so that when the time comes, they will be ready to implement them. One day these instructors likely will have control over their curriculum and pedagogy. By then, they will be well-prepared, reflective practitioners who are ready to embrace and influence whatever the classroom has in store for them.

REFERENCES

Association of American Universities. (1998). *Committee on Graduate Education: Report and recommendations*. Washington, DC: Author. Retrieved from www.aau.edu/WorkArea/showcontent.aspx?id=6720

Boice, R. (1984). The relevance of faculty development for teachers of psychology. *Teaching of Psychology, 11*(1), 3–8. doi:10.1207/s15328023top1101_1

Boye, A., & Meixner, M. (2010). Growing a new generation: Promoting self-reflection through peer observation. In J. E. Miller & J. E. Groccia (Eds.), *To improve the academy: Vol. 29. Resources for faculty, instructional, and organizational development* (pp. 18–31). San Francisco, CA: Jossey-Bass.

Brookfield, S. D. (1995). *Becoming a critically reflective teacher.* San Francisco, CA: Jossey-Bass.

Clark, D., & Redmond, M. (1982). *Small group instructional diagnosis: Final report*. Retrieved from ERIC database. (ED217954)

Cook, C. (2001). The role of a teaching center in curricular reform. In D. Lieberman & C. Wehlburg (Eds.), *To improve the academy: Vol. 19. Resources for faculty, instructional, and organizational development* (pp. 217–230). San Francisco, CA: Jossey-Bass.

Diamond, R. M. (2005). The institutional change agency: The expanding role of academic support centers. In S. Chadwick-Blossey & D. R. Robertson (Eds.), *To improve the academy: Vol. 23. Resources for faculty, instructional, and organizational development* (pp. 24–36). San Francisco, CA: Jossey-Bass.

Fletcher, J. J., & Patrick, S. K. (1998). Not just workshops anymore: The role of faculty development in reframing academic priorities. *International Journal for Academic Development, 3*(1), 39–46. doi:10.1080/1360144980030106

Gaff, J. G. (2002a, November/December). Preparing future faculty and doctoral education. *Change, 34*(6), 63–66.

Gaff, J. G. (2002b). The disconnect between graduate education and faculty realities. *Liberal Education, 88*(3), 6–13.

Gardiner, L. F. (2005). Transforming the environment for learning: A crisis of quality. In S. Chadwick-Blossey & D. R. Robertson (Eds.), *To improve the academy: Vol. 23. Resources for faculty, instructional, and organizational development* (pp. 3–23). San Francisco, CA: Jossey-Bass.

Golde, C. M., & Dore, T. M. (2001). *At cross purposes: What the experiences of today's graduate students reveal about doctoral education.* Philadelphia, PA: Pew Charitable Trusts. Retrieved from www.phd-survey .org/report%20final.pdf

Hativa, N. (2000). Becoming a better teacher: A case of changing the pedagogical knowledge and beliefs of law professors. *Instructional Science, 28*(5/6), 491–523.

Hodges, L. (2006). Preparing faculty for pedagogical change: Helping faculty deal with fear. In S. Chadwick-Blossey & D. R. Robertson (Eds.), *To improve the academy: Vol. 24. Resources for faculty, instructional, and organizational development* (pp. 121–134). San Francisco, CA: Jossey-Bass.

Kuther, T. L. (2003). Teaching the teacher: Ethical issues in graduate student teaching. *College Student Journal, 37*(2), 219–223.

Loughran, J. J. (2002). Effective reflective practice: In search of meaning in learning about teaching. *Journal of Teacher Education, 53*(1), 33–43. doi:10.1177/0022487102053001004

Marshall, E. (2003). Victims of circumstance: Academic freedom in a contingent academy. *Academe, 89*(3), 45–48.

McAlpine, L., & Weston, C. (2000). Reflection: Issues related to improving professors' teaching and students' learning. *Instructional Science, 28*(5/6), 363–385.

Meacham, J. (2002). Our doctoral programs are failing our undergraduate students. *Liberal Education, 88*(3), 22–27.

Park, C. (2002). Neither fish nor fowl? The perceived benefits and problems of using graduate teaching assistants (GTAs) to teach undergraduate students. *Higher Education Review, 35*(1), 50–62.

Prieto, L. R., & Meyers, S. A. (1999). Effects of training and supervision on the self-efficacy of psychology graduate teaching assistants. *Teaching of Psychology, 26*(4), 264–266.

Schneider, A. (1999, December 10). To many adjunct professors, academic freedom is a myth. *Chronicle of Higher Education,* pp. A18–A19.

Thompson, K. (2003). Contingent faculty and student learning: Welcome to the strativersity. In E. Benjamin (Ed.), *New directions for higher education: No. 123. Exploring the role of contingent instructional staff in undergraduate learning* (pp. 41–47). San Francisco, CA: Jossey-Bass.

Turner, J. L., & Boice, R. (1986). Coping with resistance to faculty development. In M. Svinicki, J. Kurfiss, & J. Stone (Eds.), *To improve the academy: Vol. 5. Resources for faculty, instructional, and organizational development* (pp. 26–36). Stillwater, OK: New Forums Press.

Weisbuch, R. (2004). Toward a responsive Ph.D.: New partnerships, paradigms, practices, and people. In D. H. Wulff & A. E. Austin (Eds.), *Paths to the professoriate: Strategies for enriching the preparation of future faculty* (pp. 217–235). San Francisco, CA: Jossey-Bass.

Zahorski, K. (1993). Taking the lead: Faculty development as institutional change agent. In D. L. Wright & J. P. Lunde (Eds.), *To improve the academy: Vol. 12. Resources for faculty, instructional, and organizational development* (pp. 227–245). Stillwater, OK: New Forums Press.

8

ADAPTING A LABORATORY RESEARCH GROUP MODEL TO FOSTER THE SCHOLARSHIP OF TEACHING AND LEARNING

Beth A. Fisher, Regina F. Frey, Washington University in St. Louis

A multidisciplinary group of faculty and staff formed an education research group modeled on a laboratory research group to focus on the scholarship of teaching and learning (SoTL) in science, technology, engineering, and mathematics (STEM). This group has bridged the communication and knowledge gaps between STEM and social science faculty and science education specialists, fostered the development of collaborative SoTL projects, and laid the groundwork for broader institutional support of SoTL.

Much educational research in science, technology, engineering, and mathematics (STEM) has historically been undertaken by mathematics and science education specialists who do not typically teach undergraduate STEM courses. Recently, however, STEM faculty have become more interested in educational research and have identified participation in the scholarship of teaching and learning (SoTL) as a means of bridging the gaps that often exist between STEM faculty and specialists in mathematics and science education fields (Banchoff & Salem, 2002; Coppola & Jacobs, 2002; Huber & Morreale, 2002; Wankat, Felder, Smith, & Oreovicz, 2002). As Coppola and Jacobs (2002) have argued in relation to SoTL in chemistry, faculty who teach undergraduate courses should be involved in this scholarship because "only practitioners of chemistry can recognize the common yet content-rich stumbling blocks that students face when learning chemistry" (pp. 202–203). The same argument applies to the development of SoTL in all STEM fields.

Increasing interest in SoTL among STEM faculty can also be traced to the emphasis that major funders, including the National Science Foundation, the Howard Hughes Medical Institute (HHMI), the U.S. Department of Education, and the Institute of Education Sciences, have placed on evaluation of the programs they support (Huber & Hutchings, 2005; Wankat et al., 2002). Such funding has enabled faculty to incorporate into their teaching innovative methods including active and collaborative learning (Coppola & Jacobs, 2002; Wankat et al., 2002). As more STEM faculty adopt such methods, the need has developed for them to conduct evaluative studies of their own teaching and familiarize themselves with principles of human learning that are applicable to STEM classroom and laboratory teaching. Faculty developers have responded to this need with consultations and programs that provide faculty with opportunities to design teaching innovations that are informed by, and contribute to, SoTL (Sorcinelli, Austin, Eddy, & Beach, 2006). At our university, the director of the teaching center and colleagues from across STEM disciplines developed a successful model for fostering SoTL in STEM. This Education Research Group (ERG) meets weekly in a format resembling a laboratory research group meeting. The ERG brings together a multi-disciplinary group representing faculty who teach undergraduate STEM courses, faculty who conduct research in cognitive and learning sciences, and faculty and staff who develop and implement K–12 science outreach programs.

Now in its third year, the ERG has fostered approaches to SoTL that bridge communication and knowledge gaps among groups of faculty and research staff who share a common goal of improving teaching and learning but rarely have opportunities to work together or learn from one another. The ERG has also helped to raise awareness beyond the group about the breadth of scholarship at the university and has laid the groundwork for a university center devoted to research on teaching and learning.

Although the ERG was developed in response to a specific need to evaluate in a systematic way projects funded by HHMI, it serves another, broader purpose by fostering collegial and collaborative interactions among scholars from different disciplines that the Carnegie Foundation for the Advancement of Teaching has identified as crucial to the value of SoTL (Huber & Hutchings, 2005). The group's weekly meetings define teaching and scholarship on teaching not as solitary and separate pursuits, but as mutually reinforcing work that is most productive and useful when it is undertaken within and by a community of scholars (Shulman, 1993). The ERG members share a commitment to improving teaching and learning in STEM and an interest in learning about and developing methods to evaluate teaching and learning. The group members' shared focus on teaching and learning in undergraduate STEM classrooms at the university means that, despite the fact that the group is multidisciplinary, their projects are grounded within discipline-specific contexts and content; this aspect of the group coheres with Lee Shulman's (1993) vision of teaching as "community property"—or work that is best developed and refined within intellectual communities that share specific disciplinary traditions.

We believe that the ERG model represents a useful response to challenges that prevail in nearly every discipline and at many colleges and universities. First, the scholarship of teaching and learning is still considered, for the most part, independent of the faculty reward structure, which traditionally focuses on faculty contributions to "the scholarship of discovery" (Boyer, 1990). Second, there is a dearth of institutional support for SoTL. Third, the time needed to design and conduct SoTL is a scarce resource, given the current reward structure and the multiple commitments to research and teaching that shape faculty priorities in various ways. Finally, most faculty teaching in the disciplines are not trained in the principles of human learning and the research methodologies central to SoTL (Coppola & Jacobs, 2002; Huber, 2002; Hutchings & Shulman, 1999; Middendorf & Pace, 2008; Wankat et al., 2002).

The ERG has not only fostered faculty participation in SoTL, but has also promoted a broader set of goals that faculty developers at all types of institutions have identified as priorities: "to create or sustain a culture of teaching excellence," "respond to and support individual faculty," "advance new initiatives in teaching and learning," and "foster collegiality" among faculty (Sorcinelli et al., 2006, p. 48). The ERG is a product of an approach to faculty development that prevails at our university and at many others, where teaching center staff, themselves faculty, approach their work as a collaboration with fellow faculty to develop programs and services that will enhance teaching and learning at the university (Sorcinelli et al., 2006).

History of the ERG

Faculty at our university often collaborate with colleagues to design and refine undergraduate courses in STEM. Such collaboration can include consultation with the teaching center director, who is also a professor of the practice in chemistry. Several years ago, a professor of biology began to work with the director to redesign a writing-intensive biology course, first during a teaching center workshop on teaching with writing, then in a series of consultations. The goal was to redesign her course's writing assignments and grading rubrics with a focus on determining whether students achieved the course learning objectives. Their conversations about this course led the professor and the director to think about new ways to apply this scholarly approach to teaching to the design and evaluation of a broad array of undergraduate STEM courses and programs supported by the university's multiyear grant from HHMI. Initially won in the early 1990s and continually renewed since then, the HHMI grant has been instrumental in the development of numerous initiatives in STEM education. As HHMI has increasingly emphasized the need to evaluate supported educational projects, the faculty involved in the HHMI courses and programs have become more interested in designing and conducting educational research.

In summer 2008, the biology professor met with the teaching center director and the science outreach director, also a member of the HHMI advisory panel, to discuss hiring a postdoctoral fellow to assist faculty with the design and execution of studies to evaluate the effectiveness of the HHMI-supported teaching innovations. During this discussion, they determined that what was needed was not just a single postdoctoral fellow but also a larger culture within which evaluation work could develop. To create such a culture, they decided to follow the model of a weekly laboratory research group meeting that would involve the newly hired postdoctoral fellow and faculty and staff involved in HHMI projects. This group, which they named the STEM ERG, would provide an opportunity for faculty and staff to learn how to develop effective evaluation plans for HHMI projects and would provide a venue for regular collegial discussions of teaching and learning—discussions that would ultimately improve teaching and learning across the university. The initial group consisted of faculty and staff involved in HHMI projects from the departments of biology, chemistry, mathematics, physics, science outreach, education, engineering, and the student learning center. In addition, the founders invited two faculty who were not involved in HHMI projects: a cognitive scientist and professor of psychology whose research is in learning and memory and an educational psychologist whose research is in collaborative learning. Recently the director of preservice programs in the department of education joined the group. The ERG has met every fall and spring semester since fall 2008. Approximately twenty-six individuals have participated, with a group of thirteen core members participating on a regular basis during the nearly two and a half years since its inception.

Structure of ERG Meetings

The group's weekly sessions function like laboratory research group meetings in the sciences. Each week, a group member gives a presentation on an ongoing project, which in some cases is the result of collaboration among multiple ERG members. This project is typically at one of three stages: an initial planning stage, involving the definition of the project's informing principles and objectives; a later planning stage, involving the development of evaluation methods; or a data analysis and conclusions stage. The projects range from the design and evaluation of instructional methods to the development of interdisciplinary research on learning approaches that students bring to first-year courses. The schedule of presentations for each semester is established at the end of the previous semester. Each member volunteers to present approximately once a year. The presenter may ask the group to read an article or two prior to the meeting or may use visuals, a handout, or an activity to structure the presentation and discussion during the meeting. Each presentation is brief, serving as a springboard for the discussion, the heart of each meeting. The discussion is lively and interactive, often including complex questions and vigorous debate about the project and appropriate evaluation methods. The ERG members are quick to challenge one another to develop methods and approaches that are understandable and applicable across disciplinary boundaries.

ERG Member Perspectives

To better understand the experiences of the STEM ERG members, one of us conducted interviews with all three ERG founders and with another core ERG member. The purpose of these interviews was to give these four individuals an opportunity to reflect on the group's objectives and benefits.

Shared Benefits

The ERG members report that they find great value in the energetic, collegial environment of the weekly meetings. They describe this environment as "friendly" and "open," as well as "engaging" and "challenging." One notes that the success of the meeting format is due in part to the fact that the majority of the ERG members are in disciplines in which the laboratory group meeting is a familiar model for scholarly conversation and collaboration. The ERG members are accustomed to and appreciate the scholarly give-and-take that occurs during each meeting, and they each take seriously their responsibilities to offer thoughtful feedback and questions that will help one another refine their respective projects. The ERG members agree that the cohesiveness of the group is a result of a shared sense of purpose: all participants are dedicated to, and excited about, advancing teaching and learning in STEM and improving the various types of educational research in which they are each engaged.

The ERG members value the diversity of the group. Participants bring different levels of expertise in SoTL and in research on learning. Some are just beginning to explore SoTL, and others have been conducting SoTL and science education research for many years. They also bring different perspectives on how to ask and answer questions about teaching and learning. For example, STEM faculty often approach these meetings with questions such as, "What methods or approaches can I use to help my students learn?" They focus on the learning objectives that shape their courses and on what they have learned about student learning, whether through observation or formal evaluation. Faculty who conduct research in cognitive and learning sciences bring questions such as, "What do you mean by learning?" and, "How can you measure learning?" They bring to the ERG knowledge about principles of human learning that have been identified not in classrooms but in laboratory research.

Initial group meetings quickly revealed that ERG members used different vocabularies to discuss teaching and learning. Subsequent meetings provided opportunities for the group to learn to lower the linguistic barriers that often separate faculty in STEM departments from those in social science departments and to develop ways of speaking to one another across these barriers. The conversation that occurs each week thus exemplifies the way in which multidisciplinary discussions about SoTL can establish a teaching commons—a space in which scholars from different disciplines can discuss and learn about teaching. As Huber and Hutchings (2005) describe it, the teaching commons is valuable because of its heterogeneity: "its vibrancy, like that of a city's, lies in the number, variety, and distinctiveness of its neighborhoods" (p. 71). The ERG members describe the multidisciplinary nature of the group as crucial to its value. One notes, for example, that the group offers a rare opportunity to "interact in a very scholarly and productive way with people who are in different disciplines." Participation in the ERG provides a means for members to critically examine their own disciplinary approaches and assumptions, learn about scholarship that they would not have otherwise known about, and develop valued collegial relationships across disciplines.

A Broader Perspective on Course Design and Evaluation

The professor of biology brings to the ERG expertise in developing and teaching upper-division, writing-intensive courses in the sciences. As the principal investigator on the HHMI grant and chairperson of the biology department, she brings to the group expert knowledge about university-wide and national efforts to improve undergraduate STEM education. Her presentations to the group have focused on the redesign and evaluation of her writing-intensive course. Feedback from the group at the initial stage helped this professor and her co-instructor (also an ERG member) identify ways to measure whether the course is successful at helping students develop specific cognitive and writing skills, such as formulating ideas based on evidence and explaining concepts with the context that readers require. Once the co-instructors had developed an evaluation plan, they presented this plan to the ERG and again gathered feedback. Now that the evaluation phase is under way, they plan to return to the ERG with a subsequent presentation on the results of the evaluation.

The biology professor has appreciated the group's feedback and suggestions at each stage of her project. In fact, she finds that giving multiple presentations on her project has been productive rather than repetitive; each time she discusses new developments and questions with colleagues who are familiar with the project. The sequence of presentations, she notes, allows her to make progress on the project and to "progress in [her] thinking" about the project. She points out that the laboratory group structure of the ERG allows her to learn about other projects at a deeper level than she would at a research symposium. Moreover, learning about these projects at various stages of their development has given her a broader, enriched understanding of how colleagues in other disciplines think about teaching, student learning, and the process of evaluation.

A K–20 Perspective on STEM Education

The director of science outreach is an experienced educator who is working on a doctorate in science education. She has presented to the ERG on several projects, including a challenging project to evaluate the university's master's program for high school biology teachers. In this program, teachers take intensive summer courses and then design curricula based on the content taught in those courses. The rich conversation that has resulted from her presentations has helped her develop more robust approaches to collecting and analyzing data. More broadly, the

weekly conversations with faculty who teach in STEM in higher education have informed her work helping high school teachers learn how to
prepare their students for university-level work. By the same token, her
knowledge of high school curricula and of the challenges that high school
science teachers face is valuable to the ERG's STEM faculty, who are
working to develop curricula and programs that help students make a
successful transition to university courses. The science outreach director
refers to this exchange of information as producing a K–20 perspective
on STEM education, and she sees it as one of the chief benefits of the
ERG. She also notes that participating in the ERG has helped to raise
awareness, within and beyond the group, that science outreach researchers and educators are engaged in scholarship that is integral to the university's mission. This awareness has helped to combat a common, reductive
image of science outreach as developing programs that are merely "fun"
and "supplemental," rather than integrated with the university's focus on
research and postsecondary education.

Collaborative Research on Teaching and Learning

The teaching center director, a professor of the practice in chemistry,
brings to the group expertise in effective teaching practices in STEM and
in chemical education. Her approach to the latter field is unusual: she is
a chemist who entered educational research as a faculty member teaching
in the discipline rather than through doctoral work in science education.
She has presented to the ERG on several topics, including her research on
peer-led team learning and a first-year transition program in chemistry.
Participating in the ERG has helped her develop research methods that
approximate the methodologies that ERG colleagues in the social sciences
use. At the same time, she notes that the participating STEM faculty have
helped their social science colleagues understand the extent to which clas-
sic experimental methods cannot be applied rigidly in SoTL; instead they
must be adapted to fit classroom teaching, where there are many variables and no true controls (Nummedal, Benson, & Chew, 2002).

Another result of the director's participation in the ERG is the development of a collaborative project. The genesis of this project was a presentation to the ERG by a psychology professor whose research
investigates how principles of cognitive science may be applied to
improve instruction in the classroom. The presentation focused on a
function learning test that the psychologist developed to identify two
approaches that students take to learning: an algorithmic (rote learning) approach and a conceptual (theory-based) approach. This presentation

sparked the interest of the teaching center director, who pointed out that these two approaches seemed to describe the two groups of students she has observed during many years of teaching general chemistry. These two ERG members developed a new project in which they are using the function learning test to identify the learning approaches of first-year students in the fall general chemistry course. Preliminary data show performance differences associated with these two approaches; later phases of the project will focus on developing interventions to benefit the lower-performing group.

The collaboration between these two ERG members exemplifies the benefits of the group's multidisciplinary conversations on teaching and learning. Conversations among ERG members helped the psychologist become better informed about how STEM instructional environments differ from the more controlled laboratory environments where cognitive science research is conducted, and presented cognitive science research in ways that make its relevance more clear to STEM faculty. The chemist learned to use tools from cognitive science research to provide insights into student learning in a first-year course that is a part of the core undergraduate curriculum.

Additional Collaborative Projects

Faculty participation in the STEM ERG has spurred the development of other collaborative projects, including a redesign of objectives and assessments in a microbiology course, a study of student performance and satisfaction in general physics courses that replace the traditional lecture format with mini-lectures and group problem solving, and the development of a new approach to data analysis in a project evaluating the discourse in peer-led team learning groups.

Next Steps

The format of the ERG is evolving. The weekly meetings now focus less on presentation of information and more on formal planning of HHMI projects. Starting in spring 2011, most of the meetings are conducted in a working group format, in which members discuss each project and work together to develop clear objectives, evaluation methods, and a time line. The product of each meeting is intended to be a plan that the project manager can use to advance the project. This format will be especially valuable for new ERG collaborations, such as a planned project applying tools and insights from cognitive science to evaluate three different approaches to inquiry-based learning in upper-division science laboratory courses.

The success of the STEM ERG in its first phase has laid the groundwork for institutional support of SoTL across disciplines. Three ERG members have successfully lobbied the provost for the creation of a university center, to be funded starting in fall 2011, that will bring together the expertise of cognitive scientists and faculty teaching in the disciplines to produce research on teaching and learning. The provost's support will allow the hiring of a full-time staff scientist who will design and conduct evaluative studies for educational projects that are not funded by external grants and assist faculty in writing proposals to seek external support for SoTL.

Advice on Starting an ERG

While the ERG model uses a structure that is most familiar to faculty who conduct laboratory research, this model can foster the development of scholarship of teaching and learning in any discipline. In addition, it can be successful in a variety of settings, and not only at private, research-intensive, doctorate-granting universities. We offer the following advice to faculty developers who are interested in establishing an ERG:

- Leadership and knowledge of effective pedagogy are crucial to establishing and maintaining the group's focus on classroom-based, discipline-specific issues. However, it is essential to develop and define the ERG in collaboration with one or two faculty colleagues and, when relevant, with leaders from educational outreach or student learning centers.

- Work with colleagues to define the group around a common purpose. Whether the purpose is to advance educational projects supported by a single grant or to investigate pedagogical objectives such as improving students' writing or problem-solving skills, this common purpose will help the ERG cohere and endure.

- Invite faculty and research staff from multiple departments and disciplines, and with different levels of expertise in SoTL, to participate. The different perspectives each brings to the group will create opportunities for the ERG members to think critically about the assumptions behind their respective disciplinary approaches and develop new insights that will improve their projects.

- When inviting faculty to participate, suggest how participation in SoTL can shed light on the teaching methods that they use in their own classes, as well as provide an opportunity to contribute to knowledge that can have an impact on teaching and learning beyond their own classrooms (Hutchings & Shulman, 1999). It may be helpful to explain that the collaborative work of the group could take different forms, ranging from a collegial exchange of ideas on teaching, learning, and evaluation to the development of collaborative research projects.

- Play an active role in helping faculty learn how to communicate and share ideas across disciplinary boundaries. Think about the communication and knowledge gaps that might be stumbling blocks within the group. You can help bridge these gaps by drawing on your own expertise to suggest, for example, how research on learning can be applied to the development of specific, practical teaching methods.

- Develop a structure of regular, weekly meetings and schedule topics for each meeting well in advance.

- Use faculty symposia, newsletters, and other means to inform nonparticipating faculty and upper-level administrators about the ERG and its contributions to SoTL and to improving teaching and learning.

- Develop a regular mechanism for the members to reflect on the group's progress, make any necessary changes in its purpose and structure, and explore options for broader institutional and external support to advance the group's SoTL projects.

Conclusion

At our university, the STEM ERG has helped to bridge communication and knowledge gaps among STEM faculty, science education specialists, and faculty who conduct laboratory research in cognitive and learning sciences. The group has advanced existing HHMI-funded educational projects and prompted the development of collaborative, multidisciplinary projects that will shed light on specific questions about teaching and learning in STEM. Moreover, during its first two and a half years, the ERG has broadened the definition of scholarship at the university and has raised awareness among the faculty and administration about how faculty, the director of the teaching center, and researchers in science outreach and education are conducting scholarship that advances the university's mission of excellence in both teaching and research.

REFERENCES

Banchoff, T., & Salem, A. (2002). Bridging the divide: Research versus practice in current mathematics teaching and learning. In M. T. Huber & S. P. Morreale (Eds.), *Disciplinary styles in the scholarship of teaching and learning: Exploring the common ground* (pp. 181–196). Sterling, VA: Stylus.

Boyer, E. L. (1990). *Scholarship reconsidered: Priorities of the professoriate.* San Francisco, CA: Jossey-Bass.

Coppola, B. P., & Jacobs, D. C. (2002). Is the scholarship of teaching and learning new to chemistry? In M. T. Huber & S. P. Morreale (Eds.), *Disciplinary styles in the scholarship of teaching and learning: Exploring the common ground* (pp. 197–216). Sterling, VA: Stylus.

Huber, M. T. (2002). Disciplinary styles in the scholarship of teaching: Reflections on the Carnegie Academy for the Scholarship of Teaching and Learning (orienting essay). In M. T. Huber & S. P. Morreale (Eds.), *Disciplinary styles in the scholarship of teaching and learning: Exploring the common ground* (pp. 25–43). Sterling, VA: Stylus.

Huber, M. T., & Hutchings, P. (2005). *The advancement of learning: Building the teaching commons.* San Francisco, CA: Jossey-Bass.

Huber, M. T., & Morreale, S. P. (2002). Situating the scholarship of teaching and learning: A cross-disciplinary conversation. In M. T. Huber & S. P. Morreale (Eds.), *Disciplinary styles in the scholarship of teaching and learning: Exploring the common ground* (pp. 1–24). Sterling, VA: Stylus.

Hutchings, P., & Shulman, L. S. (1999, September/October). The scholarship of teaching: New elaborations, new developments. *Change, 31*(5), 10–15.

Middendorf, J., & Pace, D. (2008). Easing entry into the scholarship of teaching and learning through focused assessment: The "decoding the disciplines" approach. In D. R. Robertson & L. B. Nilson (Eds.), *To improve the academy: Vol. 26. Resources for faculty, instructional, and organizational development* (pp. 53–67). San Francisco, CA: Jossey-Bass.

Nummedal, S. G., Benson, J. B., & Chew, S. L. (2002). Disciplinary styles in the scholarship of teaching and learning: A view from psychology. In M. T. Huber & S. P. Morreale (Eds.), *Disciplinary styles in the scholarship of teaching and learning: Exploring the common ground* (pp. 163–179). Sterling, VA: Stylus.

Shulman, L. S. (1993, November/December). Teaching as community property: Putting an end to pedagogical solitude. *Change, 25*(6), 6–7.

Sorcinelli, M. D., Austin, A. E., Eddy, P. L., & Beach, A. L. (2006). *Creating the future of faculty development: Learning from the past, understanding the present*. San Francisco, CA: Jossey-Bass.

Wankat, P. C., Felder, R. M., Smith, K. A., & Oreovicz, F. S. (2002). The scholarship of teaching and learning in engineering. In M. T. Huber & S. P. Morreale (Eds.), *Disciplinary styles in the scholarship of teaching and learning: Exploring the common ground* (pp. 217–237). Sterling, VA: Stylus.

9

INSTITUTIONAL ENCOURAGEMENT OF AND FACULTY ENGAGEMENT IN THE SCHOLARSHIP OF TEACHING AND LEARNING

Thomas F. Nelson Laird, Tony Ribera, Indiana University

Framed by Huber and Hutchings's defining features of the scholarship of teaching and learning (SoTL), the study described in this chapter examines institutional encouragement of and faculty engagement in SoTL. Faculty at forty-nine U.S. colleges and universities participating in the 2009 Faculty Survey of Student Engagement completed items about SoTL. Results suggest that institutional encouragement of and faculty engagement in the public dissemination of teaching investigations lag behind encouragement and engagement in other aspects of SoTL. Some faculty subgroups (among them, women and faculty in education) on average feel more institutional encouragement and engage in SoTL activities more than their colleagues do.

Faculty who engage in the scholarship of teaching and learning (SoTL) approach the classroom as a research site, assessing student learning and evaluating teaching methods in order to promote student learning and advance the profession (Huber & Hutchings, 2005). Essentially SoTL "is about the combining of research and teaching/learning into one activity" (Dobbins, 2008, p. 1). Pecorino and Kincaid (2007) and Shulman (2000) argue that as professional educators, all faculty have an obligation to engage in SoTL. In doing so, they not only improve their own quality of instruction but also further the teaching profession (Pecorino & Kincaid, 2007). Despite calls for faculty to engage in such work, little is known about the level of faculty engagement in SoTL.

Although engagement in SoTL seems to be on the rise, there has been no large, multicampus assessment of the extent of faculty engagement in SoTL or what faculty characteristics (gender, race, discipline, and rank) predict this type of engagement. There is also little empirical evidence about faculty perceptions of institutional support for SoTL. We use data from the 2009 Faculty Survey of Student Engagement (FSSE) to address these research questions.

SoTL Defined

As evidenced by pedagogical journals in sociology and chemistry (McKinney, 2007), scholarly work on teaching and learning has been present in certain disciplines for many years. More recently, scholars have explored scholarly work on teaching and learning in broader terms. Cross (1986) encouraged college instructors to become classroom researchers, exploring their teaching and student learning. Chism, Sanders, and Zitlow (1987) encouraged faculty to continually examine and reflect on their teaching practices by gathering feedback and discussing pedagogy with colleagues. In his significant text, *Scholarship Reconsidered: Priorities of the Professoriate*, Boyer (1990) built on these ideas. Addressing an imbalance in faculty work, Boyer encouraged professors to expand the definition of scholarship to include a scholarly approach to teaching, and by so doing to garner for SoTL the recognition and resources that had typically been reserved for traditional research (Pace & Erekson, 2006). Despite drawing much attention, Boyer's (1990) conceptualization of SoTL was met with resistance and critique (Bender, 2005). Most notably, Boyer failed to present a clear distinction between scholarly teaching and SoTL (Hutchings & Shulman, 1999; McKinney, 2004). Since Boyer, agreement has been building that scholarly teachers stay informed on current trends and issues in the field and use theory and research to inform their efforts. Such faculty members reflect on their teaching practices and assess student learning to improve their teaching (Kiener, 2009; McKinney, 2004; Shulman, 2000). However, scholarly teaching is not synonymous with SoTL, which goes beyond individual development (Boshier, 2009; Kiener, 2009). Huber and Hutchings (2005) describe four defining features of SoTL: (1) questioning, (2) gathering and exploring evidence, (3) trying out and refining new insights, and (4) going public. Thus, SoTL consists of peer-reviewed scholarship that is publicly disseminated in order to advance the scholarly efforts of others who are investigating teaching and learning (Cambridge, 2000; Cottrell & Jones, 2003; Huber, 2001; Hutchings & Shulman, 1999; Shulman, 1999).

Surveying eighty-five faculty from a large, public research university in the Northwest, Myers (2008) found that the average faculty member "sometimes" did SoTL activities like reviewing literature on teaching and learning issues and using assessment findings to inform changes to courses. Myers also found that female faculty tend to engage in SoTL more than male faculty do and that the gender gap increases with years of teaching experience. Whitman and Richlin (2007) explored SoTL across disciplines. They found that SoTL is most prevalent in the natural sciences and professions and that it is slowly becoming valued in the humanities. Although these studies provide a glimpse of faculty engagement in SoTL, more work is needed.

Methods

The Faculty Survey of Student Engagement measures faculty perceptions and expectations of undergraduate student engagement in educationally purposeful activities as well as the extent to which faculty promote student learning and development in their courses and interactions with students (Kuh, Nelson Laird, & Umbach, 2004). Faculty members at forty-nine colleges and universities across the United States were invited to complete a set of items concerning SoTL that were added to the end of the FSSE questionnaire. The participating colleges and universities that included the extra items represent a wide cross-section of U.S. baccalaureate-granting institutions. Based on the 2005 revision of the Carnegie Classification (http://classifications.carnegiefoundation.org), 24 percent of the institutions were doctoral or research universities, 39 percent were master's universities, 6 percent were baccalaureate colleges—arts and sciences, 18 percent were baccalaureate colleges—diverse, and 12 percent were other types such as schools of business and management and baccalaureate/associate's colleges). Slightly over half of the institutions were private (53 percent). Undergraduate enrollments ranged from just over two hundred students to slightly over twenty thousand, with a mean of fifty-eight hundred. Response rates ranged from 17 to 89 percent, with an average response rate of 49 percent.

After deleting cases for missing data, the sample for this study consisted of 4,229 faculty members. About 45 percent of the respondents were female. Three-fourths (76 percent) were white, with 5 percent African American, 1 percent American Indian, 5 percent Asian, 3 percent Hispanic, 1 percent other, 1 percent multiracial, and 8 percent indicated a preference not to identify race/ethnicity. Most of the respondents were U.S. citizens (92 percent). Nearly seven of ten had a doctorate (69 percent). The age of the respondents ranged from twenty-one to eighty-two, with a mean of fifty. Various ranks and employment statuses were represented, with 13 percent of the respondents being part-time instructors or lecturers, 11 percent full-time instructors or lecturers, 28 percent assistant professors, 25 percent associate professors, and 23 percent full professors. The number of courses taught by faculty during the academic year ranged from one to eighteen, with 44 percent of respondents reporting a class load between four and six. Slightly over a third of the faculty taught at least one graduate-level course.

Respondents taught in a wide range of fields. A relatively large percentage were in the arts and humanities (27 percent), while smaller percentages represented the biological sciences (5 percent), business (10 percent), education (7 percent), engineering (4 percent), the physical sciences (11 percent), professional fields (8 percent), the social sciences (14 percent), and other fields (13 percent). This subsample of the FSSE respondents mirrors the characteristics of the overall FSSE sample, which, for many characteristics, is similar to the national sample of faculty (Faculty Survey of Student Engagement, 2009).

Huber and Hutchings's (2005) defining features served as the framework for our dependent measures. The scale measuring institutional encouragement of SoTL (Table 9.1) combines items indicating how much faculty members at a respondent's campus are encouraged to systematically collect information about teaching effectiveness outside of end-of-course evaluations, use assessment findings to inform course changes, publicly present information about teaching and learning in their courses, publish on teaching and learning, and collaborate with colleagues on improving teaching and learning. Together these items constitute a reliable scale (alpha = 0.87). The faculty engagement in SoTL scale combines five items focused on how much respondents have incorporated the activities above into their own work (Table 9.1). It too was found to be a reliable scale (alpha = 0.83). Simple frequencies were used to answer our first two questions: (1) to what extent institutions encourage faculty to engage in SoTL and (2) to what extent faculty engage in SoTL. Regression analyses were used to answer the third: what predicts faculty perceptions of institutional encouragement and faculty engagement in SoTL. For the regression models, the dependent variables were standardized prior to the analyses, and the independent variables included individual-level measures similar to those in past studies of faculty teaching-related perceptions and behaviors (Nelson Laird & Garver, 2010; Umbach & Wawrzynski, 2005). In addition to characteristics such as gender, race/ethnicity, rank and employment status, course load, and disciplinary area, we added a measure of teaching effort (the average

Table 9.1 SoTL Item Frequencies

Items	Very Little	Some	Quite a Bit	Very Much
Institutional encouragement of SoTL				
Systematically collect information about the effectiveness of their teaching beyond end-of-term course evaluations	27%	32%	23%	19%
Use assessment findings to inform changes made to their courses	18	35	28	19
Publicly present (for example, lectures or workshops) information about teaching or learning	26	39	23	12
Publish on teaching and learning	30	40	20	11
Collaborate with colleagues on improving teaching and learning	18	39	27	16
Faculty engagement in SoTL				
Systematically collect information about the effectiveness of your teaching beyond end-of-term course evaluations	16	33	28	23
Use assessment findings to inform changes made to your courses	10	27	34	28
Publicly present (for example, lectures or workshops) information about teaching or learning	42	29	16	13
Publish on teaching and learning	56	24	11	10
Collaborate with colleagues on improving teaching and learning	15	34	30	22

Note. Some frequency totals do not sum to 100 percent due to rounding.

number of hours in a typical week spent preparing for class per course taught), hypothesizing that engagement in the SoTL would be positively associated with the time one devotes to teaching. Furthermore, in the model predicting faculty engagement in SoTL, we included the standardized measure of faculty members' perceptions of institutional encouragement of SoTL since much of the literature suggests that faculty engagement in SoTL (or lack thereof) results from the support (or barriers) in place at institutions (Huber & Hutchings, 2005). Due to the nested nature of the data (faculty within institutions), which violates the independence assumption of ordinary least-squares analyses resulting in misestimated standard errors, we used STATA release 10 (StataCorp, 2007) to run our regression analyses and produce robust standard errors.

Results

The frequency distributions contained within Table 9.1 suggest that most faculty members (70 percent or more) feel at least "some" encouragement from their institutions for the SoTL activities described by the items. When asked the extent to which their institutions encourage faculty to systematically collect information about the effectiveness of their teaching beyond end-of-term course evaluations, more than seven of ten respondents (73 percent) indicated their institutions do this "some," "quite a bit," or "very much." More than four of five (82 percent) indicated that their institutions provide at least "some" encouragement for using assessment findings to inform changes made to their courses and for collaborating with colleagues on improving teaching and learning. The smallest percentages of faculty members felt encouraged "quite a bit" or "very much" by their institutions to publicly present information about teaching and learning (35 percent) or publish on teaching and learning (31 percent). The equivalent percentages for the other items were 42 percent or above.

Table 9.1 also contains the distributions for items about faculty engagement in SoTL. Most faculty (between 84 and 90 percent) indicated that they incorporate systematic collection of information about teaching and learning, use assessment findings for course improvement, and collaborate with colleagues on improving teaching and learning at least "some." These percentages are greater than those for the similar institutional encouragement items, indicating that institutional encouragement may lag faculty engagement in these areas. A different pattern is apparent for the public dissemination items. While more than 70 percent indicated at least "some" encouragement for publicly presenting teaching and learning information and publishing on teaching and learning, 56 percent of respondents indicated "never" publicly presenting, and 44 percent indicated publishing on teaching and learning "some" or more.

Table 9.2 contains the results of regression analyses. For institutional encouragement of SoTL, the model explained a significant but relatively small amount of variance ($F = 28.45$, $p < 0.001$; $R^2 = 0.07$). The results suggest that after controlling for other variables in the model, women faculty and instructors on average feel their institution encourages SoTL slightly more—about a tenth of a standard deviation—than their male colleagues ($B = 0.08$, $p < 0.05$). Black or African American faculty members ($B = 0.22$, $p < 0.05$) and Asian/Pacific Islander faculty members ($B = 0.36$, $p < 0.001$) reported significantly higher institutional encouragement when compared to their white peers. Non-U.S. citizens reported greater institutional encouragement ($B = 0.18$, $p < 0.01$), and those with a doctorate indicated less institutional encouragement than those without a doctorate ($i = -0.15$, $p < 0.001$).

Course load had a small, positive effect ($B = 0.04$, $p < 0.001$), indicating that, on average and holding constant the other measures in the model, teaching an additional course would correspond to a sense of institutional encouragement for SoTL four one-hundredths of a standard deviation higher. A faculty member's field affected his or her sense of institutional encouragement. Education faculty, on average and after controlling for the other variables in the model, indicated the highest sense of institutional encouragement. Faculty in other fields scored below education faculty by between two-tenths of a standard deviation ($B = -0.19$, $p > 0.05$ for professional fields) and over six-tenths of a standard deviation ($B = -0.60$, $p < 0.001$ for social science; $B = -0.63$, $p < 0.001$ for biological science). The number of hours spent in a typical week preparing for each course, our measure of teaching effort, was significant in the institutional encouragement model, but the effect was close to zero. Differences by age, rank, and whether one taught graduate students were small and insignificant.

For faculty engagement in SoTL, the model explained a sizable and significant amount of variance ($F = 214.68$, $p < 0.001$; $R^2 = 0.39$). After controlling for the other factors, women, on average, engaged in SOTL over one-tenth of a standard deviation more than their male peers ($B = 0.12$, $p < 0.001$). Racial/ethnic differences were evident. Asian/Pacific Islander faculty ($B = 0.15$, $p < 0.05$) and faculty who preferred not to respond to the race/ethnicity question ($B = 0.14$, $p < 0.01$) reported significantly more engagement than their white counterparts did. Age had a negative effect on engagement. On average and holding the other variables in the model constant, a faculty member ten years older than another would score four one-hundredths of a standard deviation

Table 9.2 Institutional Encouragement of and Faculty Engagement in SoTL Regression Results

	Institutional Encouragement of SoTL			Faculty Engagement in SoTL		
		Robust			Robust	
	B	SE	Significance	B	SE	Significance
Constant	0.29	0.14	*	0.18	0.10	
Female	0.08	0.03	*	0.12	0.04	***
Race/ethnicity						
White	*reference group*			*reference group*		
Black/African American	0.22	0.09	*	−0.00	0.04	
Asian/Pacific Islander	0.36	0.08	***	0.15	0.06	*
Hispanic	0.03	0.10		0.10	0.08	
Other race/ethnicity	0.17	0.10		0.19	0.06	**
Prefer not to respond	0.18	0.06		0.14	0.04	**
Non-U.S. citizen	0.18	0.06	**	0.00	0.07	
Age (in decades)	−0.01	0.00		−0.04	0.00	***
Doctorate earned	−0.15	0.04	***	0.04	0.04	
Rank/employment status						
Part-time lecturer	*reference group*			*reference group*		
Full-time lecturer	−0.08	0.07		0.04	0.06	
Assistant professor	−0.07	0.07		0.13	0.06	*
Associate professor	−0.12	0.07		0.14	0.05	*
Full professor	−0.05	0.06		0.15	0.06	*
Course load	0.04	0.01	***	0.02	0.01	**
Taught graduate students	0.00	0.05		0.10	0.03	**
Field						
Arts and humanities	−0.50	0.07	***	−0.43	0.05	***
Biological science	−0.63	0.08	***	−0.51	0.08	***
Business	−0.41	0.09	***	−0.38	0.05	***
Education	*reference group*			*reference group*		
Engineering	−0.51	0.12	***	−0.41	0.08	***
Physical science	−0.58	0.09	***	−0.39	0.06	***
Professional	−0.19	0.10		−0.28	0.05	***
Social science	−0.60	0.07	***	−0.45	0.05	***

Other fields	−0.45	0.09	***	−0.35	0.06	***
Preparation per course	0.02	0.01	***	0.02	0.00	**
Institutional encouragement of SoTL	—	—		0.57	0.01	***
R^2		0.07			0.39	
F		28.45***			214.68***	
Root MSE		.97			.78	

Note. $N = 4{,}229$. Dependent variables standardized prior to running the model. The standardized measure of institutional encouragement of SoTL was used in the faculty engagement model. B = regression coefficient; robust SE = robust standard error of the regression coefficient; significance: $*p < 0.05$, $**p < 0.01$, $***p < 0.001$. Constant = the constant term from the regression equation; F = F statistic for the regression model; root MSE = root mean squared error, which is equivalent to the standard deviation of the error term.

lower than the younger faculty member ($B = -0.04$, $p < 0.001$). Since our study is not longitudinal, we cannot determine whether this difference is related to getting older (as faculty get older, they decrease their engagement in SoTL), a cohort effect (due to differences in socialization, today's younger faculty tend to do these activities more than today's older faculty), or a change in practice (older faculty did not receive as much training in studying teaching and learning as their younger peers).

All of the position characteristics were significant in the faculty engagement model. Holding all else constant, tenure-track faculty participated in SoTL activities more than their non-tenure-track colleagues did. Assistant ($B = 0.13$, $p < 0.05$), associate ($B = 0.14$, $p < 0.05$), and full ($B = 0.15$, $p < 0.05$) professors participated, on average, over a tenth of a standard deviation above part-time lecturers, while the difference between full-time and part-time lecturers was small and insignificant ($B = 0.04$, $p > 0.05$). Faculty who taught graduate students participated in SoTL activities a tenth of a standard deviation more than those who did not teach graduate students ($B = 0.10$, $p < 0.01$). Field was again a major factor, with education faculty reporting the greater engagement in SoTL activities. Holding the other variables constant, faculty from other fields averaged engagement scores between nearly three-tenths of a standard deviation ($B = -0.28$, $p < 0.001$ for professional fields) and just over five-tenths of a standard deviation ($B = -0.51$, $p < 0.001$ for biological science) less than their education colleagues, which is not surprising since studying teaching and learning is essential to many education faculty members' disciplinary research.

Teaching effort, as measured by average hours per week spent per course taught, had a small but significant effect. For each additional hour of preparation per course, a faculty member would be expected to participate in SoTL activities two-hundredths of a standard deviation more ($B = 0.02$, $p < 0.001$), holding all else constant. The strongest predictor in the model was institutional encouragement of SoTL. On average and controlling for other factors, faculty members who sensed institutional encouragement one standard deviation more than other faculty would have participated in SoTL activities nearly three-fifths of a standard deviation more than those other faculty ($B = 0.57$, $p < 0.001$).

Discussion and Implications

The results of this study have implications for faculty and those who support SoTL (for example, academic administrators and faculty development professionals). With a sizable proportion (more than 20 percent) of faculty respondents reporting incorporating the systematic collection of information about teaching effectiveness and using assessment findings to improve their teaching "very much" and most faculty (over 80 percent) doing this type of activity at least "some," our study suggests that SoTL-type activities are part of faculty members' work and, for some, a significant part. This is encouraging for the improvement of teaching and for those who have worked to promote SoTL.

While a similar proportion of faculty report collaborating with colleagues on improving teaching and learning, a potential avenue for going public with one's SoTL work, the proportion of faculty involved in the public presentation and publication of teaching and learning investigations appears to be quite a bit smaller. It is worth noting that having 10 percent of faculty reporting that they have incorporated publishing on teaching and learning into their work "very much" perhaps represents a significant achievement by the SoTL community. However, our results suggest that more work needs to be done to get faculty more involved in going public. To aid in this work, researchers should examine faculty members' awareness of teaching and learning journals and conferences within their fields, as well as their awareness of on-campus opportunities for disseminating research on teaching and learning. Faculty developers can promote awareness among faculty by providing resources and suggesting venues for disseminating research on teaching and learning.

In addition, there is value in understanding what encourages faculty engagement in SoTL. Our study lends empirical evidence to the claims that institutional support for SoTL is one crucial element (it was the largest predictor in our model of faculty engagement in SoTL). Still, more research is needed to understand what particular practices influence faculty members' sense of support and encouragement and which institutions seem to be effective at encouraging faculty engagement (unfortunately, our sample of institutions was too small to adequately address the question). Furthermore, since our model predicting institutional encouragement of SoTL indicates differences by gender, race, citizenship status, and field, future investigations must examine the various representations and filters of institutional support. Findings from this study suggest that faculty who are often marginalized in higher education (females, Asian/Pacific Islanders) report a higher sense of encouragement to engage in SoTL. What are we to make of this considering the marginalized status of SoTL work at many colleges and universities (Boyer, 1990; Huber & Hutchings, 2005)? Are institutions actively encouraging marginalized faculty to engage in marginalized research? Or are the mechanisms more indirect? For example, if, as its proponents say, SoTL is an effective educational practice (Huber & Hutchings, 2005), then the finding that women, faculty of color, and younger faculty incorporate SoTL into their work is consistent with other research showing that these groups engage in effective practices more than their counterparts do (Kuh et al., 2004; Umbach & Wawrzynski, 2005). What is interesting, however, is that these effects remain significant even after controlling for faculty perceptions of institutional encouragement of SoTL and the other measures in the model. Using gender as an example, our results suggest that a female faculty member is more likely to do SoTL than a male who feels equal levels of support, comes from the same field, and is at the same rank. Faculty developers can use these findings to target populations in promoting scholarly work on teaching and learning.

This same analysis applies to position characteristics. Holding perceptions of institutional support and other characteristics constant, tenure-track faculty participate in SoTL more than non-tenure-track faculty do. More research is needed to understand why this effect exists. Are non-tenure-tack faculty simply less likely to use effective educational practices in general (Umbach, 2007) and therefore SoTL in particular, or are there barriers to engagement in SoTL that could be removed by institutions? Faculty developers seem well positioned to both pursue this line of inquiry and play a role in removing these potential barriers.

As with other investigations using FSSE (Nelson Laird & Garver, 2010), our results suggest that academic field is important. Our findings show that faculty and instructors in education perceive greater institutional encouragement of SoTL and, even if perception of institutional encouragement and other factors are held constant, engage in this type of scholarship more than most of their colleagues in other fields. These results could speak to the closer connection between the scholarships of discovery and teaching in education and, possibly, that disciplinary training is important for increasing SoTL work.

Conclusion

The results of our study suggest that SoTL is embedded in the work of many faculty members and that faculty doing this work do so with at least some sense of support from their institutions. That said, researchers, faculty, and faculty developers have work to do to understand how to encourage SoTL among all faculty, particularly the presentation and publication of investigations into teaching and learning.

Shapiro (2006) and others (Huber & Hutchings, 2006) argue that a shift is needed in promotion and tenure processes in order to encourage SoTL among faculty. In order for SoTL to be institutionalized in academe, it must be practiced and rewarded (Hatch, 2006; Kreber, 2003). Doing so will ensure that faculty pose and answer questions about teaching and learning, contribute to the profession, and increase the status of teaching in higher education (Trigwell & Shale, 2004). It will also ensure that educational quality will be in a constant state of improvement, something all faculty and institutions should support.

REFERENCES

Bender, E. T. (2005, September/October). CASTLs in the air: The SoTL "movement" in mid-flight. *Change, 37*(5), 40–49.

Boshier, R. (2009). Why is the scholarship of teaching and learning such a hard sell? *Higher Education Research and Development, 28*(1), 1–15.

Boyer, E. L. (1990). *Scholarship reconsidered: Priorities of the professoriate.* San Francisco, CA: Jossey-Bass.

Cambridge, B. L. (2000). The scholarship of teaching and learning: A national initiative. In M. Kaplan & D. Lieberman (Eds.), *To improve the academy: Vol. 18. Resources for faculty, instructional, and organizational development* (pp. 55–68). San Francisco, CA: Jossey-Bass.

Chism, N., Sanders, D., & Zitlow, C. (1987). Observations on a faculty development program based on practice-centered inquiry. *Peabody Journal of Education, 64*(3), 1–23.

Cottrell, S. A., & Jones, E. A. (2003). Researching the scholarship of teaching and learning: An analysis of current curriculum practices. *Innovative Higher Education, 27*(3), 169–181. doi:10.1023/A:1022303210086

Cross, K. P. (1986, September). A proposal to improve teaching or what "taking teaching seriously" should mean. *AAHE Bulletin, 39*(1), 9–14.

Dobbins, K. (2008). Enhancing the scholarship of teaching and learning: A study of the factors identified as promoting and hindering the scholarly activities of academics in one faculty. *International Journal for the Scholarship of Teaching and Learning, 2*(2), 1–8.

Faculty Survey of Student Engagement. (2009). *FSSE 2009 overview.* Bloomington: Indiana University, Center for Postsecondary Research.

Hatch, T. (2006). *Into the classroom: Developing the scholarship of teaching and learning.* San Francisco, CA: Jossey-Bass.

Huber, M. T. (2001, July/August). Balancing acts: Designing careers around the scholarship of teaching. *Change, 33*(4), 21–29.

Huber, M. T., & Hutchings, P. (2005). *The advancement of learning: Building the teaching commons.* San Francisco, CA: Jossey-Bass.

Huber, M. T., & Hutchings, P. (2006, May/June). Building the teaching commons. *Change, 38*(3), 24–31.

Hutchings, P., & Shulman, L. S. (1999, September/October). The scholarship of teaching: New elaborations, new developments. *Change, 31*(5), 10–15.

Kiener, M. (2009). Applying the scholarship of teaching and learning: Pursuing a deeper understanding of how students learn. *InSight: A Journal of Scholarly Teaching, 4,* 21–27.

Kreber, C. (2003). The scholarship of teaching: A comparison of conceptions held by experts and regular academic staff. *Higher Education, 46*(1), 93–121.

Kuh, G. D., Nelson Laird, T. F., & Umbach, P. D. (2004). Aligning faculty and student behavior: Realizing the promise of greater expectations. *Liberal Education, 90*(4), 24–31.

McKinney, K. (2004). The scholarship of teaching and learning: Past lessons, current challenges, and future visions. In C. M. Wehlburg & S. Chadwick-Blossey (Eds.), *To improve the academy: Vol. 21. Resources for faculty, instructional, and organizational development* (pp. 3–19). San Francisco, CA: Jossey-Bass.

McKinney, K. (2007). *Enhancing learning through the scholarship of teaching and learning: The challenges and joys of juggling.* San Francisco, CA: Jossey-Bass.

Myers, C. B. (2008). College faculty and the scholarship of teaching: Gender differences across four key activities. *Journal of the Scholarship of Teaching and Learning, 8*(2), 38–51.

Nelson Laird, T. F., & Garver, A. K. (2010). The effect of teaching general education courses on deep approaches to learning: How disciplinary context matters. *Research in Higher Education, 51*(3), 248–265.

Pace, D., & Erekson, K. A. (2006). The scholarship of teaching and learning history comes of age: A new international organization and Web site/newsletter. *History Teacher, 40*(1), 75–78.

Pecorino, P., & Kincaid, S. (2007). Why should I care about SOTL? The professional responsibilities of post-secondary educators. *International Journal for the Scholarship of Teaching and Learning, 1*(1), 1–6.

Shapiro, H. N. (2006, March/April). Promotion and tenure and the scholarship of teaching and learning. *Change, 38*(2), 38–43.

Shulman, L. S. (1999, July/August). Taking learning seriously. *Change, 31*(4), 10–17.

Shulman, L. S. (2000). From minsk to pinsk: Why a scholarship of teaching and learning? *Journal of Scholarship of Teaching and Learning, 1*(1), 48–53.

StataCorp. (2007). *Stata statistical software: Release 10.* College Station, TX: Author.

Trigwell, K., & Shale, S. (2004). Student learning and the scholarship of university teaching. *Studies in Higher Education, 29*(4), 523–536.

Umbach, P. D. (2007). How effective are they? Exploring the impact of contingent faculty on undergraduate education. *Review of Higher Education, 30*(2), 91–123. doi:10.1353/rhe.2006.0080

Umbach, P. D., & Wawrzynski, M. R. (2005). Faculty do matter: The role of college faculty in student learning and engagement. *Research in Higher Education, 46*(2), 153–184.

Whitman, P. D., & Richlin, L. (2007). The status of the scholarship of teaching and learning in the disciplines. *International Journal for the Scholarship of Teaching and Learning, 1*(1), 1–17.

10

DEFINING CRITICAL THINKING IN HIGHER EDUCATION

DETERMINING ASSESSMENT FIT

Martha L. A. Stassen, Anne Herrington, Laura Henderson,
University of Massachusetts Amherst

Critical thinking is an important learning outcome for higher education, yet the definitions used on campuses and national assessment instruments vary. This article describes a mapping technique that faculty and administrators can use to evaluate the similarities and differences across these definitions. Results demonstrate that the definitions reflected by standardized tests are more narrowly construed than those of the campus and leave dimensions of critical thinking unassessed. This mapping process not only helps campuses make better-informed decisions regarding their responses to accountability pressures; it also provides a stimulus for rich, evidence-based discussions about teaching and learning priorities related to critical thinking.

Critical thinking has emerged as an essential higher education learning outcome for both external audiences focused on issues of accountability and for colleges and universities themselves. One of the most recent national efforts to respond to accountability pressures, the Voluntary System of Accountability (VSA), requires campuses to use one of three standardized tests to measure and report student learning gains on critical thinking and written communication (Voluntary System, 2010, para. 17). In its survey of employers, the Association of American Colleges and Universities (AAC&U, 2008) found that 73 percent of employers wanted colleges to "place more emphasis on critical thinking and analytic reasoning" (p. 16). In a recent survey of AAC&U member colleges and universities, 74 percent of respondents indicated that critical thinking was a core learning objective for the campus's general education program (AAC&U, 2009, p. 4).

While there is general agreement that critical thinking is important, there is less consensus, and often lack of clarity, about what exactly constitutes critical thinking. For example, in a California study, only 19 percent of faculty could give a clear explanation of critical thinking even though the vast majority (89 percent) indicated that they emphasize it (Paul, Elder, & Bartell, 1997). In their interviews with faculty at a private liberal arts college, Halx and Reybold (2005) explored instructors' perspectives of undergraduate thinking. While participants were "eager to promote critical thinking" (p. 300), the authors note that none had been specifically trained to do so. As a result, these instructors each developed their own distinct definition of critical thinking.

Perhaps this variability in critical thinking definitions is to be expected given the range of definitions available in the literature. Critical thinking can include the thinker's dispositions and orientations; a range of specific analytical, evaluative, and problem-solving skills; contextual influences; use of multiple perspectives; awareness of one's own assumptions; capacities for metacognition; or a specific set of thinking processes or tasks (Bean, 1996; Beyer, Gillmore, & Fisher, 2007; Brookfield, 1987; Donald, 2002; Facione, 1990; Foundation for Critical Thinking, 2009; Halx & Reybold, 2005; Kurfiss, 1988; Paul, Binker, Jensen, & Kreklau, 1990). Academic discipline can also shape critical thinking definitions, playing an important role in both the forms of critical thinking that faculty emphasize and the preferred teaching strategies used to support students' development of critical thinking capacities (Beyer et al., 2007; Huber & Morreale, 2002; Lattuca & Stark, 2009; Pace & Middendorf, 2004).

The Dilemma for Student Learning Outcomes Assessment

External accountability pressures increasingly focus on using standardized measures of student learning outcomes as comparable indicators of institutional effectiveness, and students' critical thinking performance is among the outcomes most often mentioned (see VSA, 2010, as an example). The range of critical thinking dimensions and the lack of one agreed-on definition pose a challenge for campuses working to align their course, program, and institution-wide priorities for critical thinking with appropriate national or standardized assessment methods. Among the questions facing these institutions are these three: (1) What dimensions of critical thinking do national and standardized methods emphasize? (2) To what extent do these dimensions reflect campus-based critical thinking instructional and curricular priorities? (3) What gaps in understanding students' critical thinking performance will we encounter when we use national or standardized tools?

Answers to these questions are important to any campus that wants to develop assessment strategies that accurately reflect teaching and learning priorities and practices on campus. A focus on the alignment of assessment tools with campus priorities is also essential for engaging faculty in the assessment decision-making process. It is unlikely that faculty will use evidence to inform changes in instructional practices and curricular design unless they have been involved in the assessment design and believe the tools and results accurately represent instructional priorities and practices.

Methods

To determine the alignment of current assessment tools with institutional instructional priorities, we conducted a qualitative content analysis of five representations of the critical thinking construct and identified the common and distinct dimensions across the five sources. The five sources used for this study represent two different contexts for defining critical thinking: an internal definition developed by a group of general education instructors on our campus and a number of external sources representing the primary tools currently under discussion for national assessments of critical thinking in higher education.

Internal Source

To represent our campus's operational definition of critical thinking, we use a definition developed by a group of general education instructors and administrators at a large public research university. The definition was developed as a part of a campuswide workshop on teaching critical thinking in general education and was generated by collecting the responses of groups of participants to the following question and prompt: "What learning behaviors (skills, values, attitudes) do students exhibit that reflect critical thinking? Students demonstrate critical thinking when they . . ." Participant responses were then clustered by researchers in the campus's Office of Academic Planning and Assessment into twelve dimensions of critical thinking, listed in Table 10.1 in the "Results" section. A post-hoc confirmation of these dimensions was done by comparing the categories to the definitions of critical thinking present in the literature (see Office of Academic Planning, 2007, for the full set of responses and the links to the literature).

External Context

Critical thinking definitions from four external sources were used, which include three national standardized tests of critical thinking currently being used as a part of the VSA.

STANDARDIZED TESTS

ACT's Collegiate Assessment of Academic Proficiency (CAAP) comprises six independent test modules, of which the writing essays and critical thinking are relevant to this study. The critical thinking assessment is a forty-minute, thirty-two-item, multiple-choice test that, according to ACT, measures "students' skills in clarifying, analyzing, evaluating, and extending arguments" (ACT, 2011). The writing essays consist of two twenty-minute writing tasks, which include a short prompt that provides the test taker with a hypothetical situation and an audience.

The Collegiate Learning Assessment (CLA) is the Council for Aid to Education (CAE)'s testing instrument. Varying in length between ninety minutes (for the performance task) and seventy-five minutes (for the make-an-argument and critique-an-argument tasks, taken together), these written tests require students to work with realistic problems and analyze diverse written materials. CLA measures students' critical thinking skills with respect to analytic reasoning, problem solving, and effectiveness in writing. CLA is unique among the three standardized tests in its view of writing as integral to critical thinking.

Educational Testing Service (ETS) offers the Proficiency Profile (PP), a test of four skills, including reading and critical thinking. The PP is available in a standard form (two hours, 108 questions) and an abbreviated form accepted by VSA (forty minutes, 36 questions). Reading and critical thinking are measured together on a single proficiency scale.

NATIONAL ASSESSMENT TOOL

The fourth external source, the Valid Assessment of Learning in Undergraduate Education (VALUE) rubrics, is a set of scoring rubrics faculty or other reviewers can use to assess student work. The rubrics provide specific criteria for each of fifteen learning outcomes, two of which are relevant to this study: critical thinking, and inquiry and analysis (AAC&U, 2010a).

Three-Phase Content Analysis

Using these five sources, our research team conducted a three-phase content analysis.

PHASE ONE: IDENTIFYING THE DEFINITIONS

In order to compare our internal definitions with those of the external sources, we had to identify what aspects of critical thinking serve as the focus of each external assessment tool. We used a number of approaches to gather this information for the three standardized tests. To ascertain each testing agency's working definition of critical thinking, we used the most detailed descriptions available, drawing from promotional materials, information on their websites, and communication with company representatives.

ACT (2010) describes the skills tested within each of three content categories: analysis of elements of an argument (seventeen to twenty-one questions, 53 to 66 percent of the test), evaluation of an argument (five to nine questions, 16 to 28 percent of the test), and extension of an argument (six questions, 9 percent of the test). Since it is not accessible through ACT's website, we obtained this document through a representative of ACT.

For ETS's PP, we selected passages from the User's Guide (Educational Testing Service, 2010): an introductory section that describes the abilities that the critical thinking questions measure and a more detailed description of the skills measured in the area of reading and critical thinking at the intermediate and high proficiency levels.

For the CLA, we began with the skills contained in the CLA Common Scoring Rubric (Council for Aid to Education, 2008). This rubric is divided into two categories: (1) critical thinking, analytic reasoning, and problem solving and (2) written communication. In spring 2010, we learned that CAE was in the process of implementing new critical thinking rubrics: analytic reasoning and evaluation, problem solving, and writing effectiveness. We analyzed these new descriptions (CLA II) alongside the older rubric (CLA I). In fall 2010, after the research described here was completed, CAE published a more detailed version of the critical thinking scoring rubric that is now available on its website. While differently formatted, the descriptors we used for this analysis are similar to the categories in this new rubric.

We were able to use the actual measures in the VALUE rubrics because they are the components of the rubric used to review and assess students' work (AAC&U, 2010b). We incorporated both the critical thinking and the inquiry and analysis rubrics in our analysis. We chose to include them because this category seemed particularly relevant to the conceptualization of critical thinking emerging from our campus discussions.

PHASE TWO: CODING FOR COMMONALITIES WITH CAMPUS CRITICAL THINKING DEFINITION

To understand the commonalities between the four external sources and our campus's own critical thinking definition, we used our internal definition as the anchor definition and coded the external sources in relation to the categories present in that internal definition. The research team reviewed each descriptor of the four external source definitions and coded each for its alignment with one or more of the twelve dimensions of our internal definition. For example, the CLA listed "constructing cogent arguments rooted in data/information rather than speculation/ opinion" (Council for Aid to Education, 2008) as one descriptor of their critical thinking/writing effectiveness definition. In our analysis, we coded this descriptor as falling into the judgment/argument dimension of the campus-based definition. In conducting this coding, we used two approaches. First, to develop common understandings of the process, we worked as a team (three coders) to code two of the external sources (CAAP and PP). We then individually coded the CLA and VALUE sources and met to confirm our coding. In both approaches, we identified areas of disagreement and worked together for clarity in our standards, coming to mutually agreed-on final codes.

Once the coding was completed, we sorted the individual descriptors by dimension and reviewed them again for consistency. For example, we checked to see if the items we had coded as evidence-based thinking all reflected our deepening understanding of the construct. This stage helped us further clarify distinctions among the dimensions.

PHASE THREE: ANALYSIS OF PATTERNS
Once the coding and checking were complete, we arrayed the results in a table to facilitate a comparative analysis. We calculated how many of each tool's descriptors referenced each of the twelve dimensions in our campus definition and, to get a sense of the relative emphasis each tool gave to each of the twelve dimensions, we calculated the proportion of all descriptors listed that reflect each dimension. In this way, we denote what proportion of each tool's definition reflects each of the twelve campus-based critical thinking dimensions.

Results

Table 10.1 summarizes the commonalities and gaps among the various definitions. This table indicates how many of the critical thinking dimensions listed in each of the external assessment tools reflect each of the twelve campus critical thinking dimensions. To provide a very rough estimate of the relative emphasis or importance of these dimensions in our campus definition, we counted how many descriptors emerged in the workshop for each dimension and calculated the proportion of all descriptors that this dimension represents (under the assumption that the number of descriptors of a dimension generated by a group of faculty

Table 10.1 Relationships Between Campus Critical Thinking Definitions and Four External Sources

Campus-Based Definition	Campus		Collegiate Learning Assessment I		Collegiate Learning Assessment II		Proficiency Profile		Collegiate Assessment of Academic Proficiency		Value	
	N	%	N	%	N	%	N	%	N	%	N	%
Judgment/argument	8	15	24	80	6	55	10	56	8	73	6	55
Synthesizing	6	12	2	7	2	18	2	11	0	0	4	36
Problem solving	2	4	1	3	1	9	1	6	0	0	0	0
Evidence-based thinking	3	6	7	23	3	27	5	28	6	55	1	9
Drawing inferences	2	4	1	3	2	18	3	17	3	27	2	18
Perspective taking	7	14	3	10	1	9	0	0	1	9	3	27
Suspend judgment	1	2	0	0	0	0	0	0	0	0	0	0
Application	10	19	0	0	0	0	0	0	0	0	0	0
Metacognition	5	10	0	0	0	0	0	0	0	0	1	9
Questioning/skepticism	4	8	0	0	0	0	0	0	0	0	1	9
Knowledge/understanding	3	6	0	0	0	0	1	6	0	0	1	9
Discipline-based thinking	1	2	0	0	0	0	0	0	1	9	2	18
Total items in definition	52	100	30	100	11	100	18	100	11	100	11	100

Note. Percentages provided as an indicator of relative importance or emphasis of each construct across sources. Numbers represent duplicate counts across categories—one item in a list can reflect more than one campus-related CT category. The "total" numbers in the bottom row of the table reflect the unduplicated count of the descriptors.

reflects greater centrality or emphasis for this dimension). Note that looking at the campus definition this way highlights the relative emphasis
(10 percent or more of the descriptors) placed on five dimensions of critical thinking: judgment/argument, synthesis, perspective taking, application (representing the most emphasis with 19 percent of the descriptors
reflecting this particular dimension), and metacognition. We followed the
same method to determine the relative emphasis of each dimension in
the external assessment tools. Looking at the CLA I column as an example, we found that twenty-four of the thirty descriptors listed in the
CLA I definition of critical thinking reflect our campus's construct of
judgment/argument. These twenty-four occurrences represent 80 percent
of the dimensions in the CLA I list.

As the results in Table 10.1 illustrate, judgment/argument is the predominant component of critical thinking reflected in all of the external
assessment options (accounting for between one-half to over three-quarters
of all the descriptors associated with critical thinking). For the three standardized tests and VALUE, there is also a substantial emphasis on drawing
inferences. Evidence-based thinking is emphasized in all three standardized tests. To varying degrees, synthesizing, problem solving, and perspective taking also receive some attention from the external sources.

In our analysis, a number of the campus dimensions receive no attention from any of the standardized tests: application, suspending judg-
ment, metacognition, and questioning/skepticism. Of those that are
missing from the standardized tests, the VALUE rubrics do reflect metacognition and questioning/skepticism.

The results suggest differences among the four external sources. The
CAAP appears the most focused or limited in scope, with primary emphasis on judgment/argument, use of evidence, and drawing inferences.
The VALUE rubrics are the most expansive, with references to nine
of the twelve dimensions from the campus-based definition. Two of the
three dimensions that are not included, problem solving and integrative
and applied learning, are actually present as separate VALUE rubrics
(AAC&U, 2010b), so their absence from the rubrics used in this analysis
is not surprising.

In addition to providing us with one perspective on the relationship
between the four external assessment tools and our campus's critical
thinking definition, this analysis also provided us with the opportunity to
revisit the campus definition. Our analysis helped us clarify a number
of our dimensions in relationship to the four external sources. For example, our category of multiple perspectives/perspective taking emerged as

the dimension where we coded all external source descriptions that referenced "dealing with complexity" in addition to items that indicated "addressing various perspectives." As we coded, we also noted that our campus descriptions of perspective taking tended toward the positive dimension of multiple perspectives (that is, taking into account these perspectives) but did not include more critical aspects of this dimension (that is, critiquing or refuting a perspective that is weak or uninformed, "considering *and possibly refuting* [italics added] alternative viewpoints" [CLA II]). We also were made aware of dimensions of critical thinking present in the external sources that are not present in the campus definition.

Limitations

It is important to acknowledge that this analysis is not a study of test item validity. Instead, it focuses on how the basic construct of critical thinking is defined, and the dimensions emphasized, within both contexts and across the five sources. Obviously these definitions and emphases drive item development and have important implications for the appropriateness of each assessment tool as an indicator of institutional effectiveness as measured by students' critical thinking performance. However, the technique we used to determine definitional emphases is limited.

The limitations fall into two categories: those having to do with the campus definition and those having to do with the sources used for the external definitions. First, to represent the campus definition, we used the results of a collaborative brainstorming session conducted as part of a campuswide workshop on critical thinking in general education. The definition that emerged is multidimensional, and the elements correspond to common elements of critical thinking as defined in various sources in the literature. However, the campus definition has not been systematically vetted or tested against the responses of other groups of faculty, so it is still very much an emerging document on our campus. Still, many of the dimensions of this definition are identified in other faculty-generated statements of general education learning objectives, including the learning objectives for the campus's junior-year writing requirement (an upper-division writing requirement that addresses the writing conventions of the student's major) and the results of a survey where instructors report emphasizing these objectives in their general education courses (Office of Academic Planning and Assessment, 2008). The definition also does not definitively reflect the faculty's beliefs about the relative importance of each of these constructs. We used the number of references as a rough indicator of importance, but this is certainly not a systematically tested assumption.

With respect to the external sources, the characteristics we used for the three standardized tools (CLA I and II, PP, and CAAP) come from each test company's description of the critical thinking components covered in their test. We took these descriptors and coded each against our campus-based definition. Because we do not know the relative emphasis on each component in the test itself (that is, the number of test items, or scoring weights, for each item), we considered each descriptor of equal importance and looked at the number of them that reflect each of our campus categories. Once they were coded, we then looked to see what proportion of the items reflect each campus construct. While we believe this was the most appropriate step to take given the available information, it may misrepresent the actual emphasis of the test. Conducting a more finely tuned analysis would require us to look at the actual tests and, for those with open-response items, the evaluative rubrics and weights used. This, of course, is an analysis of even greater complexity, requiring us to address proprietary constraints with the testing companies. The public relations representation of the test substance is the information most academics would use to make such determinations, so we felt it was a relevant source to use and dissect.

Discussion

We set out to understand the relationship between our campus's emerging definition of critical thinking and the definitions used by four external tools for assessing students' critical thinking. This exploratory analysis was intended to help us understand the relevance (or fit) of each of these tools to our faculty's priorities for students' critical thinking development. The analysis process also ended up challenging us to clarify our own expectations for student performance and assessment. Finally, this research offers an analytical and evidence-based process for engaging faculty in reviewing teaching and learning priorities within the context of responding to external accountability demands.

Focusing first on the issue of fit between the four external sources and our campus definition, the results suggest that all three standardized tests address a narrow set of constructs present in the campus definition, with the primary focus on judgment/argument, evidence-based thinking, and drawing inferences. The VALUE rubrics provide more comprehensive coverage of the campus definitions, touching on nine of the twelve dimensions. Two that are not included (application and problem solving) are referenced in separate VALUE rubrics, which could be used to address the fuller range of campus dimensions.

These results help inform the campus discussion of which assessment options would be most appropriate. For example, if the faculty on our campus determine that judgment/argument is appropriate as the focus of our externally driven assessment, then any of the standardized tests might be acceptable. But if we decide we want our assessment strategy to reflect more of the dimensions of critical thinking present in the campus definition, the VALUE rubrics might be a better choice but would not necessarily reflect the same relative importance of these constructs as emerged from our faculty workshop results. This discrepancy could be remedied in part by including the integrative and applied learning VALUE rubric to the assessment since it would address the dimension that received the most attention from faculty application.

It should be noted, however, that selecting the VALUE rubric tool would not be sufficient for fulfilling the current VSA requirements for a standardized assessment method. VALUE rubrics also require more faculty time and expertise than standardized tests since rubrics require raters to be trained and then to assess samples of student work. The standardized tests have other costs (testing fees, incentives for the students, and staff effort in recruiting respondents) that, if used for VALUE analysis instead, would defray the costs described above. Clearly, associated costs also need to be a part of the campus's decision-making process.

Our analysis has raised another essential question that the faculty need to address: What sort of evidence of students' critical thinking is appropriate? The various descriptors of critical thinking used in these five sources (both the internal and the external sources) suggest the different kinds of performance tasks being used. The PP and CAAP rely on multiple-choice tasks—and their descriptors reflect identifying and recognizing aspects of an argument—for example, "identify accurate summaries of a passage" (Educational Testing Service, 2010) and "distinguish between rhetoric and argumentation" (ACT, 2010). The CLA, on the other hand, requires students to craft an argument. The CLA definition uses descriptors that reference creating an argument—for example, "constructing organized and logically cohesive arguments," "considering the implications of decisions and suggesting additional research when appropriate" (Council for Aid to Education, 2010). In this test, however, the parameters of student-generated responses are limited in scope. Students write answers to a set of narrowly focused prompts that address specific elements of the task and evidence presented.

The VALUE rubrics were designed specifically to assess portfolios of students' work from their courses—tasks that would be varied in focus, content, and types of writing contexts. The items in these rubrics reflect the comprehensiveness of these types of student work, referencing contextual analyses, identifying and describing a problem, and articulating the limits of one's position. Students' responses in this case would be unconstrained, reflecting the variety of ways one demonstrates a range of critical thinking dimensions across an array of courses and assignments.

Finally, our campus definition came from the discussions of a diverse group of instructors who responded to the prompt they were given by, quite naturally, thinking about the evidence of critical thinking they see in the assignments and tasks they ask of their students. Therefore, their responses focus to a larger degree on the doing: the creation of arguments, the application of theory to new settings, and the identification of evidence to support those arguments or assertions. The focus of these faculty-derived definitions, based as they are on what students are actually asked to do in the classroom, seems particularly distant from the tasks associated with the standardized multiple-choice tests that focus more on identifying and selecting over creating and constructing.

Another complexity emerges that is particularly relevant to assessment methods that use open-ended or constructed responses that are scored by sources outside the control of the faculty or the campus (like the CLA tasks and the CAAP and CLA essays). In these cases, it is important to make a distinction between what the assessment task is and what actually gets scored for performance assessment purposes. For example, the CLA task certainly seems to qualify as representing critical thinking application since it asks students to apply their analysis of various sources of information to a real-world question. It is therefore interesting that in our analysis, we did not find evidence of application in the CLA critical thinking definition—the elements of critical thinking they say their test addresses. Instead, their critical thinking descriptors focus primarily on judgment/argument, evidence-based thinking, synthesizing, and drawing inferences (CLA II).

Without more specific information about how the constructed responses are actually scored (that is, what elements of performance actually count) it is unclear whether application, for example, is actually a performance factor that is assessed or only the frame through which the performance of interest is stimulated. For example, is the student's capacity to judge the relevance of evidence to a particular context scored, or is the focus on being able to make the distinction between correlation and causation? Both would be a reflection of evidence-based thinking.

However, the first would also be a more complex or advanced form of critical thinking that reflects application. The second reflects a somewhat more basic but still important component of evidence-based thinking but would not reflect application as we have conceived it in our campus definition. This is an important point in reminding ourselves that the assessment task itself is only one component of the consideration of fit. When student performance is scored by parties removed from the campus context, it is also particularly important to be clear about what elements of student performance are included in the final score.

The importance of taking account of the types of tasks and the scoring criteria is illustrated in a recent study conducted by the University of Cincinnati and highlighted in an AAC&U publication (AAC&U, 2010a). Researchers compared first-year students' performance on the CLA with those students' performance on an e-portfolio assignment, assessed by faculty at the university using a slightly modified version of the VALUE rubrics. Researchers found no significant correlation between the two sets of assessment results, suggesting that the two assessment tools capture very different elements of students' critical thinking performance. These results raise an important question for campuses to consider: Does our assessment strategy capture the kind of student learning and performance we emphasize and value? Tools that do not effectively measure what matters to faculty are not appropriate sources of evidence for promoting change or for accurately reflecting instructional and curricular effectiveness.

Connecting Research and Practice: A Note to Faculty Developers

Finally, and perhaps most important, this method of inquiry leads to productive and engaging faculty discussions of critical thinking teaching, learning, and assessment. This project illustrates a way to address external accountability pressures while also generating joint faculty and administration discussions and insights into campus-based teaching and learning priorities. The first example of this productive inquiry was the workshop activity that produced the cross-disciplinary definition of critical thinking for our campus. Having this definition in place made it possible to pursue the line of inquiry described here, which served as an essential starting point for our campus's consideration of how to assess critical thinking in ways that are internally valid and externally legitimate.

The exercise of mapping our critical thinking dimensions against the definitions of the four assessment tools sparked a rich discussion among the coders. It was as we tried to code the external definitions using our internal critical thinking categories that we began to clarify the meaning of our own definition and see both the gaps and strengths of that definition. During this process, we also discovered the essential links between our definition and our faculty's pedagogical values in facilitating students' critical thinking. We believe that workshops that provide groups of faculty and administrators the opportunity to conduct this kind of analysis together can generate an important evidence-based dialogue about expectations for student learning, the assessment tools that most appropriately reflect those expectations, and the trade-offs inherent in making those kinds of decisions. The coding process opens up a conversation about what we mean when we use the term *critical thinking,* a process of clarification that informs one's own teaching as well as the larger campus conversation about critical thinking assessment.

REFERENCES

ACT. (2010). *CAAP critical thinking content categories and subskills.* Iowa City, IA: Author.

ACT. (2011). *Critical Thinking Test.* Retrieved from www.act.org/caap/test_thinking.html

Association of American Colleges and Universities. (2008). *Our students' best work: A framework for accountability worthy of our mission* (2nd ed.). Retrieved from www.aacu.org/publications/pdfs/studentsbestreport.pdf

Association of American Colleges and Universities. (2009). *Learning and assessment: Trends in undergraduate education.* Retrieved from www.aacu.org/membership/documents/2009MemberSurvey_Part1.pdf

Association of American Colleges and Universities. (2010a). Assessing learning outcomes at the University of Cincinnati: Comparing rubric assessments to standardized tests. *AAC&U News.* Retrieved from www.aacu.org/aacu_news/AACUNews10/April10/

Association of American Colleges and Universities. (2010b). *VALUE: Valid assessment of learning in undergraduate education.* Retrieved from www.aacu.org/value/rubrics/index.cfm

Bean, J. C. (1996). *Engaging ideas: The professor's guide to integrating writing, critical thinking, and active learning in the classroom.* San Francisco, CA: Jossey-Bass.

Beyer, C. H., Gillmore, G. M., & Fisher, A. T. (2007). *Inside the undergraduate experience: The University of Washington's study of undergraduate education*. San Francisco, CA: Jossey-Bass.

Brookfield, S. D. (1987). *Developing critical thinkers: Challenging adults to explore alternative ways of thinking and acting*. San Francisco, CA: Jossey-Bass.

Council for Aid to Education. (2008). *Common scoring rubric*. Retrieved from www.cae.org/content/pdf/CLA_Scoring_Criteria_%28Jan%202008%29 .pdf

Council for Aid to Education. (2010). *CLA scoring criteria*. Retrieved from www.collegiatelearningassessment.org/files/CLAScoringCriteria.pdf

Donald, J. G. (2002). *Learning to think: Disciplinary perspectives*. San Francisco, CA: Jossey-Bass.

Educational Testing Service. (2010). *ETS Proficiency Profile user's guide*. Retrieved from www.ets.org/s/proficiencyprofile/pdf/Users_Guide.pdf

Facione, P. (1990). *Critical thinking: A statement of expert consensus for purposes of educational assessment and instruction* [Executive summary]. Retrieved from ERIC database. (ED315423)

Foundation for Critical Thinking. (2009). *Our concept of critical thinking*. Retrieved from www.criticalthinking.org/aboutCT/ourconceptCT.cfm

Halx, M. D., & Reybold, L. E. (2005). A pedagogy of force: Faculty perspectives of critical thinking capacity in undergraduate students. *JGE: The Journal of General Education*, 54(4), 293–315. doi:10.1353/ jge.2006.0009

Huber, M. T., & Morreale, S. P. (Eds.). (2002). *Disciplinary styles in the scholarship of teaching and learning: Exploring common ground*. Sterling, VA: Stylus.

Kurfiss, J. G. (1988). *Critical thinking: Theory, research, practice and possibilities* (ASHE-ERIC Higher Education Report No. 2). Retrieved from ERIC database. (ED304041)

Lattuca, L. R., & Stark, J. S. (2009). *Shaping the college curriculum: Academic plans in context* (2nd ed.). San Francisco, CA: Jossey-Bass.

Office of Academic Planning and Assessment, University of Massachusetts Amherst. (2007). *Defining critical thinking: Participant responses*. Retrieved from www.umass.edu/oapa/oapa/publications/gen_ed/critical_ thinking_definitions.pdf

Office of Academic Planning and Assessment, University of Massachusetts Amherst. (2008). *Gen ed curriculum mapping: Learning objectives by gen ed course designations*. Retrieved from www.umass.edu/oapa/oapa/ publications/gen_ed/instructor_survey_results.pdf

Pace, D., & Middendorf, J. (2004). Decoding the disciplines: A model for helping students learn disciplinary ways of thinking. In D. Pace & J. Middendorf (Eds.), *New directions for teaching and learning: No. 98. Decoding the disciplines: Helping students learn disciplinary ways of thinking* (pp. 1–12). San Francisco, CA: Jossey-Bass.

Paul, R., Binker, A., Jensen, K., & Kreklau, H. (1990). *Strategy list: 35 dimensions of critical thought.* Retrieved from www.criticalthinking.org/page .cfm?PageID=466&CategoryID=63

Paul, R., Elder, L., & Bartell, T. (1997). *Study of 38 public universities and 28 private universities to determine faculty emphasis on critical thinking in instruction.* Retrieved from www.criticalthinking.org/research/Abstract-RPAUL-38public.cfm

Voluntary System of Accountability Program. (2010). *Participation agreement.* Retrieved from www.voluntarysystem.org/docs/SignUp/ VSAParticipationAgreement.pdf

CURRICULUM REVISION AND CULTURAL CHANGE

A JOINT FACULTY DEVELOPMENT AND FACULTY

GOVERNANCE APPROACH

Terre H. Allen, David A. Horne, Ingrid M. Martin, Michael E. Solt, California State University, Long Beach

Typically faculty development is not closely aligned with faculty governance. However, faculty development and faculty governance can find opportunities to work together to achieve transparent, rapid, and systematic curriculum revision and cultural change. Specifically, we describe the process of revision of a master's of business administration (M.B.A.) curriculum in which faculty development and faculty governance worked together to provide continuous assistance, opportunities for frequent discussion, periodic review, and faculty programming to achieve curriculum and course redesign for integrative learning and integrative teaching practice.

Curriculum revision is one of the most contentious issues in academia (Johnson, 2001). Many faculty come only reluctantly to the table to negotiate curriculum revision with attitudes that can be characterized as, "If you change it, don't change my course," and, "This is my course and I've been teaching it this way, and it's been working." Nevertheless, global, societal, and legislative mandates require that universities prepare students for twenty-first-century work. Business executives and business educators agree that M.B.A. learners require an integrative curriculum because business problems are not limited to a single academic domain (Latham, Latham, & Whyte, 2004; Rapert & Curington, 2010). However, little is known about best practices in curriculum change for such cross-functional academic programs.

Johnson (2001) studied how 147 school districts engaged in curriculum revision and provided a set of best practices for accomplishing revision and change. The project explored in this chapter applied John-son's best practices to establish a multilevel yet rapid process for curricu-lum revision in a large, multidepartment college of business.

Establishing the Need for Curriculum Revision

The curriculum revision process began in a typical fashion, with prepara-tion for an accreditation visit to the College of Business Administration (CBA) at California State University, Long Beach. The Association to Advance Collegiate Schools of Business required the college to establish a student learning task force to evaluate the strengths and weaknesses of the undergraduate and graduate curricula. Results indicated low alumni satisfaction with their learning in the M.B.A. program and prompted an urgent focus on the M.B.A. curriculum. A task force was established to examine the attributes of the M.B.A. curriculum and review how other M.B.A. programs were addressing graduate business education. The task force recommended a complete revision of the M.B.A. curriculum to meet the needs of students and the demands of the local and global business community.

The M.B.A. task force:

- Undertook review of the core curriculum of five top M.B.A. pro-grams, five comparable M.B.A. programs, and ten M.B.A. pro-grams in the region with which we directly compete

- Conducted alumni surveys and focus groups

- Held interviews and focus groups with current M.B.A. students

- Participated in Association to Advance Collegiate Schools of Business conferences on curriculum innovation

- Held discussions with administrators from other programs that had undergone curriculum revision

- Engaged in open discussions and brainstorming sessions with small groups of faculty across the college

- Conducted discussions with university administrators

- Consulted with external curriculum experts

Results indicated that one of the most profound weaknesses in the M.B.A. program was its lack of focus on student ability to think criti-cally. The task force recognized that instead of encouraging students to think critically across disciplinary boundaries, our faculty were forcing memorization of compartmentalized information. Lorange (2010) suggests that "academics must work across boundaries to create learning, teaching, and research environments that embrace a 'we, we, we' spirit . . . where business is seen as a whole, not as a series of parts" (p. 38). In a similar vein, Bisoux (2009) notes that the challenge is to create programs that are flexible, integrated, and experiential. The dean, the M.B.A. director, and the M.B.A. curriculum committee envisioned a curriculum that integrated the functional areas of the M.B.A. program.

The M.B.A. task force identified integrative learning as the ideal approach to achieve the vision (Bisoux, 2009; Lorange, 2010). The common denominator of integrative learning programs is a problem-based approach that simulates the business world, allowing students to hone their critical thinking skills in a business decision-making environment that crosses functional areas. Such a dramatic curricular redesign meant that there had to be a corresponding change in pedagogical tools and strategies to teach the new courses, necessitating that faculty learn to teach outside their comfort zones. In addition, the proposed change would require that faculty coordinate regularly across departments to exchange ideas and information and work together both in and out of the classroom. Faculty would need to look beyond courses and their own functional silos to focus on business problems and processes.

The M.B.A. task force next conducted a SWOT analysis, looking at strengths (S) and weaknesses (W) of each program and the opportunities (O) and threats (T) in the market for each program. The result was a succinct set of points that was mapped onto a two-by-two SWOT matrix. This team passed its work to the graduate curriculum committee to establish program-level learning outcomes:

> *Critical thinking skills.* Students will demonstrate conceptual learning, critical thinking, and problem-solving skills.
>
> *Interpersonal, leadership, and team skills.* Students will demonstrate interpersonal communication and leadership skills to work in a dynamic and diverse world independently and in a team environment.
>
> *Social responsibility skills.* Students will demonstrate awareness and knowledge of social responsibility, ethical leadership, and corporate citizenship in the domestic and global environment.
>
> *Business functions.* Students will demonstrate knowledge of today's dynamic business environment (business functions, practices, and related theories) and be able to integrate this functional knowledge in order to address business problems.

Domestic and global environment. Students will demonstrate knowledge of today's dynamic business environment (legal, regulatory, political, cultural, and economic), especially the links between our region and the global business world.

Quantitative and technical skills. Students will demonstrate the quantitative and technical skills needed to analyze, interpret, and communicate business data effectively and to improve business performance.

Initially many faculty voiced opposition to the proposed substantive changes in the curriculum. The dean recognized the need to change the culture of teaching and learning in the college and recommended that the graduate curriculum committee chair and the M.B.A. program director meet with the university faculty development director for suggestions and recommendations on how to bring resistant faculty to the table to discuss their issues, and navigate curriculum, teaching, and learning changes simultaneously. As Latta (2009) suggested, the prospect of working toward M.B.A. curriculum revision and cultural change in teaching and learning presented an important opportunity for faculty development to support broad strategic goals of the college.

University trustees had earlier established a professional fee assessed to students of the M.B.A. programs that would be used to maintain accreditation, expand career services for M.B.A. students, and recruit a more diverse M.B.A. student body. The fee provided funds for the faculty development required to be successful in a curriculum revitalization process. The provost and dean argued that the use of the fee constituted an investment in the future of our program.

The dean established a cultural change team based on Kotter's (2001) assertion that the linchpin between ideas and action is aligning people who understand the vision and are committed to its achievement. The cultural change team was made up of the dean, the M.B.A. program director, the chair of the M.B.A. curriculum committee, and the university faculty development director. The team included the university faculty development director because the dean wanted to ensure that sufficient professional development opportunities would be designed specifically to meet the needs for curriculum and cultural change to a learner-centered and integrative M.B.A. program of study.

Navigating Curriculum and Cultural Change

Johnson's (2001) best practices were selected as the guiding principles for navigating curriculum and cultural change among the CBA faculty. The team adopted four guiding principles for our work:

1. Administrators, faculty, students, alumni, and community partners must be involved in the curriculum revision process.

2. The time frame for revision and training should be short in duration; our goal was to launch a pilot cohort group at the end of the second year of internal study.

3. Participants should have access to continuous assistance, opportunity for frequent discussion, and periodic review throughout the entire process.

4. Curricular revitalization would necessitate changes in classroom instructional practices. In addition, the team recognized that a multitude of administrative issues required attention and that the process required simultaneous actions on multiple fronts.

We implemented these principles in the three phases of our project.

Phase 1: Setting the Stage for Change

Johnson's (2001) guiding principles provided the framework for a series of events aimed at simultaneous curriculum and cultural change. The events were designed to involve faculty, students, alumni, local businesses, and administration actively throughout the change process. The events were distinct, each with a definite purpose and audience. They were spread over an academic year, timed at deliberate intervals; held away from the college in university facilities designed to accommodate conferences; and provided breakfast and lunch. All events were planned, coordinated, and facilitated by the cultural change team and the faculty development director.

The first event, the M.B.A. retreat, was organized around the theme, "Is Change in the M.B.A. Curriculum Necessary?" The retreat provided a context for engaging the faculty and introducing Johnson's (2001) principles. All faculty (tenured, tenure track, and adjunct) were invited to attend; more than sixty of the seventy-five participated. The first half of the session was a moderated open discussion about the existing program and the results of the M.B.A. task force analysis. A general consensus emerged that the curriculum was out of step with the business world, and change was necessary. Next, faculty were divided into discussion groups to explore possible alternatives of how to achieve curriculum change. Each table presented its ideas to the group, and a question-and-answer period followed. Recognizing the importance of socializing as a means to build relationships and foster a culture of inclusion and collaboration, we built into the event a social hour after the meeting.

The M.B.A. curriculum committee used oral and written feedback from this event to continue drafting the revitalized M.B.A. curriculum. The second event, the M.B.A. Revitalization Conference, was presented in an academic conference format. Johnson's (2001) principle of engaging administration, faculty, students, alumni, and community provided the foundation for planning this event. More than one hundred faculty, alumni, current students, advisory board members, high-level university administrators, and community leaders participated. Four panel presentations, each with a moderator and faculty presenters, explored specific possible format changes of the revitalized program: orientation, discipline-based core, integrative core, and integrative electives. Faculty panelists also demonstrated that proposed changes had academic integrity and that faculty from different departments could work together on curriculum revision. Faculty panel participants received a stipend for attending two half-day faculty development workshops to coordinate the panel presentations. A question-and-answer session at the event's conclusion resulted in a spirited discussion of what should be included in a twenty-first-century M.B.A. curriculum. Faculty, alumni, current students, and community business leaders engaged in public dialogue about the proposed changes and program learning outcomes.

The first two events resulted in sufficient feedback and idea generation that the graduate curriculum committee and M.B.A. director formulated a revised curriculum plan (Table 11.1). Johnson's (2001) second and third principles recommend a short time frame and access to continuous assistance; therefore, within two months, the cultural change team quickly followed up the revitalization retreat with a third half-day workshop. Prior to the workshop, faculty were asked to suggest topics that would serve as potential themes for integrative M.B.A. courses—for example, sustainability, global enterprise, and innovation. The graduate curriculum committee identified two types of courses from those suggested by faculty: narrow integrative courses, comprising two departments or areas of study; and broad integrative courses, spanning three or more departments or areas of study.

The Revitalized M.B.A. Workshop, attended by more than sixty faculty, served as a hands-on demonstration of turning cross-disciplinary ideas into potential integrative courses. It began with an empowering message from the dean, an overview of the purpose and plan for the workshop activities, and brief presentations on integrative course design and assessment. Participants were assigned to specific theme tables based on their specified interests to draft ideas as to how each theme could evolve into an integrative course. Faculty teams presented their ideas to

Table 11.1 Original and Revitalized M.B.A. Curricula

Original M.B.A. Curriculum (based on three-unit courses)		Total Units	Revitalized M.B.A. Curriculum (based on four-unit courses)	Total Units
A. First year Orientation (Optional)		0	Orientation (required)	2
Core courses— for nonbusiness undergraduates or if taken more than three years earlier	Basic courses in accounting, finance, management, and marketing	0 to 12	Online diagnostic tests and tutorial program for prerequisite skills	0
Core courses required for all M.B.A.s	Courses in accounting (one), finance (one), human resource management (one), information systems (two), marketing (one)	21	One course each in accounting, finance, information systems, management, and marketing	20
B. Second year Elective courses	Four required from twenty-four available: accounting (two); finance (four), human resource management (three), information systems (two), management (four), marketing (six)	12	Integrative core: two eight-unit sequences required: Sustainable Business Organizations and Customer Relationship Management; and an integrative elective course (one required from six available)	16 4
International	NA	NA	International experience/study abroad	3
Capstone	Capstone course	3	Practicum— community-based project	3
Total		36–48		48

the entire group; prizes and friendly competition contributed to the fun and excitement. The workshop resulted in a noticeable cultural shift from, "Why should we do this?" to, "How can we do this?" Certainly not every faculty member embraced these initiatives, and some faculty voiced concerns about how to design integrative learning experiences that would produce the desired learning outcomes. This event operationalized Johnson's (2001) third principle, access to continuous assistance, by providing faculty with an opportunity to review the feedback and work accomplished thus far and work together on idea generation for curriculum-centered activities.

The cultural change team met to review progress and faculty feedback from the workshop. In accordance with Johnson's (2001) third principle, the team determined that a systematic faculty development program for designing integrative courses was necessary to move revitalization forward. The faculty development director drafted, and the dean and the M.B.A. curriculum committee approved, a proposal for a blended learning (face-to-face and online) course called Designs4Integration. The dean and the graduate curriculum committee decided that faculty who would teach in the revised curriculum would be required to participate in the course and would be awarded a three thousand dollar stipend for course completion. Requirements for completion were that each team submit a standard course outline, syllabus, assignments, and recommended assessments ready for curriculum approval at the department, college, and university levels. Reflecting our commitment to Johnson's (2001) first principle, a community partner who was also an alumnus was asked to review the Designs4Integration proposal. He gave his enthusiastic endorsement and provided some recommended resources.

Phase 2: Providing Faculty Development

The deliverables for curriculum approval required that faculty from different functional areas (accounting, finance, information systems, marketing, and management) collaborate to design integrative courses. Collaborative course design, collaborative teaching, and integrative learning were all new concepts to the vast majority of faculty in the college. Naturally most faculty were uneasy about putting the ideas of integrative learning into practice. As such, the university faculty development director worked toward designing a learning experience that would produce the intended outcomes and deliverables and educate faculty about integrative learning, collaborative course design, and collaborative teaching practices.

Designs4Integration is conducted over three weeks, with three face-to-face half-day sessions. It is housed on our learning management system. All faculty were enrolled as students; in summer 2010, thirty-four participated, and in winter 2011, fifteen did so. The course has seven developmentally sequenced modules:

Module 1: Introduces faculty to the course and intended outcomes and deliverables.

Module 2: Provides a variety of readings exploring integrative learning and integrative learning practices.

Module 3: Addresses issues in collaborative teaching for integrative learning and includes readings on cultivating colleagueship, collaborative course design, and collaborative teaching strategies.

Module 4: Addresses culturally responsive pedagogy by situating case method practices (www.hbs.edu/teaching/case-method-in-practice/) as a culturally responsive way to achieve integration of course content in the classroom.

Module 5: Addresses technology in integrative learning.

Module 6: Designing Your Course, adapted from Fink (2003), which leads faculty teams through a variety of activities that result in specific deliverables. Each course team, working within a theme area, was led through a collaborative process of building strong primary components (determining learning goals, building learning activities, building assessment and feedback), assembling those components into a coherent whole (designing the course structure, the standard course outline and syllabus), and finalizing the learning material for review (university policies and practices).

Module 7: Asked teams to reflect on their process and consider feedback and leadership issues.

Face-to-face sessions were half-day workshops that provided time for discussion of module specifics, questions, and teamwork. Blended instruction allows team members to work in collaborative online groups and to house all documents and resources (curriculum information, assessment information, accessibility requirements, academic journal websites, campus policy statements) at one point of access. In addition, groups posted deliverables on the course site for all participants to review. The summer 2010 offering of Designs4Integration resulted in seven integrative course proposals: Sustainability and the Business Enterprise, Customer Relationship Management, e-Commerce, Global Investments,

Innovation and the Business Enterprise, Financial Statement Analysis, and Mergers and Acquisitions.

Feedback from the summer 2010 offering indicated that faculty were most apprehensive about sharing their teaching time with other faculty. In addition, faculty remained unsure about how to ensure that students integrate information from the areas of study presented in the class. Reflecting Johnson's (2001) fourth principle, changes in instructional processes, the faculty development director developed a second course, Teaching4Integration, to help faculty create learner-centered and integrative classroom experiences. Again, we asked our alumni community partner to review the Teaching4Integration proposal, and he gave it enthusiastic support.

Teaching4Integration leads faculty through a three-part model (content delivery, active learning for integration, and reflection, synthesis, and application) of class organization and delivery. Each part is accompanied by recommended student work, activities, and assessment. Faculty spend the least amount of time delivering content individually. Active learning for integration is facilitated and coordinated by both or all faculty together, as is the reflection, synthesis, and application portion of the class. Harvard Business School case studies provide the basis for content integration. During the Teaching4Integration workshop, teaching teams work toward establishing comfort and competence in collaborative teaching, a paradigm shift in pedagogy for most faculty.

Phase 3: Bringing It All Together

Bringing the process to fruition in the form of a completed curriculum required some planning at a strategic level and included a curriculum matrix, assessment, and sustaining support.

DEVELOPING THE CURRICULUM MATRIX

Deans may lead and manage, but the college constitution specifies that approval of a new curriculum requires a vote of tenured and tenure-track faculty. An important step toward gaining faculty acceptance was the development of a curriculum matrix. Faculty were asked to address a map of course topics that contributed to the newly defined M.B.A. program outcomes. Numerous content redundancies were revealed during this process. Faculty began to buy into the idea that curriculum revision might reduce redundancies across courses and functional areas and might be acceptable since topics and concepts were reorganized into new courses and not dropped from the new curriculum.

Curriculum matrices from each department were combined to develop the overall M.B.A. curriculum map that delineated the full set of concepts, topics, and theories by functional area. Faculty had to come together to discuss how and where concepts could be integrated within the new curriculum. By charting what should be taught, when it should be taught, and how it should be configured, faculty produced a plan for achieving learning that could be used with assessment data to inform further modifications in the curriculum.

ASSESSING PROGRAM-LEVEL OUTCOMES

Another important step toward the acceptance of M.B.A. revitalization was the explicit recognition that assessment had to be built into the new program in a manner that would link learning objectives, accreditation requirements, and the shortcomings uncovered in our SWOT analysis. The college associate dean for accreditation guided the development of the assessment process. She identified an outside expert who worked with the curriculum committee to design and implement a portfolio assessment plan that was integrated into the new curriculum. The works collected include students' expectations about their M.B.A. education as related to the learning goals, their participation in various projects and efforts, their self-reflections, samples of their work related to outcomes being assessed, and documents that demonstrate their growing mastery of the M.B.A. curriculum. The portfolio is not merely a tool to assess the learning impact of the revitalized curriculum but also a marketing tool for M.B.A. students as they search for employment after graduation.

SUSTAINING SUPPORT

We reached out to other business schools that had undertaken this type of major educational paradigm shift. The most important piece of advice that we received was to engage as many participants as possible in the change process with the understanding that there would always be a few who would never join the shift to a new way of teaching and learning. The stakeholder engagement process needed to be constant, and it needed to address the points of resistance, concern, and risks that faculty and others identified.

Early in the curriculum revision process, college administrators recognized that the proposal for M.B.A. revitalization required significant support from other units on campus. Specifically, the university process for proposing any new course, let alone an entirely new curriculum, was a well-defined procedure with established time lines, policies, and deadlines. The aggressive timetable established early in the process had the goal of offering the new curriculum in the next academic year. This timetable meant that classes that were only being dreamed of had already passed the usual approval deadlines. Other obstacles emerged during cross-campus discussions, and each presented unique challenges to keep the effort on track. Each time an obstacle emerged, the cultural change team met to strategize a solution, and one or more team members followed through on making the solution a reality.

Obtaining acceptance across the campus required constant communication with university leaders. Most administrative service units appreciated consultation about implementation issues that they would need to accomplish. Numerous suggestions about how various components would or would not work within the current university system altered some elements of the overall intended results, but the changes were minor. All in all, working with the administration demonstrated that truly good ideas do not always have to adhere to the rigid rules of the institution, but with the proper level of support across the university, they can be given a chance.

Conclusions and Recommendations

The three phases outlined in this chapter represent significant milestones of successful and swift curriculum revitalization and cultural change. The process involved faculty development and faculty governance for continuous assistance, opportunities for frequent discussion, periodic review, and faculty development for curriculum design, course redesign, integrative learning, and integrative teaching practice. The phases outlined in this chapter can be replicated or adjusted to meet the needs of any group working toward curriculum revision or paradigm shift.

Johnson's (2001) guiding principles were central to establishing events and activities that fostered the changes we desired. They enabled us to assess our processes and to plan for future events. Specifically, we included administration, faculty, students, alumni, and community partners in our processes whenever possible (principle 1). The process took place from fall 2009 (M.B.A. Revitalization Retreat) through summer 2010 (Designs4Integration). Thus, a new curriculum was conceived and new courses were developed and moved through the curriculum process in one academic year (principle 2). A new cohort of students started the revitalized M.B.A. in fall 2010.

The two faculty development courses that supported curriculum change reflect principles 3 and 4. Making faculty development an integral part of curriculum change situates faculty development as a provider of continuous assistance. Housing both faculty development courses on the learning management system provides faculty with continuous access to learning material, curriculum material, assessment material, and course material. The semester prior to teaching a new integrative M.B.A. course, faculty use Teaching4Integration, which reflects principle 4 in that it is focused on changes in instructional processes.

The events and activities documented in this process represent strategic efforts to generate excitement, foster meaningful dialogue, demonstrate cooperation, engage participants, and provide social opportunities for relationship building and collaborative partnerships. The planning for each component involved significant efforts from the college leadership, the faculty development expert, faculty governance groups, and staff. The results were impressive. Each event was well attended and had people asking, "What's next?" Each event earned the attention of the university administration, and they are encouraging other university colleges to duplicate this curriculum and cultural change process.

Faculty development professionals need not be involved in large-scale cultural change to use the ideas and resources found in Designs4Integration and Teaching4Integration. However, Latta's (2009) call for faculty developers to support broader university efforts provides a valuable recommendation. Teaming with campus partners to support strategic change efforts adds value and visibility to faculty development activities. Faculty development and faculty governance indeed make good partners for curriculum revision.

REFERENCES

Bisoux, T. (2009, May/June). Next generation education. *BizEd, 8,* 24–30.

Fink, D. L. (2003). *Creating significant learning experiences: An integrated approach to designing college courses.* San Francisco, CA: Jossey-Bass.

Johnson, J. A. (2001). Principles of effective change: Curriculum revision that works. *Journal of Research in Education Leadership, 1*(1), 5–18.

Kotter, J. P. (2001). What leaders really do. *Harvard Business Review, 12,* 3–12.

Latham, G., Latham, S. D., & Whyte, G. (2004). Fostering integrative thinking: Adapting the executive education model to the M.B.A. program. *Journal of Management Education, 28*(1), 3–18. doi:10.1177/1052562903252647

Latta, G. F. (2009). Maturation of organizational development in higher education. In L. B. Nilson & J. E. Miller (Eds.), *To improve the academy: Vol. 18. Resources for faculty, instructional, and organizational development* (pp. 32–71). San Francisco, CA: Jossey-Bass.

Lorange, P. (2010, January/February). A new model for management education. *BizEd, 1,* 38–41.

Rapert, M. I., & Curington, W. P. (2010). Navigating the sea of change: Developing and implementing an interdisciplinary undergraduate core curriculum. *Journal of Innovative Educational Strategies, 1*(1), 38–46.

BROADENING THE CAMPUS CONTEXT

12

ACADEMIC DISHONESTY AMONG INTERNATIONAL STUDENTS IN HIGHER EDUCATION

Krishna K. Bista, Arkansas State University

University instructors address and want to eschew student academic misconduct. These educators presume that students understand fully what cheating and plagiarism are. However, the issue of academic dishonesty among international students is complex and difficult. This study investigated the perceptions of international undergraduate and graduate students in a southern U.S. university about possible causes for academic misbehavior. Results reveal several causal variables: previous learning style, English language proficiency, unfamiliarity with American academic cultures, relationship between student and teacher, and availability of technical and educational resources associated with academic dishonesty.

Academic misconduct in higher learning institutions remains prevalent among students at both the undergraduate and graduate levels (Lipson & McGavern, 1993; Love, 1997). Academic misconduct is more prevalent among international students than students educated in English-speaking countries (Arkoudis, 2007; Park, 2003). As is typical of many institutions, the University of Alberta (2010) defines academic dishonesty as cheating (using unauthorized notes or study aids on an examination), plagiarism (using others' work as their own without acknowledging the contribution of the author), fabrication (falsifying any information or

Thanks to Charlotte Foster and David Cox at the Center for Excellence, Arkansas State University, and Barry S. Davidson and Andrew Creamer at the College of Education at Troy University.

data, unauthorized access, misuse of availability of computer system or alteration of computerized records), deception (providing false information to the instructor), and sabotage (preventing others from completing their course work).

Variables Affecting Plagiarism

Some researchers have suggested that academic honesty offenses may result from misunderstanding of course policy or definitions of misbehavior such as plagiarism rather than a deliberate intention to cheat (Bamford & Sergiou, 2005; Evans & Youmans, 2000). Broadly speaking, scholars have categorized plagiarism into two groups: intentional and unintentional (Bamford & Sergiou, 2005; Hammond, 2002; Larkham & Manns, 2002; Park, 2003). Hall (2004) found several reasons for plagiarism, such as differing cultural values, personality factors, stress, peer pressure, and contextual factors. Studies conducted in China, Latvia, Lithuania, and the United States revealed historical, political, economic, and technical influences as major variables of plagiarism (Russikoff, Fucaloro, & Salkauskiene, 2003). A study at the University of Alberta (2010) mentioned poor time management and organizational skills, strong home culture, pressure for scholarship and jobs, and misunderstanding of course rules and regulations leading individuals to acts of plagiarism. McCabe, Trevino, and Butterfield (2001) suggest contextual factors such as peer behavior as the most powerful influence to educational cheating.

Previous Learning Style and Culture

In many cultures, the ability of learners to integrate the words of others in harmony with one's own was considered an academic practice (Cammish, 1997). Fleck (2000) investigated the concept of cheating in urban and rural Nepal from an ethnocentric perspective. He found that the underlying causes of cheating were grounded in Nepal's hierarchical cultural values: education is considered a status or rank rather than a process of learning, and cheat sheets, whispers, and copied answers were examination reality in many of Nepal's public schools. Such academic practices occur in many ethnic-oriented tribal communities, as Ballard and Clanchy (1991, cited in Hall, 2004, p. 4) explained: "In a Confucian, Buddhist, Hindu or Islamic society, for example, the ability to quote from sacred writings, from the saying of the ages, from the words of leading scholars, is the essence of scholarship."

Nazir and Aslam (2010) studied perceptions of academic dishonesty among Pakistani undergraduate and graduate students in different universities and found that more than half of the students studied were involved in dishonest acts such as helping other students copy homework assignments, exam papers, or graded project reports. These students believed that cheating and copying were not serious offenses and that there was no penalty for such behaviors.

In the Western world, knowledge acquisition is an intellectual exercise whereby one applies and manipulates information and data from various sources (Hellsten & Prescott, 2004). However, in non-Western cultures, rote learning and memorization are still widely practiced, and the degree of plagiarism is higher in graduate students than in undergraduate students due to the greater demand for critical and analytical writing (Scheyvens, Wild, & Overton, 2003). Some scholars have focused on the fact that many international students have already fossilized their learning attitudes into culturally influenced beliefs and behaviors from years of schooling at their home university, and it appears they may be unable to alter those behaviors in the American classroom (Carroll, 2002; Ryan, 2000).

Academic attribution and the use of others' published material is greatly influenced by culture. Russikoff et al. (2003) found common economic practices in communist and post-Soviet settings to be influential in plagiarism. These researchers found students copying from each other and comparing composition lengths on a free-writing assignment in a Latvian institution of higher learning. When questioned by the researchers, students responded, "We do it this way! We always do it this way! We copy and our teachers all know we just do it!" (p. 110). Chinese students state that plagiarism and copying is "a pedagogical practice" (Russikoff et al., 2003, p. 112). Fleck (2000), studying the nature of cheating in Nepal's public schools, found that students preferred copying answers from each other in free-writing assignments.

Communication Difficulties

The lack of English language proficiency and awareness of standard English citation conventions may contribute to plagiarism and cheating (Hyland, 2001; Park, 2003). Language barriers (Biggs & Burville, 2003) and difficulties in separating one's own thoughts from information gathered from texts and properly acknowledging the sources can also lead to plagiarism (Hall, 2004). In addition, international students may not have adequately developed such skills as essay writing, note taking, group work, and presentation, leading them to take academic shortcuts on academic tasks. Robertson, Line, Jones, and Thomas (2000) mentioned difficulties in comprehending the content of lectures, difficulties in understanding subject-specific terminology, high speed of delivery in lectures and seminars, and difficulties in interpreting the English language as reasons that international students plagiarize.

Lack of Familiarity with the Culture of Academics

The cultural difference of what constitutes public knowledge versus private knowledge is a central phenomenon of academic misconduct in some Asian and European educational settings. Some cultural groups do not regard plagiarism as a serious violation (Cammish, 1997). The University of Alberta (2010) suggested that 60 percent of international students interviewed stated they could not distinguish between paraphrased and plagiarized text. Carroll (2002) and Ryan (2000) highlighted the problems of such students who did not fully understand the differences among quoting, embedding sources, and plagiarism. In some cultural contexts, cheating is considered a learned behavior (DiPietro, 2010). For example, Italian students viewed copying from other sources as acceptable and as a mark of respect to the original author (cited in Hyland, 2001). Hammond (2002, cited in Hall, 2004, p. 1) listed the following reasons international students gave for plagiarizing:

"I couldn't keep up with the work."
"The lecturer/tutor doesn't care, so why should I?"
"I have to succeed. Everyone expects me to succeed, and I expect it, too."
"I don't understand what I'm expected to do to avoid plagiarism."
"I can't do this! I will have to copy."
"But you said, 'Work together.'"
"But paraphrasing would be disrespectful."
"I got desperate at the last moment."

Both international and domestic students indicate that normal academic pressures can lead to academic misconduct. Russikoff et al. (2003) found basic reasons that some individuals plagiarize: "It takes less time to complete an assignment, the ideas and writing are better, it is easier than having to produce original work, and teachers do not care" (p. 113).

Student-Teacher Relationship

Student-teacher relationships play a crucial role in determining the degree of academic dishonesty for international students. Teachers are highly respected authority figures in Bhutan, China, India, Japan, Nepal, and other Asian countries. Students in such cultures often consider teachers' opinions or information from books as the ultimate truth without question, and they reproduce this type of information verbatim (Ninnes, Aitchison, & Kalos, 1999; Robertson et al., 2000). Ryan (2000) points out that students from some cultures believe it is impolite to quote a reference or information from other sources because "this indicates that the teacher does not know that the text exists" (p. 23). Hall (2004) suggests that in any collectivist culture, the teacher determines the types of information that his or her students require to become successful. Knowledge in such cultures is considered "communal property" that anyone can use without acknowledgment (Carroll, 2002; Ryan, 2000).

Little research has been conducted on how undergraduate and graduate students are socialized in behaviors and attitudes related to academic misconduct. In a 1984 study at the undergraduate level, Nuss found that 53 percent of faculty surveyed indicated they rarely or never discussed university policies related to cheating and plagiarism with their students. A study by Love (1997) with six international graduate students found that they did not have any orientation experiences focused on the American writing culture.

Access to Educational Resources

Having access to the electronic and print versions of educational materials is essential for both educators and learners to maximize learning. However, many learners in technologically underdeveloped countries lack easy access to these resources. Limited teaching resources such as lecture notes and textbooks place burdens on instructors and students alike in China, India, and Nepal (Biggs, 1996; Fleck, 2000; Ninnes et al., 1999). In addition, poor quality of teaching aids, ineffective class management, inappropriate assessment, lack of expertise in education, and an authoritarian approach have all been associated with academic misbehavior (Fleck, 2000; Hellsten & Prescott, 2004).

It is often argued that students in American and other Western universities are highly involved in academic misconduct because they have easy access to Internet resources (Russikoff et al., 2003). However, students and instructors in poor Asian countries without easy access to the Internet or library resources are also prone to cheating and plagiarism.

Psychological Pressure and Adjustment Issues

Psychological pressures that international students face in the process of transitioning to study in the United States are associated with academic performance and misconduct. After arrival in a new country, international students face a number of challenges in adjusting to living and learning, including culture shock and financial problems, which may have an impact on their study plans, academic motivation, and attention to assignments and course work. These adjustment problems can vary by country of origin, race, ethnicity, English language proficiency, and collective versus individualist cultural orientation (Constantine, Anderson, Berkel, Caldwell, & Utsey, 2005; Poyrazli & Grahame, 2007).

The American university can also contribute to adjustment difficulties and the pressure to cheat when its international student services fall short by not making social connections to international students' home cultures, language, food, and social life. As a result, international students may experience negative psychological responses such as tension, confusion, depression, homesickness, disorientation, feelings of isolation, alienation, and powerlessness (Poyrazli & Grahame, 2007), often leading to lower academic achievement (Poyrazli & Grahame, 2007; Rai, 2002; Ying, 2002). Eisenberg, Golberstein, and Gollust (2007) indicate that 37 to 84 percent of international students did not receive free counseling, mental health services, or psychotherapy. When international students experience psychological, social, and academic pressures, they may be at greater risk of not following the standards and guidelines of American academic honesty requirements.

Much has been written about academic dishonesty and plagiarism among college students, but little has been done to study the causes of plagiarism among international students. As we have seen, international students with different culture, language, and learning environment backgrounds face several academic and nonacademic problems. I conducted a study of international students to answer the following questions:

- What are the major adjustment challenges for international students who are seeking academic degrees in the United States?

- Do social, cultural, and economic issues and psychological stress make international students prone to increased rates of plagiarism?

- Do home country teaching and learning styles contribute to documentation and citation difficulties?

- How do international students perceive cheating and plagiarism?

Methodology

I gathered data from international students studying at a southern university in 2010 using a questionnaire distributed by e-mail and in person. The questionnaire surveyed demographic factors such as gender, nationality, educational degree, and issues related to academic dishonesty. The focus of the study was to better comprehend the social, cultural, and psychological backgrounds of international students. Of the 300 international students invited to respond, 230 participated in the questionnaire, distributed by country of origin as follows: Australia (4), Azerbaijan (1), Belarus (1), China (66), Japan (10), India (30), Kenya (10), Malaysia (5), Morocco (4), Nepal (36), New Zealand (2), Norway (2), Poland (5), the Netherlands (4), Togo (2), Turkey (2), Saudi Arabia (23), South Korea (16), and Sweden (3). Four participants did not mention their country of origin. Female participants (51.6 percent) slightly outnumbered male participants (48.4 percent). Academically, 58.3 percent of the students were undergraduates, 33.3 percent were graduate students, and 8.3 percent were in English as a Second Language programs.

Findings

The data obtained from the study were analyzed from the perspective of student learning styles and cultures. The findings of this study fall into six main categories.

Previous Learning Style and Culture

Some international students have learning styles that may be different from those observed in traditional American classrooms. In many emerging Asian countries, teachers and educators follow traditional modes of instruction in the class. In a response to a question regarding previous learning and exam preparation in their home country, 93.3 percent of international students admitted that they primarily memorized information, 43.3 percent acknowledged use of group study, 50 percent were encouraged to prepare by rote learning, and 10 percent experienced collaborative testing and sharing answers for exams.

In response to a question on writing and information-finding conventions, 76.7 percent of respondents admitted that they did not follow the American Psychological Association or Modern Library Association writing format on class assignments in their previous work at their home university. This indicates that the majority of survey participants followed standard writing formats only in American schools. Similarly, 16.7 percent agreed that it was acceptable to consult with a friend when writing or studying, 26.7 percent believed that finding answers from online sources was acceptable, and 30 percent shared that getting help from others in taking an online exam or completing a take-home test was appropriate.

Incompetence and Other issues

This study indicated that English was a major language barrier for foreign students. More than half (58 percent) of the participants were undergraduate students, and their level of English proficiency was rated as just "satisfactory." Of the remaining participants, 10 percent rated themselves as a limited user, 11 percent as a moderate user, 12 percent as a good user, and 8 percent as a very good user.

When students are not interested in their programs of study, they are likely to slack off on their academic course work. For example, when asked what academic problems they faced in their course work, 27.5 percent of respondents supported the statement, "I didn't have a high enough score on the TOEFL/IELTS [Test of English as a Foreign Language/ International English Language Testing System] and I had to do ESL [English as a Second Language] program"; 10 percent selected, "I did a prerequisite or foundation course as I changed my major"; 2.5 percent chose, "I dropped the course because I wasn't interested"; and 37.5 percent responded, "I am just doing this program because I didn't have any other choice." In addition, 45 percent responded, "I found my own English not good enough." These responses suggest that many international students were pursuing university study without a particular interest in the academic field. Students may not progress well academically when they do not enter the program or take courses of their choice. The method of classroom instruction in secondary schools and universities in their home country plays a vital role in determining English competency for many international students. The survey showed that 69 percent of students were taught in a non-English local dialect or native language. In addition, 50 percent interacted with their professors in the local language while they were in their home country. These factors indicate that international students may not be acquiring strong language competence in English in their home countries. For most international students, face-to-face encounters with native English speakers did not occur until their entry into the United States. As a result, many students cannot express themselves comfortably, have low self-esteem, and fear making mistakes when they approach their professors in an American classroom setting (Cammish, 1997).

Being Unfamiliar with the Culture of Academics

In response to the question, "Why do you think that many students copy materials from the Internet and textbooks while doing reports, course assignments, or theses?" more than half of the students (56.7 percent) indicated that they lacked knowledge of what plagiarism is. Nearly half (46.7 percent) indicated that they were unfamiliar with the academic culture of American schools. Forty percent admitted cheating on exams or course assignments because of the pressures of timed exams. Furthermore, 10 percent cheated on the tests and admitted taking advantage of the instructor's permissive leniency . The results of this study support the findings of previous research that international students do not know what plagiarism truly means (Cammish, 1997; DiPietro, 2010; Hall, 2004; University of Alberta, 2010).

Student-Teacher Relationship

Cultural values that international students hold determine the form and style of communication, interpersonal behavior, and interaction between students and teachers. In the collective culture of Asian countries, learners may have a unique classroom demeanor—very polite, respectful, and obedient. Many foreign students find American classroom cultures disorienting when they have to navigate unfamiliar customs such as casual dress, students eating in class, direct communication, and calling professors by their first names.

This conflict of classroom culture is supported by student responses to the question about student-teacher interaction. Students indicated that their home country behavior practices still influenced their U.S. classroom interactions. Seventy percent responded, "I listen more and speak less"; 40 percent said, "To be silent is a part of a good discipline in the class"; and 13.3 percent responded, "There were no questions and interaction in the class," and, "I never made eye-to-eye contact while speaking." This indicates that international students in this study bear similar cultural features to those in previous studies.

Access to Educational Resources

International students, especially from developing countries such as Bhutan, China, India, Nepal, and Pakistan, may not have had access to a computer or research library in their previous academic experiences (Neuman, Khan, & Dondolo, 2008; Rennie & Mason, 2007). In response to the question, "How often did you use a library, computer or references while preparing term papers and class assignments in your previous study at your home university?" 26 percent reported "always," more than half (53 percent) answered "seldom," and 20 percent replied "rarely." In response to another question about their previous learning experiences in their home countries, 53 percent reported that their teachers asked them to memorize, read, and take comprehensive tests. Twenty percent of respondents said that their teachers read directly from the text with little or no explanation of content materials, whereas nearly half (49 percent) of the respondents stated that teachers at their previous schools did not use computers, did not conduct research, and did not assign project work. This lack of exposure to educational resources suggests that some international students are at greater possible risk for academic misinterpretation of established college norms in American institutions of higher learning.

Psychological Pressure and Adjustment Issues

Many international students experience anxiety, homesickness, and cultural and social isolation, which occur not only in the immediate transitional adjustment phase but also for many months that follow. Many students from developing countries also face financial challenges paying for academic and living expenses. Although it is illegal for international students to work off campus, some feel compelled to engage in any kind of work to support their unmet needs.

Students have a difficult time excelling in their studies and paying attention to school work if they are not socially, mentally, and economically ready. In this study, 57 percent of new international students indicated that they feared making mistakes, and 50 percent reported they did not express themselves most of the time. Nearly half (47 percent) of respondents shared that they felt awkward and found it difficult to speak with others, and another 37 percent suggested that anxiety impeded their ability to articulate their thoughts exactly and correctly.

Almost one in four students (23 percent) expected their friends could share course work with them.

When a professor asks a question in class, international students sometimes take longer to collect their thoughts or formulate an answer. Beginning instructors may not be aware that some foreign students are mentally translating words before speaking. When possible, international students like to use "beautiful sentences" from books or other resources to include in their writing to compensate for these language difficulties.

Implications

The findings from this study and previous research highlight the fact that academic misconduct is a complicated issue for international students.

Many students do not know what plagiarism is, and their cultural and social beliefs cloud the issues of improperly borrowed sources. The goal of the instructor is to have a positive impact on learning, as well as improve communication with their students (Evans & Youmans, 2000), and it is essential that educators teaching international students understand the social, cultural, and pedagogical background of their students and how they may or may not be aligned with U.S. academic values and behaviors (Grey, 2002). Instructors need to explain how to avoid improper documentation in college writing, and providing positive reinforcement with corrective action, instead of punishment, should become the norm. One possible solution is to offer an integrated bridge course on academic writing techniques and pitfalls for international students. Felix and Lawson (1994) and Bamford and Sergiou (2005) recommend conducting cultural reorientation programs focused on proper reference citation for international students. Ryan (2000, p. 56) makes these suggestions for reducing plagiarism among international students:

- Discuss what plagiarism is, and give examples.
- Explain the difference between paraphrasing and plagiarism.
- Demonstrate to students how to paraphrase, synthesize, and weave other sources into their own work.
- Show students how they are supposed to meet referencing requirement and why the requirements exist.
- State what is not permitted, describing what it is and why it is unacceptable.
- Explicitly state the consequences of not complying with the rules against plagiarism.

Changing improper writing habits of foreign students in regard to proper citation and plagiarism is hard work. Classroom educators must provide clear and explicit instructions to students about what is acceptable and what is not in writing in an academic setting. Arkoudis (2007) recommends that all teachers of students who are not native English speakers use a variety of educational approaches to avoid plagiarism.

Conclusion

The results of this study indicate that academic misconduct and plagiarism are prevalent among international students. According to the literature review and survey responses, external social, economic, and psychological pressures are the main causes of plagiarism. Many international students do not know what plagiarism is due to complex cultural differences as well as the learning and teaching styles of their home country. It is difficult to break the routine habits of international students (Bamford & Sergious, 2005), and they must receive direct, explicit instruction concerning plagiarism in the preparation of research papers as well as course work. It is important for faculty to understand the divergent linguistic and cultural backgrounds of their international students. Special attention should be given to students suffering from social and psychological discomforts such as anxiety, homesickness, or cultural disorientation in the cross-cultural adjustment process. The notion of academic dishonesty must be addressed from a perspective that recognizes that international students, especially those from developing countries, come from distinct cultural, economic, and educational backgrounds.

REFERENCES

Arkoudis, S. (2007). *Teaching international students: Strategies to enhance learning.* Melbourne, Australia: Center for the Study of Higher Education, University of Melbourne.

Ballard, B., & Clanchy, C. (1991). *Teaching students from overseas.* Melbourne, Australia: Longman Cheshire.

Bamford, J., & Sergiou, K. (2005). International students and plagiarism: An analysis of the reasons for plagiarism among international foundation students. *Investigations in University Teaching and Learning, 2*(2), 17–22.

Biggs, J. (1996). Western misconceptions of the Confucian-heritage learning culture. In D. Watkins & J. Biggs (Eds.), *The Chinese learner: Cultural, psychological, and contextual influences* (pp. 45–67). Hong Kong, China: University of Hong Kong.

Biggs, J., & Burville, J. (2003). *Teaching for quality learning at university: What the student does* (2nd ed.). Buckingham, England: Society for Research into Higher Education & Open University Press.

Cammish, N. K. (1997). Studying at advanced level through English. In D. McNamara & R. Harris (Eds.), *Overseas students in higher education: Issues in teaching and learning* (pp. 143–155). London, England: Routledge.

Carroll, J. (2002). *A handbook for deterring plagiarism in higher education.* New York, NY: Oxford University Press.

Constantine, M. G., Anderson, G. M., Berkel, L. A., Caldwell, L. D., & Utsey, S. O. (2005). Examining the cultural adjustment experiences of African international college students: A qualitative analysis. *Journal of Counseling Psychology, 52*(1), 57–66. doi:10.1037/0022-0167.52.1.57

DiPietro, M. (2010). Theoretical frameworks for academic dishonesty: A comparative review. In L. B. Nilson & J. E. Miller (Eds.), *To improve the academy: Vol. 28. Resources for faculty, instructional, and organizational development* (pp. 250–262). San Francisco, CA: Jossey-Bass.

Eisenberg, D., Golberstein, E., & Gollust, S. E. (2007). Help-seeking and access to mental health care in a university student population. *Medical Care, 45*(7), 594–601.

Evans, F. B., & Youmans, M. (2000). ESL writers discuss plagiarism: The social construction of ideologies. *Journal of Education, 182*(3), 49–65.

Felix, U., & Lawson, M. (1994). Evaluation of an integrated bridging course on academic writing for overseas postgraduate students. *Higher Education Research and Development, 13*(1), 59–69. doi:10.1080/0729436940130106

Fleck, C. (2000). Understanding cheating in Nepal. *Electronic Magazine of Multicultural Education, 2*(1). Retrieved from www.eastern.edu/publications/emme/2000spring/fleck.html?

Grey, M. (2002). Drawing with a difference: Challenges faced by international students in an undergraduate business college. *Teaching in Higher Education, 7*(2), 153–166. doi:10.1080/13562510220124268

Hall, B. (2004). *International students and plagiarism: A review of the literature*. Retrieved from www.bournemouth.ac.uk/cap/documents/Plagiarism percent20and%20International%20Students.pdf

Hammond, M. (2002). *Cyber-plagiarism: Are FE students getting away with words?* Retrieved from www.leeds.ac.uk/educol/documents/00002055.htm

Hellsten, M., & Prescott, A. (2004). Learning at university: The international student experience. *International Educational Journal, 5*(3), 344–351.

Hyland, F. (2001). Dealing with plagiarism when giving feedback. *ELT Journal, 55*(4), 375–381. doi:10.1093/elt/55.4.375

Larkham, P., & Manns, S. (2002). Plagiarism and its treatment in higher education. *Journal of Further and Higher Education, 26*(4), 339–349.

Lipson, A., & McGavern, N. (1993, May). *Undergraduate academic dishonesty at MIT: Results of a study of attitudes and behavior of undergraduates, faculty and graduate teaching assistants.* Paper presented at the 33rd annual forum of the Association for Institutional Research, Chicago, IL.

Love, P. G. (1997, November). *The meaning and mediated nature of cheating and plagiarism among graduate students in a college of education.* Paper presented at the 22nd annual meeting of the Association for the Study of Higher Education, Albuquerque, NM.

McCabe, D. L., Trevino, L. K., & Butterfield, K. D. (2001). Cheating in academic institutions: A decade of research. *Ethics and Behavior, 11*(3), 219–232.

Nazir, M. S., & Aslam, M. S. (2010). Academic dishonesty and perceptions of Pakistani students. *International Journal of Educational Management*, 24(7), 655–668. doi:10.1108/09513541011080020

Neuman, S. B., Khan, N., & Dondolo, T. (2008). When I give, I own: Building literacy through READ community libraries in Nepal. *Reading Teacher*, 61(7), 513–522. doi:10.1598/RT.61.7.1

Ninnes, P., Aitchison, C., & Kalos, S. (1999). Challenges to stereotypes of international students' prior educational experience: Undergraduate education in India. *Higher Education Research and Development*, 18(3), 323–342. doi:10.1080/0729436990180304

Nuss, E. M. (1984). Academic integrity: Comparing faculty and student attitudes. *Improving College and University Teaching*, 32(3), 140–144.

Park, C. (2003). In other words: Plagiarism by university students—Literature and lessons. *Assessment and Evaluation in Higher Education*, 28(5), 471–489.

Poyrazli, S., & Grahame, K. M. (2007). Barriers to adjustment: Needs of international students within a semi-urban campus community. *Journal of Instructional Psychology*, 34(1), 28–45.

Rai, G. (2002). Meeting the educational needs of international students. A perspective from US schools. *International Social Work*, 45(1), 21–33.

Rennie, F., & Mason, R. (2007). *The development of distributed learning techniques in Bhutan and Nepal*. Retrieved from ERIC Database. (ED496159)

Robertson, M., Line, M., Jones, S., & Thomas, S. (2000). International students, learning environments and perceptions: A case study using the Delphi technique. *Higher Education Research and Development*, 19(1), 89–102. doi:10.1080/07294360050020499

Russikoff, K., Fucaloro, L., & Salkauskiene, D. (2003). Plagiarism as a cross-cultural phenomenon. *CAL Poly Pomona Journal of Interdisciplinary Studies*, 16, 109–120.

Ryan, J. (2000). *A guide to teaching international students*. New York, NY: Oxford Center for Staff and Learning Development.

Scheyvens, R., Wild, K., & Overton, J. (2003). International students pursuing postgraduate study in geography: Impediments to their learning experiences. *Journal of Geography in Higher Education*, 27(3), 309–323. doi:10.1080/0309826032000145070

University of Alberta. (2010). *Why students plagiarize: Guide to plagiarism and cyber-plagiarism*. Retrieved from www.library.ualberta.ca/guides/plagiarism/why/index.cfm

Ying, Y.-W. (2002). Formation of cross-cultural relationships of Taiwanese international students in the United States. *Journal of Community Psychology*, 30(1), 45–55. doi:10.1002/jcop.1049

13

FORTY PERCENT OF 2 MILLION

PREPARING TO SERVE OUR VETERANS WITH DISABILITIES

Bruce C. Kelley, Ernetta L. Fox, Justin M. Smith, Lisa A. Wittenhagen, University of South Dakota

On August 1, 2009, the Post-9/11 Veterans Educational Assistance Act of 2008 was passed, and as a result, almost 2 million veterans returning from Iraq and Afghanistan will soon enroll in postsecondary education. Up to 40 percent of these veterans are estimated to have disabilities. This chapter examines some of the characteristics of this group, the challenges that veterans face as they transition into life as college students, and how faculty developers can help faculty better serve these incoming veterans.

John (named changed to protect identity) is medically retired from the Air Force, having served in both Operation Enduring Freedom (OEF) and Operation Iraqi Freedom (OIF). He has major depression and social phobia. Despite these challenges, he has decided to get a bachelor's degree in alcohol and drug studies:

> I do pretty well but the depression hits me every so often and it makes it difficult for me to study. I'm also so highly medicated at times that I can't really function. I may spend most of the week in bed and my attention and focus aren't that well. I was a 3.8 grade point average student but because of my depression I've fallen to a 2.5 grade point average. I've gotten a couple of F's since I fell

The material in this chapter was developed under a congressionally directed grant administered through the U.S. Department of Education. However, it does not necessarily represent the policy of the Department of Education and does not assume endorsement by the federal government.

so far behind that I couldn't catch up. I've also failed most of my correspondence courses since I really lack the motivation and since I don't have deadlines I put everything off and just focus on my online classes so I don't fall behind. I really struggle between the depression, or maybe I'm just not motivated. I know with having social phobia I'll never use my degree but it's a goal in life and it gives me something to keep me going. . . . I've never used the disability services. I've always felt like I wouldn't qualify.

John's story is far from unique. As of the 2007–2008 academic year, military veterans, active-duty service members, and reserves (referred to throughout the rest of this chapter as student veterans) constituted 4.2 percent of the total undergraduate population in the United States—875,000 students enrolled nationwide (Radford & Wun, 2009). The Post-9/11 Veterans Educational Assistance Act of 2008 (post-9/11 GI bill) was passed on August 1, 2009, and as a result, almost 2 million veterans returning from the Iraq and Afghanistan wars will soon enroll in postsecondary education (American Council on Education, 2008). Veterans returning from OEF and OIF are different from those of past generations. Advances in body armor, vehicle protection, medical procedures, and treatment mean that up to 40 percent of these veterans will be enrolling in college with both visible and invisible disabilities (Grossman, 2009). Forty percent of 2 million: Are we, as faculty developers, ready to help our faculty serve these incoming student veterans? What do faculty need to know about this incoming surge of students who will have such unique challenges?

Characteristics of Veterans Returning to Higher Education

Veterans returning to school under the post-9/11 GI bill are demographically different from the typical incoming first-year student. Of all military undergraduates in the classroom, 84.5 percent are older than the traditional college student, 47.3 percent are married, and 47.0 percent of them have children, including 14.5 percent who are single parents (Radford & Wun, 2009). As a group, military members and veterans seek associate degree programs at two-year colleges at a higher rate than the traditional college population. An astounding 76.6 percent of them do not attend school full time for an entire academic year, and only 37.7 percent of military undergraduates used veterans' education benefits during the 2007–2008 academic year, although the post-9/11 GI Bill may change this dramatically (Radford & Wun, 2009).

Veterans and Disabilities

Veterans returning to higher education are doing so with a variety of physical and psychological disabilities. Bilmes (2008) estimates that

> more than 70,000 have been wounded in combat, injured in accidents, or airlifted out of the region for emergency medical care. More than a third of the 750,000 troops discharged from the military so far have required treatment at medical facilities, including at least 100,000 with mental health conditions and 52,000 with post-traumatic stress disorder [PTSD]. According to a recent U.S. Army estimate, as many as 20 percent of returning soldiers have suffered mild brain injuries, such as concussions. More than 20,000 troops have survived amputations, severe burns, or head, spinal, and other serious injuries. (p. 84)

Veterans may also return to higher education with hearing disorders (Lew et al., 2007) and eye injuries (Thatch et al., 2008). Warden (2006) found that 28 percent of all individuals medically evacuated to the Walter Reed Army Medical Center had traumatic brain injury (TBI), and Kennedy et al. (2007) found that between January 2003 and February 2007, 29 percent of the patients medically evacuated to Walter Reed Army Medical Center had evidence of both TBI and PTSD. Hoge, Auchterlonie, and Milliken (2006) reported that

> the prevalence of reporting a mental health problem was 19.1% among service members returning from Iraq compared with 11.3% after returning from Afghanistan and 8.5% after returning from other locations. . . . Thirty-five percent of Iraq war veterans accessed mental health services in the year after returning home; 12% per year were diagnosed with a mental health problem. (p. 1023)

Many of the soldiers who need treatment often do not even report mental health problems or seek help due to the stigma of seeking psychiatric assistance, especially in a volunteer army where many are seeking to advance their careers (Hoge et al., 2004; Litz & Orsillo, 2004).

TBI and PTSD deserve special mention, for they are in some respects invisible. Students suffering from TBI or PTSD are not as clearly identifiable to a faculty member as someone with, say, an amputation. TBI produces a number of symptoms, many of them similar to common types of learning disabilities According to Okie (2005), "Cognitive changes . . . may include disturbances in attention, memory, or language, as well as delayed reaction time during problem-solving. Often, the most troubling symptoms are behavioral ones: mood changes, depression, anxiety, impulsiveness, emotional outbursts, or inappropriate laughter" (pp. 2045–2046). PTSD can affect students in a variety of ways. It can inhibit interaction with peers during discussion and group work because students with PTSD are often reluctant to share their thoughts and opinions, and some course topics might cause extreme anxiety for them. It can cause a student discomfort in classes where seating is not the same from week to week or in classes that are exceptionally large, and it has an impact on the student's ability to focus in a timed setting when there are distractions in the room such as shuffling noises or people in the hallway. The disorder can also cause difficulty in concentrating and reading for extended periods of time and has been linked to substance abuse, acute stress disorder, somatoform disorders, depression, and other mood and anxiety disorders (Cozza et al., 2004). One of the most difficult challenges of PTSD is that it sometimes has a delayed onset (Hoge et al., 2008), and symptoms of the disorder can begin to manifest themselves after the student has transitioned into higher education.

Large numbers of veterans are returning from OIF and OEF with varying types and degrees of disabilities. It is to the benefit of both these veterans and higher education to create supportive environments for these men and women if we wish to fulfill the promise this country makes to educate its veterans. As Duane (2007) succinctly states, "Those who have sacrificed so much for our country deserve physical and mental health care, educational opportunities, and a real chance to live fulfilling lives" (p. 2123).

Transitions

The transition of a veteran from the military into higher education produces a unique set of experiences, challenges, and stresses. Some of these are positive; the experience of serving can provide "greater self-efficacy, enhanced identity and sense of purposefulness, pride, camaraderie, etc." (Litz & Orsillo, 2004, p. 21). The experience can also have negative impacts on life, work, and learning in both the short and long terms. Some of the challenges veterans face as they transition to higher education can include (University of Michigan–Flint, 2010):

- Insomnia
- Difficulty concentrating
- Recurring thoughts and memories of war experiences

- Hyperalertness (difficulty relaxing or feeling safe even in an unthreatening environment) and startle reactions
- Grief and sadness over losses
- Guilt (surviving when others died)
- Anger
- Impatience and low tolerance for frustrations (civilian rules may seem irrelevant or meaningless)
- Difficulty connecting with and trusting others, especially those without war zone experience
- Anxiety about being redeployed

Student veterans must learn to develop an identity that goes beyond that of the military, and as they merge into the nonveteran student population, they must deal with a variety of issues—for example (University of Michigan–Flint, 2010):

- Difficulty relating to and connecting with traditional college students
- Difficulty finding importance and meaning in experiences and ideas that are not life or death
- Difficulty negotiating the structural and procedural differences between the military and higher education bureaucracies
- Making a greater number of decisions in a far more complex world (the number of independent decisions that must be made— when to get up, where to eat, and what to do that day—are far more limited in the military than for traditional college students)
- Developing a sense of safety on campus (sitting in areas of the classroom that give them a clear view of who is going in and out of the door)
- Struggling with boredom (few classes compare with a firefight in terms of excitement)

Student veterans with disabilities discover that even language about disability changes as one navigates through the military, the Veterans Administration (VA), and the Americans with Disabilities Act (ADA). The military defines a disability as a service-connected physical or mental impairment that renders a member unfit to perform his or her required duties, while the VA defines disability as a mental or physical disease or injury resulting from or aggravated by military service. Broadly speaking, the amended ADA defines disability as a physical or mental impairment, a history or record of such an impairment, or being regarded by others as having an impairment (Miller & Smith, 2011). The subtle differences in these definitions mean that student veterans are sometimes considered able by one agency and disabled by another. The ADA tends to be broader in scope, and service members who receive only a partial disability under VA regulations may be entitled to full accommodations in higher education. The result of this complex situation is that students should not base their eligibility for academic accommodations on their disabilities classification through the military or the VA.

There has been a growing awareness that higher education needs to be better prepared to serve student veterans. Some notable initiatives include the Minnesota State College and University system's My Military Education Program, the University of Arizona's Supportive Education for Returning Veterans Program, Cleveland State University's Veteran Student Success Program, Montgomery College's Combat2College Program, and George Washington University's Yellow Ribbon Program. In general, however, there has been little emphasis on preparing faculty, staff, and administration to serve veterans with disabilities. Momentum for providing on-campus support for, and increased retention of, these veterans currently lags efforts to get them on campus in the first place.

Preparing Faculty to Better Serve Veterans

It is important for faculty to recognize the transitional challenges that student veterans must overcome as they move to higher education. We have identified three broad, and at times overlapping, areas where faculty developers can suggest specific strategies to enable faculty to better serve veterans with disabilities: course structure and design, learning activities, and classroom environment. The strategies, which we describe next, will improve the chances for academic achievement for all students, but they are especially important in enabling student veterans with disabilities to succeed in higher education. Keep in mind that every veteran is unique, and that the generalizations we describe will not apply to all student veterans or even to every student veteran with a disability.

Course Structure and Design

Structural elements that faculty should be aware of fall along a continuum that ranges from specific design elements for individual courses at one end to university-wide instructional policies regarding the disability accommodations at the other. The structure of individual courses should be reevaluated in light of the unique challenges student veterans face and redesigned where appropriate. Faculty generally do not need to know the intimate details of VA medical processes, for example, but they should be informed that the system is not at all like scheduling an appointment with a family physician. VA appointments, if cancelled, often cannot be rescheduled until months later. Faculty should develop attendance and class participation policies that do not penalize student veterans who have to miss class because of VA appointments. Military obligations, such as weekend training for National Guard units, should be regarded as the same type of excused absence that faculty would extend to sports-related absences. Assignments should all be clearly defined in the syllabus, for student veterans have been trained to communicate in a clear, direct manner and to work toward specific goals. Rubrics and assignment templates that are included with the basic course materials can help provide that clarity. Consider scaffolding longer assignments, such as term papers, as a series of several smaller tasks with specific deadlines. Many students, including student veterans, struggle with structuring their time to finish larger academic tasks.

Emphasizing the reflective quality of academic work is important as well. The military trains its members to make rapid decisions, and "student veterans with disabilities will benefit from experiences that help them in learning that rarely will they need to make such harrowing split second decisions and that when a decision needs to be made, they should spend the necessary time to do so" (Branker, 2009, p. 62). Student veterans will benefit from a course structure that encourages them to take their time with assignments and to be deliberately thoughtful in their academic activities. Asynchronous communication, through the use of learning management discussion boards, wikis, blogs, or tweets, can help student veterans build in time for this reflection (Grabinger, 2010).

At a larger structural level, instructors should be aware of institutional policies regarding students with disabilities. Faculty developers should develop a working relationship with their institution's office of disabilities services (ODS) and should encourage their faculty to do so as well. Faculty should know how the process of granting accommodation works at their institution and should be given basic information about the most common disabilities that veterans experience. This is especially true of TBI and PTSD, for they can manifest themselves in ways that often appear to be common learning disabilities and may have a delayed onset. A student veteran who did not have a learning disability prior to deployment may not understand why he or she is now having trouble concentrating or memorizing and may be resistant to using disability services. Students who grow up with learning disabilities often discover them in elementary school, and by the time they have reached college, they have had a number of years to master the language of accommodation and understand their rights and their responsibilities. Student veterans with disabilities are unlikely to have this familiarity and may need to be encouraged to seek information from the ODS. At the very least, every faculty member should include a statement on the syllabus regarding the ADA. Finally, the principles of universal design can provide faculty with numerous ways to better serve all students with disabilities, including those who are student veterans. These principles include making course materials available in a variety of formats, providing a fully accessible physical environment, and assessing students through a variety of measures. Burgstahler and Cory (2008) provide the definitive exploration of universal design in higher education.

Learning Activities

Numerous specific teaching strategies and styles can have a positive impact on the learning experience of student veterans with disabilities. Because they are typically older, many student veterans are interested in practical and hands-on types of activities, such as service-learning projects, case studies, simulations, and field research. Team projects, if they are clearly defined and have unambiguous goals, can enhance the educational experience of student veterans, for they have been trained to work as a team to accomplish specific missions. Branker (2009) recommends that "an intentionally designed educational environment for student veterans with disabilities should emphasize collaboration, not competition and isolation" (p. 62). Assignments that foster teamwork are one way to provide this environment.

Student veterans may also struggle with the difference in communication styles between the military and the typical college classroom. The military teaches a brief and direct communication style. Faculty therefore may need to spend extra time with student veterans, mentoring them on how to communicate in a voice that is more appropriate for an academic setting. Activities that encourage students to argue ideas or explore issues from different viewpoints can help veterans learn a more academic communication style.

One of the foundational principles of universal design is to let students demonstrate knowledge in multiple ways. Faculty should consider constructing a wide variety of assignments within each course, such as weekly question cards, study guides, self-assessments, attendance at campus events, participation in community service projects, writing assignments, oral presentations, small-group multimedia projects, and exams (Higbee, 2008). A wide variety of assignments ensures that students who struggle with specific methods of assessment (for example, test taking or in-class writing assignments) will have other options to show mastery of course materials and activities. An array of assessment strategies benefits all students, but is especially important for students with disabilities, such as a student veteran who has recently lost his or her primary writing hand.

Activities that make use of educational technology can provide numerous benefits to student veterans with disabilities. Multiple versions of course content can be created through the use of streaming video (especially if close-captioned), podcasts, narrated slides, and course-related websites. Students in turn can create content through a variety of media. Social media and online collaborative writing tools can provide an engaging learning experience for all students, including student veterans with disabilities.

Classroom Environment

Faculty should be aware that the success of student veterans is often tied to the physical and emotional environment of the classroom. Student veterans who have recently returned from conflict often feel insecure in large classrooms or in classrooms with multiple doors. They have been trained to secure rooms, meaning that everything is searched and all exits closed or watched. The general hubbub and commotion of 150 students (with their unsearched backpacks) interacting in a room can be intimidating or distracting for student veterans, especially those with neurological disorders. Some student veterans want to sit in a location (such as the back row of the room) where they can easily watch everyone and where their "back" is secure. For that reason, rooms with lots of windows or glass walls or that are generally open can be distracting. Faculty may need to work with their ODS to find ways of best serving student veterans who are struggling with the physical classroom environment. Student veterans often find the behavior of their fellow students disruptive. Whispering, texting, or Web surfing (in ways unrelated to course content) are foreign to the typical military briefing and can be highly distracting for student veterans.

The emotional environment of the class is also an essential element in the success of student veterans. While faculty should foster an atmosphere that encourages direct communication with all their students, this is especially important with veterans. First-year noncombat veterans reported that they were less engaged with faculty than their peers were, and combat and noncombat veterans who were academic seniors reported significantly lower student-faculty interaction and less support from their campus environment than did nonveteran students (National Survey of Student Engagement, 2010). In light of these results, faculty should make concentrated efforts to interact with their student veteran population both in and outside the classroom. Many student veterans are quietly proud of their military service and are uncomfortable with overt displays of recognition (positive or negative) that single them out from their classmates. Faculty may wish to devise nonintrusive ways of identifying these students—perhaps by collecting information from all students on note cards or through an online survey. Student veterans have experienced the world in many ways that most other students have not, and developing assignments and activities that draw on this experience will provide a supportive environment that enriches the entire class.

Faculty should thoughtfully consider how they handle in-class issues related to the global war on terror in general and the Middle East in particular. Within the veterans' community itself, there are many opinions about our current wars, from unwavering support to unswerving criticism. As a result, faculty should find ways of discussing current events and Middle Eastern policies in a way that distinguishes political policies and military strategies from individuals who have had to carry out those policies. Finally, faculty need to understand that certain questions should never be asked of a student veteran, including, "Did you kill anyone?" "Did you see anyone die?" and other intrusively personal questions. Advise faculty to avoid asking these questions in class, and if students ask them, they should step in immediately to redirect the question, as they would with any patently offensive statement made in that environment.

Conclusion

There is a great need for faculty, staff, and administration to better understand the challenges that veterans returning from OEF and OIF face, and faculty developers need to be prepared to help faculty better serve those veterans who are entering higher education with disabilities. As Cook and Kim (2009) state, "Veterans are not necessarily looking to be isolated or have special programs created on their behalf. More than anything, they are looking for an educational environment that provides the tools and resources that allow them to succeed" (p. 29). When we provide student veterans with disabilities with the opportunity for an extraordinary education, we also add immeasurably to the educational experiences of the entire academic community.

Terry (named changed to protect identity) is a service-connected veteran with a disability. This is his story, in his own words:

> No two experiences veterans have are the same, but we share many things in common when returning to school. In my case the ED[ucation] graduate program I started in 2001 was interrupted for two years for OEF/OIF from 2003–2005. When I returned home to South Dakota I no longer had the finances to complete the program as I had two of my own children in college. Four long years later a G.I. Bill for Reservists was passed and in 2009 I resumed taking classes to complete the program I had started in 2001. The School of Education faculty had changed, and my advisor and entire committee had either retired or left in those intervening years. I applied/appealed for an extension to complete my program. My situation is not unique and only because of an understanding School of Ed Department head and tenacity and commitment on my part was I able to [continue my program].

With the proper support, our veterans with disabilities can thrive. As of this writing, Terry is only four weeks away from graduation, a success story that makes us all proud.

REFERENCES

American Council on Education. (2008). *Serving those who serve: Higher education and America's veterans*. Retrieved from www.acenet.edu/Content/NavigationMenu/ProgramsServices/MilitaryPrograms/serving/index.htm

Bilmes, L. J. (2008). Iraq's 100-year mortgage. *Foreign Policy, 165*, 84–85.

Branker, C. (2009). Deserving design: The new generation of student veterans. *Journal of Postsecondary Education and Disability, 22*(1), 59–66.

Burgstahler, S. E., & Cory, R. C. (Eds.). (2008). *Universal design in higher education: From principles to practice*. Cambridge, MA: Harvard Education Press.

Cook, B. J., & Kim, Y. (2009). *From soldier to student: Easing the transition of service members on campus*. Washington, DC: American Council on Education.

Cozza, S. J., Benedek, D. M., Bradley, J. C., Grieger, T. A., Nam, T. S., & Waldrep, D. A. (2004). Topics specific to the psychiatric treatment of military personnel. In *Iraq war clinician guide* (2nd ed., pp. 4–20).

Washington, DC: U.S. Department of Veterans Affairs, National Center for PTSD. Retrieved from www.ptsd.va.gov/professional/manuals/iraq-war-clinician-guide.asp

Duane, J. F. (2007). True patriotism. *American Journal of Public Health*, *97*(12), 21–23. doi:10.2105/AJPH.2007.125237

Grabinger, S. (2010). A framework for supporting postsecondary learners with psychiatric disabilities in online environments. *Electronic Journal of e-Learning*, *8*(2), 101–110.

Grossman, P. D. (2009). Forward with a challenge: Leading our campuses away from the perfect storm. *Journal of Postsecondary Education and Disability*, *22*(1), 4–9.

Higbee, J. L. (2008). The faculty perspective: Implementation of universal design in a first-year classroom. In S. E. Burgstahler & R. C. Cory (Eds.), *Universal design in higher education: From principles to practice* (pp. 61–72). Cambridge, MA: Harvard Education Press.

Hoge, C. W., Auchterlonie, J. L., & Milliken, C. S. (2006). Mental health problems, use of mental health services, and attrition from military service after returning from deployment to Iraq or Afghanistan. *Journal of the American Medical Association*, *295*(9), 1023–1032.

Hoge, C. W., Castro, C. A., Messer, S. C., McGurk, D., Cotting, D. I., & Koffman, R. (2004). Combat duty in Iraq and Afghanistan, mental health problems, and barriers to care. *New England Journal of Medicine*, *351*(1), 13–22.

Hoge, C. W., McGurk, D., Thomas, J. L., Cox, A. L., Engel, C. C., & Castro, C. A. (2008). Mild traumatic brain injury in U.S. soldiers returning from Iraq. *New England Journal of Medicine*, *358*(5), 453–463.

Kennedy, J. E., Jaffee, M. S., Leskin, G. A., Stokes, J. W., Leal, F. O., & Fitzpatrick, P. J. (2007). Posttraumatic stress disorder and posttraumatic stress disorder-like symptoms and mild traumatic brain injury. *Journal of Rehabilitation Research and Development*, *44*(7), 895–920. doi:10.1682/JRRD.2006.12.0166

Lew, H. L., Jerger, J. F., Guillory, S. B., & Henry, J. A. (2007). Auditory dysfunction in traumatic brain injury. *Journal of Rehabilitation Research and Development*, *44*(7), 921–928. doi:10.1682/JRRD.2007.09.0140

Litz, B., & Orsillo, S. M. (2004). The returning veteran of the Iraq war: Background issues and assessment guidelines. In *Iraq war clinician guide* (2nd ed., pp. 21–32). Washington, DC: U.S. Department of Veterans Affairs, National Center for PTSD. Retrieved from www.ptsd.va.gov/professional/manuals/iraq-war-clinician-guide.asp

Miller, W. K., & Smith, J. (2011, January). *Student veterans with disabilities: Transition to higher education.* Paper presented at the Fides: Developing the Academic Promise for Our Student Veterans Workshop, Vermillion, SD.

National Survey of Student Engagement. (2010). *Major differences: Examining student engagement by field of study—Annual results 2010*. Bloomington: Indiana University, Center for Postsecondary Research.

Okie, S. (2005). Traumatic brain injury in the war zone. *New England Journal of Medicine, 352*(20), 2043–2047.

Radford, A. W., & Wun, J. (2009). *Issue tables: A profile of military service members and veterans enrolled in postsecondary education in 2007–08*. Retrieved from http://nces.ed.gov/pubs2009/2009182.pdf

Thatch, A. B., Johnson, A. J., Carroll, R. B., Huchun, A., Ainbinder, D. J., Stutzman, R. D., Blaydon, S. M., . . . Fannin, L. A. (2008). Severe eye injuries in the war in Iraq, 2003–2005. *Ophthalmology, 115*(2), 377–382.

University of Michigan–Flint. (2010). *For the returning war veteran*. Retrieved from http://beta-www.umflint.edu/studentveterans/for_the_returning_war_veteran.htm

Warden, D. (2006). Military TBI during the Iraq and Afghanistan wars. *Journal of Head Trauma Rehabilitation, 21*(5), 398–402.

14

WORKING EFFECTIVELY WITH PSYCHOLOGICALLY IMPAIRED FACULTY

Carolyn B. Oxenford, Marymount University

Sally L. Kuhlenschmidt, Western Kentucky University

More than one-fourth of all residents of the United States experience mental health disorders in any given year. Evidence suggests that faculty are more likely to suffer from psychological impairment than the general population. This chapter reviews evidence on faculty stress and impairment and helps faculty developers recognize signs that mental health issues may be affecting faculty performance. It also will help faculty developers understand legal issues in relation to faculty impairment and help them work effectively with colleagues who are coping with psychological impairments.

Based on the most recent National Comorbidity Survey Replication (Lacey, 2005), more than one-fourth of U.S. adults reported symptoms severe enough to constitute a diagnosable mental disorder during a given twelve-month period. Over half of those disorders were classified as serious or moderate, and thus likely to impair the individual's effective functioning. The same survey estimated that approximately half of Americans will experience symptoms of a diagnosable mental disorder over their lifetime. In a survey of faculty, Schwebel (2009) found that 20 to 25 percent of respondents experienced some form of mental illness at any given time.

Psychological distress appeared to be more common in academic staff than in the general population in an Australian study (Winefield, 2000). A sample of British academic staff self-reported higher levels of burnout, depression, and anxiety than the general population did (Kinman, 2001). Slightly over half of those assessed in this study were found to need mental health intervention. A recent *Chronicle of Higher Education* report indicated that 12 to 13 percent of U.S. college employees, including staff, who went on disability did so for mental health reasons, compared to 7 percent in other professions (Ruark, 2010).

Because this research suggests that faculty members are at least slightly more likely than the general population to experience psychological distress, faculty developers should expect to encounter colleagues whose mental health is having a negative impact on their performance. While many aspects of working with psychologically impaired colleagues are similar to other consultations, some unique situations need to be recognized and handled differently.

Stress and the Professorial Personality

Although university teaching has often been viewed as a low-stress job, recent research suggests increasing stress levels over the past three decades (Gillespie, Walsh, Winefield, Dua, & Stough, 2001). Studies of Australian academic staff suggest a marked increase in stress over a five-year period and found that academic staff experienced more stress and negative health effects due to stress than did nonacademic staff (Gillespie et al., 2001). Academic staff involved in both teaching and research experienced higher levels of stress than those who were engaged in only one of those functions (Winefield & Jarrett, 2001). Kinman (2001) found cognitive impairments, increased behavioral problems such as absenteeism and substance abuse, and physical and psychological symptoms associated with higher levels of stress in the United Kingdom. In the United States, Hogan, Carlson, and Dua (2002) found that stress correlated positively with behavioral, cognitive, and physiological symptoms and with negative emotionality.

A number of common sources of stress in academia were identified in these studies and others (Abouserie, 1996; Blix, Cruise, Mitchell, & Blix, 1994; Dua, 1994; Winefield et al., 2003):

- Increasing workloads and higher accountability demands
- Ambiguous tenure and promotion standards
- Increased competition for grants, publications, and positions
- High-stakes peer assessments and public criticism
- Unsupportive administrators and reduced autonomy
- Fiscal pressures, including reduced funding, salary freezes, furloughs, and delayed retirement

- For some, an expectation of independent work and sole authorship
- Increased research and publication pressures
- Increased work-home conflict due to work pressures

Some research suggests that individuals attracted to academic careers have characteristics that may exacerbate the effects of environmental stressors. In particular, faculty tend to be highly intelligent and prone to maladaptive perfectionism, defined as "punishing and unattainable standards that reflect an inadequate sense of self and that can lead to unyielding self-criticism and an inability to experience pleasure through normal accomplishments" (Dunn, Whelton, & Sharpe, 2006, p. 511).

Most studies have found stress levels to be highest in untenured and female faculty (Blix et al., 1994; Hogan et al., 2002; Winefield & Jarrett, 2001). No gender effect was found in a Welsh university sample (Abouserie, 1996); however, the lack of sample detail makes comparisons difficult. Machell (1988) described a debilitating sequence he called professional melancholia. This progressive deterioration of self-esteem and emotional health begins when young professors with unrealistic expectations of perfection and approval discover that they are no longer star students. Professional competition and inevitable rejections lead to increasing levels of hurt, resentment, and frustration. The faculty member begins to build a self-protective wall that leads to further loss of motivation, decreased scholarly interest, and lowered self-esteem. At its most extreme, professional melancholia can result in contempt for students and colleagues, deep alienation, elitism, and arrogance.

High continuing stress levels are associated with a variety of psychological symptoms in academic staff, including withdrawal, cynicism, burnout, dissatisfaction, and health complaints (Dua, 1994; Hogan et al., 2002; Winefield et al., 2003). Stress also can exacerbate underlying mental health disorders. Individuals with significant mental health issues usually show lowered creativity, problem-solving, decision-making, and concentration skills, and they are less productive and less accessible to students and colleagues (Boston University, n.d.).

Recognizing Mental Health Issues

A mental disorder is an extreme version of common behaviors. These behaviors reach the level of disorder when they actively interfere with a person's effectiveness or happiness (American Psychiatric Association, 1994). Professor A forgets to return papers but eventually does so and grades them appropriately. Students are annoyed but not harmed.

Professor B loses papers repeatedly and cannot recall conversations with students or colleagues. Grades are missing or seem randomly assigned. Students are upset, and departmental work is undone.

The boundary between eccentricity and disorder depends on environmental norms. Some university environments tolerate highly eccentric behavior. Faculty with mental health issues can continue to function, but their problems can become fairly severe before tolerance is exhausted. Other institutions or departments may tolerate very little eccentricity or view differences as weakness, leading to a loss of resources or respect for the faculty member, which has the effect of encouraging faculty to hide their problems. Due to their intelligence and creativity, faculty members can be good at adapting to their environments. Given time and support, they may resolve their own issues. They can also be good at hiding their problems and therefore not get the help they need.

In order to help psychologically impaired faculty, it is not necessary for a faculty developer to become a clinician, but it helps to be aware of behavior patterns that might signal mental health issues. The sections that follow offer a broad overview of behavioral signs for the most frequently diagnosed clusters of mental health disorders (American Psychiatric Association, 1994; Lacey, 2005). Individuals without mental health problems also display these behaviors, and at some level, most of them are reasonable responses to specific situations. Many of us find echoes of ourselves in the following list, but it is the particular combination of symptoms, their severity, and disrupted functioning that creates cause for concern. A faculty member showing many of the signs for one or more of these disorders should alert the faculty developer that referral to a mental health professional may be needed.

Anxiety Disorders

These include phobias, panic disorder, obsessive-compulsive disorder, and posttraumatic stress disorder (PTSD). Common symptoms are excessive worrying, repetitive behaviors, frequent illness, obvious tension and jumpiness, reluctance to change routines, and avoidance of certain situations. Rigid, moralistic, or perfectionist attitudes are common in some of these disorders. In the classroom, faculty may display excessive nervousness, overly detailed preparation that interferes with performance, a focus on perfection in their own and students' work, rigidity about class rules and routines, avoidance of activities (such as public speaking, night teaching, or participating in new initiatives), overreaction to plagiarism, or difficulty managing student problems calmly. High levels of structure and predictability help these individuals function, but change may trigger deterioration.

Mood Disorders

Mood disorders include major depression, dysthymia (mild, chronic depression), bipolar disorder, cyclothymia (persistent pattern of periods of elevated, expansive, or irritable mood alternating with periods of dysthymia), and seasonal affective disorder. Depressed individuals may show flat or sad affect, low energy, fatigue, concentration problems, hopelessness (sometimes including suicidal thoughts), altered eating or sleeping patterns, and loss of interest in pleasurable activities. For those who are bipolar, periods of depression alternate with periods of agitation, high energy, inflated self-esteem, distractibility, unrestrained behavior, and racing thoughts. Moods may swing rapidly or more slowly and vary in their extremity. At the most extreme ends, mood disorders may appear psychotic. Signs of faculty depression might include dismissing class early, missing meetings or classes, and failure to make progress on scholarship. Lack of concentration and organization is also likely. Manic individuals may dominate conversations excessively and make unrealistic promises. Creating grandiose plans that are never completed also characterizes individuals with manic disorders. Mild depression and mania may not meet full diagnostic criteria but are still disruptive. Depression also can accompany events such as the loss of a loved one or the loss of a source of self-esteem and gratification (such as stepping down from a prestigious position or health problems).

Impulse-Control Disorders

These include hostile outbursts out of proportion to the provocation. A faculty member may shout at students or throw papers or other objects. Impulse control problems also may be caused by brain trauma.

Substance-Related Disorders

These disorders are generally characterized by physical evidence of drug use, erratic and unreliable behavior, flimsy excuses, and disheveled appearance. Early signs may include missing classes, failure to remember conversations or to show up for scheduled obligations, and increasingly unconvincing excuses. These symptoms may alternatively signal depression or dementias such as Alzheimer's disease. Coming to class hung over or under the influence of psychoactive substances may indicate a deteriorating situation or a crisis.

Schizophrenia

Schizophrenia is characterized by the presence of odd or unusual symptoms such as hallucinations, delusions, paranoia, and bizarre behaviors or by the absence of appropriate emotional reactions, withdrawal from social contact, loss of motivation, and failure to maintain personal hygiene. A faculty member with schizophrenia may be disorganized and difficult to follow in lecture or conversation. In particular, he or she may not be connecting explanations from one concept to the next, or they may be extremely obscure. The individual may have difficulty recognizing and responding to others' emotional states, may comment on experiences that seem to have no basis in reality, or may withdraw from people entirely. Symptoms may worsen during stressful periods of the semester or at times of change and transition.

Dementias

A dementia such as Alzheimer's disease is usually first noticeable due to increasing forgetfulness, particularly for recent memories. The individuals may react to forgetting with anger or denial. In class, these individuals may repeat themselves, forget to complete tasks, or lose student work. High levels of structure and stability will help those with dementia maintain their functioning, but changes in the environment are difficult for them to manage. Some organic brain disorders show similar behavioral patterns.

Brain Trauma

These traumas, often caused by strokes or accidents, can present very differently depending on the location of the damage. Common problems include poor impulse control, shortened attention span, and behavioral inconsistencies. Blackouts and abrupt changes in handwriting or other motor skills, particularly on only one side of the body, may indicate stroke. The individual may experience depression as a side effect of the damaged brain function or as a result of awareness of the loss of functioning. Brain trauma can be particularly difficult to manage in an academic environment since typical academic work requires high-level cognitive processing that even mild impairment can disrupt. Faculty may show distractibility, angry outbursts, inappropriate sexual behaviors not present prior to the trauma, or a lack of efficiency. Abilities may fluctuate noticeably, with one stack of papers completed correctly, while the other remains undone. Apparently stubborn or uncooperative behaviors may reflect difficulty handling change or the need for a simplified environment.

Developmental Disorders

This category includes learning disabilities, attention deficit/hyperactivity disorder (ADHD), and Asperger's syndrome.

Faculty with learning disabilities have an area of academic functioning that is significantly below their other capacities. An instructor with a learning disability in math may resist numerical grading schemes, and one with a written language disability may avoid assigning papers or serving on committees that require intensive reading and writing. An instructor with ADHD may have great difficulty organizing or finishing work, grading papers, or monitoring students. They may seem to daydream at inappropriate times.

Those with Asperger's syndrome have difficulty interpreting others' behaviors, especially in emotional situations. Many have a narrow but intense intellectual focus that lends itself to specialization in highly technical fields. Individuals with Asperger's may avoid eye contact, have difficulty with conversational exchanges (tending to dominate the conversation), and trouble filtering comments. They may be highly sensitive to sensory stimuli (light, sound, touch) and generally are rule bound. These individuals may need extensive coaching to understand the emotional communications in classroom discussions and engage in long classroom monologues. They may irritate colleagues with their rule-bound, rigid, and pedantic style.

This brief summary of mental health disorders and their possible ramifications is not meant to be exhaustive. Consider an anonymous consultation with a mental health professional to gain additional information specific to an individual case.

If there is reason to believe that a faculty member's job difficulty has a significant mental health component, what is the next step?

Faculty Mental Health and the Role of the Faculty Developer

When faculty mental health issues begin to affect the campus environment, there are several important roles that faculty developers may be called on to perform. These include educating faculty and other members of the campus community about the potential impact of mental health issues on teaching and learning; recognizing instances when mental health issues may be affecting the learning environment and helping to develop plans to cope with those instances; and consulting with appropriate campus offices to make sure that policies and procedures support both the impaired faculty and stakeholders such as colleagues and students.

Prevention and Education

There are several steps faculty developers can take to build healthy campus awareness of mental health situations among faculty, staff, and students. These are particularly useful for prevention and education:

- Develop policies and procedures before there is a crisis. Many campuses have no clear guidelines for handling a mental health emergency. Faculty developers may be in the best position to bring together human resources, the disability services officer, faculty affairs, counseling staff, legal counsel, and the campus police to develop policies and working relationships.

- Develop or locate resources that can be sent out when a trauma occurs—for example, "Tragedy in the College Classroom" (www.wku.edu/teaching/booklets/tragedy.htm), "Teaching and Learning in a Time of Crisis" (www.wku.edu/teaching/booklets/crisis.html), or "Stressed for Success!" (www.wku.edu/teaching/booklets/stress.htm). Although ostensibly these materials are for faculty who are dealing with problem students, they can also inform and support faculty who struggle with mental health issues. Similarly, holding a seminar for faculty on safety in the classroom or student mental health disabilities can serve a dual function.

- Identify stressful points during the semester that may be particularly difficult for faculty with mental health issues and provide programming or other support open to all faculty, such as seminars on coping with student complaints right before midterms. Career transition programming and general stress management sessions also can be helpful.

When Problems Occur

Faculty developers may become aware of colleagues' mental health issues in several ways. Classroom problems can be an early manifestation of mental health issues and result in referral to the faculty developer. Or the faculty member may self-refer as a way to cope without acknowledging mental health concerns. Even if classroom problems have not emerged, the faculty developer may suspect mental health issues during routine interactions with the person or through grapevine comments from students or colleagues. Finally, faculty members may self-disclose mental health problems during consultations. Faculty members may trust the faculty developer more than their departmental colleagues, chairpersons, or deans since developers likely have no formal evaluative role. In addition, the typical confidentiality of the developer-faculty relationship can increase faculty willingness to self-disclose.

Given the likelihood of encountering faculty who are experiencing mental health issues, advance thought about if, when, and how to intervene is wise. What are the boundaries of practice for faculty developers who suspect mental health issues? What steps should faculty developers consider taking to best help everyone involved?

Establishing Boundaries and the Limits of Confidentiality

It is vitally important to understand the boundaries of the faculty developer role. Most faculty developers are not mental health professionals, and those who are cannot function ethically as therapists or psychodiagnostic experts with colleagues. We are educational experts. Unlike therapists or clergy, our confidentiality claims have no legal basis. Describing the limits of confidentiality can help both faculty and faculty developers understand the boundaries of their relationship. (See "Discussing Confidentiality in Faculty Development Settings" for sample language for a confidentiality discussion.)

Understanding the Americans with Disabilities Act

Faculty developers who are working in the United States should review the policies and procedures in place at their institution for compliance with the Americans with Disabilities Act (ADA) before proceeding. The ADA exists to prevent discrimination against disabled individuals in hiring and job performance, and many mental health disorders can be covered under ADA. Having a general understanding of ADA will help protect all parties involved.

If a faculty member has an eligible mental health disability and can perform essential job functions, then ADA requires the university to accommodate the disability unless the accommodation causes an undue hardship to the employer or the employee's behavior creates a

Discussing Confidentiality in Faculty Development Settings

Whether and when to address confidentiality issues is a risk management question for faculty developers. If someone wants to know about getting funding or how to get teams to function better, it's probably not necessary. However, if the consultation is likely to be sensitive (for example, if the individual is upset because of poor course evaluations or referred by the department head), consider discussing the limits of the relationship between faculty member and faculty developer verbally or in writing. What follows could be used to create a verbal script or a written document. If you prefer a verbal discussion, document when the conversation occurred and what was said. With either format, make sure that the faculty member's questions and concerns are discussed. Here is a sample script:

> Before we get started, I want to briefly discuss confidentiality with you so you understand the conditions under which we operate and so you can choose what to say and how much. Unlike a therapist or clergy, in this setting, we don't have any legal protections. So far, the administration has respected the limits when I say to them that I don't share information about our consultations. So we have some reasonable expectation of confidentiality based on past history. However, there are some situations in which confidentiality could be broken. The most important situation is if you say you are going to hurt yourself or someone else. In that case, I would work with you to keep everyone safe, and that could include talking with other responsible parties. The other condition in which confidentiality cannot be upheld is if I get a properly worded court order to release documents. This could happen if there were some personnel action, for example, if you sued the university.

In some states, a court order has to be properly worded (that is, setting out specific dates and naming the specific types of documents). Your situation may be different, however, so you should check with legal counsel to determine relevant laws.

When discussing confidentiality issues, strive for calm and reassuring body language, and be alert to signs of discomfort. Don't treat the situation as a joke, but help the faculty member understand that this is a necessary procedure for his or her protection. If the faculty member cannot work under these circumstances, offer to end the session and suggest options, such as a trusted friend or a professional.

direct threat to themselves or others. The ADA can support a faculty member who needs reasonable adjustments but is having trouble getting administrative cooperation. To claim ADA protection, faculty must disclose their disability to the university. While they may choose not to disclose their status for valid reasons, including fear of stigmatization and loss of privacy, they should be aware of what they are giving up in making that choice.

If a faculty member does not disclose a disability but the faculty developer suspects one is causing job-related problems, it is important to be cautious about labeling the faculty member. Suggesting to a faculty member that he or she has bipolar disorder or PTSD would be considered labeling and could open the faculty developer and the university to discrimination complaints and litigation. Taking a descriptive, behaviorally focused approach is more useful and does not carry this risk.

Lee and Ruger (2003) provide an excellent overview of ADA issues in university settings. Always discuss the specific policies and procedures in place at your institution with ADA personnel so you can deal effectively with any at-risk faculty.

Assessing the Situation and Determining Dangerousness

In any faculty consultation, evaluation comes first. Those who are working with psychologically impaired faculty should consider the following specific questions to address, including the potential danger of the situation and the appropriate level of intervention:

1. Ascertain the faculty member's behaviors and behavioral patterns as concretely as possible. When is the situation occurring? At the start, middle, or end of class? At meetings? With whom is the problem behavior occurring? Students only? Colleagues only? Everyone all the time? What might be triggering or encouraging the behavior?

2. How intense is the behavior? Who is bothered by it? How upset is the person? This may be hard to ascertain if the faculty member is unconcerned about or unaware of the impact he or she has on others.

3. Is there any danger to students, to colleagues, or to the faculty member himself or herself? This is an anxiety-provoking possibility for many faculty developers. If the assessment process suggests possible danger, these are the steps that should be taken:
   - Prepare for the possibility. Talk to appropriate campus officials to decide on a protocol before action is required. This conversation

will likely include participation by the university legal counsel. Also consider involving the institution's employee assistance program, campus mental health professionals, the human resource department, supervisors, or the campus or community police in formulating a plan. This process will also educate you as to how best to work with these individuals if a problem arises, and when to refer them.

- If a faculty member appears to be a potential threat to self or others, do not avoid the issue. Calm, nonjudgmental honesty is the best route. Clearly state the behaviors or comments that are causing concern and encourage the individual to talk—for example, "I'm really worried about you. You seem so down when we talk, and your comments about not being around next semester concern me. I'm worried that you are thinking about hurting yourself. Are you?" With potentially suicidal individuals, a rough estimate of lethality is the level of detailed planning. An individual who vaguely refers to "not being around" is less likely to cause self-harm than someone who has purchased a gun and ammunition. Although both individuals are at risk, immediate steps should be taken to ensure the safety of the second individual such as taking him or her to the hospital or arranging for a family member or professional to do so. A person who says, "I'm so mad at that guy," is of less concern than one who admits to stalking or has planned other threatening behaviors. If the level of concern is low, try to refer the person for treatment. Empathetically repeat what he or she has said about the distress, and reinforce the idea that seeking expert advice for problems is a wise course that can help relieve personal distress.

- If the person does not seek treatment or you are concerned about possible dangerous behavior, it may be time to reach out to other campus resources. One way to do this is to meet jointly with the department chairperson, dean, or other appropriate supervisor; the faculty member; and a counselor if possible. Ideally the faculty developer will be present at this meeting because people are known to change their statements in the presence of others. If the faculty member alters or denies earlier statements, the faculty developer can repeat nondefensively what was said and describe the behavioral indicators that triggered the meeting. Typically those who are in distress are appreciative when someone notices and reaches out with respect. Sometimes the faculty member may become angry or alienated, but at this point, safety has to be the main concern and justification for action.

- In rare situations there may be an urgent and strongly credible threat of danger—for example, if the person has a weapon with him or her. In this case, contacting the police and protecting yourself and others without escalating the emotional situation is the priority.

Giving Feedback and Cocreating an Action Plan

Once the faculty developer has assessed the situation and determined that dangerous behavior is not an issue, the faculty member can benefit from feedback that focuses on specific, observable behaviors that are having a negative impact in the workplace—for example, "I noticed in the classroom that when a student asked a question, you answered it, but your tone of voice seemed stern to me, and you then commented about laziness. How do you think the students responded?" Stay away from "you" comments that are based on personality judgments, such as, "You're rude to students." Describing problem behaviors and discussing how to change either the behaviors or the situation allows the faculty developer to avoid labeling while at the same time recognizing and addressing the problem. A videotape of a class session may provide the most objective feedback, but may be difficult for the faculty member to view. Once the issues of concern have been jointly identified and accepted, the discussion can move to possible interventions. Whether or not the individual has acknowledged the presence of a disorder, identifying specific behaviors that are problematic for the person's success on the job can lead to productive discussions about how to change those behaviors. What would be an acceptable outcome for this situation? Is it realistic? Does the faculty member also perceive this outcome as acceptable?

So far, the approach outlined here is common to many consultations. However, several issues are more likely to arise with an underlying mental health component to a problem:

- The individual may request a referral for psychological help. Being prepared to make such referrals can reassure the faculty member that others do not find their situation unusually troubling. Talk with the campus employee assistance program, counseling center, or other mental health professionals to obtain local referral options.

- The individual may say he or she will make a change and then does not or cannot. Now the discussion shifts to what is preventing the faculty member from making productive changes. This conversation may well lead to acknowledgment of deeper issues that the faculty member needs to address, perhaps in treatment. Another outcome might be recognition that the job requirements are too much for the faculty member to handle at this time. The faculty developer can help plan a coping strategy—for example, requesting a temporary leave or course reduction, finding another type of position, or requesting ADA-based accommodations.

- The individual may show dramatic fluctuations in behavior or signs of deterioration, increased distress, or potential threat to self or others. At this point, it may be beyond the faculty developer's role to continue to work with the individual. Recognizing the downhill trend, stepping aside from the situation, and making appropriate referrals may be the most effective steps.

Keeping Appropriate Records

Documenting the discussions and decisions of a faculty consultation is good practice in any case, but documentation is particularly important when dealing with the sensitive situations that can arise when mental health issues are involved. Following these guidelines will result in accurate, helpful, and legally sound records:

- Record and date notes on the same day the interaction occurred. Records that were made days or weeks later are less reliable and less useful if a situation does become litigious.

- Describe observable behaviors, actions, and comments, and avoid commentary. If someone cried, note that but do not label the person as "depressed." If someone says he has PTSD, write, "John said he had PTSD," rather than, "John has PTSD," so it is clear who is making this attribution.

- Do not include information that is not relevant to the matter at hand. Always write as if these notes might end up on the Internet or in a court of law. Keep personal opinions private.

- Document all recommendations. This is particularly important if it becomes necessary to demonstrate that appropriate actions were taken.

- If there is a potential risk of danger to anyone, record the reasons for believing this, stressing the behaviors and statements that led to this conclusion, and describe the preventive steps that were taken—for example, "John stated that he has a gun at home and sometimes loads it. I walked him to the counseling center."

- Reread your notes. Have you said just enough to convey what happened objectively but not elaborated beyond that standard? If so, then sign or initial them directly below the last sentence to document their authenticity.

Working with psychologically impaired faculty is something that faculty developers are already doing, perhaps without realizing it. By becoming aware of the signs and symptoms of distress, we have the opportunity to intervene and refer in meaningful ways that will result in faculty getting the support they need, and students getting the quality educational experiences they expect.

REFERENCES

Abouserie, R. (1996). Stress, coping strategies and job satisfaction in university academic staff. *Educational Psychology, 16*(1), 49–56. doi:10.1080/0144341960160104

American Psychiatric Association. (1994). *Diagnostic and statistical manual of mental disorders* (4th ed.). Washington, DC: Author.

Blix, A. G., Cruise, R. J., Mitchell, B. M., & Blix, G. G. (1994). Occupational stress among university teachers. *Educational Research, 36*(2), 157–169.

Boston University, Center for Psychiatric Rehabilitation. (n.d.). *How does mental illness interfere with work performance?* Retrieved from www.bu.edu/cpr/reasaccom/employ-func.html

Dua, J. K. (1994). Job stressors and their effects on physical health, emotional health, and job satisfaction in a university. *Journal of Educational Administration, 32*(1), 59–78.

Dunn, J. C., Whelton, W. J., & Sharpe, D. (2006). Maladaptive perfectionism, hassles, coping, and psychological distress in university professors. *Journal of Counseling Psychology, 53*(4), 511–523.

Gillespie, N. A., Walsh, M., Winefield, A. H., Dua, J., & Stough, C. (2001). Occupational stress in universities: Staff perceptions of the causes, consequences and moderators of stress. *Work and Stress, 15*(1), 53–72. doi:10.1080/02678370117944

Hogan, J. M., Carlson, J. G., & Dua, J. (2002). Stressors and stress reactions among university personnel. *International Journal of Stress Management, 9*(4), 289–310. doi:10.1023/A:1019982316327

Kinman, G. (2001). Pressure points: A review of research on stressors and strains in UK academics. *Educational Psychology, 21*(4), 473–492. doi:10.1080/01443410120090849

Lacey, J. (2005). *Prevalence and severity of mental illness in the United States* [Press release]. Retrieved from www.eurekalert.org/pub_releases/2005–06/jaaj-pas060205.php

Lee, B. A., & Ruger, P. R. (2003). *Accommodating faculty and staff with psychiatric disabilities.* Washington, DC: National Association of College and University Attorneys.

Machell, D. F. (1988). *A discourse on professorial melancholia.* Retrieved from ERIC database. (ED304063)

Ruark, J. (2010, February 16). In academe, mental health issues are hard to recognize and hard to treat. *Chronicle of Higher Education.* Retrieved from http://chronicle.com/article/In-Academe-Mental-Health-I/64246/

Schwebel, D. (2009). Impaired faculty: Helping academics who are suffering from serious mental illness. *Academic Leadership: The Online Journal, 7*(2). Retrieved from www.academicleadership.org/article/impaired-faculty-helping-academics-who-are-suffering-from-serious-mental-illness

Winefield, A. H. (2000). Stress in academe: Some recent research findings. In D. Kenny, J. Carlson, F. McGuigan, & J. Sheppard (Eds.), *Stress and health: Research and clinical applications* (pp. 437–446). Amsterdam, Netherlands: Harwood Academic.

Winefield, A. H., Gillespie, N., Stough, C., Dua, J., Hapuarachchi, J., & Boyd, C. (2003). Occupational stress in Australian university staff: Results from a national survey. *International Journal of Stress Management, 10*(1), 51–63. doi:10.1037/1072-5245.10.1.51

Winefield, A. H., & Jarrett, R. J. (2001). Occupational stress in university staff. *International Journal of Stress Management, 8*(4), 285–298.

15

NEXT GENERATION @ IUPUI

A LEADERSHIP DEVELOPMENT PROGRAM FOR
FACULTY OF COLOR

Megan M. Palmer, Julianna V. Banks, Joshua S. Smith, Sherree A. Wilson, Indiana University–Purdue University Indianapolis

Next Generation @ IUPUI is an intensive one-year leadership program designed to develop the leadership potential of faculty of color. The program expands the pool of faculty who are ready to assume leadership positions. In addition to addressing higher education administration theories and trends, participants receive individualized coaching and mentoring to develop a broad network of peers.

Since the civil rights movement, universities have made efforts to diversify their student bodies, faculty, and administration. While student bodies have become increasingly diverse by race, ethnicity, and gender (Kuh, 2006; Rankin & Reason, 2005) and more minorities and women have entered the academy (Dailey-Hebert, Donnelli, & Mandernach, 2010; Thompson, 2008; Trower, 2009), faculty and administrators have remained disproportionately white and male (Antonio, 2003; Jayakumar, Howard, Allen, & Han, 2009; Villalpando & Delgado Bernal, 2002). Nationally, underrepresented faculty make up only 16 percent of the full-time professoriate (National Center for Education Statistics, 2008). Furthermore, only 5.3 percent of full professors are African American, Hispanic American, or Native American (Ryu, 2008; Thompson, 2008).

The path to leadership for faculty from underrepresented populations is difficult (Schuster & Finkelstein, 2006). Increasing pressure to publish,

---

For a fuller description of the Next Gen program and an outline of the curriculum, contact the authors.

teach heavy course loads, adopt new pedagogies, meet tenure and promotion standards, and assume heavy service commitments dissuade many from pursuing leadership positions. For some faculty, the tension between work and life has resulted in decisions to seek alternative positions or leave altogether (Rosser, 2004).

Indiana University–Purdue University Indianapolis (IUPUI) aspires to exceed peer institutions in its representation of gender and underserved minorities in its faculty and staff. The university's 2009 State of Diversity Report ranked the institution's performance on this goal as "unacceptable . . . but likely to improve in 1–2 years" (IUPUI Diversity Cabinet, 2009, p. 12). However, unless university administrators address barriers and avoid overly broad solutions, the diversity of the student and faculty bodies will continue to fall below expectations.

In an effort to counteract several of the barriers already noted, accelerate the development of faculty from underserved populations, and expand the pool of faculty who are ready to assume leadership positions, the Indiana University School of Medicine's Office of Faculty Affairs and Professional Development (OFAPD) launched the Next Generation @ IUPUI program (Next Gen). The program is designed to provide professional development with special emphasis on leadership, self-awareness, communication, institutional change, and career planning. It specifically examines higher education administration theories, trends, and best practices; provides individualized coaching and mentoring; and creates opportunities to expand professional networks across the campus. Although all faculty may benefit from this type of leadership program, the demands and struggles that faculty of color face make this an especially important matter.

Literature Review

Diverse faculty benefit college campuses by providing support to students from diverse backgrounds (Allen, Eby, & Lentz, 2006; Villalpando & Delgado Bernal, 2002); symbolizing the interest that institutions have in diverse populations; creating role models for increasingly diverse student populations (Allen et al., 2006); broadening epistemological frameworks; developing opportunities for collaboration; and ensuring that faculty are actively engaged in institutional change (Jayakumar et al., 2009; Thomas, 2001). Despite these benefits and the changing demographics of those earning the doctorate, leadership in American higher education lacks diversity.

Chilly Climates

The climate, culture, and collegiality that faculty encounter on entering academe are principal determinants of their capacity to excel as scholars and leaders (Trower, 2009). Studies show that many underrepresented faculty exit the academy prior to tenure decisions due to an array of campus climate issues (Bach & Sorcinelli, 2010; Griffin, 2008; Maher & Thompson Tetreault, 2007; Stanley, 2006; Suh, 2008; Thompson, 2008). These include limited opportunities to participate in decision making; excessive teaching, service, and committee assignments; limited access to leadership appointments; marginalization or devaluation of scholarship; lack of mentors; and limited guidance on professional expectations, networking, and promotion and tenure processes (Griffin, 2008; Jayakumar et al., 2009; Turner, 2002; Yoshinaga-Itano, 2006).

The limited representation of diverse faculty in academia influences policies, procedures, and expectations, and it perpetuates a climate that impedes the development of future diverse leaders. The intersection of race and gender compounds pressures for female faculty of color (Hollenshead & Thomas, 2001; Turner, 2002). Similarly, minority faculty encounter challenges when other faculty devalue their scholarship by virtue of outlets or topics of inquiry. The subsequent isolation of minority faculty further excludes them from information and support that are important in acquiring resources and securing opportunities for leadership and career advancement (Aguirre, 2000; Thompson, 2008).

Mentoring Underrepresented Faculty

Mentoring and leadership programs mitigate the negative impacts of campus climate and improve professional outlook and career outcomes. Benefits of mentoring are prominent throughout the career development literature (Allen, Eby, Poteet, Lentz, & Lima, 2004; Spencer & Tribe, 2004; Wasburn, 2007) highlighting the importance of mentoring in the academic profession as it is the means by which faculty are socialized into and become familiar with organizational structures and culture (Casto, Caldwell, & Salazar, 2005; Fayne & Ortquist-Ahrens, 2006; Kirchmeyer, 2005; Snelson et al., 2002). Mentoring has the capacity to increase scholarly productivity (Mundt, 2001), faculty retention (Lottero-Perdue & Fifield, 2010), and faculty diversity (Davidson & Foster-Johnson, 2001) and may also help minority faculty manage and challenge inequality in academia (Green & King, 2001; Moody, 2004). Instead, mentoring can empower faculty to serve as change agents within the institution (Angelique, Kyle, & Taylor, 2002; Lottero-Perdue & Fifield, 2010).

Faculty benefit from engaging multiple mentors (Dixon-Reeves, 2003; King & Cubic, 2005; Packard, Walsh, & Seidenberg, 2004). Such models are based on Higgins and Kram's (2001) concept of mentoring as a developmental network and are deliberately designed for women and minorities and employ "peer mentoring to deemphasize [power differences] (McGuire & Reger, 2003) . . . or [to construct] empathetic communities of support (Chelser & Chelser, 2002; Green & King, 2002)" (Lottero-Perdue & Fifield, 2010, p. 45).

Developing Faculty Leaders

Academe has traditionally devoted little effort to selecting leaders, chairs, and deans and spends even less time preparing them for the responsibilities they assume (Carroll & Wolverton, 2004; Meyer & Kaloyeros, 2005; Wolverton & Ackerman, 2006). In fact, in national surveys between 1990 and 2000, only 3 percent of more than two thousand academic leaders reported they had any type of leadership training or preparation (Gmelch, 2000).

Many institutions appoint department leaders based on the assumption that if a faculty member performs well in the faculty role, then he or she will perform well (or at least well enough) as a leader (Wolverton & Ackerman, 2006). But the skill sets required for research or instruction and those necessary for leadership are, with few exceptions, different. Teaching and research are generally conducted in isolation or within small clusters of like-minded faculty who thrive on autonomy (Wolverton & Ackerman, 2006). In contrast, effective leading is a collective venture. Communication, interpersonal skills, and rapid but thoughtful response are among the skills required of leaders and administrators. Although management tasks such as budgeting and conflict resolution can be learned fairly quickly (Hecht, 2004; Thomas & Schuh, 2004), leadership skills such as the ability to anticipate needs, plan strategically, and develop vision are more challenging to acquire, require significantly more time, and are rarely examined in faculty development (Thomas & Schuh, 2004; Wolverton & Ackerman, 2006).

Typical faculty development programs comprise a series of workshops that provide exposure to educational principles or instructional strategies with opportunities to apply and practice skills. Such programs are narrow in scope and limited in duration, and they tend to address immediate self-efficacy, teaching improvement, and curriculum development (Gruppen, Frohna, Anderson, & Lowe, 2003). Short-term workshops may be less effective in promoting educational leadership among faculty because of their limited scope. More innovative formats linking extended workshops to programs that target a broader range of leadership issues and outcomes are encouraged in preparing faculty for active roles in leadership and governance (Gruppen et al., 2003).

There are emerging and successful leadership development programs for faculty (see, for example, Michigan State University's Academic Leadership Program, http://fod.msu.edu/Leadership/about.asp). However, because underrepresented faculty play vital roles in an institution's education, research, and service functions, campus leaders and faculty developers must recognize that in order to achieve excellence in each of these areas, they must develop and draw on the intellectual vitality and innovation that come from a racially and ethnically diverse professoriate (Moreno, Smith, Clayton-Pederson, Parker, & Teraguchi, 2006). Given the current state of affairs, OFAPD launched the Next Gen program.

The Next Gen Program

The Next Gen Program was founded at an urban university with more than twenty-five hundred faculty in over twenty schools and two hundred degree-granting programs. The campus is home to several nationally ranked programs and is distinguished by its commitment to research, service, and civic engagement. Over the course of the one-year program, the founding cohort provided information and feedback on the impact of program participation.

Participants

All faculty of color on campus were invited to submit applications (personal statement, letter of support, curriculum vitae) to participate in the 2009–2010 program. Of the approximately sixty applications received, members of the Next Gen advisory board reviewed and selected five male and nine female faculty members representing three American minority groups: three African or African American, six Latino/a, and six Asian or Asian American. Other program participants hailed from India, China, Burma, Argentina, Mexico, Brazil, and Puerto Rico.

Faculty from the United States of Chinese and African American descent also participated. The schools of medicine, dentistry, engineering, health, informatics, law, liberal arts, and physical education were represented. Some participants were relatively junior faculty without much formal leadership experience, while two others were about to take on the role of department chair.

Assessment

A semistructured interview was conducted with each participant early in the program and again at the end of the one-year experience to develop a rich understanding of the cohort group, including challenges that impede promotion to leadership positions. Sample questions included, "What are your expectations for this experience, or rather, what do you expect to gain professionally and personally?" and, "How will this prepare you to become a leader in your field?" The follow-up interviews conducted at the end of the program assessed participant perspectives of the program's impact and gathered feedback on the utility of the curriculum, resources, opportunities, and support provided.

To evaluate the program's format, structure, curriculum, and group dynamics, observations of each workshop session were conducted by the third author. He was part of the advisory board that reviewed applications and oversaw the implementation of the program. Following each workshop, he reflected on his experience and the interaction that participants had with one another and the workshop facilitators.

Data Analysis

The data analysis procedure was guided by the constant comparative method (Glaser & Strauss, 1967), which involved sorting individual units of data and then grouping and categorizing them into more general conceptual themes. The initial coding scheme followed an open coding model that loosely corresponded to the overarching questions in the two interview protocols. Observation field notes were coded separately and then combined with emerging interview themes where appropriate.

Outcomes

A strong bond among faculty emerged early in the Next Gen program, and although participants came from different disciplines and had diverse leadership experiences and years of service, personal connections and a shared commitment to support one another were evident in the passionate disclosures of concerns and accomplishments. Participants were genuinely enthusiastic about the program and entered with a desire to increase their leadership skills and gain awareness of their own strengths and weaknesses. Participants identified people skills, including oral communication and how to deal with conflict, as intended outcomes of the program, along with a desire to obtain knowledge of leadership opportunities at the university and network with faculty who experienced similar challenges. Despite the fact that the participants were part of a leadership program, associate and full professors alike consistently stated that they had no intention of seeking higher posts and noted their distaste for the politics, bureaucracy, and the limitations formal leadership posts had on scholarly production.

Early in the program, the general feeling was that leadership was associated with formal administrative roles that often required an abundance of meetings, responding to university-wide demands, and being pulled away from the day-to-day functions of a faculty member. These perceptions were complicated by specific barriers faculty faced as they considered their current and future roles within the university. Participants described significant challenges in their respective fields, including a lack of time, racial and gender discrimination, and unrealistic role expectations.

All of the Next Gen participants consistently commented on service to other students and faculty of color in their departments and schools and across the university. One African American woman stated, "I think the biggest barrier for faculty of color is we tend to get involved and do a lot of service. . . . A lot of committees . . . need 'representation.' They ask us." During program discussions, the "they" often referred to were university administrators who would contact faculty of color and "invite" them to be on a committee, chair a committee, or advise a student group. The pressure of the invitation was subtle, but the entire group felt that saying no would not bode well for them. In addition to the committee work, participants spoke of countless hours supporting, advising, and mentoring other faculty and students of color. There was consensus that although recognition for committee work was nominal, mentoring students and faculty was not viewed favorably. However, there was an overwhelming sense that it was important to give back. All participants reported that time pressure and role expectations contributed to their decisions not to pursue formal and informal leadership roles on campus.

Personal accounts of racial and gender discrimination involving administrators, peers, and students surfaced in more than half of the interviews. Several participants reported that they had not personally experienced racial or gender discrimination as a barrier but thought they were "lucky" or the "exception." Issues of race and gender were included in curricular materials, incorporated into presentations, or brought up by individual participants.

Although feedback regarding the program was overwhelmingly positive, only a few participants thought the Next Gen program would have a direct impact on barriers that minority faculty face. As one faculty member put it, "It is not going to change the barriers, because it is people [current leaders] who are the barriers. They either don't know what this program is doing, or they are against it." Others echoed this sentiment but acknowledged the potential for the program to diminish some of the obstacles to promotion and tenure. "Opportunities are there; we just don't know how to go and get them," explained one participant, who went on to say that the program helped remove a barrier by exposing minority faculty to the system and the positions available throughout the institution. Another participant indicated that the program itself constituted recognition on the part of the university that minority faculty and "their contributions to the university are things that are valued." She suggested that this may inspire minority faculty to take on more challenging positions.

Specific benefits associated with participating in the program included expansion of professional networks, applied skills, latent knowledge, and preparation and access to leadership positions. Participants established positive connections with other program members, their mentors, and program coordinators. Many indicated that they had a better understanding of the upper levels of the system. One participant noted, "I have been exposed to some of the people in administration that I would not normally have been exposed to." Newly acquired knowledge clarified misconceptions about the roles of executive administrators and access to such positions. Several participants appeared more open to leadership positions as a result of their participation in the program. One participant insisted that being an administrator "was the furthest away from what I ever want to do. Then when I agreed to come to the program, I was on the fence. My program participation helped me understand what an administrator does and doesn't do. I understand what the opportunities for administration are on campus."

Throughout the sessions, the observer noted that faculty were reticent about aspirations to high-level positions of leadership. When asked by a guest speaker what their dream position was, the vast majority cited their current role or earning the next tenure rank within the same unit. Explanations for the rather conservative aspirations of these exemplary faculty members included that they were comfortable in their positions or did not fully trust the fact that these opportunities are a reality for faculty of color.

By the end of the program, three participants had already accepted new committee or council appointments, directorships, and advanced teaching positions. For other participants, the Next Gen program had a clear impact on their decisions to assume leadership positions. One participant, who was "very hesitant" to accept a chair position, admitted that had it not been for the program, he might not have accepted. Others indicated that the program helped them become more confident and settled in their current leadership roles.

Most participants applied skills learned in the Next Gen workshop sessions, reporting that they were improving time management, opening communication with colleagues, building teams in their current positions, using a strengths-based approach, and learning to be more selective about research and service opportunities. In the area of communication, they developed an understanding of the perspectives of others and improved their ability to collaborate with diverse groups. One participant noted, "It also helped me understand better who I am and how I operate." Another participant likened academia to a "wheel where we just keep running without ever kind of having the chance to stop" and valued the program for providing time to "come up with a plan."

Although not all faculty identified specific ways they had applied the lessons gleaned from the workshop sessions, over two-thirds suggested that the knowledge, though currently lying dormant, would be "converted into actions in the future." One participant summed this up by saying, "Now I am armed with knowledge," while another indicated that she now had "an arsenal." Another participant described the program as an aha! moment because it forced her to realize that if she wanted to become a leader, she needed a plan. "If you are going to be wishy-washy about the whole thing," she said, "you are going to go nowhere. If you are going to do it, what is your plan?" The Next Gen program was a call to action that provided the space to map out a future in leadership and the tools to complete the job successfully.

Committing time to the program meant cutting out other work. However, all of the participants indicated that they felt the sacrifice was worthwhile. Absences from workshops were rare and attributed only to faculty illness or previously scheduled conferences. This reflects the personal drive and responsibility of the faculty, but also the fact that the Next Gen curriculum required active participation that was meaningful, timely, and engaging.

Participants had mixed feelings about the impact of the mentoring aspect of the program. Two participants never established working relationships with their mentors, while others met regularly and found the mentoring relationship extremely useful. One positive experience was described this way: "Without my mentoring sessions, I don't know where I would be. I just have great mentors. They really take the time . . . keep me on task. They respond quickly and directly, and they will tell me I am not going to help you because you should do this yourself. Or they will tell me, 'Here are the steps you need to take before I can help you.'" Several maintained strong mentoring relationships throughout the program, and a few others never found a successful match. Implicit in their comments about mentoring was the idea that a good mentor could meet regularly, provide honest feedback, help solve problems, and connect their mentees to other people and resources.

Discussion

The findings suggest that participation in the Next Gen program leads to increased interest in seeking leadership among program participants and confidence to be successful in these positions. As we continue to follow participants, we will be able to better ascertain if participation in the program helps the institution develop a culture that embraces diversity and one in which leaders are chosen from a wider range of races and cultures. Given the diverse population of students in colleges and universities, we must strive to ensure that leadership in American higher education reflects the diversity of the student body and communities where they are located.

IUPUI has an opportunity to cultivate emerging leaders for the campus specifically and higher education in general. The first cohort of the Next Gen program was diverse, not only in race, ethnicity, and gender, but also in terms of academic discipline. Since leadership can take many forms and does not have to be defined or determined solely based on position title, we recommend that campus administration consider how the expertise of the cohort members can benefit the institution. It is entirely possible to be engaged in leadership development in rather informal ways such as chairing campuswide or search committees; serving on campus teams in national workshops or institutes; asking the faculty to read, write, and provide commentary on issues of relevance to the campus; serving on review or accreditation teams; or seeking input from faculty regarding policy deliberations. If we expect to develop faculty of color and diversify leadership, our focus must be on cultivating a welcoming climate that fosters full participation from its members.

The early impact of the Next Gen program is promising. If similar programs were adopted at other colleges and universities, we may more quickly meet our goal of having a more diverse group of campus leaders.

REFERENCES

Aguirre, A. (2000). *Women and minority faculty in the academic workplace: Recruitment, retention, and academic culture.* San Francisco, CA: Jossey-Bass.

Allen, T. D., Eby, L. T., & Lentz, E. (2006). Mentorship behaviors and mentorship quality associated with formal mentoring programs: Closing the gap between research and practice. *Journal of Applied Psychology, 91*(3), 567–578.

Allen, T. D., Eby, L. T., Poteet, M. L., Lentz, E., & Lima, L. (2004). Career benefits associated with mentoring for protégés: A meta-analysis. *Journal of Applied Psychology, 89*(1), 127–136.

Angelique, H., Kyle, K., & Taylor, E. (2002). Mentors and muses: New strategies for academic success. *Innovative Higher Education, 26*(3), 195–209. doi:10.1023/A:1017968906264

Antonio, A. L. (2003). Diverse student bodies, diverse faculties. *Academe, 89*(6), 14–17.

Bach, D., & Sorcinelli, M. D. (2010). The case for excellence in diversity: Lessons from an assessment of an early career faculty program. In L. B. Nilson & J. E. Miller (Eds.), *To improve the academy: Vol. 28. Resources for faculty, instructional, and organizational development* (pp. 310–326). San Francisco, CA: Jossey-Bass.

Carroll, J. B., & Wolverton, M. (2004). Who becomes a chair? In W. H. Gmelch & J. H. Schuh (Eds.), *New directions for higher education: No. 126. The life cycle of the department chair* (pp. 3–10). San Francisco, CA: Jossey-Bass.

Casto, C., Caldwell, C., & Salazar, C. F. (2005). Creating mentoring relationships between female faculty and students in counselor education: Guidelines for potential mentees and mentors. *Journal of Counseling and Development, 83*(3), 331–336.

Dailey-Hebert, A., Donnelli, E., & Mandernach, B. (2010). Access to success: A new mentoring model for women in academia. In L. B. Nilson & J. E. Miller (Eds.), *To improve the academy: Vol. 28. Resources for faculty, instructional, and organizational development* (pp. 327–340). San Francisco, CA: Jossey-Bass.

Davidson, M. N., & Foster-Johnson, L. (2001). Mentoring in the preparation of graduate researchers of color. *Review of Educational Research, 71*(4), 549–574. doi:10.3102/00346543071004549

Dixon-Reeves, R. (2003). Mentoring as a precursor to incorporation: An assessment of the mentoring experience of recently minted Ph.D.s. *Journal of Black Studies, 34*(1), 12–27. doi:10.1177/0021934703253680

Fayne, H., & Ortquist-Ahrens, L. (2006). Learning communities for first-year faculty: Transition, acculturation, and transformation. In S. Chadwick-Blossey &

D. R. Robertson (Eds.), *To improve the academy: Vol. 24. Resources for faculty, instructional, and organizational development* (pp. 277–290). San Francisco, CA: Jossey-Bass.

Glaser, B. G., & Strauss, A. L. (1967). *The discovery of grounded theory: Strategies for qualitative research.* Chicago, IL: Aldine.

Gmelch, W. H. (2000, February). *Rites of passage: Transition to the deanship.* Paper presented at the American Association of Colleges for Teacher Education Conference, Chicago, IL.

Green, C. E., & King, V. G. (2001). Sisters mentoring sisters: Africentric leadership development for black women in the academy. *Journal of Negro Education, 70*(3), 156–165.

Griffin, K. A. (2008). *Can reaching back push you forward? A mixed methods exploration of black faculty and their relationships with students* (Unpublished doctoral dissertation). University of California, Los Angeles.

Gruppen, L. D., Frohna, A. Z., Anderson, R. M., & Lowe, K. D. (2003). Faculty development for educational leadership and scholarship. *Academic Medicine, 78*(2), 137–141.

Hecht, I.W.D. (2004). The professional development of department chairs. In W. H. Gmelch & J. H. Schuh (Eds.), *New directions for higher education: No. 126. The life cycle of the department chair* (pp. 27–44). San Francisco, CA: Jossey-Bass.

Higgins, M. C., & Kram, K. E. (2001). Reconceptualizing mentoring at work: A developmental network perspective. *Academy of Management Review, 26*(2), 264–288.

Hollenshead, C., & Thomas, G. D. (2001). Resisting from the margins: The coping strategies of black women and other women of color faculty members at a research university. *Journal of Negro Education, 70*(3), 166–175.

IUPUI Diversity Cabinet. (2009). *State of diversity 2009: Chancellor's message.* Retrieved from www.iupui.edu/~divrsity/docs/Diversity%20Report-April%202009.pdf

Jayakumar, U. M., Howard, T. C., Allen, W. R., & Han, J. C. (2009). Racial privilege in the professoriate: An exploration of campus climate, retention, and satisfaction. *Journal of Higher Education, 80*(5), 538–563. doi:10.1353/jhe.0.0063

King, C. A., & Cubic, B. (2005). Women psychologists within academic health systems: Mentorship and career advancement. *Journal of Clinical Psychology in Medical Settings, 12*(3), 271–280. doi:10.1007/s10880-005-5746-3

Kirchmeyer, C. (2005). The effects of mentoring on academic careers over time: Testing performance and political perspectives. *Human Relations, 58*(5), 637–660. doi:10.1177/0018726705055966

Kuh, G. D. (2006). Making students matter. In J. C. Burke (Ed.), *Fixing the fragmented university: Decentralization with direction* (pp. 235–265). San Francisco, CA: Jossey-Bass.

Lottero-Perdue, P., & Fifield, S. (2010). A conceptual framework for higher education faculty mentoring. In L. B. Nilson & J. E. Miller (Eds.), *To improve the academy: Vol. 28. Resources for faculty, instructional, and organizational development* (pp. 37–62). San Francisco, CA: Jossey-Bass.

Maher, F. A., & Thompson Tetreault, M. K. (2007). *Struggling to diversify: Privilege and diversity in the academy.* New York, NY: Routledge.

Meyer, H. D., & Kaloyeros, A. E. (2005, June 10). What campuses can do to pick up the pace of decision making. *Chronicle of Higher Education,* p. B16.

Moody, J. (2004). *Faculty diversity: Problems and solutions.* New York, NY: RoutledgeFalmer.

Moreno, J., Smith, D., Clayton-Pederson, A., Parker, S., & Teraguchi, D. (2006). *The revolving door: Underrepresented minority faculty in higher education.* San Francisco, CA: James Irvine Foundation.

Mundt, M. H. (2001). An external mentor program: Stimulus for faculty research development. *Journal of Professional Nursing, 17*(1), 40–45. doi:10.1053/jpnu.2001.20241

National Center for Education Statistics. (2008). *Digest of educational statistics 2007.* Washington, DC: U.S. Department of Education.

Packard, B. W-L., Walsh, L., & Seidenberg, S. (2004). Will that be one mentor or two? A cross sectional study of women's mentoring during college. *Mentoring and Tutoring, 12*(1), 71–85. doi:10.1080/1361126042000183039

Rankin, S. R., & Reason, R. D. (2005). Differing perceptions: How students of color and white students perceive campus climate for underrepresented groups. *Journal of College Student Development, 46*(1), 43–61.

Rosser, V. J. (2004). Faculty members' intentions to leave: A national study on their work-life and satisfaction. *Research in Higher Education, 45*(3), 285–309.

Ryu, M. (2008). *Minorities in higher education 2008: 23rd status report.* Washington, DC: American Council on Education.

Schuster, J., & Finkelstein, M. (2006). *The American faculty: The restructuring of academic work and careers.* Baltimore, MD: Johns Hopkins University Press.

Snelson, C. M., Martsolf, D. S., Dieckman, B. C., Anaya, E. R., Cartechine, K. A., Miller, B., . . . Shaffer, J. (2002). Caring as a theoretical perspective for a nursing faculty mentoring program. *Nurse Education Today, 22*(8), 654–660.

Spencer, C., & Tribe, K. (2004). *Mentoring made easy: A practical guide* (3rd ed.). Retrieved from www.une.edu.au/od/files/mentoring_made_easy.pdf

Stanley, C. A. (2006). Coloring the academic landscape: Faculty of color breaking the silence in predominantly white colleges and universities. *American Educational Research Journal, 43*(4), 701–736. doi:10.3102/00028312043004701

Suh, S. A. (2008). *The significance of race for Asian Americans: Access, rewards, and workplace experiences of academics* (Unpublished doctoral dissertation). University of California, Los Angeles.

Thomas, G. (2001). The dual role of scholar and change agent. In R. O. Mabokela & A. L. Green (Eds.), *Sisters of the academy: Emergent black women scholars in higher education* (pp. 80–91). Sterling, VA: Stylus.

Thomas, J. R., & Schuh, J. H. (2004). Socializing new chairs. In W. H. Gmelch & J. H. Schuh (Eds.), *New directions for higher education: No. 126. The life cycle of the department chair* (pp. 11–25). San Francisco, CA: Jossey-Bass.

Thompson, C. (2008). Recruitment, retention, and mentoring faculty of color: The chronicle continues. In N.V.N. Chism (Ed.), *New directions for higher education: No. 143. Faculty at the margins* (pp. 47–54). San Francisco, CA: Jossey-Bass.

Trower, C. A. (2009, September/October). Toward a greater understanding of the tenure track for minorities. *Change, 41*(5), 38–45.

Turner, C.S.V. (2002). Women of color in academe: Living with multiple marginality. *Journal of Higher Education, 73*(1), 74–93. doi:10.1353/jhe.2002.0013

Villalpando, O., & Delgado Bernal, D. (2002). A critical race theory analysis of barriers that impede the success of faculty of color. In W. A. Smith, P. G. Altbach, & K. Lomotey (Eds.), *The racial crisis in American higher education: Continuing challenges for the twenty-first century* (pp. 243–269). Albany: State University of New York Press.

Wasburn, M. H. (2007). Mentoring women faculty: An instrumental case study of strategic collaboration. *Mentoring and Tutoring, 15*(1), 57–72. doi:10.1080/13611260601037389

Wolverton, M., & Ackerman, R. (2006). Cultivating possibilities: Prospective department chair professional development and why it matters. *Planning for Higher Education, 34*(4), 14–23.

Yoshinaga-Itano, C. (2006). Institutional barriers and myths to recruitment and retention of faculty of color: An administrator's perspective. In C. A. Stanley (Ed.), *Faculty of color: Teaching in predominantly white colleges and universities*. San Francisco, CA: Jossey-Bass.

16

DIFFUSING THE IMPACT OF TOKENISM ON FACULTY OF COLOR

Yolanda Flores Niemann, Utah State University

In addition to the expected challenges related to teaching, research, service, and the tenure and promotion process, faculty of color often experience the impact of token status, or tokenism. This chapter describes the personal, psychological, and career-damaging impacts of tokenism and provides guidelines for professional development professionals that may diffuse these negative impacts by assisting department heads to mentor faculty of color.

University faculty face similar experiences and challenges related to teaching, research, service, and the tenure and promotion process. In addition to these expected challenges, faculty of color are vulnerable to token status, or tokenism. Tokenism occurs, in part, when those in the numerical minority account for 15 percent or less of the total workforce in a given context (Kanter, 1977; Mullen, 1991; Niemann, 2003; Niemann & Dovidio, 1998a). More than numerical status, a critical but insufficient identifier of tokenism, tokenized contexts impose negative personal, psychological, and career-damaging effects on faculty of color (Gutierrez y muhs, Niemann, Gonzales, & Harris, in press). Symptoms of tokenized contexts include the collective and damaging effects of isolation and loneliness, visibility and distinctiveness, representativeness and role encapsulation, stereotype threat, and attributional ambiguity (Niemann, 1999, 2003; Niemann & Dovidio, 1998a). These impacts are especially pervasive in predominantly white institutions that lack a numerical critical mass of faculty of color, and they are exacerbated in predominantly white communities (Niemann & Dovidio, 1998a).

Faculty development professionals can help minimize the roots of tokenism and negative experiences associated with tokenized contexts for faculty of color. They can intercede to diffuse symptoms of tokenism, primarily through their influence on department head training. Department heads are the main lifeline for faculty as their primary administrator, advocate, and professional development mentor, but their lack of training belies this critical role. Most department heads assume their roles without the skills or experience needed to mentor faculty of color. Faculty development professionals' understanding of the university context, along with their skills and experience in effecting change in that context, makes them critical players in training department heads to mentor of faculty of color.

Isolation, Loneliness, and Alienation

Faculty of color in token contexts may experience isolation, loneliness, and alienation (Johnsrud, 1993; Niemann, 1999, 2003; Niemann & Dovidio, 1998a; Washington & Harvey, 1989). Universities and their departments may be oppressive without conscious maliciousness and subject people of color to subtle and overt experiences of racism (Niemann, 2003; Niemann & Dovidio, 1998a). In tokenized contexts, the burdens of institutional and individual racism weigh heavily, but the psychological safety associated with numbers is not available to persons who work in these isolated situations (Washington & Harvey, 1989). Faculty of color often do not have opportunities to form relationships with persons who understand the impacts of being a member of a minority group that is subjected to intentional or unintentional discrimination and "isms."

Tokens report feelings of isolation that result in part from pressures to assimilate and doubts from their majority group counterparts regarding their competency (Fontaine & Greenlee, 1993). They spend time and cognitive energy ruminating about these experiences and their responses, or lack of responses, to the situation (Lord & Saenz, 1985; Niemann, 1999; Saenz & Lord, 1989; Steele, 1997, 2010). The more that tokens ruminate about experiences or events not directly related to their work, the more stressed and isolated they become, which begins a vicious circle (Ellsworth, 1993; Niemann, 2003).

Tokens are culturally isolated. In predominantly white institutions, the cultural values and mores may be very different from those of communities of color. Tokens must attempt to acclimate and, in some cases, assimilate to fit in with the predominant culture. Often as a result, they experience symptoms of loneliness, isolation, alienation, and burnout that include intense cynicism, seeing life activities as valueless, pressure to dissociate themselves from others, and arrogance (Machell, 1988–1989).

Distinctiveness

Due to their low numbers, tokens work in situations that make them particularly distinctive and visible (Cota & Dion, 1986; Fiske & Taylor, 1991; Kanter, 1977; McGuire, McGuire, Child, & Fujioka, 1978; Niemann, 1999, 2003, in press; Niemann & Dovidio, 1998a; Pollak & Niemann, 1998). Their novelty within groups often makes tokens feel as if they are in a glass house (Kanter, 1977; Niemann, 2003, in press; Niemann & Dovidio, 1998a), and they attract disproportional attention and causality (Taylor & Fiske, 1976), or responsibility for outcomes. That is, because tokens are so visible, their words and behaviors are easier to recall than are those of more homogeneous group members. This attention is reflected in group members' general, but not specific, recollection of the group experience. Consequently when things go well, token group members receive some credit, but when outcomes are not good, they receive much of the blame (Taylor & Fiske, 1976). For instance, when only one person of color is part of a committee discussion, that person's statements will be the ones most recalled. If a committee's outcomes are positive, the person of color will be praised; when the outcomes are negative, the person of color will be blamed, even when his or her statements or actions are ancillary to the decisions or outcomes (Mullen, 1991; Taylor & Fiske, 1978).

The distinctiveness that tokens describe is largely negative. It is not the type of distinctiveness felt by a Nobel Prize winner or high-ranking officer of the university (Niemann, 2003). Tokens' salience creates psychological discomfort and places them on constant guard about the implications of their words, behaviors, and very presence. They feel a stressful sense of having no privacy or freedom to be themselves. This distinctiveness becomes uncomfortable to the extent that tokens report fearing visibility (Kanter, 1977; Niemann, in press).

The distinctiveness of tokens results in exaggeration of differences between faculty of color and their white colleagues (Fiske & Taylor, 1991). Tokens must often pretend that racial differences do not exist or have no implications (Niemann, 1999). Their white colleagues will often assert that they are "color-blind," not realizing that such comments are considered insulting by their very denial of tokens' identity and experiences in the institution (Niemann, 2005). At times, tokens may don a "white mask" to fit in with white colleagues (Alexander-Snow & Johnson, 1999). Distinctiveness and visibility are so uncomfortable that faculty of color often forgo their cultural selves when they are in their faculty roles and portray the cultural behaviors and preferences of their white colleagues in an effort to blend in with the racial or ethnic majority.

Consistent with feelings of distinctiveness, tokens often believe that they are evaluated under different, and more stringent, criteria than their white colleagues are. Their actions and words are heavily scrutinized. Faculty of color report increased pressure to outperform others and to outshine and outthink their colleagues (Fontaine & Greenlee, 1993). Everything they do and say, from their attire, to their choice of music, to their opinions on political or controversial matters, to their latest research project, will become public knowledge quickly. In contrast, typical faculty within the same department generally do not know the research topics of their white colleagues.

Due to their distinctive salience and the added stress induced by these situations, tokens may engage in self-monitoring (Snyder, 1979) and defensive impression management strategies to establish particular attributes in the eyes of others (Tedeschi & Norman, 1985). Tokens' self-protective attributions exacerbate a state of cognitive busyness (Crocker & Major, 1989), resulting in more memory and problem-solving deficits than nontokens have (Lord & Saenz, 1985; Salvatore & Shelton, 2007; Schmader, Forbes, Zhang, & Mendes, 2009), which may have an impact on their job performance. These deficits are interpreted to be a function of their cognitive busyness with their minority status rather than with any inherent personal deficits (Lord & Saenz, 1985). That is, simultaneously managing their distinctiveness and the task at hand strains tokens' cognitive resources.

Tokens' individuality seems nonexistent as their racial, ethnic, group, or social identity becomes increasingly salient. As tokens become preoccupied with issues pertaining to self-distinctiveness and self-presentation strategies, they feel less satisfied with their jobs (Niemann & Dovidio, 1998a).

Representativeness, Stereotyping, and Role Encapsulation

As the size of the minority group decreases relative to the majority, tokens not only become perceived as increasingly distinctive from the majority, they are perceived as homogeneous (Mullen, 1991), which fuels their stereotyping and role encapsulation. Stereotypes are "pictures in our heads" (Lippmann, 1922) that contain a structured set of beliefs, including perceivers' organized knowledge, beliefs, and expectancies about some human group (Fiske & Taylor, 1991). Because of stereotypical attributions, tokens may be type-cast as specialists in ethnic matters rather than being perceived as qualified in their particular disciplines (Kanter, 1977; Niemann, 1999; Spangler, Gordon, & Pipkin, 1978). This stereotypical perception leads to tokens' placement in limited and caricatured roles, such as "diversity" committees, or committees where a "person of color voice" is considered beneficial. Tokens report feeling as if they are in special mascot-like roles (Gutierrez y muhs et al., in press; Niemann, in press). They are often deliberately thrust into the limelight as the institution's representative when it is in the interest of the institution to demonstrate a belief in diversity (Kanter, 1977; Niemann, 1999).

Tokens are perceived as symbolic representatives of their ethnic or racial groups (Kanter, 1977; Pollak & Niemann, 1998). They serve as symbols of their group when they fumble and as unusual examples of their kinds when they succeed (Fiske & Taylor, 1991; Kanter, 1977; Kunda, 2000). The pressure and stress from this representativeness may be constant, as tokens are often asked to provide a point of view representing their ethnic or racial group. There is a general assumption that they know what "their" group wants or thinks. Faculty of color believe that due to colleagues' biases and their situational visibility and representativeness, they are not allowed any missteps. They must hit the ground running to justify their hiring by white colleagues. Any sign that they are less than the perfect hire will justify racist, stereotypical beliefs that people of color are not qualified for the professoriate or for high-ranking positions in academia (Gutierrez y muhs et al., in press; Niemann, in press). Whether or not they wish to be, they are seen as representatives of their distinctive racial or ethnic group in the university environment. Observers assume that their imperfections and mistakes are reflective of their group. Simultaneously, due to the powerful and stigmatizing impact of negative stereotypes, their successes are seen as exceptions to the rule and as anomalies that are not reflective of their group (Pinel, 1999). Tokens must therefore be continually aware of putting their best foot forward so as not to have a negative impact on others' perceptions of members of their demographic groups.

Tokens become representative of government programs such as affirmative action (Niemann & Dovidio, 1998b). They are presumed to be in the employ of the institution because of affirmative action policy, and not because they are qualified (Crosby & Clayton, 1990). Tokens may thus carry a stigma of incompetence that accompanies the affirmative action label (Heilman, Block, & Lucas, 1992), in addition to being objects of racial bias. Role stress represented in role encapsulation and representativeness has been linked to feelings of tension, decreased job satisfaction, and employee turnover (Niemann & Dovidio, 1998a).

Stereotype Threat

Tokens may experience stereotype threat, defined as the possibility of proving true the stereotypes about one's group (Steele, 2010). For people of color, especially African Americans and Latinos/as, stereotypes related to intelligence and educational achievement are largely negative, thereby exacerbating the damaging impact of tokenism in the academic context (Garza, 1992; Niemann, 2001). Stereotypes and efforts to avoid being seen as representative of their group may lead tokens to operate in a state of reflective expectancy, a psychological state associated with persistent feelings of anxiety, fear of proving the accuracy of negative racial stereotypes, and living in fear of making a mistake. This state inhibits their work and may even stop their progress toward tenure (Niemann, 2003; Niemann & Dovidio, 1998a; Pollak & Niemann, 1998; Steele, 1997, 2010).

For women of color in token situations, the intersections of race or ethnicity and gender are particularly pronounced. They are subjected to greater degrees of discrimination than white women and are doubly disadvantaged in their efforts to advance (Fontaine & Greenlee, 1993). Because women of color tend to be exoticized in predominantly white environments, they are at particular risk for sexual harassment. They may be stereotyped as easy or passive targets who want the attention of white men, while also experiencing sexism from members of their own ethnic or racial groups, especially those from patriarchal communities (McKay, 1988) in which women are traditionally expected to be subordinate to male group members.

Their awareness that others perceive them in a stereotypical manner can have damaging consequences for tokens' interactions and relations with department colleagues and other institutional personnel. It can have an impact on their job performance and hinder the formation of friendships that could alleviate feelings of isolation and loneliness. It can also preclude formations of alliances and relations with potential mentors, and have strong implications for their success of these minority faculty.

Attributional Ambiguity

Tokens live in a state of attributional ambiguity, which refers to not knowing the intentions of the feedback or actions toward or against them (Crocker, Voekl, Testa, & Major, 1991; Niemann, 1999, 2003). They do not know if negative feedback is racist, or if positive feedback is overly kind and patronizing from unconscious racists who do not have the confidence or courage to provide negative feedback to members of underrepresented groups. Not knowing whether feedback from whites is genuine or is related to prejudice makes it difficult for the stigmatized to predict their future outcomes, select tasks of appropriate difficulty, or accurately assess their own skills and abilities (Crocker & Major, 1989; Dovidio, Gaertner, Niemann, & Snider, 2001; Niemann, 1999; Niemann & Dovidio, 1998a).

Attributional ambiguity can stop the progress of people of color. A key component of success for faculty is mentoring that sees them through the institutional ranks. This mentoring includes constructive, critically analytical feedback on their work from majority white colleagues and supervisors. Not to have trusted feedback is to not know how to improve. Attributional ambiguity results in isolation from collaborative work and intellectual and professional stimulation (Hall, 1990).

Guidelines for Faculty Developers and Administrators

The effects of tokenism are interconnected. So too are the guidelines that can diffuse or minimize these effects. The guidelines that follow may be implemented to minimize situations that create tokenized contexts and create a more positive university climate and job experience for faculty of color:

- *At upper institutional levels, facilitate the establishment of social networks and encourage grassroots organizations of faculty of color.* The university president or provost can host gatherings of faculty of color at his or her home to provide opportunities for these faculty to get to know one another. These gatherings provide a university-sanctioned means for faculty of color to find cultural communities and share similar experiences and advice from more senior faculty. Relationships formed in these groups facilitate a sense of belonging and retention (Olmedo, 1990).

- *Engage faculty in department meetings, committees, teams, and work groups.* During department meetings, seek the participation of all faculty. These interactions provide faculty of color an opportunity to be known beyond group stereotypes and to form meaningful relationships and friendships.

- *Facilitate department, disciplinary, college, and university unity and identity.* These collective identities help diffuse racial stereotypes and identification.

- *As part of mentoring, include concrete deadlines, goals, and schedules.* A specific, impending goal will help keep focus on productivity and away from ruminations that expend time and energy.

- *Facilitate the establishment of reading groups for junior faculty.* These groups should contain people who will not be involved in any evaluative process for group members. For that reason, people from outside the member's department will be trusted to provide feedback on drafts of research papers and creative works.

- *Ask faculty to select formal mentors rather than assigning mentors.* Provide enough flexibility to all faculty to change mentors as they form relationships with colleagues or when they establish research-based alliances.

- *Train mentors of faculty of color to understand the unique experiences associated with tokenism.*

- *Encourage persons in upper-level ranks, such as presidents, provosts, and deans, to mentor faculty of color.* Some of the best informal (nonassigned) mentors for faculty of color are high-status members of the institution who are not competing in any way with their mentees.

- *Do not assume that faculty of color are prepared to teach about diversity issues* or have the interest or qualifications to serve on diversity-related committees and tasks.

- *Ensure that white faculty serve on diversity-related committees.* Faculty of color should not be the only persons advocating for diversity-related concerns.

- *Value teaching social justice issues.* Make sure that white faculty, and not just faculty of color, are assigned to teach this curricular content.

- *Protect faculty of color from excess service, unwanted summer teaching, and paid and unpaid overload teaching.* At the same time, understand that their cultural values will motivate and inspire them to engage in service to the community at large and to individual and student group advising. Consider providing release time to ensure equitable time for their attention to their scholarship and teaching. Be forthright about which of their service contributions will be taken into consideration for tenure, promotion, and salary increases.

- *Conduct searches with the intention of diversifying the faculty.* When conducting searches, do not equate merit with elite institutions; most faculty of color did not achieve their formal education at Ivy League universities. Ensure that committee members understand federal affirmative action policy and the implications of the policy for faculty searches (Persico, 1990). Being intentional about diversifying the faculty will contribute to the university climate for faculty of color and minimize impacts of tokenism. Rarity and scarcity, rather than being an ethnic or racial minority, shape the environment and set the stage for tokenization. In more ethnically balanced groups that include a critical mass of faculty of color, members have freedom to assume nontraditional roles (Rozell & Vaught, 1988).

- *Express a belief in the added value of diversity and affirmative action* rather than relaying the message that the policy is being forced upon the unit (Fine, 1992).

- *Acknowledge that intersectionality (for example, intersections of gender, race, socioeconomic status, and sexuality) has implications for faculty's perception of the university climate* (Bowleg, 2008; Shields, 2008). Understand that women of color are particularly vulnerable to sexual harassment, and act immediately on accusations of harassment.

- *Provide opportunities for frank discussion regarding issues of racism and stereotyping.* When faculty of color have colleagues with whom to discuss these issues, they will feel less isolated and may spend less time ruminating about the negative token experiences on their own.

- *Do not dismiss issues and experiences related to perceived racism, sexism, and stereotyping.* Faculty of color have a unique reality based largely on their tokenized status.

- *Acknowledge white privilege.* Do not pretend to be color-blind. Be color conscious, noting the added value of faculty of color. Be aware of your own white privilege and aversive racism. Consider taking the implicit association test (https://implicit.harvard.edu/implicit/demo/) and facing your own prejudices and stereotypes.

- *Use your privileged position to combat practices that subordinate others,* including inappropriate jokes, demeaning group identities and accomplishments, dismissal of affirmative action policy, and disregarding the accomplishments of certain colleagues. Be aware that all persons unconsciously hold stereotypes until they consciously deconstruct their prejudices (Devine, 1989).

Conclusion

Tokenism is a psychological state imposed on faculty of color. It is a function of a social-ecological context that faculty of color are typically left on their own to navigate. In some cases, these faculty, especially those new to the academy, may not have the experience or understanding to be conscious of the effects of token status or to understand how to minimize the negative aspects of the situation. The same is true for their white colleagues, who may want faculty of color to succeed, but lack the knowledge to help their colleagues diffuse the damaging ramifications of tokenism. Professional development professionals, working collaboratively with university administrators and department heads, can promote change that affords faculty of color opportunities to succeed and to have a good quality of life in predominantly white academic institutions.

REFERENCES

Alexander-Snow, M., & Johnson, B. J. (1999). Perspectives from faculty of color. In R. J. Menges & Associates, *Faculty in new jobs: A guide to settling in, becoming established, and building institutional support* (pp. 88–117). San Francisco, CA: Jossey-Bass.

Bowleg, L. (2008). When black + lesbian + woman = black lesbian woman: The methodological challenges of qualitative and quantitative intersectionality research. *Sex Roles, 59*(5/6), 312–325. doi:10.1007/s11199-008-9400-z

Cota, A. A., & Dion, K. L. (1986). Salience of gender and sex composition of ad hoc groups: An experimental test of distinctiveness theory. *Journal of Personality and Social Psychology, 50*(4), 770–776. doi:10.1037/0022-3514.50.4.770

Crocker, J., & Major, B. (1989). Social stigma and self-esteem: The self-protective properties of stigma. *Psychological Review, 96*(4), 608–630.

Crocker, J., Voelkl, K., Testa, M., & Major, B. (1991). Social stigma: The affective consequences of attributional ambiguity. *Journal of Personality and Social Psychology, 60*(2), 218–228.

Crosby, F., & Clayton, S. (1990). Affirmative action and the issue of expectancies. *Journal of Social Issues, 46*(2), 61–79. doi:10.1111/j.1540-4560.1990.tb01923.x

Devine, P. G. (1989). Stereotypes and prejudice: Their automatic and controlled components. *Journal of Personality and Social Psychology, 56*(1), 5–18.

Dovidio, J. F., Gaertner, S. L., Niemann, Y. F., & Snider, K. (2001). Racial, ethnic, and cultural differences in responding to distinctiveness and discrimination on campus: Stigma and common group identity. *Journal of Social Issues, 57*(1), 167–188. doi:10.1111/0022-4537.00207

Ellsworth, E. (1993). Claiming the tenured body. In D. Wear (Ed.), *The center of the web: Women and solitude* (pp. 63–74). Albany: State University of New York Press.

Fine, T. S. (1992). The impact of issue framing on public opinion: Toward affirmative action programs. *Social Science Journal, 29*(3), 323–334. doi:10.1016/0362-3319(92)90025-D

Fiske, S. T., & Taylor, S. E. (1991). *Social cognition.* New York, NY: McGraw-Hill.

Fontaine, D. C., & Greenlee, S. P. (1993). Black women: Double solos in the workplace. *Western Journal of Black Studies, 17*(3), 121–125.

Garza, H. (1992). Academic power, discourse, and legitimacy: Minority scholars in US universities. In M. Romero & C. Candelaria (Eds.), *Community empowerment and Chicano scholarship* (pp. 35–52). San Jose, CA: National Association of Chicano Studies.

Gutierrez y muhs, G., Niemann, Y. F., Gonzales, C., & Harris, A. (Eds.). (in press). *Presumed incompetent.* Logan: Utah State University Press.

Hall, C.C.I. (1990). Qualified minorities are encouraged to apply: The recruitment of ethnic minority and female psychologists. In G. Stricker, E. Davis-Russell, E. Bourg, E. Duran, W. R. Hammond, J. McHolland, . . . B. E. Vaughn (Eds.), *Toward ethnic diversification in psychology education and training* (pp. 105–111). Washington, DC: American Psychological Association.

Heilman, M. E., Block, C. J., & Lucas, J. A. (1992). Presumed incompetent? Stigmatization and affirmative action efforts. *Journal of Applied Psychology, 77*(4), 536–544.

Johnsrud, L. K. (1993). Women and minority faculty experiences: Defining and responding to diverse realities. In J. Gainen & R. Boice (Eds.), *New directions for teaching and learning: No. 53. Building faculty learning communities* (pp. 3–16). San Francisco, CA: Jossey-Bass.

Kanter, R. M. (1977). *Men and women of the corporation.* New York, NY: Basic Books.

Kunda, Z. (2000). *Social cognition: Making sense of people.* Cambridge, MA: MIT Press.

Lippmann, W. (1922). *Public opinion.* New York, NY: Harcourt, Brace.

Lord, C. G., & Saenz, D. S. (1985). Memory deficits and memory surfeits: Differential cognitive consequences of tokenism for tokens and observers. *Journal of Personality and Social Psychology, 49*(4), 918–926.

Machell, D. F. (1988–1989). A discourse on professorial melancholia. *Community Review, 9*(1/2), 41–50.

McGuire, W. J., McGuire, C. V., Child, P., & Fujioka, T. (1978). Salience of ethnicity in the spontaneous self-concept as a function of one's ethnic distinctiveness in the social environment. *Journal of Personality and Social Psychology, 36*(5), 511–520.

McKay, N. Y. (1988). Minority faculty in [mainstream white] academia. In A. L. Deneef, C. D. Goodwin, & E. S. McCrate (Eds.), *The academic's handbook* (pp. 48–64). Durham, NC: Duke University Press.

Mullen, B. (1991). Group composition, salience, and cognitive representations: The phenomenology of being in a group. *Journal of Experimental Social Psychology, 27*(4), 297–323. doi:10.1016/0022-1031(91)90028-5

Niemann, Y. F. (1999). The making of a token: A case study of stereotype threat, stigma, racism, and tokenism in academe. *Frontiers: A Journal of Women Studies, 20*(1), 111–135.

Niemann, Y. F. (2001). Stereotypes about Chicanas and Chicanos: Implications for counseling. *Counseling Psychologist, 29*(1), 55–90. doi:10.1177/0011000001291003

Niemann, Y. F. (2003). The psychology of tokenism: Psychosocial realities of faculty of color. In G. Bernal, J. E. Trimble, A. K. Burlew, & F. T. Leong (Eds.), *The handbook of racial and ethnic minority psychology* (pp. 110–118). Thousand Oaks, CA: Sage.

Niemann, Y. F. (2005). Color blindness: Its ironies, impossibilities, and contradictions. In Y. F. Niemann, C. R. Lugo-Lugo, J. Alamillo, L. Guerrero, R. Ong, & J. Streamas (Eds.), *Racial crossroads: A reader in comparative ethnic studies* (pp. 217–228). Dubuque, IA: Kendall Hunt.

Niemann, Y. F. (in press). Presumed incompetent: Lessons learned from the experiences of race, class, sexuality, gender, and their intersections in the academic world. In G. Gutierrez y muhs, Y. F. Niemann, C. Gonzales, & A. Harris (Eds.), *Presumed incompetent.* Logan: Utah State University Press.

Niemann, Y. F., & Dovidio, J. F. (1998a). Relationship of solo status, academic rank, and perceived distinctiveness to job satisfaction of racial/ethnic minorities. *Journal of Applied Psychology, 83*(1), 55–71.

Niemann, Y. F., & Dovidio, J. (1998b). Tenure, race/ethnicity and attitudes toward affirmative action: A matter of self-interest? *Sociological Perspectives, 41*(4), 783–796.

Olmedo, E. L. (1990). Minority faculty development: Issues in retention and promotion. In G. Stricker, E. Davis-Russell, E. Bourg, E. Duran, W. R. Hammond, J. McHolland, . . . B. E. Vaughn (Eds.), *Toward ethnic diversification in psychology education and training* (pp. 99–104). Washington, DC: American Psychological Association.

Persico, C. F. (1990). Creating an institutional climate that honors diversity. In G. Stricker, E. Davis-Russell, E. Bourg, E. Duran, W. R. Hammond, J. McHolland, . . . B. E. Vaughn (Eds.), *Toward ethnic diversification in psychology education and training* (pp. 55–63). Washington, DC: American Psychological Association.

Pinel, E. C. (1999). Stigma consciousness: The psychological legacy of social stereotypes. *Journal of Personality and Social Psychology, 76*(1), 114–128.

Pollak, K. I., & Niemann, Y. F. (1998). Black and white tokens in academia: A difference of chronic versus acute distinctiveness. *Journal of Applied Social Psychology, 28*(11), 954–972. doi:10.1111/j.1559-1816.1998 .tb01662.x

Rozell, E., & Vaught, B. C. (1988). The interaction effects of women in groups: A review of the interaction and implications. *Arkansas Business and Economic Review, 21*(3), 1–15.

Saenz, D. S., & Lord, C. G. (1989). Reversing roles: A cognitive strategy for undoing memory deficits associated with token status. *Journal of Personality and Social Psychology, 56*(5), 698–708.

Salvatore, J., & Shelton, J. N. (2007). Cognitive costs of exposure to racial prejudice. *Psychological Science, 18*(9), 810–815. doi:10.1111/j.1467-9280.2007.01984.x

Schmader, T., Forbes, C. E., Zhang, S., & Mendes, W. B. (2009, May). A metacognitive perspective on the cognitive deficits experienced in intellectually threatening environments. *Personality and Social Psychology Bulletin, 35*(5), 584–596. doi:10.1177/0146167208330450

Shields, S. A. (2008). Gender: An intersectionality perspective. *Sex Roles, 59*(5/6), 301–311. doi:10.1007/s11199-008-9501-8

Snyder, M. (1979). Self-monitoring processes. In L. Berkowitz (Ed.), *Advances in experimental social psychology* (Vol. 12, pp. 85–125). Orlando, FL: Academic Press.

Spangler, E., Gordon, M. A., & Pipkin, R. M. (1978). Token women: An empirical test of Kanter's hypothesis. *American Journal of Sociology, 84*(1), 160–170.

Steele, C. M. (1997). A threat in the air: How stereotypes shape intellectual identity and performance. *American Psychologist, 52*(6), 613–629.

Steele, C. M. (2010). *Whistling Vivaldi: And other clues to how stereotypes affect us*. New York, NY: Norton.

Taylor, S. E., & Fiske, S. T. (1976). The token in a small group: Research findings and theoretical implications. In J. Sweeney (Ed.), *Psychology and politics, collected papers* (pp. 110–117). New Haven, CT: Yale University Press.

Taylor, S. E., & Fiske, S. T. (1978). Salience, attention, and attribution: Top of the head phenomena. In L. Berkowitz (Ed.), *Advances in experimental and social psychology* (Vol. 11, pp. 249–288). Orlando, FL: Academic Press.

Tedeschi, J. T., & Norman, N. (1985). Social power, self presentation, and the self. In B. R. Schlenker (Ed.), *The self and social life* (pp. 293–321). New York, NY: McGraw-Hill.

Washington, V., & Harvey, W. (1989). *Affirmative rhetoric, negative action: African American and Hispanic faculty at predominantly white institutions*. Washington, DC: George Washington University, School of Education and Human Development.

DIFFICULT DIALOGUES AND TRANSFORMATIONAL CHANGE THROUGH CROSS-CULTURAL FACULTY DEVELOPMENT

Elizabeth Roderick, University of Alaska Anchorage

Across the globe, our current way of life is taking us to the edge of the cliff. The systems and consciousness that we have used to try to solve problems are not working. Young people need to think and work in new ways.

—Larry Merculieff, Project Director, Warriors for a New Era

A unique partnership between two universities sought to improve the learning climates on both campuses, making each more inclusive of minority voices and ways of knowing and safer places for the free exchange of ideas. Faculty development intensive workshops introduced a wide range of strategies for engaging controversy through difficult dialogues in the classroom. The process, strategies, and results were documented in a handbook. A second-level intensive workshop tackled difficult dialogues between indigenous communities and the academy. The results were transformative, establishing an atmosphere where all viewpoints were respected and freeing both faculty and students to explore new ideas.

Given the role that higher education needs to play in preparing young people to tackle daunting global and national issues, this call to action could have been issued on any college campus. In this instance, it was

---

The project described in this chapter was supported by the Ford Foundation Difficult Dialogues Initiative.

made by an Aleut (Alaska Native) leader at the University of Alaska Anchorage (UAA) during a panel discussion prompted by a joint faculty development project on engaging difficult dialogues in higher education. As we worked to promote civil discourse, safer classrooms, and stronger ties and trust between Alaska Native communities and Western universities through a project funded by the Ford Foundation, faculty and staff discovered that new ideas and ways of approaching problems may be found in the ancient traditions of Alaska's First Peoples.

There were two phases to our efforts, each funded by a separate Ford Foundation Difficult Dialogues grant. The first involved two faculty development intensive workshops aimed at increasing skill levels among faculty for introducing difficult dialogues into the classroom, a Books of the Year program, and the creation of a handbook of best practices for engaging controversial topics in higher education classrooms. The second introduced our faculty to key difficult dialogues between the academy and indigenous communities and to traditional indigenous best practices for teaching and learning. The approaches we used can be adapted anywhere to help faculty connect with other invisible or underrepresented groups, build understanding, open faculty to exciting new (and ancient) approaches to teaching, and improve student learning.

Background

In 2006, UAA, a public four-year open access institution, partnered with Alaska Pacific University (APU), a neighboring small private university, on a proposal to the Ford Foundation's Difficult Dialogues initiative. As the Ford Foundation website explains, "Difficult Dialogues is a program designed to promote academic freedom and religious, cultural, and political pluralism on college and university campuses in the United States" (www.difficultdialogues.org). One of twenty-six two-year projects funded by the initiative, the UAA/APU program aimed to engage faculty and students in constructive dialogue about sensitive political, religious, racial, and cultural issues. Such cooperation between these two usually competitive campuses was an enormous step in successfully negotiating our own difficult dialogues.

In applying for the Ford Foundation grant, UAA was responding to a survey conducted by UAA psychology professor Claudia Lampman: it had revealed that the majority of UAA faculty members had experienced some form of student harassment in the classroom, ranging from open displays of disrespect or disdain to stalking and threats. These incidents had had a measurably negative effect on faculty performance, productivity, and job satisfaction, particularly among female faculty. The study showed that 19 percent of female faculty felt physically afraid, 29 percent grew anxious or depressed, and 33 percent had difficulty sleeping. Fifteen percent suffered a loss in productivity, 13 percent admitted to changing an assignment or their teaching style, and 9 percent dropped a controversial topic altogether (Lampman, Phelps, Bancroft, & Beneke, 2008). Although some incidents of student harassment of faculty did stem from discussions of controversial topics in class, no clear link was established between those two factors. However, significant numbers of faculty indicated a tendency to avoid or downplay certain topics in class in an attempt to prevent unmanageable classroom tensions from arising. Clearly faculty members needed to understand and deal with harassment more effectively.

There was reason to believe that these encounters were also poisoning the learning environment for students. On the 2006 National Survey of Student Engagement, UAA's benchmark mean scores in the Enriching Educational Experience questions ranked below its Carnegie peers' national scores. Students reported few, if any, serious conversations with others who have different religious beliefs, political opinions, or personal values or who come from a different race or ethnicity. More alarming, they ranked the university low on encouraging such contacts.

Learning How to Talk

Before we could engage successfully with controversial topics in or out of the classroom, we needed training. Faculty come to the university as experts in their fields, but many do not have much training on how to teach and little, if any, preparation on how to deal effectively with, let alone introduce, controversy in the classroom. "If we want our universities to remain vital training grounds for engagement in a democratic society, we must model ways to conduct civil discourse in the classroom," Lauren Bruce, director of the UAA Center for Advancing Faculty Excellence, wrote about the project (Landis, 2008, p. v). To build faculty skills and support for engaging tough topics in the classroom—whether those topics involved gay marriage, resource development, or racism— we decided to design and offer two week-long faculty development intensives.

A faculty committee from both campuses and a variety of disciplines (rhetoric, religious studies, communication, and Alaska Native studies) designed the intensive curriculum; committee members also served as presenters during the intensive itself. The curriculum addressed academic freedom, how to prevent or respond to disruptive students, and multicultural ways of knowing, in addition to a wide variety of strategies and techniques for introducing controversial topics and conducting effective civil discourse in the classroom.

Faculty members from both universities applied to participate and were paid for their time. Thirty-two fellows, representing both relatively new and seasoned professors, were selected from eighteen disciplines across the two institutions. The goal was to create a committed cohort that would attend the intensive and serve as a support network for each other after the project concluded. Participants were contractually obligated to apply, document, and assess what they learned in their classrooms the following year; engage students in one or more difficult dialogues; and field-test one or more new techniques. They were also required to submit at least two short reflective essays on strategies, topics, or philosophical issues related to teaching controversial topics and report on their experiences to their colleagues. Finally, participants needed to organize and conduct one university or community workshop on a topic related to difficult dialogues.

We used group exercises extensively in the intensive; faculty became learners of the structures and strategies proposed for possible use in their own classrooms. We began with the strategies outlined in *Discussion as a Way of Teaching: Tools and Techniques for Democratic Classrooms* (Brookfield & Preskill, 2005), which served as the text for the faculty intensives.

Week-long faculty development intensives were chosen as a format because they afforded participants and designers two key things. The first was the luxury of time. Academic life makes relentless demands on faculty time. Taking on a new challenge that requires deep learning, and sometimes unlearning, takes focus and, above all, time. The week-long format allowed faculty the time to absorb the new material and consider how to apply it in their courses, practice new skills with peers, and process the emotional and intellectual challenges evoked by controversial topics. The format also provided faculty the opportunity to bond with a new cohort and develop the sense of safety needed to allow themselves to be vulnerable and honest enough to take meaningful risks. With sufficient grounding in the material, the group formed ongoing learning communities and support networks within and across the two campuses.

The second was a mechanism for overcoming faculty resistance to addressing certain topics, particularly race. The intensive was promoted to faculty as an opportunity to learn skills and strategies for addressing controversial topics in the classroom. Faculty who applied were asked to indicate the kinds of issues they wished to address. Due to the range of disciplines represented by selected participants, the topics of interest were wide ranging, including environmental controversies, evolution, racism, and gender-related issues. Faculty who attended rarely had much awareness of, or exposure to, the kinds of controversial topics and difficult dialogues (or even disruptive student behaviors) that colleagues in very different disciplines might encounter on a routine basis. Someone who teaches physics, for example, might never have had the time or opportunity to think deeply about issues related to gender, whereas an English professor might not have given much thought to the challenge of responding to evangelical Christian students who attack the theory of evolution.

Inviting faculty to participate in a week-long intensive in which all of these difficult dialogues were addressed allowed them to become better acquainted with the range of controversies and challenges facing the academy. It also ensured that faculty who might usually decide that "that topic [say, race and racism] has nothing to do with my subject or students or teaching" would have the opportunity to participate in discussions and exercises that could begin to clarify the relevance of these issues to all learning communities at the universities. Such challenging topics, in which faculty might be required to more deeply explore their own biases and how those biases might affect their teaching and students, were placed midway through the week. Doing so ensured that participants would have established some sense of safety and community and that they had sufficient time invested in the project so they were less likely to drop out if things became uncomfortable.

Shared Texts as Catalysts for Difficult Dialogues

Concurrently with participants' efforts to apply what they learned in their classrooms, the two universities launched a Books of the Year program in which selected texts served as a framework and catalyst for guided explorations on common controversial topics. The books selected that first year were *The Spirit Catches You and You Fall Down* (Fadiman, 1997) and *The Tortilla Curtain* (Boyle, 1995), both of which address multiculturalism, immigration, assimilation, and otherness. Events included public forums, guest speakers, art programs and performances, and faculty development workshops on best practices for teaching the selected books. Reader's guides were developed for each book to help guide discussions. Faculty voluntarily included all or part of the books in their syllabi.

"We use our Books of the Year program to provoke serious discussions at all levels throughout the curriculum," explained John Dede, special assistant to the senior vice provost at UAA, one of the administrators in the project. The discussions created cross-disciplinary interactions that had rarely occurred among faculty. It even produced some novel interactions between classes. For example, two philosophy courses joined forces to have their students role-play scenes from the Fadiman book, with students teaming up to represent various characters in the book and improvising sequels to incidents described in it. Students were so enthusiastic that they stayed after class for an extended period of time, continuing the discussion.

UAA and APU are now in the fifth year of the Books of the Year program. Subsequent themes have included religion and politics, Alaska Native issues, and responding to climate change. The 2010–2011 theme is service in a foreign land, which explores the responsibility of the individual to other human beings. The books are *This Is Not Civilization* (Rosenberg, 2004) and *Mountains Beyond Mountains* (Kidder, 2004).

Sharing What We Learned

After a year of using the new pedagogical tools, it was time to share what we had learned. Faculty experiences, curricula, materials, and resources, as well as insights from the facilitator, were compiled into an easy-to-use manual aimed at faculty, *Start Talking: A Handbook for Engaging Difficult Dialogues in Higher Education* (Landis, 2008). This best practices handbook was distributed to faculty at both universities and to selected universities nationwide.

As project director, I have been invited to speak to faculty and faculty developers across the country about the program. Everywhere I travel, people are hungry for resources to help them effectively engage students, colleagues, and communities in the most critical issues of the day. Those issues often involve charged and challenging discussions between individuals or groups with very different perspectives and backgrounds. Higher education is one of the only places in which we can both model for and train each new generation how to respectfully and civilly engage in the give-and-take between diverse viewpoints and populations so necessary for a healthy democracy.

Assessing Our Efforts

We used four methods to assess the initial project:

1. A pre- and posttest during the faculty intensive, and a test a year later of participant perceptions of their new skills and knowledge of difficult dialogues practice and of the roles and responsibilities related to academic freedom

2. End-of-term evaluations of student outcomes in those classes testing difficult dialogue techniques

3. Extensive qualitative review and self-assessment by participating faculty members

4. Qualitative assessments by staff of the campus and community activities centering upon the Books of the Year

The data showed that faculty members felt significantly more knowledgeable, well prepared, and confident about facilitating discussions on difficult or controversial topics. There was also significant improvement in a faculty member's likelihood of teaching controversial issues. Significant gains were also noted in the ability to create inclusive classrooms where students could safely talk about issues without fear of being sanctioned by other students or the teacher. The faculty gained significantly greater understanding and confidence in addressing disruptive students in the classroom. The data indicated that the faculty development initiative was so much of a success so that we continued it for two successive cohorts using internal funds.

Student outcomes were also positive, based on end-of-term course evaluations from the classes participating in the project. Students were significantly more comfortable speaking openly about a controversial topic and felt the instructor was effective in creating opportunities for difficult dialogue. Although only 240 out of 500 students completed the evaluations, many others were exposed to the classroom practices and community dialogues generated by our project.

Continuing the Conversation: Difficult Dialogues with Alaska Native Communities

The positive assessments were encouraging, but even after four faculty development intensives, two Books of the Year programs, and the creation of the *Start Talking* handbook, everyone felt we had just begun the conversation. This was especially true with respect to the tensions between our Alaska Native communities both on and off campus, which many faculty had become acutely aware of through participating in the intensives. We felt ready to move to a deeper level of dialogue, understanding, and action. The Ford Foundation agreed and included us in the group of thirteen out of the original twenty-six designated for funding for a more focused difficult dialogue.

The two-year renewal grant enabled us to continue introducing the lessons learned through the faculty development intensives and other learning communities using the *Start Talking* handbook. Two faculty from the original intensives conducted a six-session faculty learning community on engaging difficult dialogues based on *Start Talking*. Faculty who attended five of the six sessions received modest stipends for the purchase of materials at the UAA/APU Consortium Library.

More important, we chose to deepen our focus on a subset of difficult dialogues related to Alaska Native issues and constituencies and incorporated books by and about Alaska Native peoples into the Books of the Year program. The original intensives briefly addressed difficult dialogues related to race, ethnicity, and culture, using Alaska's Native peoples as a case study. For many faculty members, even this degree of focus on issues related to Alaska's indigenous communities (beyond the general concern over improving the retention rate for Alaska Native and other minority students) was new. Most of the professors who teach in Alaskan universities—like most of the general population in the state—come from "Outside" in the "Lower 48" states. Beyond the general concern for retaining Alaska Native (and all other) students, indigenous issues were not something to which our faculty had given much thought.

Alaska Native people make up 16 percent of the total population in Alaska, 8 percent of UAA students, and only 1.6 percent of faculty. They comprise 14 percent of APU's student body, but APU currently has no Alaska Native faculty. Both universities have invested significant resources in recruitment and retention measures for this important segment of Alaska's population, though retention rates remain well below the university averages. However, most retention initiatives aimed to make Alaska Native students and faculty more successful within the existing institutional culture. By contrast, the Difficult Dialogues project was designed not only to help non-Native faculty begin to understand and introduce into their courses key difficult dialogues between Alaska's Native communities and Western institutions of higher education, but also help them begin to incorporate traditional Alaska Native ways of teaching and learning into their teaching repertoires. The purpose of the latter focus was twofold: (1) to preempt or otherwise head off difficult dialogues that need not occur if faculty demonstrated a better understanding of and respect for traditional indigenous worldviews and issues and (2) to open faculty to the possibility that non-Native educators have as much or more to learn from Alaska Native elders, leaders, educators, and community members as indigenous peoples do from the mainstream. The intention was to establish a sense of mutuality so that genuine dialogue (difficult or not) could begin to take place between the two communities. We hoped that offering non-Native faculty a chance to enter more deeply into and appreciate the ways of teaching, learning and knowing of an "Other" (in the form of Alaska Native cultures) could also serve as a case study for learning from and interacting respectfully with other forms of difference. Such learning might offer transformational possibilities for higher education—possibilities everyone truly committed to education seeks and, as the Aleut leader cited at the opening to this chapter pointed out, are critical for our times.

Native Ways of Teaching and Learning

In conjunction with the project director (myself, a white woman), Alaska Native leaders, elders, educators, and community members designed a new faculty intensive using much the same structure as the previous intensives, but centered around Alaska Native issues and learning strategies. We recruited a second cohort of eighteen faculty fellows from among the participants in the previous four Difficult Dialogues cohorts, based on their demonstrated leadership, motivation, and commitment. Again, these fellows were expected to apply what they learned in the classroom, participate in assessment activities, and share their learning with their colleagues. Assignments were given to small groups of faculty to develop strategies for applying several of these ways of teaching and learning in at least one of their courses.

Faculty were introduced to several traditional Alaska Native ways of teaching and learning, including experiential and applied learning, place- and community-based learning, nonverbal learning, storytelling, and an organic earth-based pace, incorporating silences and pauses that provide time to reflect. They also participated in key difficult dialogues between Alaska Native communities and the academy concerning such topics as sustainability of life systems, the role of spirituality in education, the relationship between Western science and research and Alaska Native communities, institutional racism, and the lack of Alaska Native faculty and ways of teaching in the academy.

One day of the intensive took place on tribal lands some twenty miles north of the campuses. Alaska Native elders from four different indigenous nations spoke to the group, and each represented tribe made a presentation about its history and lands. An Alaska Native dance group performed and engaged the faculty in dancing, and faculty members presented nonverbal stories derived from their lives. At the end of the day, the group ate traditional foods together outside on the land. At various times during the week, guest presenters from the Alaska Native community shared their experience and expertise on topics ranging from our first-ever Alaska Native charter school for kindergarten to sixth grade, to Alaska Native storytelling, to what our Alaska Native students need today. In addition, Alaska Native faculty and staff participated in a fish-bowl exercise in which they shared their experience of institutional racism at one of the universities and how they believe that racism affects Alaska Native students. Interactive theater was employed to help faculty participants grapple with incidents involving institutional racism.

Online Teaching Portfolios

As a way of ensuring that the learning that resulted from participation in the intensive was not limited to these few faculty members, participants were required to create and post an electronic teaching portfolio based on the principles of the scholarship of teaching and learning (SoTL). They attended two training sessions in SoTL prior to the intensive that were designed to help them think about how best to introduce indigenous content and pedagogies into their courses. They also received technical assistance to help put the portfolios together and upload them onto the website. These portfolios can be viewed at www.uaa.alaska.edu/cafe/portfolios/index.cfm.

In one portfolio, Dorothy Shepard Dunne of APU describes how she introduced place-based learning and time for reflection into a writing assignment for her online human services course, Discussing Diversity and Discrimination. Each student was asked to find a place outdoors and spend at least an hour alone closely observing the surroundings and letting go of other thoughts. Dunne suggested a breathing exercise to help them let go. After their time outdoors, they were to write down what they had observed in as much detail as they could, how they felt during the exercise, and any meaning found in what they observed. Since the course was offered online, students were located in many different locations, including Virginia. The results were surprising and touching. Several wrote that they had never had this kind of experience before. These busy, plugged-in students had learned a powerful lesson about how to slow down and pay attention. And if they could hear the birds chattering and the sound of their own feet crunching on the brittle fallen leaves, feel the wind brushing their skin, and notice the texture of the clouds and the sky above, maybe they could listen with an open mind and heart to people who might look different than they do or hold a different point of view.

Don Rearden, assistant professor in UAA's College of Preparatory and Development Studies, used a similar exercise in his preparatory writing course with equally powerful results. Students deemed highly at risk academically by the institution produced lyrical, impassioned writings that brought tears to the eyes of Rearden's colleagues from the intensive when he shared them at one of the regular support sessions for participants.

A Life-Changing Experience

Project results have been impressive. UAA's Lampman designed qualitative and quantitative assessment programs for both faculty and students to track success. Pre- and posttests documented significant shifts in attitudes related to teaching strategies. For example, faculty and students increased their belief that slowing the class pace and covering less material at a deeper level would be beneficial for student learning. All groups involved with the intensive were also more likely to endorse the notion that course material should be tied to the sustainability of the earth's systems and that sharing personal stories relevant to class material should be encouraged. In addition, significant numbers of faculty shifted with respect to Alaska Native–specific questions; for example, 65 percent felt that their classrooms were now more likely to be places where all students would feel comfortable talking about Alaska Native issues, and 71 percent agreed more strongly that institutional racism is an important explanation for why some Alaska Native students have difficulty completing college. Qualitative data confirmed the transformative impact that the experience had on faculty, both personally and professionally. One faculty member offered these comments in the postintensive evaluation, "This has been a life-changing intensive . . . the experience will affect not only my teaching, but also my parenting and my citizenship." Another wrote, "This was a perspective-shifting, life-altering experience and I know that it will enable me to do my part in helping all students, and particularly Alaska Native students."

Why Start Talking?

While one of the primary motivations for the original initiative was to create classrooms safe for students and faculty to explore a full range of ideas and subjects, another reason we invested in this effort was to improve how we teach. Most of us are clear about the value of cross- and intercultural learning for our students, but fewer of us have focused on the similar value of developing cross-cultural faculty development programs. Such programs allow faculty to become temporarily "uncoupled from the stream of cultural givens" (Habermas, 1990, p. 162), allowing them to think critically about their own teaching practices and the ways in which they may be culturally bound. They help faculty become more aware of how unconscious biases and assumptions may be shaping our classroom environments and pedagogies in spite of our best efforts. They serve to challenge the ways in which faculty development programs, like teaching practices, can unknowingly serve to reproduce the unequal power structures in educational institutions.

We want to design programs that help faculty ensure that all students succeed, not just those who have already accumulated considerable cultural capital. We want to deliver programs that help faculty prepare students to think critically about the status quo and find ways to make society more just, healthy, and sustainable. It is difficult for faculty to do this if they have not had the opportunity to experience other ways of thinking, seeing, speaking about, and organizing the world themselves. Cross-cultural faculty development programs offer that opportunity.

For example, most faculty rarely consider it part of their responsibility to outline for students the connections between their discipline and the fate of the biosphere on which we depend for continued human existence. In indigenous educational systems, making those connections is central. "Our educational mission is to produce human beings who are at home in their place, their environment, their world," says Yup'ik faculty member Angayuqaq Oscar Kawagley. Native Alaskan educators challenge their mainstream colleagues to reconsider the very purpose of the educational endeavor. If we are not creating human beings who can ensure a sustainable environment for future generations, they ask, then what are we doing?

Learning from Alaska Native educators, community members, leaders, and elders reversed the usual faculty view in which professors tended to see their role as one of "helping" Alaska Native students succeed within the dominant culture. Instead, participants became aware that many indigenous students (and their communities) do not necessarily want to become more like the dominant culture. They learned that many students experience great losses as well as gains by "succeeding" in higher education—losses of language, oral traditions, ties to rural communities and elders, experience in subsistence harvesting practice—and that many elders fear that attending university makes their young people "stupid." Our faculty also learned that if Alaska Native students, communities, and cultures are embraced as full partners in higher education, they can contribute perspectives and practices that could radically improve the educational system for all our students.

The best practices in teaching and learning of nondominant cultures bring fresh, time-tested ideas into the academy. Some, like active, experiential learning, small group work, and contextualized learning, parallel those identified by Western research as the most effective ways of teaching for most students. Others, like the indigenous focus on shaping citizens aware of their interdependency with and responsibility to the ecosystems that support life, may be different and transformative.

What If You Do Not Have a Specific Minority Group to Work With?

Many, if not most, faculty development programs do not have a specific minority community with which to work closely to develop an effective cross-cultural faculty development program or module. What can we do in such cases?

First, there are indigenous communities near many universities that are largely invisible to the university community. Invisibility is a key component in the oppression of indigenous peoples, the inevitable result of centuries of policies of assimilation. Begin to research the indigenous nations in your region, where they live, and where their young people attend college. Often a tribal college has been formed because indigenous students do not feel at home in mainstream universities. Identify the indigenous student population at your institution, however small, and reach out to the people and programs that serve them. Ask them to help you find ways to help your faculty learn from those communities and cultures.

Second, begin to build relationships, if you do not already have them, with your faculty of color, international faculty, or community leaders from different cultural backgrounds. Invite them to meet with you to educate you about the best practices in teaching and learning from their cultural backgrounds. Set up opportunities for them to meet with faculty at your institution to share that knowledge. Nurture these relationships over time, and you will begin to develop resources on and off campus for cross-cultural faculty learning.

Finally, in your current faculty development work, emphasize teaching practices that are designed to make learning environments inclusive: varying teaching techniques, permitting multiple ways for learners to show that learning has occurred, using cooperative and collaborative teaching and learning styles, creating occasions for authentic human exchanges, relating course material to learners' lives, using inclusive language, employing problem-solving goals, and asking for feedback from learners about behaviors, practices, and policies that discriminate. These approaches and others have been demonstrated to create learning environments in which students "who have been marginalized by the educational system in this culture" (Tisdell, 1995, p. 84) can thrive (Tisdell, 1995; Wlodkowski & Ginsberg, 1995).

Next Steps

> *The purpose of a university is to make students safe*
> *for ideas—not ideas safe for students.*
>
> —Clark Kerr, former president, University of California

When we began this journey, we were not sure where it would take us. The dedication and belief in the process by university leadership, faculty developers, faculty members, and staff combined to create a process that organically built on itself and led us through each stage. We made progress toward our goals of improving the learning climates on both campuses, making them more inclusive of minority voices and ways of knowing, and providing a safer place for learning and the free exchange of ideas. We discovered that through thoughtful faculty development that built skills to introduce difficult dialogues into and enhance pluralism within our classrooms, we not only touched and challenged students but transformed and energized faculty. By establishing an open atmosphere where all viewpoints and beliefs are respected, we saw first-hand that both faculty and students are freed to explore new ideas and, in the words of our Aleut elder, "Think and work in new ways." Isn't that the role of the university?

How Do You Start Talking?

- Visit http://difficultdialoguesuaa.org to view *Start Talking: A Handbook for Engaging Difficult Dialogues in Higher Education* (Landis, 2008). Link to additional resources and campus initiatives, and learn more about the UAA/APU project
- Start a faculty learning community based on *Start Talking*.
- Become part of the national conversation (www.difficultdialogues. org) about integrating difficult dialogues into higher education across the country.

REFERENCES

Boyle, T. C. (1995). *The tortilla curtain*. New York, NY: Penguin Books.

Brookfield, S. D., & Preskill, S. (2005). *Discussion as a way of teaching: Tools and techniques for democratic classrooms* (2nd ed.). San Francisco, CA: Jossey-Bass.

Fadiman, A. (1997). *The spirit catches you and you fall down: A Hmong child, her American doctors, and the collision of two cultures*. New York, NY: Farrar, Straus, & Giroux.

Habermas, J. (1990). *Moral consciousness and communicative action* (C. Lenhardt & S. W. Nicholsen, Trans.). Cambridge, MA: MIT Press.

Kidder, T. (2004). *Mountains beyond mountains: The quest of Dr. Paul Farmer, a man who would cure the world*. New York, NY: Random House.

Lampman, C., Phelps, A., Bancroft, S., & Beneke, M. (2008). Contrapower harassment in academia: A survey of faculty experience with student incivility, bullying, and sexual attention. *Sex Roles, 60*(5/6), 331–346. doi:10.1007/s11199-008-9560-x

Landis, K. (Ed.). (2008). *Start talking: A handbook for engaging difficult dialogues in higher education*. Anchorage: University of Alaska Anchorage and Alaska Pacific University.

Rosenberg, R. (2004). *This is not civilization: A novel*. New York, NY: Houghton Mifflin Harcourt.

Tisdell, E. J. (1995). *Creating inclusive adult learning environments: Insights from multicultural education and feminist pedagogy*. Columbus, OH: ERIC Clearinghouse on Adult, Career and Vocational Education.

Wlodkowsi, R. J., & Ginsberg, M. B. (1995). *Diversity and motivation: Culturally responsive teaching*. San Francisco, CA: Jossey-Bass.

SECTION FOUR

DEVELOPING OUR CRAFT

18

FACULTY DEVELOPMENT BEYOND INSTRUCTIONAL DEVELOPMENT

IDEAS CENTERS CAN USE

Mary Deane Sorcinelli, University of Massachusetts Amherst

Tara Gray, New Mexico State University

A. Jane Birch, Brigham Young University

Most faculty development programs focus on the faculty member as teacher. However, faculty seek support in many areas, including orientation, mentoring, scholarly writing, time management, career advancement, leadership, and service. Research and practice also suggest that faculty and faculty development programs benefit from an integrated approach to professional development. This chapter fills a gap in faculty development practice by suggesting ways that centers can create programming that goes beyond instructional development, thereby supporting a more expansive range of faculty work.

A large-scale study of the field of faculty development indicates that many programs focus primarily on enhancing teaching and learning (Sorcinelli, Austin, Eddy, & Beach, 2006). Quality teaching and learning is critical for student development, and it has become increasingly complex, requiring new skills of faculty members and faculty developers.

We thank the following people who graciously read and responded to earlier drafts of this chapter: Kate Brinko, Tom Brinthaupt, Jo Clemmons, Jean Conway, Rene Hadjigeorgalis, Mark Hohnstreiter, Pam Hunt, Cathy Luna, Laura Madson, and Lynn Sorenson.

At the same time, research indicates that early-career faculty members, especially women and faculty of color, encounter challenges beyond their teaching role that can have a negative effect on their productivity and career advancement. These roadblocks include getting oriented, finding mentors, excelling in scholarship, creating work-life balance, navigating the tenure track, and leading effectively (Rice, Sorcinelli, & Austin, 2000; Yun & Sorcinelli, 2009). A comprehensive faculty study that Schuster and Finkelstein (2006) conducted also concludes that the nature of faculty work is increasingly multifaceted, thereby requiring professional development in more areas.

Faculty developers are well aware of expectations for faculty to fulfill new and expanding roles and responsibilities. Some have called for faculty development programs that better align with organizational goals (Morahan, Gold, & Bickel, 2002; Palmer, Dankoski, Brukiewicz, Logio, & Bogdewic, 2010). Others note that centers need to create multiple entry points for faculty development by serving needs other than instructional development: "A broad mandate . . . may give faculty more reasons to use the center" (Gray & Shadle, 2009, p. 8). Indeed, some faculty development centers have already adopted broader missions and ventured into additional programming areas, most notably new faculty orientation and mentoring programs. Fewer faculty development centers have engaged in scholarly writing, career advancement, time management, work-life balance, and leadership development, including department head training (Lee, 2010).

In this chapter, we explore ways that developers can address the roadblocks to faculty success by implementing programs that go beyond instructional development. We present ideas that have proven successful in terms of participation rates and ratings of overall effectiveness (assessment data are available from the authors). These efforts have been tested at three very different universities: New Mexico State University (NMSU), Brigham Young University (BYU), and University of Massachusetts Amherst (UMass). These universities differ in student enrollment, faculty, research classification, and private or public designation. Their centers also differ in size of staff devoted to faculty development beyond instructional development: 1.5 professional full-time equivalent (FTE) at NMSU, 3.5 at BYU, and 2.5 at UMass.

Each of these universities has created opportunities for faculty to get oriented, find mentors, strengthen scholarly writing, manage time, navigate the tenure process, and develop leadership skills. We encourage developers to venture into these emerging areas of practice, adapting ideas to the goals and resources of their own centers and institutions and thereby embody a more holistic, multifaceted definition of faculty development.

Getting Oriented

New faculty members are an important clientele for every faculty development center. Serving new faculty well during their initial year on campus establishes a solid platform for continued engagement with them throughout their careers. New faculty are especially open to assistance, and women and faculty of color, who often lack more informal support systems, are particularly well served by formal programs that help them negotiate a new environment (Sorcinelli & Yun, 2007). Also, helping faculty get off to a good start is a smart investment for institutions. The hiring process is time-consuming and expensive; the university profits when new faculty flourish and are retained (Bensimon, Ward, & Sanders, 2000).

New faculty orientations can take many forms. New or small centers might consider piloting a modest program. For example, at NMSU, the center provides two half-day orientations for new faculty so that they are not overloaded with information on arrival. These short orientations feature the provost and several other speakers and panels on topics such as teaching, scholarly writing, research, and promotion and tenure. In addition, new faculty members are encouraged to choose from more than one hundred workshops, courses, and short courses provided to all faculty each year that address a range of professional and institutional questions.

At UMass, the center's new faculty orientation extends across two semesters, helping newcomers develop both academic and social networks. Just prior to fall semester, new faculty (tenure-track and full-time contract faculty) spend a day getting to know each other and the campus, hearing from a panel of near peers, and experiencing a "progressive luncheon" with key service providers from the library, academic computing, faculty development, research affairs, and student life. The chancellor then hosts a reception at his home where new faculty, their spouses and partners, and senior administrators are introduced to each other. In spring semester, the chancellor and associate provost for faculty development invite all new tenure-track faculty to small group breakfasts, providing them a chance to take stock, ask questions, and reconnect with peers. All new faculty are also invited throughout the year to participate in workshops and apply for internal grants related to their context-specific professional needs.

BYU offers a multiformat eighteen-month program for all new tenure-track professors. The program begins with seven lunch sessions during fall semester, featuring topics that serve the needs of new faculty during their initial year. By the start of second semester, new faculty members choose a faculty colleague to serve as their mentor. Mentors and protégés come together to a February training meeting and are encouraged to meet regularly thereafter. In May, the new faculty members attend an intensive two-week seminar (meetings in the morning, homework in the afternoon). During the seminar, participants explore an array of faculty issues in greater depth, as well as connect with each other and key administrators. They also work on individual development plans and design three projects to pursue in the upcoming year (one each in teaching, scholarship, and service). The program concludes the following March with project reports and a celebratory banquet. To encourage participation, BYU provides a stipend of two thousand dollars to each participant who completes the program.

Mentoring

Mentoring helps new faculty members in many ways, resulting in better teaching evaluations, socioemotional support, political savvy, research productivity, and career success (Boice, 1990; Johnsrud & Atwater, 1993; Johnson, 2007). Unfortunately, spontaneous mentoring occurs for only about 30 percent of all new faculty (Boice, 2000; Goodwin & Stevens, 1998), and "nontraditional hires and newcomers who struggled most were even more likely to go unmentored" (Boice, 2000, p. 238).

Formal mentoring programs need not match protégés with one partner, as is the tradition. Some of the most successful mentoring programs allow the protégé to select his or her own mentor. In fact, research suggests that more successful mentoring relationships occur after the protégé meets with several possible mentors before choosing one (Boice, 2000). Furthermore, several recent studies suggest that faculty with multiple mentors reap greater career benefits than those with just one (van Emmerik, 2004; Yun & Sorcinelli, 2009) and that a networking model of mentoring may be more inclusive of women and minorities (Sorcinelli & Yun, 2007). Therefore, mentoring programs should encourage faculty to develop a broad, flexible network of mentoring relationships and to consider peers, near peers, and senior colleagues as potential mentoring partners.

New Mexico State University hosts a large (more than one hundred faculty) multiyear mentoring program designed to give pretenure faculty members a mentor from their first year through tenure. In this program, new faculty members are paired with more senior faculty by a committee of faculty members who know many faculty members across campus. In addition, two luncheons and two mixers are hosted each year so that participants in the program can network. NMSU also offers first- and second-year faculty a more intensive team mentoring program. In regular meetings, protégés receive help from their peers, as well as from the director of the faculty development center. Protégés interview three potential mentors before selecting one (Gray & Birch, 2008).

Many new faculty need mentoring as soon as they are hired and before they are in a position to select an appropriate mentor. At BYU, the center encourages department chairs to assign an experienced faculty member to assist new faculty during their first semester. New faculty are then encouraged to get to know colleagues, build relationships, and choose a long-term mentor by the beginning of the second semester. Before inviting someone to serve as their mentor, new faculty must have their choice approved by their department chair, who may be aware of reasons that a particular mentor would not be the best choice. After mentors are chosen, mentors and their protégés participate in joint training to help them learn how and think about how to establish a successful mentoring relationship. During this training, the mentoring pair discusses their goals for the relationship and determines a specific day and time they can meet regularly. They are encouraged to make this a mutually beneficial relationship by, for example, working on joint projects that serve both partners' interests.

The center at UMass directs a mutual mentoring initiative that promotes an innovative hybrid of traditional mentoring and professional networking. Unlike the traditional one-on-one mentoring relationship between a tenured faculty member and pretenure protégé, mutual mentoring encourages the development of a nonhierarchical network of support in which early-career faculty work with a range of mentoring partners to share their areas of experience and expertise for mutual benefit. The model is carried out through two grant programs. Team grants are for large group mentoring that support faculty-designed projects at the departmental, college, interdisciplinary, or interinstitutional levels. Microgrants are for small group mentoring that encourages early-career faculty to identify areas for professional growth and develop the necessary mentoring relationships to make such change possible. Partners focus on a wide array of self-selected topics, including research productivity, teaching development, tenure preparation, and work-life balance. Mentoring networks demonstrate every possible variation of mentoring: peer, near peer, senior to junior, one-on-one, small group, large group, face-to-face, and online. (Mentoring exemplars and a guide for mentoring partners and department chairs are available at www.umass.edu/ofd/ mentoring/Mutual%20Mentoring%20Guide%20Final%2011_20.pdf.)

In addition to formal programs, centers can help faculty widen their network of mentoring partners in other ways. Center workshops and seminars should be designed to help early-career faculty get to know each other and meet experienced faculty and key administrators. Faculty developers help build collegial networks by using name tags, sharing names and e-mail lists with participating faculty, emphasizing learning communities or workshop series versus one-time offerings, and providing informal opportunities to network such as meals and receptions. All of these strategies encourage the development of mentoring relationships and possible teaching and scholarly collaborations.

Scholarly Writing

Faculty members need support for scholarly writing and publishing. Three interventions that help faculty produce more and better scholarship are workshops on writing productivity, writing groups, and writing coaches. For each of these interventions, when pre- and postdata were available, publication rates improved at least twofold (McGrail, Rickard, & Jones, 2006). Writers' retreats can also help jump-start writing, provide synergy to writers, and help writers push through barriers they encounter (Elbow & Sorcinelli, 2006; Murray & Newton, 2009).

Boice (1997) found that academics, regardless of discipline, teaching load, or type of institution, produce more scholarly writing when they engage in daily writing, keep records of their writing, and hold themselves accountable to someone for doing so. Boice (1989) compared two groups of scholars and found that those who subscribed to these three practices produced more scholarly writing in a year than those who did not by a factor of nine.

Centers may want to include some or all of these practices as part of any intervention to improve scholarly productivity. For example, NMSU and BYU regularly host a writing expert to conduct a four-hour writing workshop on their campuses. The workshop helps faculty and graduate student scholars write daily, keep records, organize their paragraphs around topic sentences, and get meaningful help on their prose from others. After the opening workshop, writing circles of three or four writers meet for one hour weekly for the rest of the semester to support each other in their daily writing and to get feedback on a few pages that they have written each week (Gray, 2010; Gray & Birch, 2000).

UMass offers a portfolio of scholarly writing programs for faculty that includes writing retreats, writing spaces, and summer online writing fellowships. Writing retreats have evolved over the years from offering formal writing workshops to offering time and space to help faculty work on their scholarly writing. The center and university library collaborated to create a faculty-only teaching commons in the library that hosts a variety of large-scale and mini-writing retreats throughout the year. These include a long-standing A Room of Your Own retreat in June to help faculty jump-start their summer writing projects; a retreat in August for faculty to prepare for the upcoming semester; a January retreat to make effective use of writing time during winter break; and monthly mini-writing retreats so that faculty can schedule regular, distraction-free writing time. These events feature a quiet, comfortable, fully wired place in which to work. Such writing spaces with few interruptions are important for writing productivity (Boice, 2000), and centers might work with their libraries or other units to establish such spaces. Finally, the center provides summer online writing fellowships facilitated by an experienced local writing coach. Two-month fellowships are offered in June and July. Fellows establish concrete summer writing goals, track their writing progress online, receive online guidance from their coach and fellow peers in the program, and may interact with the writing coach and other participants through an in-person kick-off meeting or a midmonth consultation with the writing coach.

Time Management and Work-Life Balance

"Finding enough time to do my work" stands out as one of the predominant sources of stress reported in many studies of early-career faculty (Boice, 1992; Rice et al., 2000; Yun & Sorcinelli, 2009). Difficulties in balancing new responsibilities for teaching, research, and service usually head the list of faculty concerns. Concern about lack of time is a new faculty member's most consistent source of stress across time. One study (Olsen & Sorcinelli, 1992) found that over their first five years on the job, new faculty became increasingly comfortable with teaching and gained greater clarity and direction in their research agenda. However, their satisfaction with their ability to find enough time to do quality work and to balance the conflicting demands of research, teaching, and service steadily declined. Midcareer and senior faculty also report that work-related stress is frequently related to time constraints—feeling overloaded with work and having little or no time for personal matters (Chu, 2006).

Centers that address time management can help faculty cope with stress and also boost faculty morale and productivity. Effective time management solutions can be found in the interventions described in earlier sections, for example, providing just-in-time information at orientation, expediting the development of a network of mentors, and encouraging faculty to carve out time to write daily. In addition, centers can host an academic time management consultant. NMSU, BYU, and UMass have all hosted such individuals for campuswide professional development seminars. Such consultants can offer practical strategies to help participants integrate work and personal life and to consciously organize and manage paper, e-mail, and electronic files. Centers may also want to consider linking their website to campus policies and resources for work-life balance. At UMass, these links include help in areas as varied as child care, parental leave, postponement of the tenure decision year for new parents, accommodations for dual-career couples, and elder care.

Even more critical than specific programs, developers may want to consider how their centers' activities can emphasize the importance of managing professional roles and personal lives. One recommendation is to thread this issue throughout other activities provided to faculty by addressing it explicitly or implicitly. Faculty developers may want to ask presenters to keep this issue in mind as part of the context of their remarks for almost any faculty development topic. For example, some faculty choose collaborative work in scholarship as an explicit means to enable them to accomplish each scholar's career goals while also enhancing their personal lives. It is important to recognize and acknowledge that faculty members cannot do it all. They must prioritize, make choices about how to organize their work and their lives, and occasionally say no. Our job as faculty developers is to reassure them that this is true of all faculty members and to help provide support, including guidelines and resources, role models, and constant sensitivity to the complexity of their lives.

Navigating the Tenure Process

Three problems most commonly identified by early faculty regarding the process of tenure are expectations for performance, feedback on progress, and the collegial review structure (Rice et al., 2000). First and foremost, pretenure faculty members are troubled by unclear, shifting, and conflicting expectations for performance. The lack of clarity around expectations can be exacerbated by insufficient, unfocused, or unclear feedback on performance. Pretenure faculty also believe the problem with feedback and evaluation is intensified by several flawed aspects of the tenure and review process itself, which include frequently rotating department chairs, turnover in the membership of personnel committees, and closed committee meetings (Rice & Sorcinelli, 2002; Tierney & Bensimon, 1996). Clearly, support in navigating the tenure process is needed. One expert (Lieberman, 2002) calls such assistance indispensable. Nonetheless, sponsoring workshops on the topic of promotion and tenure may move centers closer to the firewall between faculty improvement and faculty evaluation than any other activity. The decision to offer tenure-related programming should be carefully considered and the programs thoughtfully planned with the help of college and university administrators. This initiative might be best launched by longer-standing centers that have considerable respect and support from faculty and administrators.

UMass organizes tenure preparation seminars that directly address pretenure faculty members' concerns about expectations, feedback, and the review process. The center traditionally sponsored a campuswide tenure preparation seminar, but faculty expressed interest in having more local information. As a result, the center now works directly with colleges to cosponsor and custom-design tenure preparation workshops in which college administrators, department chairs, and faculty help to design and exclusively lead the seminars. In this way, the center is seen as enabling the sharing of best practices rather than having any involvement in personnel processes. Workshops typically include a welcome from the dean, a step-by-step overview of the tenure process by an associate dean, and a panel discussion with a department chair and past members of the department and school and college personnel committees. The formal program concludes with a panel discussion with three or four recently tenured faculty members who share general strategies for achieving tenure. A reception follows the event so that pretenure faculty members can talk with their chairs, deans, and personnel committee members in a relaxed setting.

The NMSU center hosts two university-wide half-day pretenure workshops a year. During the fall and spring workshops, participants listen to the provost and several other speakers and panels. Participants are seated by college and bring their promotion and tenure packets along with questions to ask their deans and promotion and tenure committee members, who also attend. In the summer, the center offers a week-long tenure portfolio workshop. Participants meet for two hours a day for feedback on successive drafts from a mentor chosen by their college dean. (Often this mentor is the head of the college promotion and tenure committee.) The center also keeps a set of current promotion and tenure packets in its library for reference, and the skeleton of these packets is available online. The center director and one associate director are available on request to help faculty prepare their packets.

As an alternative, developers can shape existing programs to help new faculty make progress toward tenure. For example, at BYU, promotion and tenure is a topic that comes up frequently during the eighteen-month new faculty program. During this program, the center helps faculty frame their priorities so that they are striving for excellence in their professional responsibilities rather than just jumping through hoops to get tenure. Assuming the goals are worthy and faculty succeed in accomplishing them, promotion and tenure should largely take care of themselves. Nevertheless, it is important to make sure the university's expectations are clear. New faculty and chairs are encouraged to meet regularly to discuss expectations. During the first semester and again during the two-week seminar in May, the associate academic vice president talks to new faculty about managing the evaluation process. The center also collaborates with college-level administrators to provide college-specific meetings on promotion and tenure during the May seminar. Finally, the center maintains an ongoing discussion with university administrators, providing research and advice to help improve the promotion and tenure process for all faculty members, including reviewers.

Leadership and Service

Just as graduate school does not prepare one to be an assistant professor, achieving tenure does not prepare one to be a midcareer faculty member. Service and administrative duties begin to take up considerable faculty time right after tenure (Baldwin, Lunceford, & Vanderlinden, 2005). Faculty who are asked to assume a range of administrative roles after tenure often have little leadership experience or training. The steep learning curve and time required to feel confident as an academic leader can have a negative impact on the overall quality of a university's day-to-day functioning.

New chairs, heads, and directors of programs take on roles with an influence that in many ways can rival that of a chancellor (Chu, 2006). Because the department is the locus for a great deal of the university's work, these administrators are called on to make serious personnel, budget, and curricular decisions. Faculty developers recognize the importance of supporting departmental leadership and have offered aspiring, new, and seasoned leaders the opportunity to share ideas, discuss problem situations, and brainstorm solutions in a safe environment (Sorcinelli et al., 2006).

When teaching centers provide this help, Lucas (2002) notes that they increase their impact.

UMass has developed two year-long programs: one to support new department chairs, heads, and directors and one to expose assistant professors to administrative careers in an effort to develop our own academic leaders. The chair leadership program offers monthly luncheon seminars led by seasoned chairs and administrators and focuses on topics selected by participants, such as budgeting during difficult times, time management, and managing conflict, as well as a campus update and feedback session with the provost and dean of the faculties. On behalf of the chancellor's office, the center also coordinates the Chancellor's Junior Faculty Fellows Program, which fosters an exchange of ideas between the campus's central administration and promising new faculty members who might be interested in campus leadership in the future. As part of the program, fellows meet regularly each semester with the chancellor to discuss the university's direction and how the central administration can assist pretenure faculty as they accomplish their professional goals.

Alternately, centers may want to focus leadership efforts on tenured faculty leaders as well as sitting department chairs. NMSU's center directs a year-long leadership program designed to help campus leaders (including department chairs) become familiar with university issues and get hands-on experience in identifying and solving university-wide problems. The program begins with a two-day retreat based on the principles of Stephen Covey's 7 *Habits of Highly Effective People* (1989). The retreat is followed by a series of three-hour monthly meetings in which participants hear from various administrators for an hour and work for the next two hours on a Provost's Project. This is a research project that the participants undertake collectively to help the provost with a campus-wide problem. The topic is selected by the participants in consultation with the provost. Previous topics include campuswide communication, reallocation of faculty lines, academic integrity, and why NMSU faculty leave and why they stay. At the end of the year-long project, the Provost's Project is presented to the provost with recommendations for institutional improvement in areas such as communication and shared governance, resulting in policy and procedural changes on campus. In addition, the new provost at NMSU has asked the center to establish a department head academy, which will provide one or two programs monthly and a two-day retreat in May for both deans and department heads.

A multilayered set of programs supports department chairs at BYU, where a department chair coordinating council directs department chair training.

A website, which is accessible to other campus administrators, provides information on all chair tasks with attendant policies, forms, calendars, directories, and other resources. Events are organized around policy, dialogue, and leadership. Policy events consist of regular seminars for new chairs, directed by the associate academic vice president for faculty. Topics cover core aspects of chairing associated with policy: hiring, annual reviews, promotion and tenure, finances, and budgets. Dialogue events facilitate informal interactions among chairs through brown bag discussions held monthly to address topics selected by chairs and one-on-one lunches (paid by the center) to which a new chair can invite a veteran chair. Example dialogue topics include setting academic standards, departmental governance, and giving and receiving feedback. Leadership events consist of occasional workshops to which all academic administrators are invited; these often feature someone of prominence from off campus. Example leadership topics include building functional teams and handling difficult conversations.

First Steps and Concluding Thoughts

When faculty development programming goes beyond instructional development, faculty benefit by having opportunities to develop in their multiple roles; faculty developers benefit because participation at these events tends to be higher and spills over into instructional development events; and institutions benefit through improved faculty performance and satisfaction. As developers consider whether to respond to emerging areas of practice, they might wonder if their center is large enough or well-enough established to tackle these issues, how to prioritize expansion efforts, or whether they will just invite "mission creep." Center personnel might begin by reflecting on the following questions: What are the noticeable gaps in supporting faculty work on campus that your center might fill? Does the initiative fit within your mission and values? Will it represent your center well? What are the needed resources—staff time and budget? Is this a good use of those resources? How broad an audience will this initiative reach? Can your center work in partnership with other units (say, research affairs or the library) or academic leaders (such as department chairs, deans, or the provost) to further mutual agendas for enhancing faculty careers?

In getting started, very new and small centers might begin by addressing new faculty orientation, scholarly writing, or time management, issues that are central to faculty life and for which programming is relatively easy to put together. Larger, more mature centers are more likely to have the resources and experienced faculty development professionals to address mentoring, career advancement, leadership, and service. Ideally, responding to a broader mission will not only allow a center to better address the needs of the whole faculty member and the broader institution, but also expand the expertise, reach, and potential of the center itself.

REFERENCES

Baldwin, R. G., Lunceford, C. J., & Vanderlinden, K. E. (2005). Faculty in the middle years: Illuminating an overlooked phase of academic life. *Review of Higher Education, 29*(1), 97–118. doi:10.1353/rhe.2005.0055

Bensimon, E. M., Ward, K., & Sanders, K. (2000). *The department chair's role in developing new faculty into teachers and scholars.* San Francisco, CA: Jossey–Bass.

Boice, R. (1989). Procrastination, busyness and bingeing. *Behavior Research Therapy, 27*(6), 605–611. doi:10.1016/0005-7967(89)90144-7

Boice, R. (1990). Mentoring new faculty: A program for implementation. *Journal of Staff, Program, and Organizational Development, 8*(3), 143–160.

Boice, R. (1992). *The new faculty member: Supporting and fostering professional development.* San Francisco, CA: Jossey-Bass.

Boice, R. (1997). Strategies for enhancing scholarly productivity. In J. M. Moxley & T. Taylor (Eds.), *Writing and publishing for academic authors* (pp. 19–34). Lanham, MD: Rowman & Littlefield.

Boice, R. (2000). *Advice for new faculty members: Nihil nimus.* Needham Heights, MA: Allyn & Bacon.

Chu, D. (2006). *The department chair primer: Leading and managing academic departments.* San Francisco, CA: Jossey-Bass.

Covey, S. R. (1989). *The seven habits of highly effective people: Powerful lessons in personal change.* New York, NY: Simon & Schuster.

Elbow, P., & Sorcinelli, M. D. (2006, November/December). The faculty writing place: A room of our own. *Change, 38*(6), 17–22.

Goodwin, L. D., & Stevens, E. A. (1998). An exploratory study of the role of mentoring in the retention of faculty. *Journal of Staff, Program, and Organizational Development, 16*(1), 39–47.

Gray, T. (2010). *Publish and flourish: Become a prolific scholar.* Las Cruces: New Mexico State University, Teaching Academy.

Gray, T., & Birch, A. J. (2000). Publish, don't perish: A program to help scholars flourish. In D. Lieberman & C. Wehlburg (Eds.), *To improve the academy: Vol. 19. Resources for faculty, instructional, and organizational development* (pp. 268–284). San Francisco, CA: Jossey-Bass.

Gray, T., & Birch, A. J. (2008). Team mentoring: A participatory way to mentor new faculty. In D. R. Robertson & L. B. Nilson (Eds.), *To improve the academy: Vol. 26. Resources for faculty, instructional, and organizational development* (pp. 230–241). San Francisco, CA: Jossey-Bass.

Gray, T., & Shadle, S. E. (2009). Launching or revitalizing a teaching center: Portraits of practice. *Journal of Faculty Development, 23*(2), 5–12.

Johnson, W. B. (2007). *On being a mentor: A guide for higher education faculty.* Mahwah, NJ: Erlbaum.

Johnsrud, L. K., & Atwater, C. D. (1993). Scaffolding the ivory tower: Building supports for faculty new to the academy. *CUPA Journal, 44*(1), 1–14.

Lee, V. (2010). Program types and prototypes. In K. J. Gillespie, D. L. Robertson, & Associates, *A guide to faculty development* (2nd ed., pp. 21–34). San Francisco, CA: Jossey–Bass.

Lieberman, D. (2002). Nurturing institutional change. In C. M. Schroeder & Associates, *Coming in from the margins: Faculty development's emerging organizational development role in institutional change* (pp. 60–73). Sterling, VA: Stylus.

Lucas, A. (2002). Increase your effectiveness in the organization: Work with department chairs. In K. J. Gillespie (Ed.), *A guide to faculty development: Practical advice, examples, and resources* (pp. 2–8). San Francisco, CA: Jossey-Bass.

McGrail, M. R., Rickard, C. M., & Jones, R. (2006). Publish or perish: A systematic review of interventions to increase academic publication rates. *Higher Education Research and Development, 25*(1), 19–35. doi:10.1080/07294360500453053

Morahan, P. S., Gold, J. S., & Bickel, J. (2002). Status of faculty affairs and faculty development offices in U.S. medical schools. *Academic Medicine, 77*(5), 398–401.

Murray, R., & Newton, M. (2009). Writing retreat as structured intervention: Margin or mainstream? *Higher Education Research and Development, 28*(5), 541–553. doi:10.1080/07294360903154126

Olsen, D., & Sorcinelli, M. D. (1992). The pretenure years: A longitudinal perspective. In M. D. Sorcinelli & A. E. Austin (Eds.), *New directions for teaching and learning: No. 50. Developing new and junior faculty* (pp. 15–25). San Francisco, CA: Jossey-Bass.

Palmer, M. M., Dankoski, M. E., Brukiewicz, R. R., Logio, L. S., & Bogdewic, S. P. (2010). Rx for academic medicine. In L. B. Nilson & J. E. Miller (Eds.), *To improve the academy: Vol. 28. Resources for faculty, instructional, and organizational development* (pp. 292–309). San Francisco, CA: Jossey-Bass.

Rice, R. E., & Sorcinelli, M. D. (2002). Can the tenure process be improved? In R. P. Chait (Ed.), *The questions of tenure* (pp. 101–124). Cambridge, MA: Harvard University Press.

Rice, R. E., Sorcinelli, M. D., & Austin, A. E. (2000). *Heeding new voices: Academic careers for a new generation.* Sterling, VA: Stylus.

Schuster, J. H., & Finkelstein, M. J. (2006). *The American faculty: The restructuring of academic work and careers.* Baltimore, MD: Johns Hopkins University Press.

Sorcinelli, M. D., Austin, A. E., Eddy, P. L., & Beach, A. L. (2006). *Creating the future of faculty development: Learning from the past, understanding the present.* San Francisco, CA: Jossey-Bass.

Sorcinelli, M. D., & Yun, J. (2007, November/December). From mentor to mentoring network: Mentoring in the new academy. *Change, 39*(6), 58–61.

Tierney, W. G., & Bensimon, E. M. (1996). *Promotion and tenure: Community and socialization in academe.* Albany: State University of New York Press.

van Emmerik, I.J.H. (2004). The more you can get the better: Mentoring constellations and intrinsic career success. *Career Development International, 9*(6), 578–594. doi:10.1108/13620430410559160

Yun, J. H., & Sorcinelli, M. D. (2009). When mentoring is the medium: Lessons learned from a faculty development initiative. In L. B. Nilson & J. E. Miller (Eds.), *To improve the academy: Vol. 27. Resources for faculty, instructional, and organizational development* (pp. 365–384). San Francisco, CA: Jossey-Bass.

19

GO FOR THE GOLD

FUNDRAISING FOR TEACHING CENTERS

Mark A. Hohnstreiter, Tara Gray, New Mexico State University

At New Mexico State University Teaching Academy, we have developed a comprehensive model to raise funds from faculty and others for our teaching center, which has resulted in a culture of giving. The payoff from a fundraising effort is huge, not only in terms of money, but in terms of the personal investment of participants, both valuable in difficult economic times. We explain in this chapter how to establish a fundraising program so that your teaching center can go for the gold.

Small budgets are one of the major challenges facing teaching centers. Although faculty developers may assume that it is the job of university advancement to do their fundraising, very few such units fundraise for departments as small as teaching centers. Thus, centers may want to initiate their own fundraising to supplement allocations from central administration.

At the New Mexico State University (NMSU) Teaching Academy, we have raised funds from university units and individuals. We reasoned that it would be easier to get some money from many sources rather than a lot from central administration and that deans would be especially supportive given their faculty's participation in our activities. In 1998, we began soliciting from deans and directors amounts ranging from $3,000 to $20,000 (Gray & Conway, 2007). In 2004, we began systematic efforts to raise additional money from faculty and other interested individuals from the university community and beyond. As of 2010, our annual donations have grown to $30,000 a year, given by more one hundred regular donors. Our center also obtained three exceptional future gifts

We thank the following people for their sage responses to earlier drafts of this chapter: Lockett Ford Ballard Jr., A. Jane Birch, Jean Conway, Ereney Hadjigeorgalis, Erika Kustra, Laura Madson, and Ben Wu.

Figure 19.1 Fundraising Plan Flowchart

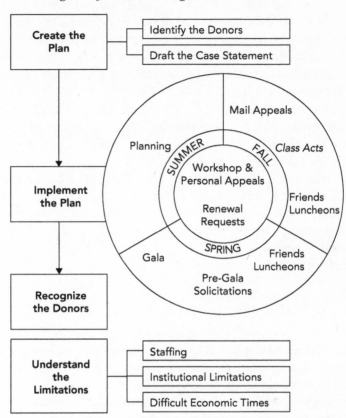

Note. Class Acts is a Teaching Academy newsletter.

totaling more than $375,000 to start an endowment. We estimate that we have raised four times what we have spent on fundraising.

A start-up fundraising program requires thorough planning (Weinstein, 2009), as depicted in Figure 19.1. First, we identified potential donors and crafted a statement seeking their support. Second, we solicited gifts through mail appeals, personal appeals, and fundraising events. Third, we recognized donors to thank them and encourage repeat giving. The plan needed to be realistic, so we considered and addressed potential limitations.

Identifying the Donors

Identifying the right potential donors gives the fundraising plan the greatest chance of success (Sargeant & Jay, 2004). Donors for traditional fundraising can be private individuals, corporations, foundations, government, and private agencies and, in the case of a teaching center, the participants themselves. At NMSU, we decided to focus first on potential donors who were nearest and dearest to our program: our members. Entry-level members are those who participate ten hours or more in Teaching Academy programming; sustaining members, twenty hours; and distinguished members, forty hours. Although most centers do not have a membership program, it is essential to identify regular participants before launching an advancement effort (Pitman, 2007). We started our fundraising program by approaching all three groups of members. Because they are on the university payroll, they had the additional option of giving through payroll deduction.

Subsequently we broadened our appeals to selected community members, including emeriti faculty, retired educators in the community, the American Association of University Women, and major university donors we happened to know well. Furthermore, we asked our board for the names of potential prospects. Three community donors made all the difference with their planned gifts of bequests (Ashton, 2004).

Making the Case for Support

Donors are savvy and will naturally question the need for giving to a teaching center as opposed to other worthwhile charities. Therefore, launching a sound advancement plan requires a succinct case for support; this is the case statement. Donors want to know why their gifts are needed, what purpose they will serve, how to give, and what amounts to give. A good case statement includes the essence of the mission and vision of the teaching center (Ahern, 2007). It tells why the teaching center is necessary and spells out opportunities rather than problems (Barbato & Furlich, 2000). In addition, the case statement is the primary document distributed to donors and friends. Portions of its text will be used in fundraising appeals and grant applications. Finally, the process of creating the case statement creates buy-in from constituents, heightens awareness of the teaching center's needs, can overcome institutional reluctance, and may generate initial gifts (Hecht, 2008).

In the NMSU Teaching Academy case statement (Exhibit 19.1), we crafted an argument for supporting our unit, provided some statistics, and made an appeal. Our argument was threefold: (1) teaching and learning are vital components of the university mission; (2) the Teaching Academy builds community for NMSU educators through training, mentoring, and networking; and, perhaps most important, (3) the Teaching Academy ultimately benefits all university students through enhanced learning.

Exhibit 19.1 Case Statement

"Giving a student a scholarship means changing the world one student at a time; giving a teaching scholarship means changing the world many students at a time."

The NMSU Teaching Academy offers donors the opportunity to have an institution-wide impact on the NMSU campuses. Some 50% of University faculty members participate in at least one NMSU Teaching Academy activity a year. The Center provides training, networking, and mentoring to NMSU faculty, staff and graduate student teachers. It supports teachers, enhances learning, and builds community. The Teaching Academy helps educators develop extraordinary teaching lives embedded in exceptional careers. All members of the University community, especially NMSU students, benefit through enhanced learning.

Formally organized in 2003, the NMSU Teaching Academy is modeled on other successful initiatives at United States colleges and universities and is the most advanced teaching center in the state of New Mexico. The Teaching Academy serves more than 1,000 educators and provides over 8,000 hours of professional development per year. Offerings have included short courses, such as Team Mentoring and Publish & Flourish, and workshops on teaching, learning, and distance education.

Gifts of all sizes are valuable because they provide ongoing support for the Academy. The Academy provides several significant donor opportunities, and both its director and advancement officer would be pleased to describe them in greater detail.

Scholarship Support: $100,000

The Teaching Academy seeks scholarships for faculty to attend national teaching conferences and institutes. Such scholarships enhance teaching, which benefits all members of the University community and especially NMSU students. Many newer faculty members do not have the discretionary salary or support to otherwise attend these valuable professional development opportunities.

Capital Opportunities: $250,000

The Teaching Academy maintains a spacious and well-equipped classroom to conduct its programs. It is the site of an event every day throughout the school year, conducted by educational leaders from NMSU and across the country. Naming the classroom would provide a donor significant recognition, as well as ensure that the room would be equipped with the latest teaching technology, including computers, projectors, and other furnishings critical to the teaching process. In addition, the Teaching Academy maintains an extensive teaching library used by NMSU educators and other participants in the Academy's programs.

Named Endowments: $2 million

While NMSU maintains a strong institutional commitment to its Teaching Academy, endowments would provide perpetual support and ensure that the Academy receives funding far into the future. In this way, the Academy would be permanently institutionalized in the fabric of the teaching culture at NMSU. Such endowments could include naming the Academy, or providing an endowed chair or professorship to support faculty or graduate student fellows at the Academy. *The Teaching Academy has already established an endowment fund through the NMSU foundation, and gifts of any size are welcome.*

Statistics are also persuasive. For example, about 50 percent of our seven hundred full-time faculty members participate in at least one NMSU Teaching Academy offering a year, and about 30 percent of the three hundred NMSU Teaching Academy members are donors. A particularly compelling appeal was borrowed from the Texas A&M Center for Teaching Excellence: "Giving a student a scholarship means changing the world one student at a time; giving a teaching scholarship means changing the world many students at a time."

Soliciting Gifts

We seek gifts throughout the school year through mail appeals; one-on-one solicitations; and pitches at workshops, Friends Luncheons, and the Teaching Academy gala. Our annual cycle of activity has become routine, making the fundraising program easier to schedule and manage. Members and other friends of the Teaching Academy receive solicitations at selected points in the academic year. Thus, prospective donors are given multiple opportunities to give, with each appeal generating new and increased givers (Greenfield, 2002).

Mail Appeals

To start our fundraising effort, a campus mail appeal (Exhibit 19.2) was sent to all past and present members (Greenfield, 2002). We developed letters of solicitation to accompany either our giving envelope (for non-university employees) or the university's payroll deduction form (for faculty and staff) (Lowenstein, 1997). Payroll deduction, an automatic way of giving, proved popular with faculty and is convenient for us because many of these gifts renew from year to year.

Exhibit 19.2 Mail Appeal

Each fall, we write to our Teaching Academy members to ask for your financial support of our efforts. The University provides us with the important core support we require to maintain our activities. To do even more, we rely on the generosity of our members.

Our donors help support scholarships to teaching workshops, new materials for our library, attracting nationally recognized speakers, and developing even more innovative programs. For example, this year we launched *Tenure and Promotion Portfolios*, a weeklong intensive, immersion workshop to assist faculty in documenting their greatest accomplishments in teaching, scholarship and service.

We invite you to join more than 100 of your colleagues who have already chosen to lend their support to the Teaching Center. We thank you for your kind consideration.

Our solicitation materials guide donors to give in specified amounts. Without giving categories, the tendency is for donors to make smaller gifts than they are capable of (Sargeant & Jay, 2004). The annual recognition categories we developed were based on a pay period every two weeks: backers (five dollars per pay period), builders (ten dollars per pay period), founders (twenty-five dollars per pay period), and benefactors (fifty dollars per pay period). We also give donors the option of making cash gifts outright, and we specify corresponding amounts.

Typically the advancement officer and director have jointly written our appeals. Recently we asked an enthusiastic faculty benefactor to write because changing authors draws more attention to our appeals (Ahern, 2007). We have followed the cue of many charities in asking for upgraded giving. Upgrade mailings (Exhibit 19.3) are personalized, asking our backers to become builders and our builders to become founders (we ask our founders to become benefactors in person only). Asking for upgrades has resulted in increased gifts.

One-on-One Solicitations

Of course, direct one-on-one solicitations are more successful than mail requests (Panas, 2002). In fact, peer-to-peer conversations can be among the most effective tools fundraisers have available (Reid, 1998). Resources are readily available to guide volunteers and new fundraisers in these solicitations. A faculty developer who does not feel comfortable

Exhibit 19.3 Upgrade Letter

We value your financial support of our Teaching Academy. You are demonstrating your commitment to our important work of training, mentoring, and networking with your regular gift of $XX/month.

We appreciate your generosity and we would like to ask you to consider increasing your support to help us in what may be our most challenging financial year. Like many units of the University, and especially smaller ones like ours, we face challenging times. As you well know, NMSU has had to make difficult decisions about its support of various colleges, departments, and centers.

The Teaching Academy is no exception to budget reduction. We have had to make several difficult decisions. In the past we have funded travel for faculty to attend national conferences, such as *Boot Camp for Profs* and the Madison *Distance Education Conference*. We have featured many national speakers, the most popular being Larry Michaelsen (Team-Based Learning) and Meggin McIntosh (Time Management). More than 50 faculty and staff attended our grant-writing workshops mentored by Ron Stewart. And we have offered stipends to participants in our short courses. We regret that we will not be able to continue all of these activities in 2010. Certainly this is no reflection on NMSU's support of our Teaching Academy. We continue to receive accolades and encouragement from the president's and provost's offices, as well as deans, department heads, and faculty. However, the reality is that our budget has been cut by a full 30%.

Our donor giving makes up 25% of our total budget. If we can increase this, we might be able to reinstate some of these valuable activities. We hope that you will consider augmenting our resources by adding to your contribution. We are including a payroll deduction form for you, should you choose to do so. We hope you will.

making such visits may want to team with a teaching center board member, a committed donor or volunteer, or a member of the university advancement staff (Schneiter, 1985). Panas (2002) describes how to make a personal request, word by word and step by step.

Pitches at Workshops

Another successful way to seek gifts is to have donors give pitches at workshops. We arrange such pitches at about one workshop per month (Warwick, 2009). We provide the donors with sample scripts but encourage them to give testimony from the heart (Reid, 1998). These testimonies are very productive: at the end of one week-long workshop, four out of twelve of the participants made pledges.

Friends Luncheons

Friends Luncheons are conducted in a group setting, and guests have included local legislators, emeriti faculty, representatives of community organizations, and university donors. The purpose of these events is fundraising as well as friend raising. Teaching Academy leadership and members explain the work of the center and provide testimonials about how the center has affected them. We present the need for funding tactfully, following up in writing and personally with the most promising donors. The results have included greater public awareness of the center and gifts ranging from five hundred to a thousand dollars to the exceptional six-figure planned gifts directed to the Teaching Center's endowment (Schumacher & Seiler, 2003).

The Gala

The close of the school year, as well as the conclusion of the center's annual cycle of activity, is marked by the NMSU Teaching Academy's annual gala, Champagne and Chocolate. The gala is a celebration that also serves as a high point for donor solicitation and recognition. On our guest list are all Teaching Academy members and donors for the current year, special awardees, department heads, and deans, as well as the president and provost. The gala is well publicized, as we never miss an opportunity to see ourselves in print.

The gala was not initially conceived as a fundraising event, but we now send a personalized solicitation letter (Exhibit 19.4) one month prior to the event reminding members that "your name can be here" in our gala program. In addition, we send personalized e-mail reminders to some of our most active members just before the printing deadline for the gala poster and program. Gala solicitations have proved to be among our most successful: members are eager to be recognized as donors at the event. Our e-mail response rate has been as high as 20 percent. Those who cannot give frequently write with accolades.

Recognizing Donors

Fundraising efforts do not stop once a gift is received. Donor recognition is an important part of the fundraising effort and can encourage repeat and increased giving (Sargeant & Jay, 2004). Recognition activities contain the same message as our solicitations: that giving to the NMSU Teaching Academy is important. It is also persuasive when members see

---

Exhibit 19.4 E-Mail Solicitation

Congratulations on earning a membership at the Teaching Academy this year!

Allow me to introduce myself: I'm the Teaching Academy advancement officer. I want to personally invite you to consider donating to the NMSU Teaching Academy. Your contribution would help us continue to offer the programming you are used to. Our donors help provide the Center with more than 25% of its resources—an especially valuable form of support in these difficult budgetary times.

Our payroll deduction levels are as follows:

Founders: $25.00 or more per pay period

Builders: $10.00 or more per pay period

Backers: $5.00 or more per pay period

We would love to include you among our donors. To have your name listed on our wall of honor and in the Gala program, we would need to hear back from you by April 19. *You need only email us a response at this time,* and we will then send you a payroll deduction form. Thanks for your consideration.

their peers and leaders giving. Donors are listed in newsletters by giving categories and invited to special events. Of course, a few donors desire little or no recognition, but most welcome mention of their giving.

We purposely err on the side of overrecognition. The NMSU Teaching Academy sends immediate thanks by a hand-written card from the advancement officer, as well as a formal letter (Exhibit 19.5) and an e-mail, both signed by the director and processed by an administrative assistant. The center maintains a prominent wall of honor in its classroom and on its website. Donors are recognized at the annual gala, where they wear special name tag ribbons, receive mention in the program, and are asked to stand as a group. In addition, all donors are invited to a group or individual lunch with the director, depending on the size of their gift. Donors are thanked as well by the university foundation in the same way as are all other university donors.

More than any other form of recognition, it is vitally important that any fundraising program ensures that funds raised for a stated purpose are used for that purpose. Professionals are bound to the Donor Bill of Rights, 1993, developed collaboratively by the Association of Fund-Raising Counsel, Association for Healthcare Philanthropy, Council for Advancement and Support of Education, and Association of Fundraising Professionals (Fischer, 2000).

Exhibit 19.5 Recognition Letter

Thank you so much for your personal support of the Teaching Academy. Your gifts enable us to purchase library materials, support short courses, provide scholarships to teaching conferences, and bring nationally known speakers to our Academy. Your generosity also sustains the spirits of all of us who work for this fine organization.

As you well know, our Teaching Academy mission is to provide training, networking and mentoring to all NMSU University educators in an effort to support teachers, enhance learning, and build community. We help you and your colleagues develop extraordinary teaching lives embedded in exceptional careers. All members of the university community, especially NMSU students, benefit.

You are joined by more than one hundred colleagues who have also committed their support to the Teaching Academy. The world is a better place because of generosity. We thank you for being a cheerful giver!

Fundraisers who subscribe to such organizations as the Association of Fundraising Professionals are obligated to adhere to this organization's code of ethics. The purpose of these codes is to ensure fidelity to the donor's intent. Although gifts to the NMSU Teaching Academy are unrestricted, they are intended to benefit five broad areas: national speakers, teaching scholarships, short courses taught by center staff, teaching books and equipment, and endowment. We spend these funds accordingly and communicate our allocations in donor correspondence.

Limitations

Inevitably a fundraising program will encounter challenges and limitations.

Staffing

Allocating staffing is one of the most significant challenges facing the start-up advancement program. Often a limitation at teaching centers, time and effort are precious resources. Nonetheless, there are several feasible models for assigning the fundraising task to professionals, including ours.

Some of the work of fundraising is shared by the director and administrative assistant of the center, but most is done by a designated advancement officer. The advancement officer plans and implements the fundraising program, manages the solicitation of individual gifts, coordinates efforts with other members of the university foundation fundraising team, and generates awareness of the center through publications and special events.

A faculty developer can serve in the role of advancement officer, and so can a graduate assistant. The advancement officer can be an additional staff member paid for by the teaching center. Alternatively, the university advancement office might assign one of its staff to oversee the teaching center's fundraising, with or without cost to the center. We decided to hire a quarter-time dedicated advancement officer because we felt that our new program would benefit from the guidance of a fundraising professional (Weinstein, 2009). In the beginning, we used ten hours a week of the advancement officer's time; now that the program is established, we use only five hours a week. In this way, our fundraising effort has become self-sustaining, raising more funds than it costs by a factor of four to one.

Resources available to the advancement officer include colleagues who have participated in fundraising and professionals in university advancement (Barbato & Furlich, 2000). The advancement officer could also garner guidance and peer support from professional fundraising organizations such as the Association of Fundraising Professionals or Council for the Advancement and Support of Education. Among the highly recommended print resources for fundraising are Greenfield (2002), Lowenstein (1997), Panas (2002), and Weinstein (2009).

Institutional Considerations

Because of institutional considerations, not every element of our comprehensive fundraising program may fit another faculty development unit. Some centers may be too small or too new to contemplate an aggressive fundraising effort. Faculty developers may be uncomfortable becoming part-time advancement officers or may not have time. However, our experience has been that many of these objections are more perceived than real. Often they can be overcome by taking the consensus-building step of creating a fundraising plan, including a case statement.

Other teaching centers may be explicitly discouraged from fundraising by their university advancement office. While some campuses (ours included) encourage decentralized fundraising, others take a more centralized approach (Hecht, 2008). A teaching center fundraising effort would function best in a large institution that already has a strong and established advancement office with many potential donors. Otherwise the teaching center would be perceived as being in competition for the same few donors. We argue that our efforts augment, rather than detract from, the university's overall fundraising picture: our Teaching Academy donors have given above and beyond what they may give for other university purposes.

Fundraising in Difficult Economic Times

Centers should not be dissuaded from fundraising by a depressed economic climate or curtailed budgets. Many charities (ours included) are raising as much as or more than they did before 2008 (Holcomb, 2009). Jaschik (2011) reports that charitable contributions to all colleges and universities increased by a modest 0.5 percent from 2009 to 2010. Among research/doctoral institutions, private universities saw an increase of 1.5 percent, and public universities showed an increase of 5.1 percent. Indeed, if a teaching center is facing budget cutbacks, fundraising may well be the answer to bridge the gap (Warwick, 2009). There are several valuable strategies for fundraising in challenging times (Klein, 2009). Our 2009 appeal to donors (see Exhibit 19.3) conveyed a message of the impact of budget cuts on our center and asked for increased giving, without adopting the tone of appearing ungrateful for the university's core support. This same letter was sent in a slightly different form to NMSU Teaching Academy members who were not donors. Both letters had a positive response.

Results

The NMSU Teaching Academy was reinvented from a previous faculty development unit that had fallen on hard times. We believed that the enthusiasm generated by its reinvigoration in 2003 would result in gifts, so we took a calculated risk in 2004 by hiring a part-time advancement officer who worked ten hours a week, funded by an open budget line created by the retirement of a staff member. The university's foundation supported the initiative and asked the Teaching Academy to prepare a one-page case statement to be included in the university's $150 million comprehensive campaign. The advancement officer drafted the case statement, created giving categories, and began personally visiting Teaching Academy members deemed most receptive to giving. Shortly after, mailings were sent to all Teaching Academy members. Our calculated gamble proved successful; in 2004, the Teaching Academy received eighteen payroll deduction gifts totaling $8,000, and in 2010 it received over 100 payroll deduction gifts totaling $30,000. Through outreach events such as Friends Luncheons, the Teaching Academy reached out to community members, and as a result, it received an unsolicited bequest commitment of $300,000. Two additional planned gifts followed, bringing the total to $375,000. The NMSU Teaching Academy now has an endowment to secure its future.

Conclusion

As budget continues to be one of the biggest problems facing teaching centers, many centers need augmented resources for expanded offerings and endowment. We have garnered goodwill in its most tangible form: a source of ongoing revenue that constitutes nearly a third of our budget and costs only a quarter of what we raise. We have also secured the future by building a Teaching Academy endowment. We believe that our model can be adopted at other teaching centers in whole or in part. While we pursue all of the fundraising efforts we have outlined here, there is no reason that another teaching center cannot cherry-pick from our roster of activities. For example, developing a case statement establishes the need, creates good public relations, and fosters a climate for later giving. Engaging the awareness of the university advancement office brings attention to the teaching center's giving opportunities. Mailing just one annual solicitation letter makes fundraising more palatable for developers reluctant to make face-to-face solicitations. Recognizing donor names, such as on our wall of honor, generates curiosity and interest. Organizing small, intimate Friends Luncheons garners unexpected and unsolicited gifts. An annual celebration such as our gala not only culminates the year's good work but also recognizes donors in public. Finally, mentioning the center's activities in a newsletter or other communication generates pleasant surprises. You may already have donors waiting in the wings, but they may be unsure of how and when to give. Each of these elements of our plan provides the means to make their gifts.

The value of donor commitment extends beyond dollars; it is important to the survival of a unit in a time of extreme budgetary constraint. Donors are invested in the center because they have given money to it (Sargeant & Jay, 2004). For example, in a period of severe budget cuts, a group of our faculty donors volunteered to approach the president's office with a message: cut our salaries, but do not cut our professional development!

A center's most natural donors are its participants, but they do not know how to give and have not been asked. A fundraising plan enumerates the steps needed to engage them, as well as other potential donors, from the larger community. The goal is to create an ongoing culture of giving.

Faculty members need well-honed skills. Teaching centers can and will do even more to support them, but they will need philanthropic help to augment the core support they receive from their parent institutions. Faculty developers are natural and enthusiastic communicators of their good work. Following the ideas we have outlined, this enthusiasm can be channeled into fundraising success.

REFERENCES

Ahern, T. (2007). *How to write fundraising materials that raise more money.* Medfield, MA: Emerson & Church.

Ashton, D. (2004). *The complete guide to planned giving.* Quincy, MA: Ashton Associates.

Barbato, J., & Furlich, D. (2000). *Writing for a good cause.* New York, NY: Fireside Books.

Fischer, M. (2000). *Ethical decision making in fund raising.* Hoboken, NJ: Wiley.

Gray, T., & Conway, J. (2007). Build it [right] and they will come: Boost attendance at your teaching center by building community. *Journal of Faculty Development, 21*(3), 179–184.

Greenfield, J. M. (2002). *Fundraising fundamentals: A guide to annual giving for professionals and volunteers* (2nd ed.). Hoboken, NJ: Wiley.

Hecht, I.W.D. (2008). Fund-raising: A new world for department chairs. *Effective Practices for Academic Leaders, 3*(4), 4.

Holcomb, J. R. (2009). *Continuing the good amid an economic crisis: Fund development advice for thriving during uncertain times.* Fort Worth, TX: Holcomb & Associates.

Jaschik, S. (2011, February 2). Not so full recovery. *Inside Higher Ed.* Retrieved from www.insidehighered.com/news/2011/02/02/colleges_see_very_modest_growth_in_fund_raising

Klein, K. (2009). *Reliable fund-raising in unreliable times: What good causes need to know to survive and thrive.* San Francisco, CA: Jossey-Bass.

Lowenstein, R. L. (1997). *Pragmatic fund-raising for college administrators and development officers.* Gainesville: University Press of Florida.

Panas, J. (2002). *Asking: A 59-minute guide to everything board members, volunteers, and staff must know to secure the gift.* Medfield, MA: Emerson & Church.

Pitman, M. A. (2007). *Ask without fear! A simple guide to connecting with what matters to them most.* Mechanicsburg, PA: Executive Books.

Reid, G. (1998). Engaging the faculty: A university science professor recommends getting his colleagues in deep with fund-raising programs. *Fund Raising Management, 29*(5), 32–33, 42.

Sargeant, A., & Jay, E. (2004). *Building donor loyalty: The fundraiser's guide to increasing lifetime value.* San Francisco, CA: Jossey-Bass.

Schneiter, P. H. (1985). *The art of asking: How to solicit philanthropic gifts.* Rockville, MD: Taft Group.

Schumacher, E. C., & Seiler, T. L. (2003). *Building your endowment.* San Francisco, CA: Jossey-Bass.

Warwick, M. (2009). *Fundraising when money is tight; A strategic and practical guide to surviving tough times and thriving in the future.* San Francisco, CA: Jossey-Bass.

Weinstein, S. (2009). *The complete guide to fundraising management.* Hoboken, NJ: Wiley.

20

HOW MATURE TEACHING AND LEARNING CENTERS EVALUATE THEIR SERVICES

Susan R. Hines, Saint Mary's University of Minnesota

This study investigated faculty development program evaluation practices at thirty-three established, centralized, university-funded teaching and learning centers (TLCs). My prior statewide study (Hines, 2009) revealed that limitations of time, resources, and assessment knowledge resulted in superficial evaluation practices. Since the majority of respondents in the previous study were part-time faculty developers with limited funding and staff, I assumed that established, centralized TLCs would have the knowledge and resources to conduct a more rigorous evaluation. This study reveals that established centralized TLCs have significantly stronger practices for evaluating their services.

The field of faculty development emerged from a wave of academic accountability (Centra, 1976), and yet for years, minimal attention was given to program evaluation. According to early studies by Gaff (1975) and Centra (1976), faculty development program evaluation ranged from nonexistent to the occasional use of satisfaction surveys. Chism and Szabo's (1997) nationwide faculty development study noted a significant increase in the quantity of program evaluation but superficial quality as evidenced by widespread use of satisfaction surveys and routine gathering of self-reported changes in teaching.

In 2007, I conducted a statewide study of the program evaluation practices of twenty faculty developers at public and private institutions (Hines, 2009). Paralleling Chism and Szabo's (1997) findings, results from this study indicated strong interest and limited rigor. Deficiencies in evaluation were most commonly attributed to a lack of time, resources, knowledge, and good evaluation models. Organizational factors may have contributed since the majority of the universities in the study took Minter's (2009) "point B" approach to faculty development.

Minter (2009) devised a continuum of faculty development from point A to point D. The point A approach (the "organized-centralized model" [p. 66]) is characterized by a centralized, well-organized, university-funded unit led by a full-time director and staff responsible for developing and implementing faculty development activities for the university and its faculty and for evaluating the program outcomes. A point B program is led part time by a faculty member on release time and provides a variety of "semi-planned and ad hoc" (p. 66) events and activities with limited evaluation. Point C is typified by a "totally or quasi-decentralized" (p. 66) approach in which deans or department heads plan events around their individual unit needs and budgets. Point D, the bottom of the continuum, is characterized by the absence of organized faculty development, leaving the faculty to self-direct their professional growth.

Of the twenty faculty development programs involved in my 2007 statewide study, seventeen were in the point B category and only three could be categorized as point A. Based on Minter's (2009) continuum, it was not surprising to find a preponderance of low-level evaluation practices. Therefore, the next logical step was to investigate the evaluation practices at point A teaching and learning centers (TLCs). TLCs were selected for this 2010 interview study using seven criteria: (1) a director (75 percent to full time) and staff dedicated exclusively to faculty development, (2) university funded, (3) separate and centralized location, (4) in existence for at least five years, (5) an articulated mission for the TLC, (6) a POD member, and (7) a U.S. university. These TLCs are referred to in this chapter as mature.

Study Design

Qualifying TLCs were identified through a cross-search between the list of more than nine hundred members of the Professional and Developmental Organization Network (POD) and member universities' websites. The website search and review resulted in fifty-six qualifying centers. The director of each TLC received an e-mail invitation to participate in the study, along with a request to confirm that the TLC met the seven criteria.

Thirty-three directors from qualifying TLCs agreed to telephone interviews. These interviews were chosen to allow in-depth inquiry, open-ended responses, and clarification of questions and terminology. The interviews were structured using a semiclosed, fixed-response, and open-ended questionnaire similar to those used in prior studies (Chism &

Szabo, 1997; Hines, 2009). Questions were designed to identify services offered; prevalence, type, and quality of evaluation practices; and reasons for gaps and limitations in their evaluation work. Participants received the questionnaire in advance of the interview and were asked to confirm or correct a postinterview transcript of their responses. All transcripts were then coded by the researcher and an outside coder, and interrater reliability was established through a series of independent coding and comparison sessions.

Findings

All participating TLCs could be characterized as point A on Minter's continuum. The participants were twenty-seven public and six private universities. Five had been in existence for five to nine years, seven for ten to fifteen years, thirteen for sixteen to twenty-five years, and eight for twenty-six or more years. All thirty-three were open year round. Four served fewer than one thousand faculty, thirteen served one thousand to two thousand, eleven served two thousand to four thousand, and five served more than four thousand faculty.

Types of Services

Services offered by the thirty-three TLCs were similar to those reported in Chism and Szabo's (1997) and my (Hines, 2009) studies. The majority provided seminars, workshops, brown bag sessions, conferences, and orientations, in addition to a variety of consultation services, online resources, and grant programs. Unlike the centers in the previous studies, over half of the TLCs surveyed sponsored faculty learning communities (FLCs). Approximately one-third designed customized programs such as faculty inquiry groups, academic fellowship programs, faculty writing programs, course revision programs, early and midcareer teaching programs, teaching enrichment series, interactive theater programs, and department-specific support programs.

Staff Conducting Program Evaluation

Most TLCs dispersed program evaluation duties among all staff members. The three TLCs with full-time staff assigned exclusively to evaluation indicated these were essential and fairly recent additions to their program. One director supported this recent appointment by saying,

"If you're trying to figure out what's working, what's not working, and where to invest time and money, you need one." Another indicated that the need for evaluation staff was related to projects funded by government grants. All three reported significantly higher levels of program evaluation activity than the other TLCs in the study.

Individuals outside the TLC were also involved in program evaluation. Approximately 20 percent of TLCs hired outside consultants to perform periodic program reviews. Several tapped staff from their university's office of assessment. A small number recruited their advisory committees to review their physical and online teaching and learning resources.

Prevalence of Evaluation

All TLCs engaged in some routine evaluation, although disparities appeared in the types of services being evaluated (Table 20.1). A high percentage of TLCs evaluated, at least occasionally, user satisfaction and impact on teaching resulting from their events and activities, consultation services, and mentoring programs. Almost half of the TLCs offering grant programs, consultation services, or large resource events made

Table 20.1 Percentage of TLCs Evaluating Satisfaction, Impact on Teaching, and Impact on Learning for Various Services

| Type of Service | Number of TLCs Offering the Service | Percentage Evaluating Each Program Outcome | | |
		Satisfaction	Impact on Teaching	Impact on Learning
Events and activities	33	100%	94%	45%[a]
Consultation services	26	81	81	47
Publications and resources	33	52	21	0
Grant programs	24	50	83	50
Mentoring programs	13	77	77	2%

Note. Percentages based on number of TLCs offering the service.

[a]Denotes high-impact activities only (large resource events such as writing improvement or instructional redesign)

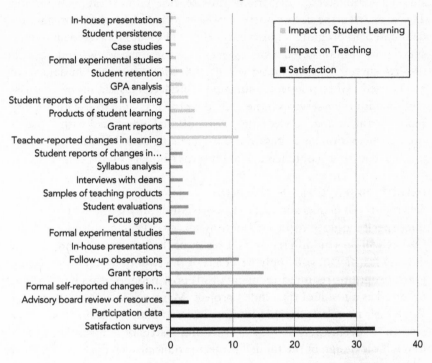

Figure 20.1 Type and Frequency of Evaluation Methods by the Participants

some effort to measure the impact these services had on student learning. There was little interest in gathering satisfaction or impact data relating to publications and resources.

Evaluation Methods

Evaluation methods most frequently consisted of satisfaction surveys, participation data, formal self-reported changes in teaching, grant reports, and formal teacher-reported changes in student learning, respectively (Figure 20.1). A variety of other methods were also implemented, although significantly less frequently.

USAGE

Participation and usage were commonly tracked. Attendance data included the department or school in which the participant taught. Usage data for online resources were frequently tracked using Google Analytics.

SATISFACTION

Satisfaction was measured through the routine use of paper or electronic surveys administered after an event or service. Almost all participating TLCs reported the use of postevent meetings to debrief on satisfaction data and plan program adjustments. Three TLCs administered an annual survey, one administered a survey every four years, and two did an end-of-term survey for consultations only. Anecdotal satisfaction data were rarely used. All respondents indicated a moderate to high level of satisfaction with their services. One TLC director was able to use an activity report listing annual services and events offered, combined with satisfaction, participation, and usage data, to persuade state legislators to avoid funding cuts that would have had a negative impact on the center.

IMPACT OF SERVICES ON TEACHING

Self-reports of changes in teaching were commonly gathered by embedding specific questions in satisfaction surveys. Typical questions were, "What will do you differently as a result of this program?" and, "What did you learn? Did you apply it?" Half of the twenty-four TLCs offering grant programs required recipients to report pedagogical changes that occurred as a result of the funded project. Many asked grant recipients to share their new instructional insights in a seminar, workshop, or poster session. Experimental data demonstrating instructional gains were collected if the design of the funded project produced such data. Evidence of pedagogical changes resulting from high-impact programs were gathered through focus groups, one-on-one interviews, and a review of instructor-created products resulting from program participation.

Besides self-reports from follow-up surveys, teaching impacts from consultation services were often evaluated through follow-up classroom observations, if appropriate and permitted by the faculty member. Student evaluations were used with similar conditions. If a faculty member requested a small group instructional diagnosis, a follow-up was sometimes performed to gather student reports of changes in teaching.

The evaluation of mentoring programs relied heavily on self-reported changes in teaching solicited through e-mail inquiries and follow-up surveys. TLC directors also reported gathering feedback from mentors and mentees through focus groups, one-on-one interviews, pre-post examinations of syllabi, and pre-post reviews of student evaluations and in-class feedback. One TLC asked mentees to write "critical account" analyses. Two designed a formal experimental study using a control group (those not in the program) and an experimental group (those in the program) and compared gains, with one using tenure ratings as a measure.

The impact of FLCs on teaching was most commonly measured through self-reported changes solicited through e-mail inquiries, focus groups, project reports, and presentations. One director conducted a retroactive faculty survey inquiring into the impact of FLCs on teaching careers over the past twenty years. A few used evidence-based measures, including teaching portfolios, classroom videos, and experimental studies, to measure gains in teaching.

IMPACT OF SERVICES ON LEARNING

Eleven of the fifteen respondents who measured impacts of events on learning solicited teacher-reported changes in student learning through surveys and interviews. FLCs were often evaluated in this manner as well. One respondent administered a five-year follow-up survey to 650 FLC participants inquiring into the perceived impact of FLC participation on student learning.

More robust evaluation efforts, reported by four respondents, targeted high-impact events where evidence demonstrating the return on the investment was required. Methods used to measure changes in learning varied by program. Programs designed to improve specific student skills (writing, for example) typically measured qualitative changes in products of student learning such as e-portfolios, writing samples, and capstone projects. Programs focused on changing instructional methods, such as large course redesigns, active learning initiatives, and cluster teaching projects, used pre-post quantitative measures of student course performance (for example, test scores, homework scores, drop-withdraw-fail rates) or overall academic success (for example, retention, persistence, grade point average). Instructional technology programs gathered reports of changes in learning through case studies, student self-reports, and student surveys. Combinations of these methods were included in reports from faculty who received instructional grants.

Program Evaluation Purpose and Strategy

Reasons for evaluation varied in frequency and type. All thirty-three TLCs studied evaluated program services for purposes of improvement: twenty-seven did so to document success, twenty-six wanted to see if their goals were met, fifteen reported that their administration required program evaluation, thirteen desired to do so, and one wanted to model evidence-based practices.

The production of an annual report summarizing program activity (participation, usage, and satisfaction) and linkage to program goals was the most common summative program evaluation practice, reported by twenty-seven of the thirty-three participants. Seven of the thirty-three participants commissioned a periodic program review conducted by individuals outside their center. Four of thirty-three improved efficiency and focus, with staggered evaluation across individual program offerings from year to year.

The most systematic practices were reported by a director who developed a staggered and staged approach to program evaluation. A three-year evaluation plan, staggered program by program, was staged to measure three outcome levels: participation, implementation, and impact. The director first tracked participation data, noting, "It's not possible and there's no point to measure impact on student learning and teaching if participation is not present." After adequate participation became evident, evidence of implementation was gathered. Once the data indicated implementation, then impact on learning was measured. Implementation data were gathered through the diligent creation of "a one page case study (like a health record) with pre- and post-assessment data to look for improvement and holes in the process." Three weeks in July are set aside to analyze the data and write up the annual report, during which time all program activities and most services cease. The director readily admits this approach "is very hard work and very time-consuming" and emphasizes the crucial need for automation and customized databases to make this work, especially with limited staff. This unique approach captured valid evidence of significant impact and yearly progress that was published in the annual report.

Reported Reasons for Gaps in Program Evaluation

Evaluation of events and activities was performed to various extents at all responding TLCs. However, events seen as informal, infrequent, irregular, or lightly attended reportedly did not justify evaluation. Consultation services were not routinely evaluated due to the desire to maintain confidentiality and also the perceived lack of time and resources. A small number believed consultation evaluation to be too difficult or unnecessary, or the services too irregular, to justify assessing. Participants reporting a lack of evaluation for their occasional services, such as online and physical resources, grant programs, and mentoring programs, most commonly cited a lack of time and resources as the cause. Other respondents indicated that evaluation was too difficult to do, it was low on the priority list, there was no good process, or the informality of the services did not justify evaluation.

The most common reason reported for gaps in evaluation regarding the impact of services on teaching was a lack of time and resources. Accompanying comments such as, "We want to, though, so we can show our dean for funding," and, "The scientist in me says it's a good approach, but between being a scientist or helpful, it's better to be helpful," highlight the conflict between desire and resource constraints. Others attributed the evaluation gap to the inherent difficulty and fear of causing survey fatigue.

The most common reason for not evaluating impacts on learning was a lack of time and resources. Several indicated that the presence of multiple confounding variables make the evaluation of impact on student learning very difficult. One respondent summed it up this way: "Being a psychologist with training in assessment, I know the level of effort it takes to do this well; anything less is a crapshoot or just a political tool."

At the conclusion of the interviews, many respondents remarked there was no reason to institute more rigorous program evaluation practices since administration already supports their work, suggesting that time, resources, and energy should go toward providing, rather than justifying, their services. An equal number of respondents reiterated the need for more staff and funding in order to develop more rigorous evaluation practices. For some, the absence of an institutional culture of assessment or leadership inconsistencies reduced their desire to improve program evaluation efforts. Others indicated that a lack of knowledge and absence of models for developing quality program evaluation plans greatly hindered their evaluation work. Disciplinary knowledge played a role and was reflected in comments such as, "We lack the knowledge in the staff. The director has a Ph.D. in social science, so there's a high standard for quality assessment with rigorous methods which we're [the rest of us are] unable to do" and "I have a Ph.D. in English, not stats. I would like to know how to do it."

Several other parting comments suggested strong interest and support for continued work in program evaluation:

> "I'm interested in assessing for viability and sustainability but just don't know how."

> "This conversation helped. We would do more evaluation if we had a better model on how to do it."

> "We are well funded but would need a FIPSE [Fund for the Improvement of Postsecondary Education] grant to make a

research report. We do need to move from self-reported changes to seeing it."

"Assessment is the future and accountability is critical, especially for federal and regional accreditation."

Discussion

Similar to the findings in Chism and Szabo's (1997) study and my own study (Hines, 2009), routine evaluation of services is prevalent among the mature TLCs studied. Unlike the previous studies, however, the mature TLCs that constituted this study group exhibited a stronger interest in extending measures beyond satisfaction and participation data to evaluation of program impact. The percentage of respondents making efforts to measure the impact of services on teaching was 20 percent in Chism and Szabo's (1997) study, 40 percent in Hines's (2009) study, and 97 percent in this study. The percentage of respondents attempting to measure the impact of particular services on learning was insignificant in Chism and Szabo's (1997) study, 20 percent in Hines's (2009) study, and 45 percent in this study. This increase in impact measures of teaching and learning is encouraging, but it is tempered by the majority reporting only superficial measures of self-reported changes. However, recognition is due to the increased prevalence of grant programs requiring evidence of changes in teaching and learning and of the implementation of periodic program reviews, both of which were rare to nonexistent in the previous two studies. In addition, this study revealed some noteworthy efforts by a select few who devoted extensive effort to gathering causal evidence of high-impact events on student learning through pre-post measures and experimental studies using multiple measures. In addition, reports of using anecdotal data were offset by substantial reports of systematic formal evaluation methods with a high reliance on technology in the form of online surveys, Google Analytics, and databases.

As has been reported for decades in the literature, many of the respondents reported gaps and superficiality in evaluation practices, with most blaming the lack of time and resources. Some individuals formally trained in assessment could not justify the time and effort to demonstrate their worth when administration already believed in them. Others felt they lacked useful models or staff with assessment knowledge.

Unlike reports from previous studies, many TLCs report efforts to overcome the obstacles of time and resources by implementing changes to their evaluation practices and staffing. The TLCs most active in evaluation have systemized their evaluation process in these ways:

- Automating attendance and online surveys
- Evaluating their programs on a staggered annual basis
- Evaluating outcomes in a staged manner
- Using random sample data collection methods
- Reserving rigorous evaluation for high-impact programs
- Leveraging support from deans or department chairs
- Creating a strong culture of assessment within the center
- Hiring full-time evaluation staff trained in program evaluation

Recommendations

Considering the findings from this and earlier studies, it appears that the most feasible and useful evaluation practices should be designed within a culture of assessment. This work can be summarized in what could be termed the four S's of program evaluation: staffing, systemization, staggered evaluation of programs, and staged outcome evaluation.

Staffing

Build staffing and institutional collaboration to support program evaluation efforts. Distribute data gathering among staff or, ideally, assign it to a full-time staff specialist hired specifically for program evaluation. In addition, collaborate with the university's office of assessment to design evaluation plans, provide readily available institutional data, and combine survey efforts.

Systemization

Create a comprehensive plan to systematically gather data for evaluating the program. Determine the goal of the program, the outcomes to be measured, the methodology and timing for data collection, and the schedule for analyzing, reviewing, and implementing the findings. Customize the plan to fit the resource limitations. Where possible, use technology such as online survey software, content management servers (such as SharePoint), database software, and student response systems (clickers) to automate the collection and analysis of data. Simplify survey distribution by standardizing surveys, using preexisting institutional data, and combining survey efforts with other institutional assessment efforts. Embed evaluation in program planning as part of standard practice along with annual reports or fact sheets to track and report program trends and success.

Staggered Evaluation of Programs

Evaluation of the entire TLC does not need to occur at one time. Stagger the evaluation of individualized programs or services on an annual basis. Create a three- to five-year plan outlining the staggered evaluation of each component of the TLC. For example, in year 1, evaluate consultation services; in year 2, evaluate the teaching certificate program; and in year 3, evaluate the mentoring program.

Staged Outcome Evaluation

Take a staged approach to the evaluation of outcomes of various programs. For example, for any given program, track participation only until a significant number is achieved. Then gather data to determine if participants are implementing the new skills. Finally, measure the impact on student learning once significant implementation is seen. Another approach could be to tailor evaluation to selected outcome measures most appropriate to the intended impact of the individual programs or services. For example, satisfaction data may suffice for ad hoc workshops, data about impact on teaching may be needed for mentoring programs, and data concerning impact on student learning may be important and feasible for grant-funded teaching projects. In other words, collect data that will add value to the center's work.

Conclusion

Directors of mature TLCs are interested in program evaluation and need feasible and useful evaluation models. The findings of this nationwide study suggest that staffing, systemization, staggered evaluation, and staged outcome measures are a useful framework for the design of evaluation methods to demonstrate the worth and inform the continuous improvement of faculty development services. Continued efforts must be put forth to share best practices in program evaluation through scholarly research, consortiums, publications, conferences, and presentations. Continued research is needed to find ways to measure the impact of faculty development on teaching and learning. Perhaps this director's closing remark best captures the need for continued research: "We're still asking, 'Does faculty development make a difference?' I don't think anyone has a good answer to that yet."

REFERENCES

Centra, J. A. (1976). *Faculty development practices in U.S. colleges and universities*. Princeton, NJ: Educational Testing Service.

Chism, N.V.N., & Szabo, B. L. (1997). How faculty development programs evaluate their services. *Journal of Staff, Program, and Organizational Development, 15*(2), 55–62.

Gaff, J. G. (1975). *Toward faculty renewal*. San Francisco, CA: Jossey-Bass.

Hines, S. R. (2009). Investigating faculty development program assessment practices: What's being done and how can it be improved? *Journal of Faculty Development, 23*(3), 5–19.

Minter, R. L. (2009). The paradox of faculty development. *Contemporary Issues in Education Research, 2*(4), 65–70.

21

FACULTY DEVELOPMENT AS A HAZARDOUS OCCUPATION

Linda B. Nilson, Clemson University

Edward B. Nuhfer, California State University, Channel Islands

Bonnie B. Mullinix, TLT Group and Greenville Technical College

"Hazardous" describes events and conditions that produce an undesired, involuntary, career-changing disruption of a developer's professional practice. While faculty development is an immensely valuable asset to an institution that knows how to make use of it, the unique nature of faculty development centers within varied academic institutions brings occupational hazards to those who direct or work in such centers. Our study synthesizes and identifies patterns among over thirty cases furnished by developers, primarily center directors, who experienced career disruptions. We conclude by offering evidence-based counsel on how to recognize the hazards and mitigate damage.

The twenty-first century began with an optimistic observation about our profession: "Never before in the history of education has greater importance been attached to the professional development of educators" (Guskey, 2000). More recently, Brownwell and Swayner (2010) advised institutions to "invest in faculty development" because instructional practices that promote student success require support and expertise to implement properly. Research increasingly shows that development helps faculty acquire the skills that promote and strengthen student learning (Nuhfer, Blodgett, Fleisher, & Griffin, 2010). Indeed, those who persist in this occupation often acknowledge that their motivation is fueled by its far-reaching power for good; helping a faculty member succeed helps every student whom that faculty member touches.

This same decade also saw the emergence of literature alerting faculty developers to their need to justify, defend, and secure their center's existence.

Publications and conference sessions suggested the importance of conducting program evaluations to document the positive impact of teaching and learning units, particularly for administrators and external audiences (Bothell & Henderson, 2002, 2003; Burkin, Chism, Frerichs, & Wehlburg, 2003; Cafarelli & Jones, 2002; Faculty and TA Development, 2004; Way, Carlson, & Piliero, 2002). Terms such as "return on investment" (Bothell & Henderson, 2002, 2003), "stakeholders," and "utilization-focused evaluation" (Cafarelli & Jones, 2002; Patton, 1998) entered the lexicon of center directors. Forums on the survival of faculty development (FD) centers (for example, Nilson, 2003; Nuhfer et al., 2003) became well-attended events at developer conferences. Ewing and Sorcinelli's (n.d.) justification for FD, "The Value of a Teaching Center," appeared in 2004 as a permanent fixture on the POD Network website. Concern was raised more broadly as well. Gosling, Chism, and Sorcinelli (2008) synthesized the results of their surveys, conducted in five separate studies, of over one thousand respondents from eighteen countries (primarily the United States, the United Kingdom, Canada, Australia, and South Africa) on the current and future challenges facing FD. They found that "organizational volatility" creates a constant disruption.

A catalyst for this second body of literature was the shock generated by the unexpected closure of one of the first American FD centers at the University of Nebraska, Lincoln (Bartlett, 2002). More center closures followed (Glenn, 2009), even as new centers and developer positions opened. The trend confirmed the risks of being a faculty developer. This organizational volatility appeared to come not from any organized national movement but from local reorganizations too numerous to ignore. It was difficult to reconcile that while assessing student achievement was becoming a national priority, the profession that directly supports instructional improvement, student success, and faculty effectiveness was being locally undercut.

Developers quickly recognized this trend in open exchanges at conferences and the POD Network listserv. Critical changes and closures were sometimes common knowledge across the profession before they were announced at the home campus. Developers who survived such career disruptions and managed to stay in the career they love understand both the hazards and how to survive them. We are three such developers—successful and survivors. This study synthesizes the case experiences of thirty other similar survivors. We thank them for their knowledge and their courage in participating in this study.

Methodology and Approach

Because career disruptions are complex and emotionally evocative, our study of the subject called for qualitative approaches and data collection strategies that guaranteed anonymity. We communicated through personal e-mail and telephone accounts, avoiding institutional accounts that are routinely archived and may be treated as public record.

Our study began with case interviews and narratives aimed at gathering thick data that could be mined for emergent themes and grounded in context-rich descriptions (Strauss & Corbin, 1998). We openly introduced our study and its purpose through an announcement on the POD listserv inviting colleagues to confidentially contact us to share their personal stories of center closures, position eliminations, or forced resignations. We used the initial communications to develop potentially generative prompts for a thirty-item case interview outline. We selectively followed up to obtain more detail, encouraging participants to address items that resonated with their experience. Responses varied widely, from a sentence or two per item, to lengthy narratives, to detailed answers to all thirty items. Grounded theory informed both the study's design and analysis strategy that relied on capturing emergent themes and allowing their growth and ongoing validation (Strauss & Corbin, 1998). Because we as researchers were also participants, the study benefited from the increased emic validity characteristic of participatory research (Freire, 1972).

This data-gathering strategy yielded thirty-three cases of center closures, position eliminations, and forced resignations from center positions. Our participants were active or recently active POD members, and thus our study omits any who left the profession. Our database consists of center directors except for one associate director, one senior consultant, and one coordinator. The vast majority of these incidents took place within the past eleven years, and three cases were from outside the United States.

Our sample of about three hazards a year over the past decade should not be mistaken as representing small impact. FD is a tiny profession of about eighteen hundred POD members and 1,267 teaching and learning centers at 933 different institutions (Kuhlenschmidt, 2011; S. Kuhlenschmidt, personal communication, January 30, 2011). To draw scalable comparisons from numbers of faculty in some common disciplines (U.S. Department of Labor, 2011), the closure of three FD centers a year is roughly equivalent to the closure of about 150 fine arts programs,

120 English departments, 90 math programs, or 40 history departments.

The thirty-three cases broke down into these subcategories:

- Twenty-three cases of closed centers, which happened twice to one person
- One case of a center that was gutted but technically not closed
- Five cases of eliminated positions, two of which happened to one person
- Four cases of directors terminated without cause

We classified as "closed" two cases of "ghost centers." These units had closed and development no longer existed, but the institutions retained the defunct centers' website.

Our study spans a wide range of Carnegie classifications. Table 21.1 shows the degree to which our U.S. sample of thirty disrupted centers represents the actual distribution of higher education institutions across Carnegie categories and the percentage of institutions in each category with a teaching and learning center, as identified by Kuhlenschmidt (2011). Our sample considerably overrepresents research universities and underrepresents associate of arts colleges. The three cases from outside of the United States were from research-oriented institutions enrolling between fifteen thousand and forty thousand undergraduate and graduate students.

The second phase of the study involved a well-attended roundtable session (Nuhfer, Mullinix, & Nilson, 2009), hereafter referred to as the roundtable. Held in a private meeting room, this session provided an opportunity to acquire data in an interactive setting. Nineteen colleagues attended; fourteen disclosed their surviving at least one career disruption. Building on preliminary findings, we developed two data collection exercises to solicit additional data: a line exercise and a themed response exercise. In the line exercise, all participants stood shoulder to shoulder in a straight line. They were instructed to take one step forward from the line if the statement that the author-facilitators read described their experience, returning to the baseline following each statement. Counts were taken of each line advancement by participants. In the themed response exercise, nine reasons for career derailments drawn from the cases and our own experiences, plus "other" and "I have no idea," were themes heading eleven blank posters on the walls around the room. Participants used sticky notes to provide details on their cases and affixed these to the posters most closely related to their experiences.

Table 21.1 Comparison of Our U.S. Study Sample with the
National Percentages of Institutions in Carnegie Categories
and National Percentage of Institutions in Each Category
with Teaching and Learning Centers

Carnegie Category[a]	Percentage of Institutions in Carnegie Category	Percentage of Institution in Each Category with Centers	Percentage of Category Represented by Disruptions in Our Study	Number of Disruptions by Category Reported in Our Study
Doctoral/*Research* Universities, Extensive				7
Doctoral/*Research* Universities, Intensive				1
Research Universities, Very High Research Activity	6.5%	22%	53%	3
Research Universities, High Research Activity				5
Master's Colleges and Universities I	15.2%	28.2%	23.3%	7
Baccalaureate Colleges, Liberal Arts/Arts and Sciences				2
Baccalaureate Colleges, Diverse Fields	17.6%	11.8%	10%	1
Special Focus Institutions	19.2%	4.6%	6.6%	2
Associate of Art Colleges	41.6%	33.5%	6.6%	2

Note. All nonsample percentages are from Kuhlenschmidt (2011).

[a]Italics in this column show the general category.

Findings from the POD Listserv Call on Career Derailments

The narratives we received revealed both the vulnerable institutional status of our profession and the personal costs to developers who suffer a disruption. They also provided contextual data that informed the exercises we led at the POD conference roundtable.

One survivor captured the experiences of several others, attributing the demise of his or her center to budget cuts: "When funding is tight, FD is the first to be cut or changed in some fashion to meet other institutional needs."

Another attested that a glowing campus reputation and data-rich program evaluations made no difference to his or her center's survival:

> Last fall the provost reviewed all the units of the [division] and came back with the finding that [the center] was the only unit of the [division] to have a uniformly positive reputation on campus. We never had acknowledgment of that finding from the new [administrator], or other feedback except for his occasional observation that [center] consulting is very labor-intensive and (by implication) very expensive. Our years of impact assessment, self-studies, regular client feedback, and annual reports don't seem to have been enough to alter this perception.

A two-time survivor (one of two) identified the disinterest of both of his or her administrations in FD:

> Neither administrators were interested in the work [of the center] because their mandate, personal or institutional, did not include the continuance of professional faculty development services. In both cases, I was told, in the end, that I was doing an "excellent job" and was "obviously well-known in my profession" and therefore could easily find another position.

The duplicity between the praise noted for doing "excellent" work and the immediate humiliation of the developer was revealed later in the narrative:

> In case B, I was literally escorted back to my desk by a campus security officer and told to pack up in an hour or two. I had my entire professional library there, so it took nearly all day to pack things up. My email access was cut off within minutes of my return to my office after the meeting. My laptop was confiscated and a copy of my hard drive made.

As we expected, survivors varied widely in how they reacted to losing their position. Fortunately, this response represented that of many: "And

I am not a loser at all, just a person caught in a web I didn't make. I will survive this." It shows a rejection of victimhood and a refusal to allow mistreatment to strip self-worth.

But another case belied a sad, entangled combination of pragmatic pessimism, self-blame, and disappointment:

> I spent XX years there, and I'm afraid I leave with much less optimism, and even a touch of bitterness. I felt through all my years in faculty development that I was there to help and serve the faculty, and I know I did good work, and helped people. But somehow I never convinced administrators that this was all worthwhile—a fundamental failure of mine, I believe. My experience in faculty development convinces me that it is indeed hazardous, and vulnerable to the winds of regime change. After all, administrators score bullet points on their résumés by starting new initiatives, not continuing existing offices, even successful ones. Would I do it over again? Faculty development was a huge part of my life for many years, but I look back on it as essentially a failure. I don't think I would want to do this again.

In contrast was this survivor's unadorned realism about how practitioners should regard their work and define their jobs:

> If [new] faculty developers go into the workplace believing that their job is to apply their passion and contribute to faculty and student learning . . . that is a pretty "novice" stance . . . and one that is going to translate to dismissal. As we develop professionally, we begin to see that part of our job description is to continually watch the landscape (and the rats) to make sure that faculty and student learning remain part of the mix in the goals of the institution.

Findings from the POD Conference Roundtable on Career Hazards

As did respondents to the listserv call, roundtable participants described center closures, position eliminations, and forced resignations. From the line exercise, we tallied fourteen survivors' perceptions of the institutional conditions and professional ramifications of the derailments and their personal feelings about the incident (Table 21.2).

As shown in part A of Table 21.2, half of the survivors had experienced more than one career disruption, and eight of them had no tenure protection. The effects of these hazards were distributed across job loss, undesired reassignment, intolerable changes, and harassment. FD services disappeared in nine cases (64 percent), most under the guise of "decentralization."

Table 21.2 Response Tally of Line Exercises Conducted During the 2009 POD Conference Roundtable

	Number	Percentage
A. The nature of the hazard		
1. You experienced as a developer a career disruption you would term a hazard that resulted from an experience beyond your control.	14	100
1.1. Take a second step forward if you experienced more than one such hazard.	7	50
2. You actually lost your livelihood for a time as result of such a hazard.	3	21
3. You did not lose your livelihood but were reassigned into another position not of your choosing.	4	29
4. You were not reassigned but removed yourself from a situation that was too distressing to tolerate.	5	36
5. The hazard involved harassment such as others trying to damage your professional reputation or credibility.	4	29
6. The development services to faculty went away after the event.	9	64
6.1. Take a second step forward if the institution claimed the services would not be curtailed but simply "decentralized."	6	43
7. You sought legal counsel.	2	14
8. Your institution reneged or tried to renege on a contract.	2	14
9. Your institution reneged or tried to renege on promises made when you accepted the position of developer.	6	43
10. You had no tenure retreat rights protection from the hazard.	8	57
B. Personal feelings		
1. You felt devastated.	8	57
2. Your confidence in your own competence was shaken.	3	21
3. You felt abandoned or betrayed by your supervisor.	9	64
4. You felt abandoned by formerly supportive colleagues.	1	7
5. Your quality of life felt significantly diminished.	9	64
6. You remained upset or angry a year or more after the event.	9	64
7. You sought professional help as a result of the event.	3	21

Six of the institutions reneged on earlier promises, and two violated contracts, prompting the survivors to seek legal counsel. In these latter cases, administrators attempted to access salary resources through intimidation, threats, reassignment, and pressuring individuals to sign contracts at lower salary levels. In the end, their lawyers successfully argued that contracts are binding; the institutions had to pay the contracts in full.

Part B of Table 21.2 details the human cost of the disruptions. Every type of injury listed was chosen by one or more survivors, validating these thematic categories while underscoring the complexity of the experiences and the strength of the emotions they evoked. The most commonly experienced emotions were feeling abandoned or betrayed by a supervisor, a significantly diminished quality of life, remaining upset a year or more after the event, and general "devastation." Yet all were true survivors, working again in a new job and actively participating at their national meeting.

The themed response exercise tallied developers' perceptions of the reasons for the disruptions they experienced (Table 21.3). With nine responses, the most common reason was "lack of recognition and understanding of the FD (faculty development) profession and its functions," followed by "budget cuts" with seven responses. Although we would expect budget issues to rank high, the apparent inability of upper-level administrators to make use of our profession reveals a need to educate them in how to use FD to further the success of their institutions. "Lack of administrative support for FD unit" attracted four comments, one of which was particularly revealing: "Looking back, I think administrators thought of FD as a nice ornament to hang out during the accreditation visit. FD got a good rating from the accreditation team, and we were the only unit in academic affairs that did. This made some above us uneasy."

Several participants expressed lingering bewilderment. As one put it, "Explicitly 'No real reason given.' Implicitly many possible unstated reasons. . . . And remember, we are all serving at the pleasure of the president." Another case of "giving no reason" centered on a new president who replaced many established administrators with appointees and targeted professional reputations in the process:

> "We can't tell you; it's a confidential personnel decision." That's what they would tell anyone they wanted to harm. Then the "confidential decision" would appear in the front page of the paper or be pumped out to the campus and the world via spam email. Sometimes the announcement appeared with the victim's campus ID photo but never with reasons or cause—just enough of a spin to make it appear the victim had done something wrong.

**Table 21.3 Response Tally of Themed Posters Exercise Conducted
During the 2009 POD Conference Roundtable**

Reasons for Career Derailment	Number	Percentage
1. Budget cuts (not reallocation)	7	50
2. Budget seizures/reallocations by new administrators (not cuts)	5	36
3. Conflicts as result of being an advocate for faculty/teaching	3	21
4. Another person wanted/awarded your job or a patronage appointment	1	7
5. Lack of administrative support for FD unit	4	29
6. Deans/chairs redefine FD as travel to meetings, etc. to get at center's funds	1	7
7. Lack of recognition and understanding of the FD profession and its functions	9	64
8. Turf perceptions—others believe they should be in charge of FD	5	36
9. Personal or stylistic conflicts between developers and others	5	36
10. Other	8	57
Personal vendettas	4	29
Supervisor of supervisor overrides supervisor	1	7
"Psychopathic" supervisor	1	7
11. "I have no idea."	5	36

Lessons Learned: Hazards

The rich qualitative data collected across the interviews, cases, and roundtable exercises provided insights to hazards that might serve as warning signs for threatened centers.

Lip-Service and Ghost Centers

Universities have evolved to regard certain components as indispensable—for instance, human resources, the general counsel, admissions, accounting, financial aid, development, and the research office. FD does not fall among these select units. Because it supports faculty and successful teaching and learning, it is only as stable as an institution's commitment to faculty and student success. While regional accrediting agencies may require FD, institutions can meet this requirement by maintaining centers through the accreditation review process and dismantling them soon afterward. During the hiatus, a center's website may remain for appearances' sake or the title "faculty development" may be given to a person or unit that does no substantial development. Such situations constitute the ghost centers we noted earlier. A few of our survivors reported witnessing and falling victim to this kind of bait and switch. Before accepting employment at an institution, it is wise to determine whether the administration ever maintained a ghost center.

Institutional Conflict and Culture Clash

Several survivors described internal conflicts between the institution's stated and enacted teaching mission or between the faculty and the administration, or both, as terminal to FD. Centers seem to fare better in a culture that is unequivocally committed to teaching and student success and is not compromised by distrust and discord between faculty and administrators. While a center can strongly influence an institution's culture, it cannot create or change its enacted mission.

A Changing of the Guard

In general, higher-level administrators change campuses more frequently than do faculty, and they bring their perceptions of FD with them when they move. In some places, the faculty developer is a full-time professional; in others, development is a part-time duty for a faculty member; and on many campuses, the faculty developer is a rotating position held by a professor for two or three years. Administrators who serve in institutions that invest in a full-time professional developer see developers differently from administrators who view FD as service. When the latter move to the former kind of campus, they will not understand the value of a full-time developer and a permanent center and will probably have other priorities. Survival after a changing of the guard may depend on expanding a center's mission and services to encompass what the new campus leaders value. Therefore, directors must be nimble enough to broaden their development programming from teaching alone to scholarly research and writing, grantsmanship, publication, student retention, leadership, assessment—whatever the new priorities may be. But the new administrators must be willing to meet with center directors regularly to learn how the developer can support their new vision. Among our survivors, the lack of willingness to meet was a sure sign of disruption to come. No matter how compelling the evidence of the center's benefits in its program evaluations, directors who lacked access to administrators were soon terminated, usually along with their entire center, without explanation.

Reorganization from the Top

A considerable number of our survivors fell victim to reorganization plans imposed from the top, with little or no faculty input or buy-in. These plans orchestrated a redistribution of resources that involved the elimination of units and positions, incompatible mergers, and unfavorable reassignments. Some were allegedly done to save money in the face of budget cuts. In our study, the most common reorganization involved FD's being "demoted" from a free-standing unit to a program within instructional technology (IT). In most such cases, the larger and wealthier IT focus drove the unit's mission, eclipsing teaching with technology.

Resentment and Destructive Gossip

A few survivors experienced some faculty resentment about their newly established center from faculty, often in a school of education or psychology department, who believed that they were more qualified to do development than the director was. They might have even been unsuccessful internal candidates for the position. One survivor raised this hazard as probably costing his or her job, and this person unwisely responded in kind to the gossip that the malcontents were spreading. Survivors who rose above such behavior by neither opposing their critics nor gossiping about them fared better. The restrained response gradually disarmed the critics and won their trust. For instance, one director read their pertinent literature, invited them to participate on a center project, and expressed respect for their contributions. Reaching out to detractors in this way can turn those who once felt disenfranchised into strong supporters as the developer's success is now theirs to share.

Exclusion from Relevant Decision-Making Forums

Many of the directors in this study noted that shortly before their career disruption, they were not being asked for input in decisions that were relevant to teaching and learning or to their centers. Some had never been invited to the table; others had been in the past. The astute directors saw such exclusion as a signal that the administration had little interest in faculty development and correctly read it as a sign of bad things to come. Being left out of regular communication and decision making diminishes any professional's ability to be effective.

Lessons Learned: Hazard Insurance

Our study suggests strategies for managing a successful FD career. Like insurance, these strategies cannot prevent hazards, but they can surely mitigate damage.

Tenured Faculty Status

While faculty status lends credibility to developers (Mullinix, 2008) and tenure facilitates survival within the academy, tenured faculty status cannot prevent disruptions in a faculty developer's career, but it can provide insurance against some effects. Ten of the thirty-three survivors we interviewed and six of the fourteen who participated in the poster exercises held retreat rights in an academic department. Remaining in the academy allowed them to retain academic credibility and provided precious income and stability while they searched for another development position. Several chose to take an FD position elsewhere, demonstrating that the desire to remain in this field can trump the security of tenure. Tenure also makes a center less attractive to an administrator who hopes to seize its resources because the salary and employer-paid benefits of any tenured personnel are unavailable for reallocation. Still, the salaries and employer-paid benefits of untenured personnel and the operating budget are vulnerable.

Center Visibility, Credibility, and Friends in High Places

In the words of one survivor, "Keeping a higher institutional profile is, in general, the best assurance of longevity. . . . If no one makes a fuss when they hear your program is threatened, it's an easy street for the administrator doing the cutting." One case described a "near-closure"—actually a one-month closure that was reversed when several deans and the faculty senate learned of the administrator's action and pressured her to reverse the decision. In essence, important parties made a fuss because the center was a well-established, high-profile, widely used fixture on the campus, and key people understood the value of its services. This happy ending, however, represents the exception, not the rule. Survivors with successful centers, professional distinction, and no shortage of faculty friends and allies still fell victim to administrative manipulations.

Supportive Professional Networks

Some survivors recounted that professional networks beyond their campus were sources of career opportunities and the strong recommendations they needed to land a new position. Network members, especially experienced survivors, provided emotional support and useful perspectives. While cultivating national, regional, and local networks of close colleagues and professional friends involves time and work—socializing at conferences, providing service to professional organizations, and participating visibly— it can be one of the best investments against career hazards.

Productive Scholarship

Tenured faculty in disciplines who let their scholarship atrophy are not mobile and cannot pursue more attractive opportunities. The same holds true for the profession of FD. As our study shows, career derailments can happen to the best of developers, no matter what their accomplishments in and outside their institution. However, the survivors who were able to recover in the shortest time had an impressive record of scholarly accomplishments, including publications, conference sessions, and invited presentations.

Conclusion

FD carries unique occupational hazards. Where developers address the hazards, disruptive and painful though they may be, they can and do survive. In spite of its hazards, the career is worth the risks. Why else would so many developers persist and respond to disruptions with such inspiring resilience?

REFERENCES

Bartlett, T. (2002, March 22). The unkindest cut: The struggle to save a teaching and learning center. *Chronicle of Higher Education*, p. A10.

Bothell, T., & Henderson, T. (2002, October). *Evaluating the return on investment of faculty development*. Preconference workshop conducted at the 27th annual Professional and Organizational Development Network in Higher Education Conference, Atlanta, GA.

Bothell, T., & Henderson, T. (2003). Evaluating the return on investment of faculty development. In C. Wehlburg & S. Chadwick-Blossey (Eds.), *To improve the academy: Vol. 21. Resources for faculty, instructional, and organizational development* (pp. 51–69). San Francisco, CA: Jossey-Bass.

Brownwell, J. E., & Swayner, L. E. (2010). *Five high-impact practices: Research on learning outcomes, completion, and quality.* Washington, DC: Association of American Colleges and Universities.

Burkin, D., Chism, N.V.N., Frerichs, C., & Wehlburg, C. (2003, October). *New horizons in assessing faculty development.* Paper presented at the 28th annual Professional and Organizational Development Network in Higher Education Conference, Denver, CO.

Cafarelli, L. K., & Jones, K. M. (2002, October). *Planning and conducting meaningful program evaluation.* Paper presented at the 27th annual Professional and Organizational Development Network in Higher Education Conference, Atlanta, GA.

Ewing, C., & Sorcinelli, M. D. (n.d.). *The value of a teaching center.* Retrieved from www.podnetwork.org/faculty_development/values.htm

Faculty and TA Development, Ohio State University. (2004). *Assessing our work: Developing an integrated data-driven evaluation system* [CD]. Columbus, OH: Author.

Freire, P. (1972). Creating alternative research methods: Learning to do it by doing it. In B. Hall, A. Gillette, & R. Tandon (Eds.), *Creating knowledge: A monopoly? Participatory research in development* (pp. 29–37). Toronto, Canada: International Council for Adult Education.

Glenn, D. (2009, August 18). Wary of budget knife, teaching centers seek to sharpen their role. *Chronicle of Higher Education.* Retrieved from http:// chronicle.com/article/Wary-of-Budget-Knife-Teaching/48049/

Gosling, D., Chism, N.V.N., & Sorcinelli, M. D. (2008, June). *The future of faculty/educational development: An international perspective.* Paper presented at the biennial meeting of the International Consortium for Educational Development Conference, Salt Lake City, UT.

Guskey, T. R. (2000). *Evaluating professional development.* Thousand Oaks, CA: Corwin Press.

Kuhlenschmidt, S. (2011). Distribution and penetration of teaching-learning development units in higher education: Implications for strategic planning and research. In J. E. Miller & J. E. Groccia (Eds.), *To improve the academy: Vol. 29. Resources for faculty, instructional, and organizational development* (pp. 274–287). San Francisco, CA: Jossey-Bass.

Mullinix, B. B. (2008). Credibility and effectiveness in context: An exploration of the issues surrounding the faculty status of faculty developers. In D. R. Robertson & L. B. Nilson (Eds.), *To improve the academy: Vol. 26.*

Resources for faculty, instructional, and organizational development (pp. 173–198). San Francisco, CA: Jossey-Bass.

Nilson, L. B. (2003, March). *Justifying our existence: Can faculty development survive the budget cutting?* Plenary session presented at the 24th annual Sharing Conference of the Southern Regional Faculty and Instructional Development Consortium, Atlanta, GA.

Nuhfer, E. B., Blodgett, M., Fleisher, S., & Griffin, J. (2010). Supporting non-tenure faculty with time- and cost-effective faculty development. *Metropolitan Universities, 21*(2), 107–126.

Nuhfer, E. B., Cunningham, T., Parnell, G., Johnston, K. M., Bothell, T. W., Henderson, T. W., . . . Nilson, L. B. (2003, October). *Reaping the priceless returns of faculty development.* Roundtable conducted at the 28th annual Professional and Organizational Development Network in Higher Education Conference, Denver, CO.

Nuhfer, E. B., Mullinix, B. B., & Nilson, L. B. (2009, October). *Faculty development as a hazardous occupation.* Roundtable conducted at the 34th annual Professional and Organizational Development Network in Higher Education Conference, Houston, TX.

Patton, M. Q. (1998). *Utilization-focused evaluation.* Thousand Oaks, CA: Sage.

Strauss, A., & Corbin, J. (1998). *Basics of qualitative research: Techniques and procedures for developing grounded theory* (2nd ed.) Thousand Oaks, CA: Sage.

U.S. Department of Labor, Bureau of Labor Statistics. (2011). *Occupational outlook handbook, 2010–11 edition, teachers—postsecondary.* Retrieved from www.bls.gov/oco/ocos066.htm#emply

Way, D. G., Carlson, V. M., & Piliero, S. C. (2002). Evaluating teaching workshops: Beyond the satisfaction survey. In D. Lieberman & C. Wehlburg (Eds.), *To improve the academy: Vol. 20. Resources for faculty, instructional, and organizational development* (pp. 94–106). San Francisco, CA: Jossey-Bass.

22

EMERGENT SHIFTS IN FACULTY DEVELOPMENT

A REFLECTIVE REVIEW

Shelda Debowski, University of Western Australia

Faculty development has largely focused on supporting the development of early-career academic skills in teaching and learning. Even recent discussions of how faculty developers might influence leaders and entire organizations have remained largely focused on teaching and learning issues. This chapter suggests the need to review and reform the role of faculty development to focus more holistically on the full nature of academic work and the evolving developmental needs of academics. It argues that the faculty developer's portfolio will need to expand to include support for academic research, career management, and leadership roles, as well as organizational development strategies to complement existing individual and instructional approaches.

From its origins in teaching and learning centers, faculty development has consolidated its focus on early-career academics and career management (Bach & Sorcinelli, 2010). Recognizing the risks of focusing solely on promoting entry-level skills, Chism (2011) offers guidance on how faculty developers can influence the decisions and processes that underpin effective development of teaching and learning. It is heartening to see open discussions around the ways in which faculty development roles are being reenvisioned and expanded. But are these moves sufficient? Do we need to reengage more deeply with the function and purpose of faculty development and its potential for enriching the capabilities and capacity of our faculty?

What Faculty Development Aims to Achieve

An academic operates across a complex range of functions: teacher, researcher, consultant, communicator, leader, change agent, author.

The expectations and standards of performance for academics have risen markedly and continue to do so. New academics have little lead time to learn the ropes and build credible profiles as both teachers and researchers. As they become established, they are also expected to consolidate their capabilities as leaders, collaborators, commentators, resource managers, and administrators. These multitudinous roles require expertise that goes significantly beyond the United States's and Australia's positioning of faculty development around support for new teachers.

The focus on teaching and learning can be traced back to the origins of faculty development in the 1970s when more students entered higher education and teaching and learning was identified as an area needing intensive support (Lee, Manathunga, & Kandlbinder, 2008; Sorcinelli, Austin, Eddy, & Beach, 2006). Pioneering work in faculty development was the foundation for, and continues to frame, much of our understanding of student learning (Tennant, McMullen, & Kaczynski, 2010). The emphasis of faculty development on teaching and learning has rarely been challenged in the ensuing years. Certainly we have seen some gradual shifts as faculty development has expanded to encompass career management, mentorship, and, to a limited extent, leadership (Fullan & Scott, 2008; Scott, Coates, & Anderson, 2008). However, discussion of these support foci remains largely situated within a teaching and learning context, and the premise that faculty development should primarily support teaching and learning appears to have been largely unquestioned. Perhaps it is assumed that other academic capabilities relating to research competence and leadership skills do not need to be supported with ongoing learning, or perhaps other support units or professional organizations are believed to be addressing these needs.

The Developmental Needs of Academics

While the progress of academics as they move from novice to expert roles is still largely unmapped, recognition is growing that academics must acquire a vast array of skills and knowledge as they move into more senior responsibilities. An early-career academic is generally expected to demonstrate basic competencies in research and teaching while acculturating to the university. As individuals progress toward more senior roles, they require higher-level capabilities in managing people, resources, relationships, and outcomes. Four key growth areas that need to be demonstrated during an academic's career relate to teaching, research, career management, and leadership.

New university teachers are given responsibility for designing and presenting instructional programs to students and must rapidly acquire entry-level capabilities in curriculum design, instructional strategies assessment, and student needs. Support for university teachers has primarily focused on offering newcomers a safe and supportive environment to develop basic capabilities (Hicks, Smigiel, Wilson, & Luzeckyj, 2010). Additional support is needed as the teacher assumes additional responsibilities such as leadership of teaching teams or initiatives, mentorship of new teachers, reform of curricula, assessment of courses and programs of study, teaching more diverse student cohorts, and designing e-learning. Teachers are also expected to engage in regular evaluation of, and research relating to, the effectiveness of their existing strategies.

Most academics are also required to undertake significant research in their disciplines. However, the completion of a Ph.D. only marginally prepares an academic for independent research (Western et al., 2007). Like those who teach, those who research need to learn many new skills as they assume responsibility for their own research; other researchers; project management; collaboration; stakeholder relationship management; innovation; and strategic leadership of groups, centers, and research programs (Cohen & Cohen, 2005; Debowski, 2007). Although grant management, research supervision of students, and research integrity are often addressed by units within the university and although national granting bodies are leading the movement to train graduate students to conduct and manage research, overall recognition of the broader capabilities required of research-active university staff is limited, and the needed capabilities are poorly supported in most university settings. A particular challenge is the determination of who should be responsible for supporting the development of research-active staff as they progress to leadership, management, and governance responsibilities.

Career management has become more necessary for academics as the competition for employment and tenure escalates. From an early focus on building a credible profile that fits institutional expectations, the academic must progressively build a strategic focus and a balanced portfolio that supports mobility and promotion by demonstrating a wide range of experiences and a depth of expertise.

Finally, academics are expected to assume more leadership responsibility as they progress in their careers. Initially focused on course or project management, these roles may gradually progress to responsibility for complex strategic outcomes, with expectations including management of issues of integrity, equity, and nurturing of effective sociocultural outcomes (Blackmore & Sachs, 2007). Leaders of academic units play an integral role in building effective academic communities through their control of resource allocations, workload, values, and outcomes, and their capacity to motivate and stimulate a vigorous academic community (Del Favero, 2006; Gibbs, Knapper, & Piccinin, 2008; Knight & Trowler, 2001). They are responsible for encouraging high-quality teaching outcomes, productive and competitive research outputs, and an environment where new academics can flourish. However, effective leaders need considerable support to build self-awareness, an understanding of their role and obligations, and a repertoire of styles and approaches that will support their faculty and student needs.

Table 22.1 summarizes the activities academics might typically undertake at different stages in their career, illustrating the transitions that may occur and the synergies across areas of activity.

As academics progress through their careers, they move toward higher-level roles in teaching, research, and leadership with responsibility for strategic deployment of people and resources. Research and teaching follow similar trajectories as academics move from building basic capabilities into the leadership and management of courses, projects, teams, and academic outcomes. At the same time, they may also assume more formal leadership roles in leading academic communities, such as discipline groups, schools, or faculties. A critical challenge in moving into a senior academic position is the coordination of teaching, research, and leadership roles to ensure that all are being well executed. Time, priorities, and career management are complex challenges, as they require a clear understanding of how academic success is measured within a particular context and more globally.

Table 22.1 highlights several key issues. First, the accommodation of the diversity of roles can be highly challenging, requiring ongoing learning to build existing capabilities. Second, the separation of support into discrete portfolios (teaching, research, career management, leadership) can be counterproductive, as the holistic nature of the development of an individual is then ignored and may lead to conflicting messages as to what is important. Third, the current focus on foundational and early-career support for academics ignores the major shifts in function and responsibility that occur as the academic moves to more influential roles. Fourth, the support offered through university development agencies is less effective if it is fragmented into different elements of the academic role. At present, for example, teaching and learning centers focus on the educational role, research units are solely focused on the research

Table 22.1 Functions of Effective Academic Work

Capabilities	Teaching	Research	Career Management	Leadership
Preentry (role orientation)				
Role familiarization	Assist, tutor, or demonstrate within teaching programs, with supervision.	Conduct supervised research; apply principles of research integrity.	Develop a curriculum vitae; learn about academic work contexts.	Undertake local leadership roles; participate in service-learning.
Foundational skills development	Become familiar with teaching and learning theory and methods.	Learn research methods.	Plan career.	Learn leadership principles and strategies.
Early career (core academic capabilities)				
Core knowledge	Increase specialist skills and knowledge.	Increase specialist skills and knowledge.	Develop a balanced portfolio of activities.	Contribute to institutional events and initiatives.
Professional skills	Design, plan, and evaluate teaching programs.	Design, plan, complete, and evaluate research projects.	Develop an academic portfolio; manage time and priorities.	Identify priorities and strategies.
Knowledge exchange	Employ teaching approaches that meet student needs; contribute to teaching networks.	Cosupervise research students; contribute to research networks.	Establish mentoring relationships; contribute to communities of practice.	Mentor others.
Collaboration	Build teaching collaborations; team-teach.	Build research collaborations; contribute to research teams.	Build local and disciplinary networks.	Contribute to university reforms and innovations.

Outcomes: funding, sponsorship, and publication	Seek external funding; publish teaching outcomes.	Seek external funding; publish research outcomes.	Seek feedback from sponsors and mentors.	Seek opportunities to learn more about leadership.
Institutional expectations	Manage equitable assessment processes; reflect quality teaching principles.	Apply research integrity principles; protect intellectual property.	Identify university promotion criteria.	Adhere to university protocols and requirements.

Additional midcareer functions (academic management)

Core role	Coordinate courses and programs of study.	Manage and execute research projects.	Increase national and international profile and impact.	Undertake institutional leadership roles.
Management skills	Coordinate teaching teams.	Coordinate research teams; supervise research students and staff.	Contribute to national and international initiatives.	Participate on committees and working bodies.
Institutional expectations	Contribute to curriculum reform and program quality assurance.	Contribute to consolidation and growth of the research community.		Reflect principles of equity and ethical practice; manage risk.
Collaborations	Develop collaborations to strengthen teaching scholarship.	Strengthen research collaborations.	Seek opportunities to expand impact; mentor junior colleagues.	Establish collaborative links with other leaders within and beyond the university.
Funding and sponsorship	Seek sponsorship for innovative teaching projects.	Establish funding history and relationships with key stakeholders.		Prepare submissions; manage budgets and staff.

Generate outcomes	Improve teaching performance and effectiveness.	Increase research impact and profile.	Monitor personal impact and performance.	Monitor group impact and performance.

Additional functions for senior academic (academic leadership)

Key role	Oversee major curriculum reform and quality outcomes from teaching and learning activities by the unit; contribute to national and international disciplinary initiatives.	Direct research programs, centers, institutes; guide new research directions and initiatives.	Maintain track record and profile; nurture and sponsor protégés; develop succession plan.	Lead academic unit in teaching and research; contribute to the growth of the university and the discipline.
Influencing function	Influence the theory and practice of teaching and learning.	Influence the theory and practice of the research domain.	Ensure a positive work environment for less senior staff.	Comment on national and international issues; advocate in the media and other forums.

process, and leadership and career management are largely unexplored in many universities. The key issue is evident: there are major gaps in support for faculty and their development.

A Case Study: The Future Research Leaders Program

In 2004 eight Australian organizational developers from the top research-intensive universities who were concerned about the evident gap in research development support interviewed thirty researchers across six universities. The human resource directors and deputy vice chancellors of research who received the resulting report recognized the need for researcher support, and their actions ultimately resulted in a million-dollar grant from the Australian government. With this money, nine online modules to assist researchers in commencing and then managing research projects were developed and rolled out to over one thousand researchers. The program continues to be sponsored by those eight universities and is now in place in other universities across two nations (www.go8.edu.au/university-staff/programs-a-fellowships/).

One of the major challenges and surprises of the project was the ownership of the development work. Amazingly, in all eight universities, faculty developers were not interested in participating in the project, despite, in some cases, strong encouragement from their deputy vice chancellors. Therefore, ownership resides with either human resource or research offices. The case highlights a risk for faculty developers of being marginalized through their disinterest in allied but different aspects of faculty support. The strong association of faculty development with teaching and learning has isolated faculty developers from the concept of also supporting other elements of academic activity. However, as the emerging discussions around leadership and organizational development illustrate (Schroeder, 2011), faculty developers can adapt and move into new roles if they see the need and relevance. Given their concern about being marginalized by university decision makers (Debowski, Stefani, Cohen, & Ho, in press), it could be time to take a fresh look at how faculty developers are positioned and future directions they might consider.

A New Framework for Faculty Development

Faculty development is a challenging field in that the role and focus can be highly variable, depending on a number of factors. Figure 22.1 offers an overview of the external drivers and internal approaches that influence the way faculty development in a particular university might operate. The model suggests four views of faculty development that influence the type of role and the methodologies adopted by developers.

First, the university expectations and context can influence how faculty development is perceived. Senior members of the university administration may have strong beliefs about priorities, leading to emphasis on particular functions. Where administrative portfolios are highly compartmentalized, so too may be the support for academics. Thus, the faculty developer role can be influenced by stakeholder expectations, institutional philosophy, and political structures. Second, the faculty development orientation that predominates is a strong influence. In Australia, for example, the majority of faculty developers see themselves as solely focused on supporting learning and teaching. There are some early signs of an emerging recognition of the holistic needs of academics and the need to recast the faculty developer role, but this could take some time to grow and gain credence. Third, the individual's role definition strongly guides what activities and priorities are supported. For example, a faculty developer who sees the role as primarily operating through the education and guidance of new academics will prioritize those activities, while another may see the need to work more intensively with academic leaders. Finally, the figure highlights the influence of research and scholarship in guiding how faculty developers view their work and their roles. A risk in this regard is that the research merely serves to reinforce existing assumptions and traditional approaches.

Figure 22.1 highlights the highly politicized context in which faculty development operates. There is potential for conflict, for example, when the university has expectations as to roles and outcomes that are differently configured from those held by the discipline or the developers. In recent years, there has been evidence of some university dissatisfaction with the way developers enact their roles, resulting in restructures,

Figure 22.1 Professional Role of Future Faculty Developers

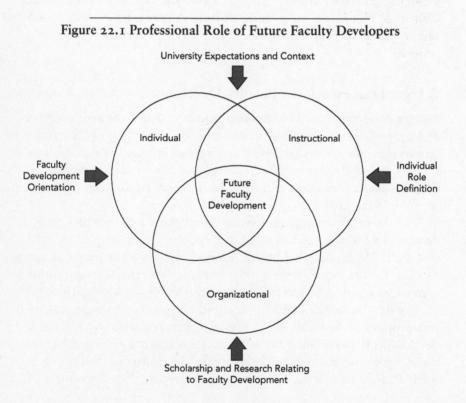

redundancies, and alternative recruitment strategies (Gosling, 2009). It could be argued that the need is increasing to build a stronger base of research, scholarship, and dialogue around the different ways in which faculty development roles may operate. In order to move from existing notions of faculty development to a more sophisticated understanding, Schroeder (2011) suggests that faculty developers need to be conversant with three levels of development: individual, instructional, and organizational.

Individual Development

Developing the early-career academic's teaching and learning capabilities has been a hallmark of faculty development for many years. Particular academics have benefited greatly from the dedication and expert support of developers as they review student feedback, develop academic portfolios, attend workshops, or address particular pedagogical challenges under the guidance of the developer. This coaching approach is time-consuming, resource intensive, and largely hidden from university leaders. It may also result in little demonstrable systemic change.

It is important to note that the successful transfer of individual learning is strongly influenced by the context in which the learner works. A negative, judgmental community, for example, will limit an individual's willingness to take risks or try new approaches. And a positive, constructive community can encourage and promote innovation and good practice as desirable outcomes. The challenge is to balance the focus on individual learning with a commensurate concern for shifting the culture and practices of the broader institutional setting. The emerging squeeze on resources challenges us to review how we operate. Is there enough impact from working with single individuals? Can we build different approaches that encourage stronger ownership by faculty members? For example, a faculty development program within faculties (Debowski, 2007) increases the engagement of the entire community and can challenge many existing assumptions around supporting new or early-career faculty.

There is considerable potential in shifting the responsibility for individual development to peers and leaders within each academic area. That is, the faculty developer role shifts from capability building to capacity building. Coaching by faculty developers may shift in emphasis from assisting junior faculty toward developing leadership and management capabilities of senior faculty and administrators who can influence entire academic communities.

Instructional Development

For many years, faculty development has emphasized programs relating to foundational skills in teaching and learning. Academic participants attend either out of personal interest or because they are required by their institutions. Obligatory attendance increases the demands on faculty developers who must ensure that sufficient access to the required programs is available to their target group. To meet this demand, there has been an increased emphasis on developing additional modes of instruction, including online delivery and graduate certification. The expansion of entry-level support to encompass career management and research strategies increases the demands on this instructional role and may require the development of additional early-career programs. The instructional development role is likely to increase in intensity and demand as the scope of faculty development work is further refined. A critical challenge for faculty developers is to remain visible and influential across the wider university community despite supporting larger numbers of entry-level academics. The shifting of support from a centralized model (where individuals attend a centralized course) to a customized model (where the developer goes to the learning community) offers many benefits for relationship building and influencing (Debowski, 2007). However, it increases the load on the developer even further. Thus, while the traditional instructional role remains critical, the scope and design of the programs could benefit from further critique and review.

Organizational Development

Faculty developers have the opportunity to influence whole faculty communities when they move into organizational development work (Debowski & Blake, 2007; Latta, 2009). Working in partnership with their academic colleagues, developers can assist in identifying critical issues and offer guidance to community leaders as consultants, coaches, mentors, and facilitators. These partnerships might focus on amending existing practices, building common messages, or encouraging stronger consistency of values, beliefs, and practices. Developers can encourage academic leaders and their communities to take ownership of issues and move toward a deeper appreciation of their influence, roles, and responsibilities in achieving robust and effective academic communities. This work can be complex, long term, and highly influential, as it often deals with complicated and interrelated issues. It may require working with leadership teams as well as individuals. In undertaking this work, faculty developers need to be conversant with university policies and context. Developers working at the organizational level benefit from an awareness of the intertwining spheres of teaching, research, leadership, and career management.

A second influential role that can be undertaken by faculty developers is to broker networks and communities of practice (Debowski & Blake, 2007). For example, targeted programs to support academic leaders are best designed as learning communities for particular cohorts, such as heads of schools or departments or faculty leaders in teaching and research spheres (Elkins & Keller, 2003; Mumford, Hunter, Eubanks, Bedell, & Murphy, 2007; Van Velsor, McCauley, & Ruderman, 2010). Such senior programs are generally less focused on skill development, instead emphasizing capacity building, reflective practice, action learning, and self-awareness. They recognize the complex setting in which academics leaders operate (Goffee & Jones, 2007), and they may require a range of strategies, including diagnostic tools, intensive feedback, and long-term implementation plans that continue beyond the end of the program.

Organizational development work is a powerful tool for building strong collaborations with deans, heads of school, and whole communities. It offers enormous potential for influencing group behaviors and having an impact on the entire university as those leaders assume more informed roles in guiding institutional practice.

Emergent Challenges for Faculty Development

The determination of how best to operate depends on a number of factors, including institutional influences and the efficacy of developers themselves. University structures, policies, political initiatives, faculty developer capabilities, and agreed-on priorities for faculty development all determine the final mix of services. Developers face challenges in working outside traditional boundaries and in refocusing their work to create a more strategic and responsive service. While the opening of discussions about potential role expansion or enrichment may seem challenging or even risky, there are also major risks attached to accepting the status quo and failing to question whether more can be achieved from an effective development service.

The extension into three levels of faculty development (and possibly a broadened scope to include research and leadership) has a number of likely implications for how we define the work we do and the priorities we emphasize:

• As the scope of faculty development expands to include research, career management, leadership, and organizational development, the ways in which we work with other service units will need to change. There is a large, invisible divide between faculty developers and organizational developers in many universities. However, the movement into organizational and leadership development support will need to draw on the professional expertise of allied professionals. Faculty developers can benefit from a larger theory base about how organizations operate and why people respond as they do to change. Diagnostic tools also enrich the evidence base that can be offered to participants. Research support units can assist in enriching learning around research strategy and outcomes. Mapping and discussion of the scope of support provided by various support units will help to identify opportunities for collaboration as well as avoid duplication.

• The promotion of organizational learning around academic work leads to informed and strong leadership across the university community. It encourages strong ownership of issues and solutions and builds learning partnerships with community leaders. This shift in focus also reduces the ascription of the developer as "the expert." Instead, developers are likely to move toward partnership models, where the desired outcomes and the pace of learning are negotiated with the learners, accommodating the particular contextual and environmental conditions that exist.

• The expansion of faculty development to include new areas of support requires better liaison with leaders across the university. Provosts and deans will need to be kept informed of new initiatives and given the opportunity to discuss strategic priorities and emergent needs. The support of these leaders can greatly improve the political positioning of the faculty development unit.

• Evaluation strategies are needed to show impact and influence. Existing measures of effectiveness will be less useful as we move toward stronger community engagement agendas. Consideration of this area is emerging (Debowski, 2011; Stefani, 2011), but more needs to be done.

• The broadening scope of faculty development requires careful prioritization of activities based on where the greatest impact can be achieved. While traditional areas of instructional and individual support are popular and well developed, they have far less impact on the larger community than organizational work does. Thus, a redesign of the service mix and its approaches may be needed.

• Many of the principles that operate in faculty development have been acquired from our understanding of how undergraduate students learn. But our clientele are experienced academics who bring considerable knowledge and expertise to their learning. Our current model is risky: new developers are commonly drawn from faculty and then simply relocated into developer roles where they learn the ropes from others or by trial and error. As we move into a broader conception of faculty development work, we will need to build rigorous accountability around how we perform our roles and the methodologies that we employ.

• The new areas discussed in this chapter require ongoing education of faculty developers. Expertise in adult learning, organizational development, leadership enhancement strategies, and research management would assist faculty developers in their roles. At present it appears that faculty developers learn about their role through self-education. More scholarship and support from professional societies would greatly assist in building a professional knowledge base.

From these brief reflections, it is apparent that faculty development has reached a crossroad. One path encourages the continuation of promoting and advancing teaching and learning as the sole professional emphasis. The other commences the process of integrating additional elements of faculty support into the professional repertoire. While the second path poses many complex challenges, it also offers considerable scope to increase the influence and recognition of the importance of faculty development work.

Ultimately the faculty development profession would benefit from a framework that articulates the professional knowledge and skills that faculty developers require to do their work. The long-established model of mirroring the practices that were applied as a faculty member is no longer acceptable as a basis for working with academics. Instead the development of organizational, instructional, and individual development skills is necessary for any faculty developer to operate with credibility. Professional societies can play a major role in guiding debate about these alternative futures and offering ongoing professional development for faculty developers. This is the next step in the process of reenvisioning the nature and function of faculty development.

Conclusion

The field of faculty development has made great strides since its beginnings in the 1970s, particularly in positioning our members as experts in learning and teaching. However, the existing model is fast approaching a point where it needs to be reviewed and challenged. We cannot continue to ignore the complex challenges that our constituents face in working as multidimensional research-intensive academics. We need additional expertise and reach to facilitate leadership and organizational learning. We need to identify the areas of influence that will be of the most benefit to our institutions and our own effectiveness.

It is time to reframe our concept of faculty development. We need to move from a traditional model to one that clearly works toward the betterment of the faculty experience and, by implication, the outcomes of the institution. It is time to review and articulate the purpose and goals of faculty development: to encourage stronger and more capable academics who can face complex challenges with confidence and courage across all areas of their work. We need to be the learning partners of choice in this ongoing process.

REFERENCES

Bach, D. J., & Sorcinelli, M. D. (2010). The case for excellence in diversity: Lessons from an assessment of an early career faculty program. In L. B. Nilson & J. E. Miller (Eds.), *To improve the academy: Vol. 28. Resources for faculty, instructional, and organizational development* (pp. 310–326). San Francisco, CA: Jossey-Bass.

Blackmore, J., & Sachs, J. (2007). *Performing and reforming leaders: Gender, educational restructuring, and organizational change.* Albany: State University of New York Press.

Chism, N.V.N. (2011). Getting to the table: Planning and developing institutional initiatives. In C. M. Schroeder (Ed.), *Coming in from the margins: Faculty development's emerging organizational development role in institutional change* (pp. 47–59). Sterling, VA: Stylus.

Cohen, C. M., & Cohen, S. L. (2005). *Lab dynamics: Management skills for scientists.* New York, NY: Cold Spring Harbor Laboratory Press.

Debowski, S. (2007). Finding the right track: Enabling early career academic management of career, teaching and research. *Research and Development in Higher Education, 30,* 138–149.

Debowski, S. (2011). Locating academic development: The first step in evaluation. In L. Stefani (Ed.), *Evaluating the effectiveness of academic development* (pp. 17–30). New York, NY: Routledge.

Debowski, S., & Blake, V. (2007). Collective capacity building of academic leaders: A university model of leadership and learning in context. *International Journal of Learning and Change, 2*(3), 307–324.

Debowski, S., Stefani, L., Cohen, M., & Ho, A. (in press). Sustaining and championing teaching and learning: In good times and bad. In J. Groccia, M.

Alsudairi, & B. Buskist (Eds.), *Handbook of college and university teaching: Global perspectives*. Thousand Oaks, CA: Sage.

Del Favero, M. (2006). Disciplinary variation in preparation for the academic dean role. *Higher Education Research and Development, 25*(3), 277–292. doi:10.1080/07294360600793069

Elkins, T., & Keller, R. T. (2003). Leadership in research and development organizations: A literature review and conceptual framework. *Leadership Quarterly, 14*(4/5), 587–606. doi:10.1016/S1048-9843(03)00053-5

Fullan, M., & Scott, G. (2009). *Turnaround leadership for higher education*. San Francisco, CA: Jossey-Bass.

Gibbs, G., Knapper, C., & Piccinin, S. (2008). Disciplinary and contextually appropriate approaches to leadership of teaching in research-intensive academic departments in higher education. *Higher Education Quarterly, 62*(4), 416–436. doi:10.1111/j.1468-2273.2008.00402.x

Goffee, R., & Jones, G. (2007). Leading clever people. *Harvard Business Review, 85*(3), 72–79.

Gosling, D. (2009). Educational development in the UK: A complex and contradictory reality. *International Journal of Academic Development, 14*(1), 5–18. doi:10.1080/13601440802659122

Hicks, M., Smigiel, H., Wilson, G., & Luzeckyj, A. (2010). *Preparing academics to teach in higher education*. Retrieved from www.altc.edu.au/resource-preparing-academics-teach-higher-education-unisa-2010

Knight, P., & Trowler, P. (2001). *Departmental leadership in higher education*. Buckingham, England: Society for Research into Higher Education & Open University Press.

Latta, G. (2009). Maturation of organizational development in higher education: Using cultural analysis to facilitate change. In L. B. Nilson & J. E. Miller (Eds.), *To improve the academy: Vol. 27. Resources for faculty, instructional, and organizational development* (pp. 32–71). San Francisco, CA: Jossey-Bass.

Lee, A., Manathunga, C., & Kandlbinder, P. (2008). *Making a place: An oral history of academic development in Australia*. Canberra, Australia: Higher Education Research & Development Society of Australasia.

Mumford, M. D., Hunter, S. T., Eubanks, D. L., Bedell, K. E., & Murphy, S. T. (2007). Developing leaders for creative efforts: A domain-based approach to leadership development. *Human Resource Management Review, 17*(4), 402–417. doi:10.1016/j.hrmr.2007.08.002

Schroeder, C. M. (2011). Faculty developers as institutional developers. In C. M. Schroeder (Ed.), *Coming in from the margins: Faculty development's emerging organizational development role in institutional change* (pp. 17–46). Sterling, VA: Stylus.

Scott, G., Coates, H., & Anderson, M. (2008). *Learning leaders in times of change: Academic leadership capabilities for Australian higher education.* Sydney: University of Western Sydney/Australian Council for Educational Research.

Sorcinelli, M. D., Austin, A. E., Eddy, P. L., & Beach, A. L. (2006). *Creating the future of faculty development: Learning from the past, understanding the present.* San Francisco, CA: Jossey-Bass.

Stefani, L. (Ed.). (2011). *Evaluating the effectiveness of academic development.* New York, NY: Routledge.

Tennant, M., McMullen, C., & Kaczynski, D. (2010). *Teaching, learning and research in higher education.* New York, NY: Routledge.

Van Velsor, E., McCauley, C. D., & Ruderman, M. N. (2010). *Handbook of leadership development* (3rd ed.). San Francisco, CA: Jossey-Bass.

Western, M., Boreham, P., Kubler, M., Laffan, W., Western, J., Lawson, A., & Clague, D. (2007). *PhD graduates 5 to 7 years out: Employment outcomes, job attributes and the quality of research training: Final report (Revised).* Queensland, Australia: University of Queensland Social Research Centre. Retrieved from http://espace.library.uq.edu.au/view/UQ:177864